The Psychoanalytic Study of the Child

VOLUME FIFTY-EIGHT

Kindly submit seven copies of new manuscripts by post
or as an e-mail attachment in MS Word to

Robert A. King, M.D.
Yale Child Study Center
230 South Frontage Road
P.O. Box 207900
New Haven, CT 06520-7900
Phone: (203) 785-5880
E-mail: robert.king@yale.edu

The
Psychoanalytic
Study
of the Child

VOLUME FIFTY-EIGHT

Yale University Press
New Haven and London
2003

Designed by Sally Harris
and set in Baskerville type.
Printed in the United States of America by
Vail-Ballou Press, Inc., Binghamton, N.Y.

Library of Congress catalog card number: 45-11304
International standard book number: 0-300-10126-0
A catalogue record for this book is available from the British Library.

The paper in this book meets the guidelines for
permanence and durability of the Committee on
Production Guidelines for Book Longevity of the
Council on Library Resources.
2 4 6 8 10 9 7 5 3 1

Contents

Memorial Note for Albert J. Solnit, M.D.

The Editorial Board deeply mourns the sudden death of Albert J. Solnit on June 21, 2002.

He was Managing Editor of this publication since 1971 and during those years he was the guiding spirit in carrying out the original aim of *The Psychoanalytic Study of the Child*. The preface of the first volume in 1945 declared: "The contribution of psychoanalysis to the study of the child covers many areas. In therapy, the range extends from child analysis to child guidance and group work; in theory, from the basic problems of genetic psychology to those concerned with the interrelation of culture and the upbringing of the child."

Dr. Solnit was well endowed for this task. He was Training and Supervising Analyst at the Western New England Institute for Psychoanalysis and Freud Professor at the Hebrew University in Jerusalem and University College, London. He was Director of the Yale Child Study Center, which he led to be an internationally recognized place for research and clinical excellence. He guided studies undertaken by the Psychoanalytic Research and Development Fund and the Anna Freud Centre, and he wrote hundreds of papers. Many of these applied psychoanalytic theory and practice to the social and medical problems of children.

Al Solnit was President of many international organizations. As an integrator of various disciplines, he reached for the widening scope of psychoanalysis and thereby opened windows for its future. He was primarily a clinician who encouraged colleagues to advance the theory and practice of psychoanalysis, or to confirm, by their own experience, its basic principles. He favored contributions that demonstrated the richness of the application of psychoanalysis.

Over the last years he expanded the scope of the content of each volume of *The Psychoanalytic Study of the Child* by organizing papers on specific themes focusing on current psychoanalytic problems and theory.

His tireless editorial attention to each paper, his generosity of spirit in encouraging scientific contributions that widened the role of psychoanalysis by facilitating interdisciplinary exchange, his energy, and his kindness will guide the Editors to continue in his path.

PETER B. NEUBAUER, M.D.
for the Editors

ALBERT J. SOLNIT AWARD OF

THE PSYCHOANALYTIC STUDY OF THE CHILD

In 2002, the Editors inaugurated the Founders Award, presented in honor of the three founders of The Psychoanalytic Study of the Child, *Anna Freud, Heinz Hartmann, and Ernst Kris. Beginning with this volume, the Editors feel it is fitting to rename the award in memory of Albert J. Solnit, M.D., longtime Managing Editor of* The Psychoanalytic Study of the Child.

Sponsored by The Psychoanalytic Study of the Child *and The Anna Freud Foundation, the award will be given annually to the author of an original paper that best exemplifies* The Psychoanalytic Study of the Child's *mission of advancing the psychoanalytic understanding of children from the clinical, developmental, theoretical, or applied research perspective (including neurobiological and genetic contributions).*

The recipient of this year's Albert J. Solnit Award is "Margo and Me II: The Role of Narrative Building in Child-Analytic Technique," by Rona B. Knight, pages 133–164.

GENDER

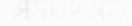

Gender and Its Clinical Manifestations

WENDY OLESKER, Ph.D.

Based on a study of five analytic cases (three reported here), and using a modern classical psychoanalytic perspective in which both biology and social forces are integrated, our study group on gender investigated why for some gender assumes a distorted and exaggerated role in the subjective sense of self. Clinical material was used because we wanted data allowing us to study patterns emerging from an exploration of patients' unconscious fantasies as they shed light on the psychological significance and function of gender. We found that in each case gender disturbances were never primary but secondary to difficulties in integration, cohesiveness, separateness, stability of solid sense of self and of the object, to depression and especially to problems with aggression and rivalry which had to be analyzed first. Conflicted gender gave rise to solutions that were literal and concrete. Not suprisingly, in each case mothers wished for a child of the opposite gender and treated gender expression in highly ambivalent ways. In terms of technique we learned that ways of coping with rejection, evolving paternal transferences which allowed for metabolysis of the maternal relationship, and

Training and supervising analyst at the New York Psychoanalystic Institute; adjunct professor, New York University Postdoctoral Program in Psychoanalysis and Psychotherapy.

I would like to thank the members of the Study Group on Gender and its Clinical Manifestations, sponsored by the Psychoanalytic Research and Development Fund, whose case material and cogent ideas are at the core of this work. The members are as follows: Sam Abrams, Rosemary Balsam, Kirsten Dahl, Sidney Furst (deceased), Edward Hartmann, Theodore Jacobs, Rona Knight, Nancy Kulish, Roy Lilleskov, Peter Neubauer, Mortimer Ostow, Ronda Shaw, Anna Wolff, and Alan Zients.

The Psychoanalytic Study of the Child 58, ed. Robert A. King, Peter B. Neubauer, Samuel Abrams, and A. Scott Dowling (Yale University Press, copyright © 2003 by Robert A. King, Peter B. Neubauer, Samuel Abrams, and A. Scott Dowling).

*ego building techniques had to take place before conflicts around gen-
der could be analyzed productively.*

INTRODUCTION

GENDER ISSUES, OF GREAT CONCERN TO MANY OF OUR PATIENTS, ARE
subject to much controversy. Freud (1905, 1933), explaining the origins of what we call gender, refuted the notion that femininity and
masculinity correspond by nature to the two biological sexes. Gender
issues came to occupy much of his attention in part because in his
mind they presented as the most intractable resistance. In women
striving to possess a male genital (penis envy) and in the male, a
struggle against a passive feminine attitude, were bedrock issues
(Freud, 1937). We no longer view these issues as bedrock or universal. At the present time there are many different psychoanalytic conceptions of gender: some writers highlight the influence of culture
and social forces (Dimen, 1991; Harris, 2000; Money and Ehrhardt,
1972), while others stress the impact of biology, anatomy, and the
body experience (Downey, 1998; Friedman and Downey, 1995). We
take a psychoanalytic developmental perspective in which both biology and social forces are integrated through the lens of the increasing gain from gender identifications in solving phase-specific conflicts.
This may suggest that, in addition to constitution and environment,
the developmental process itself is a force contributing to gender
identity as well as to character formation.

Using a modern classical psychoanalytic perspective, our study
group on gender asked why in some cases gender issues took the fore
whereas in others were minimal; why, for some, gender assumed such
an overriding part of the subjective sense of self, a central organizing
perspective by which one sees oneself and experiences with others
(Bem, 1993; Yanof, 2000). We chose only analytic cases in which gender, its constituents, its developmental path, and its transformation
were revealed in individuals through their conflicted gender issues.
Only through the analytic process could we really come to know the
meaning of gender for that individual in order to shed light on the
phenomena, to see nodal events traversed and opportunities offered
by related conflicts or the developmental process. Rather than con-
verting repeated themes into universal developmental schemes, we
wanted data affording us a glimpse of patterns emerging from an analytic lens that took into account both the observed and the subjective experience of gender. We hoped to discover whether gender

conflicts are primary and bedrock or a presentation behind which many conflicts and compromise formations lie. Only an exploration of the patient's unconscious fantasies sheds light on this question as well as on the psychological significance and function of gender.

Five cases were presented, three are reported in the papers that follow, the other two will be included in the conclusions. One was the six-year analysis of Andy, a seven-year-old boy who was brought for treatment because his friend's mother could not tolerate Andy pretending he was a girl, refusing to let her son play with Andy. Andy showed feminine proclivities since age two-and-a-half, was extremely timid, avoided competitive sports, was terrified of even minor injuries, had few friends, and was fearful of anything new. Femininity was his initial way to fortify himself from outside impingement and protect his shaky sense of his body and unstable self image. Another was Margo, a five-year-old girl who underwent a six-year analytic treatment, presenting with difficulties interacting with peers, severe mood swings, inability to control anger, and with the wish to be a boy; she also felt half male and half female, a he/she. She too suffered from problems with self and agency, attachment problems, affect regulation problems, and an inability to go beyond the dyadic in relationships. A third case was the eight-year analysis of Mona, a divorced woman in her late fifties, who sought treatment for vague complaints about other treatments not working, though the analyst sensed a profound depression. The gender problem, though not experienced as such, was a long-standing fantasy that she was half male and half female; consciously she knew she was female. Striking was the fact that the analyst could not form a coherent picture of the patient or the people in her life, leading the analyst to see Mona as suffering from a shaky sense of self and a problem with object constancy—she did not have the comfort of a solid internal image of a safe and good mothering object.

Striking in all three cases was the marked concreteness. It seemed in each case that disturbance in the self came so early when the self schema was primarily experienced in physical and bodily terms, bringing into the solution tangible body features—gender, as an umbrella to cover many other issues. In particular, as these individuals came to understand their sense of rejection, they linked it to their gender. In each case an opposite-sex sibling was seen as preferred. With each new level of development the use of gender to solve phase specific problems continued and became elaborated, a proposed solution to each new developmental phase. Thus, in these three cases the psychological organization consisted of several features: constitutionally (though not all of the cases) they had salient cross-gender features—either sturdy, aggressive female or passive, timid male. They also had difficult temperaments—one hyperalert to any changes in the environment, another with some features of Attention Deficit Disorder, and a third with bipolar tendencies. Historically the interactions with their mothers led to a sense of rejection which father did not temper enough, the timing of these features began very early, body experiences and developing sexual and aggressive fantasies augmented dispositional difficulties and pushed toward the use of gender to provide organization.

REVIEW OF THE LITERATURE

More contemporary viewpoints directly and indirectly informed our work. In contrast to Freud's (1905, 1933) proposal of an early masculine identification in both sexes, thus ascribing to the little girl a primary masculine gender identity, Stoller (1985) posits that the boy isn't born masculine and heterosexual but traverses an earlier phase in which he is merged with mother; he must first separate himself from her female body and femininity and experience a process of individuation into masculinity. Thus, for Stoller, the mother is the primary identificatory object for both genders, and the boy must free himself by disidentifying from mother and from the negative oedipal complex. (As a consequence, core gender identity might be more stable and secure in women than in men and homosexual leanings more threatening to men than to women [Kernberg, 2000]). Stoller believes there is a developmental conflict, a protofeminity, built into maleness that females are spared. There are problems with Stoller's views. First, it is noteworthy that while Stoller's clinical accounts include the subjective experience of the body as a source of pleasure and meaning, in his theoretical discussion of gender, parental behavior and attitudes are the key factors in the development of core gender identity. Second, imprinting, a nonmental mechanism acting directly on the brain, bypasses subjective experience. Third, as Person and Ovesey (1983) point out, there is no evidence that the symbiotic state prior to self-object differentiation consists of a primary identification that confers gender behavior or identity on the infant child, since there is no behavioral surface of the infant's femininity until after one year of age, when the feminine state may be covered over by masculinity, and gender markers appear. Person and Ovesey (1983) suggest that a merger fantasy, not a prolonged protofeminine state, contributes to ambiguous core identity. Such a fantasy disrupts a sense of self, object, and certain ego functions, and the resolution of separation-individuation conflicts has different consequences for each sex; males do not necessarily have more difficulty adaptively.

Along somewhat similar lines Coates, Friedman, and Wolfe (1991) emphasize that a confluence of awareness of gender differences, without establishment of self and object constancy, and with an experience of loss of mother, engenders a strong desire to be like her to regain connection with her. Feminine identification (and merger fantasy) in gender identity disorder boys was a way of handling separation and annihilation anxiety, a way of warding off aggression, a variant of identification with the lost object: these boys became mother to have mother. These investigators did not take the longer developmental perspective but focused on the earliest stages of development. Most compatible with our view is one that incorporates a full psychoanalytic developmental perspective, one that recognizes the role of constitution (biology), the environment (social and cultural forces), the interaction between constitution and environment, and the developmental process, a biological proposition in which biological potential becomes a psychological actuality as an expectable sequence of discontinuous, hierarchically ordered steps evolve in the form of discrete phases directed to a mature end point after this pull foward wanes. Development produces change by pulling new organizations and structures into existence when actualized by experience (Abrams, 1990). Applying the developmental perspective to gender some (Chused, 1999; McDevitt, 1995; Galenson and Roiphe, 1965, 1980; and Olesker, 1998) think that each new stage of development contributes and believe that the above described early experiences set the stage for intense castration anxiety that affects later conflicts and compromise formations, particularly oedipal phase and adolescence. Dahl (1989) suggests that in adolescence the girl must overcome her sexual inhibition, an expression of unconscious guilt over the oedipal implications of sexual intimacy, as well as her bisexual conflicts in relationship to her mother, in the context of the capacity for a romantic love relation. For the boy, the oedipal period is crucial to the divergent development of gender, an achievement of a separate self and different sex from mother, while father must assert himself as a rival for mother and be available as a model for masculinity (Chused, 1999). Blos (1985) emphasizes that in adolescence the boy must master his separation individuation conflicts as well as his bisexual love for his father. The boy also needs the opportunity to yearn for his mother and to fear the consequences of yearning for her: his masculinity could be taken from him. It is only after a struggle to work through oedipal conflicts that the adolescent boy is able to abandon the unconscious selection of his mother as his primary love object, to resolve ambivalence and unconscious oedipal prohibitions, and to invest in an in-depth relationship with a woman (Kernberg, 1995). While development is not always linear (Mayes, 1999), taking into account a developmental trajectory will allow the most complete understanding of gender.

CLINICAL DISCUSSION

Whatever theoretical emphasis one may have, we believed that a thorough study of analytic case material would help shed light on the multiple functions, influences, and meanings of gender. Having reviewed five cases (two as yet unreported) we found, although not generalizable beyond our sample, that in each case gender identity disturbances were secondary manifestations. When we studied the changing course of each analysis, we were struck by how gender issues were reworked and reorganized, often as one component of a symptom or character disturbance. Analytic observation did not allow for a conclusion that our notions of gender were ever bedrock, but highlighted the primacy of conflict and compromise. This is consistent with Grossman and Kaplan's (1988) finding that gender is a construction with multiple references—social, cultural, biological— that may be pulled into conflict, and that gender disturbance is yet another compromise in a developmental process, even in the gender-disordered patients we studied who used gender to mask or to solve other problems, and modified their use of it at different points in life.

In all our cases, gender issues, though a presenting problem, were not primary but secondary to difficulties with integration, cohesiveness, separateness, and stability of a solid sense of self and of the object; to struggles with depression; and to problems with aggression. Feeling identified with the opposite sex, in addition to the use of other defenses, served to handle these issues. In all our cases facilitating organization, integration, identifications, and building structure had a larger role than usual. Cross-gender identification was employed to protect the genitals: boys hid their penises via feminine identifications, and girls expressed fears of genital damage by imagining a tower or a phallus, not a hole. Each family had a mother who preferred a child of the opposite sex or rejected the sex of the child. Either blatant rejection or the parent's depressed or narcissistic state led to intense rage, sadness, despair, and/or confusion in the child.

The fathers did little to offset these attitudes, often compounding the child's feeling of rejection. Seething with more anger than ordinary defenses could contend with, all seemed to have ambivalent attachments to their parents, perhaps a source for more than usually intense reactions to anatomical differences when these came into awareness (Galenson and Roiphe, 1965). For the girls, the penis became the magic wand that would provide them with love, sexual release, strength, protection against abandonment and injury, and safety; feminine identification provided the same needs for the boy. In one boy's case, the main need was to make sure he was intact and not helpless, not necessarily female. Femininity was instituted to fortify himself against outside impingement.

Concreteness and problems with integration were present in all cases. The concreteness may have defended against body image problems. Early histories of deprivation and interference with appropriate object interaction produced problems with affect regulation, rage, and self control; problems arising so early—when the only ego is a body ego—seemed to push toward concrete body solutions. When phallic needs emerged, mastery was compromised because the child needed to fill up the emptiness or protect the body image by concretization of the penis. Since mother was absent or hostile, affect regulation was compromised, feelings of being unprotected were more intense, and thus the need for buffering was more literal. In these families intellect was downplayed, while looks and tangibles were valued, abetting concretization. Perhaps deprivation of contact with mother interfered with the girls' capacity to hold the image of mother in imagination as a comforting presence, while the boy had too much mother and had to ward her off. Without enough actual satisfaction and security in that relationship to internalize or even memorize, one's need for the concrete presence of the mothering one to prevent overwhelming anxiety is imperative. Hence, the idea of possessing, holding, and fusing with an actual object as the only way to forestall anxiety or depressive affect was probably an early development. Once this link was established, it was not a big jump from the feelings of security and ability to touch a concrete object to the need to use a transitional object that stood for mother and was comforting in that way, to a fetish whose presence is necessary to stave off quite massive anxiety. (In one male case we found a cross-gender masturbatory fantasy used as a fetishistic assist.) Perhaps concrete thinking is part of a compulsive need for a reassuring object.

The girls in our study shifted from earlier preoccupation with the penis to a focus on body attractiveness, not unusual events (Yanof,

2000). While oedipal feelings emerged in the course of these analyses, they were not obvious at the outset. One had the sense that, given their early difficulties, fear prevented competitive feelings from emerging, expressed only later in the analyses. Prephallic issues were to be worked through first. Only after anxieties over separation and aggression, coupled with the provision of a strong, solid, healing relationship with a stable and responsive maternal figure, were these triadic issues engaged more fully and deeply. Wishes for and fears of the father were not unimportant, but often secondary. Using a penis as a way of retaining father through identification served a protective function in the girls, suggesting how dense, complex, and multi-layed is the fantasy of acquiring a penis. In Margo's case, wanting a penis was not just to be a boy but to be both sexes, to have it all, to not feel depressed and inferior, to make up for all the deprivation. The imperative need to have what the opposite sex has seemed born of anxiety, especially over aggression born of frustration with mother and of retaliation for aggressive and competitive urges. All showed strong aggressive wishes to return to babyhood and be totally cared for, but all defended against feelings of dependency by assuming the role of an independent and self-sufficient child. The impulse to regress must have increased their anxiety and need for the cross-gender identification as defenses. Ultimately in each analysis the patient's anger and sadism was brought into consciousness, a necessary step toward resolution of conflict. Whether these aspects were concealed behind depression, obsessional mechanisms, a facade of self-sufficiency and pseudomaturity, or compulsive driven behavior, the symptoms modulated as the underlying conflicts were revealed. All gained insight into those warded-off aspects of their thoughts and feelings that were the source of much trouble. The processes of differentiation and internalization cannot be overestimated. The fantasied presence of the analyst seemed more important than in most cases as the organizing core that allowed growth to take place. The relationship with the analyst not only helped each patient better understand what troubled them but also aided the process of mentalization (Fonagy, 2000), the ability to know both one's own mind and the mind of another person, which was severely lacking in our patients at the outset of analysis. The relationship with the analyst offered an integrative experience, not only through the careful and accurate interpretation of distorted perceptions, troubling fantasies, defensive operations, and warded-off affects, but by experiencing the analyst in a way that allowed for critically important internalizations to take place. And without such internalizations there could be no genuine structural change, which insight and new integrative experiences worked together to effect.

All our patients yearned for sufficient structure from an early unavailable, unusually egocentric mother and a devalued, inconsistent, and/or psychologically absent father. All were exposed to mother's onslaught on their self-worth and needed tangible, concrete behavior, not just internal mechanisms, to contain their intense feelings of conflict over aggression and abandonment. The self was felt to be hopelessly defective, an object of relentless efforts at self protection or self repair. The need to be someone else was noteworthy: magical power was derived from gender so as not to be devalued and vulnerable to abandonment. In all cases early injury, deprivation, or intrusion and the ideas stimulated by these experiences led to interferences with normal narcissistic development, a deficit in the self-esteem needed to navigate the perils of childhood. Mona and Margo feared they would be rejected for not having a penis, whereas Andy feared rejection for having one; all hoped they would be more exciting (as the opposite sex). All focused on being the victim so as not to feel guilt for their rage. Mona showed an exhibitionistic component in needing an audience to provide confirmation, affection, stimulation, and validation of the cross-gender components, an audience that insured love, protected from abandonment, exerted dominance and control, and relieved guilt. Andy on the other hand needed to protect and fortify himself from outside impingement. In all, the wish for caretaking was central. All had major difficulty in organizing and integrating self and object. All suffered from intense rage, leading to a sense of unstableness of self and object, as might be expected.

Functions of gender identification, such as holding onto the object to obtain closeness, providing organization and control, expressing anger and revenge, gaining power, overcoming a sense of defectiveness, bolstering self esteem, and regulating affects, especially anxiety and depression, were found in each case. Mona used gender identification to augment the reality of her physical self, Andy used gender to protect himself from fragmentation, and Margo adapted an omnipotent he/she fantasy to protect her from feeling small and helpless. All suffered more than the usual amount of trauma, including overstimulation, neglect, and separations. All experienced an ambivalent relationship to reality, being uncertain at times about whether their thoughts and wishes could very well be true. Most used sexuality and excitement to deal with depression. All had difficult temperaments—one hyperalert to any changes in the environment, some possibly had Attention Deficit Disorder, and another perhaps with bipolar disorder. None had parents who possessed a solid mentalizing ability, an interest in what the child was like and the contents of the child's mind; they were so caught up with their own autonomy and other issues and their focus was on behavior rather than inner life. While all these factors may be important, two variables stand out in these cases where gender symptomatology was core: each mother had strong feelings about the gender and/or gender characteristics of her child, who experienced rejection of an integral part of him or herself; and no child had a father available or consistent enough to temper the pathological impact of the mother. In treatment, the analyst as a paternal figure available for attachment and identification promoted reflection and metabolization of the maternal relationship. All other factors exacerbate or may be primary but may not lead to this group of fantasies with gender emphasis as the core presentation.

Developmentally, as each new challenge arose, pathological early organization and primitive anxieties affected ego development and forestalled the child's integration of gender. Possibly because gender carried with it such rejection, compensation was in the realm of gender identification, which became the domain of magical omnipotent solution, where limitations did not have to be recognized and external reality was relegated to minor importance. It is striking that each case used an ego weakness, the unstable differentiation of gender, as a core defense.

The treatment process yielded defensive trends focused on the gender component. When gender was not solidly integrated, it assumed whatever shape was felt to repair the problematic relationship with mother, thus helping to quell annihilation and abandonment anxiety, allowing libidinal satisfaction, controlling aggression, and increasing feelings of attachment and sexual discharge. All patients used the analyst as a protector and way station to separation from mother. The analyst was not only a model for how to construe gender, but an object of identification for the basic self-regulating structures. It seemed that identification played a larger role in the therapeutic action than in many other analyses. In the initial period of treatment words seemed to be treated as objects, a concrete feeding through words. Slowly, words provided scaffolding, a structure for understanding feelings and their history; the analyst provided containment through words that helped the patients metabolize their emotions (mother had never done so), tolerate their aggression and separateness, be a reliable presence, and label their emotions. The analyst provided validation of reality, that mother hated or neglected them, which allowed them to acknowledge their own rage and alleviate the guilt over it, in part absolving them of the intensity of their guilt and rage. Other possibilities of mind opened up, since words allowed for concrete mothering in acceptable form, and the patients learned the capacity to delay, move to thoughts, and into the world of fantasy and metaphor, a sense that belittlement has limits, that one could speak the unspeakable, look at the meaning of the parental relationships instead of just feeling "I'm bad," and link emotional experience to something that happened, the foundation of interpretive work. Words then could be used to express anxiety, guilt, and conflict, all of which helped them to move on, build a new, more solid structure than the faulty, distorted gender identity provided. Since feelings of rejection because of gender were so early and so total in some cases, intolerable emotions yielded to denial of reality. Bisexual fantasies were felt as real, not wishful fantasy. These patients felt they had to change their shape to overcome rage and depression. Though they did not need outside validation of their fantasies as seen in the perversions, they did need to change reality because they could not tolerate the pain of limitations. They had to try to recover mother.

Gender went unanalyzed until later in the analyses, when it sent shock waves through the patient's system, even in those cases where gender conflict was ego-syntonic and not consciously felt to be important or pervasive. Idealization of the analyst as a person who could love and accept a child who had so much hate was an important step toward tolerating their own anger; the patients could eventually express and analyze their rage toward the analyst. Defended homosexual feelings were given more expression and understood in terms of their use in solving gender integration problems and the underlying conflicts. The analyst was perceived as opposite of the gender he/she actually was for a good part of the analyses. Person (1983) believes that gender identification precedes the phallic oedipal period and orders the fantasies attached to sexuality as well as the choice of the love object. In Andy we saw how, as he more comfortably established his masculine identity, he grew interested in girls. As Mona felt more comfortably feminine, she felt renewed excitement in heterosexuality. We saw that different periods were more salient for different people in terms of gender meanings. For Andy the early period was most important; for Margo, adolescence was a turning point, and for Mona adulthood was the period of greatest growth, though all stages of development were contributory to her problems.

In each case, even in the adult patient, the analyst as a new object—non intrusive, appreciative, emotionally available, mirroring, and articulating inner experience—was a more important element in the therapeutic action than usual, activating in each patient a progressive move to a more steady investment in a higher level of organization with its transformational potential: new ways of relating, thinking, firmer self boundaries, more advanced ego development, tempering of superego derivatives, and the understanding of cause and effect in new ways. It may be that when gender has not been integrated comfortably, basic building blocks of the self representation are not solid or cohesive, affecting delays in the unfolding of the basic structures of the personality; these need to be addressed as well as the core dynamic issues. In Andy the analytic experience of a nonintrusive object who helped him articulate his experience tapped in him the possibility for progressive internal structuralization; he gave up his symbiotic way of relating, leading to firmer self boundaries, a clearer sense of separateness, and triangular rather than dyadic relationships. In Margo opposite gender identifications were used to protect against the narcissistic injury of feeling unbearably small and helpless. When her analyst articulated her inner experience, especially her states of anger over her deprivation, she became more able to trust the analyst, and she also began to enjoy pretty clothes and flirting, later being able to take on the dangers of oedipal rivalry and triangular relationships. In Mona when the analyst articulated the feelings behind her wordless rocking on the couch and the meaning of her fears that the analyst would not return, she became able to hold a stable representation of the analyst and develop a language for feelings in addition to left out feelings in relation to the analyst and her husband.

We are not suggesting that these clinical presentations are the only form of gender disturbance, but they illustrate the defensive use of gender to deal with anxiety and depressive affect as well as attempts at repair. Sex-linked differences were observed. The males in our small sample had invasive narcissistic mothers; the boys identified with the aggressor in part to not be abandoned by mother toward whom they felt unconsiously rejected as well as reactively enraged and in part to offset the fear of mother as castrator. One boy's unconscious fantasy suggested his wish to torment and seduce his mother as well as get revenge on her, while defending against rivalrous oedipal feelings. Another boy was more dependent on a dyadic relationship, rather than sexualizing in a triadic relationship. None felt safe to express their feelings or function autonomously, but rather felt they had to submit to mother's demands. The females with absent, rejecting, and neglecting mothers tended more to denial of reality including their penisless condition. All felt that by identifying with the opposite sex they would win mother. All so feared mother's power and wanted her protection that anger toward her was suppressed lest it destroy her. All had opposite sex siblings who were viewed as preferred. Fathers were notably absent psychologically in our cases, contributing to the intensity of the ambivalence toward mother.

Different theorists have emphasized different components of gender—the biological (Freud, 1905; Galenson and Roiphe, 1965; Friedman and Downey, 1995), and the social and cultural (Money and Ehrhardt, 1972; Harris, 2000; Thompson, 1942; Sullivan, 1953). While nature and destiny can be read in so many different ways, gender is rooted in the body and biology. The "developmental constructivist" model suggests that gender differences are not essential but an artifact of the social structure, the inequality of participation in child rearing (Chodorow, 1994); the girl doesn't need to disidentify as does the boy so she has an easier time developing her gender identity. By contrast, Dimen (1991) and Harris (2000) value the dialectic between biological essentialists' and developmental constructivists' accounts as mutually enriching. Chodorow suggests that there are many masculinities and femininities, a fusion of personal and cultural meaning, and that an individual personal creation and projective emotional and fantasy animation of cultural categories create the meaning of gender and gender identity for any individual. Gender is clearly a work in progress throughout the life cycle but in analysis of our cases does not stand alone as the primary basis of character or symptomatology.

Summary and Conclusions

In summary, we questioned why gender assumed an overriding part of the sense of self in the cases presented. Our analytic explorations yielded the following findings:

1. In each case contributors to gender identity were weighted differently: the individual's experience of parental behaviors and attitudes, the body as a source of pleasure, anxiety, and meaning, the role of conflict, fantasy, and subjective experience. We found that symptomatic gender disturbances were never primary but secondary to difficulties in integration, cohesiveness, separateness, stability of solid sense of self and of the object, to depression and especially to problems with aggression and rivalry, which had to be analyzed first.

Gender confusion was part of confused identity. Gender served multiple functions, including holding onto the object, obtaining closeness, providing organization, expressing rage, gaining power, avoiding rivalry, overcoming a sense of defectiveness and regulating affects, especially anxiety and depression. Gender issues were reworked and reorganized in the course of analysis as one component of symptom or character disturbance, highlighting the primacy of conflict and compromise.

2. Conflicted gender regularly gave rise to conflict solutions that were literal and concrete. For example, Margo needed glue to fill up a hole, Mona used homosexuality to know what it felt like to be a woman, and Andy used the sensual concrete details of the female to hold onto and feel safe with mother. In these cases gender was appropriated as a solution early in development at a time when the early developing ego used body channels most readily. All subjects felt rejected because of their gender, pushing toward gender change as a solution.

3. In terms of technique we found it important to focus on the ways of handing rejection and ego building techniques before conflicts around gender could be analyzed productively. The latter included the analyst as a container of affects, allowing for the use of externalization, being a model of affect regulation, being an affectively alive, available, and accepting partner, surviving affect expression, and facilitating narrative construction to allow for the development of secure attachment, the development of a cohesive self, and a platform to work through rage and despair.

3a. Premature efforts to analyze gender conflicts were unproductive, and in every instance the above mentioned techniques were necessary before addressing gender conflict directly.

4. In all cases an integrated gender identity preceded heterosexual object choice.[1] Affects and fantasies associated with gender identity added to the erotic quality of sexual love as it developed along with the whole range of psychosexual gratification and biological/hormonal contributors. Sexual intimacy helped to overcome feelings of gender disappointment or alienation. Gender development was not established as a single temporal phase but emerged as a gradual process of refinement.

5. The psychological organization in these cases consisted of sev-

1. Because of the absence in our case material of adult homosexual object choice, we cannot make any meaningful psychological statement about the relationship of integrated gender identity in homosexuality.

eral features: a history of interactions with their mothers led to a sense of rejection which father did not temper enough, opposite sex siblings were experienced as preferred, disturbances in the self came so early when self schema was primarily experienced in physical and bodily terms bringing into the solution tangible body features—gender as an umbrella to cover many issues as development unfolded, constitutional difficulties, many with similarities to the opposite sex (aggressive sturdy female; pretty, passive, perceptually sensitive boy), difficult temperaments (one hyperalert to environmental changes, another with ADD, and a third with some aspects of bipolar disorder), and lastly, sexual and aggressive fantasies and parental behaviors that often augmented dispositional difficulties.

These are hypotheses that need to be further corroborated.

BIBLIOGRAPHY

ABRAMS, S. (1990). The Psychoanalytic Process: The Developmental and the Integrative, *Psychoanal. Quar.*, Vol. LIX: 4, 650–677.

BEM, S. L. (1993). *The Lenses of Gender.* New Haven, Conn.: Yale University Press.

BLOS, P. (1985). *Son and Father: Before and Beyond the Oedipus Complex.* New York: The Free Press.

CHODOROW, N. J. (1994). *Femininities, Masculinities, Sexualities: Freud and Beyond.* London: Free Association Books.

CHUSED, J. (1999). Male gender identity and sexual behavior, *International Journal of Psychoanalysis*, 80:1105–1118.

COATES, S., FRIEDMAN, R., & WOLFE, S. (1991). Aetiology of boyhood gender disorder: Model for integrating temperament, development, and psychodynamic, *Psychoanalytic Dialogue*, Vol. I, Issue 4:481–523.

DAHL, K. (1989). Daughters and mother: Oedipal aspects of the witch mother. *The Psychoanalytic Study of the Child*, 44:267–280. New Haven, Conn.: Yale University Press.

DIMEN, M. (1991). Deconstructing difference: Gender, splitting, and transitional space, *Psychoanalytic Dialogues*, 1:335–352.

DOWNEY, J. (1998). Female homosexuality and classical theory reconsidered, *Journal of the American Psychoanalytic Association*, 46:471–506.

FONAGY, P. (2000). Attachment and borderline personality disorder, *J. Amer. Psychoanal. Assn., 48:1129–1146.*

FREUD, S. (1905). Three essays on the theory of sexuality. *Standard Edition* 7:125–245.

——— (1933). Femininity. *Standard Edition* 22:112–125.

——— (1937). Analysis terminable and interminable. In *Collected Papers*, Vol. 5, pp. 316–357. New York: Basic Books, 1959.

FRIEDMAN, R. & DOWNEY, J. (1995). Biology and the Oedipus complex. *Psychoanalytic Quarterly*, 64:243–264.

GALENSON, E. & ROIPHE, H. (1965). Some suggested revisions concerning early female development. *J. Amer. Psychoanal. Assn.*, 24:27–67.

——— (1980). The preoedipal development of the boy. *J. Amer. Psychoanal. Assn.*, 28:805–829.

GROSSMAN, W. & KAPLAN, D. (1988). Three commentaries on gender in Freud's thought: A prologue to the psychoanalytic theory of sexuality. In *Fantasy, Myth, and Reality: Essays in Honor of Jacob A. Arlow*, Madison, Conn.: International Universities Press, Inc.

HARRIS, A. (2000). Gender as a soft assembly: Tomboys' stories, *Studies in Gender and Sexuality*, 1(3):223–250.

KERNBERG, O. (2000). The influence of the gender of patient and analyst in the psychoanalytic relationship. *J. Amer. Psychoanal. Assn.*, 48:859–883.

MAYES, L. (1999). Clocks, engines, and quarks—love, dreams, and genes: what makes development happen? *Psychoanalytic Study of the Child*, 54:169–192. New Haven, Conn.: Yale University Press.

McDEVITT, J. (1995). Preoedipal determinants of an infantile gender disorder, *Psychoanalytic Study of the Child*, 50:79–105. New Haven, Conn.: Yale University Press.

MONEY, J. & EHRHARDT, A. (1972). *Man and Woman Boy and Girl.* Baltimore: Johns Hopkins Press.

OLESKER, W. (1998). Conflict and compromise in gender identity formation: A longitudinal study, *Psychoanalytic Study of the Child*, 53:212–232.

PERSON, E. & OVESEY, L. (1983). Psychoanalytic theories of gender identity. *Journal of the American Academy of Psychoanalysis* 11:203–226.

STOLLER, R. J. (1985). *Presentations of Gender.* New Haven, Conn.: Yale University Press.

SULLIVAN, H. (1953). *The Interpersonal Theory of Psychiatry.* New York: Norton.

THOMPSON, C. (1942). Cultural pressures in the psychology of women. In: *Essential Papers on the Psychology of Women*, ed. C. Zanardi. New York: New York University Press, 1990, 207–220.

YANOF, J. (2000). Barbie and the tree of life: The multiple functions of gender in development. *J. Amer. Psychoanal. Assn.*, 48:1439–1466.

Andy

A Boy Who Thought He Needed to Be a Girl

ALAN B. ZIENTS, M.D.

In presenting the case of Andy, I hope to demonstrate the complicated multidetermined functions of feminine identifications and strivings in a boy with a diagnosable gender identity disorder. My patient's fantasies of wishing and needing to be a girl were not just the result of the influence of parental behavior and attitudes. Equipmental problems resulting from inborn factors and interferences with optimal development due to ongoing interaction with his environment were major contributing influences. Andy's experience of his body and his psychological elaboration of certain childhood events as well as his sexual and aggressive fantasies strongly influenced his feminine desires.

Associate Clinical Professor of Psychiatry at New York University College of Medicine, Training and Supervising Analyst and Supervisor in Child and Adolescent Analysis at the NYU, Columbia, and New York Psychoanalytic Institutes.

Many of the ideas that are presented in this paper were discussed in a study group sponsored by the Psychoanalytic Research and Development Fund entitled "Gender and Its Clinical Manifestations." The chairperson of this group was Wendy Olesker. Additional members included Sam Abrams, Rosemary Balsan, Kirstein Dahl, Sidney Furst (deceased), Ed. Hartmann, Ted Jacobs, Rona Knight, Mortimer Ostow, Anna Wolff, Roy Lilleskov, Nancy Kulish, Ronda Shaw, Peter Neubauer and Alan Zients. I am especially appreciative of the assistance and suggestions provided by Wendy Olesker in the preparation of this manuscript.

The Psychoanalytic Study of the Child 58, ed. Robert A. King, Peter B. Neubauer, Samuel Abrams, and A. Scott Dowling (Yale University Press, copyright © 2003 by Robert A. King, Peter B. Neubauer, Samuel Abrams, and A. Scott Dowling).

HISTORY

ANDY, A SEVEN-YEAR-OLD BOY, WAS BROUGHT FOR TREATMENT BY HIS parents subsequent to a neighborhood incident in which the mother of his friend demanded that he no longer play with her son. The friend's mother could no longer tolerate Andy's coquettishly pretending that he was a girl. His feminine proclivities began early. By two-and-a-half, Andy enjoyed dressing in his sister's clothes and was fascinated by his mother's cosmetics. An extremely timid boy, he assiduously avoided competitive sports and had a cataclysmic reaction to the most minor of injuries.

Andy had few friends, much preferring to play alone in his room designing elaborate room arrangements for his dollhouse and totally absorbed with his extensive collection of Barbie dolls. He seemed walled off, preoccupied with fantasies, the content of which he rarely revealed.

Andy's short stature and his being less physically developed than the other boys in his second grade classroom also concerned his parents. Although psychological testing suggested a superior intellectual endowment, his academic achievement was average.

Andy's mother showed little capacity to recognize his separateness insisting that he not make the mistakes that she had made growing up. Perceiving Andy as identical to her, she demanded in an uncompromising manner that he realize his intellectual and musical potentials, something she reproached herself for not having accomplished.

An extremely anxious and fearful child, Andy responded to anything new or unexpected with inordinate anxiety and regression. Troubled by night fears, he thought that a strong masculine arm would reach through the floor under the bed and injure him in an unspecified but terrifying manner. His nighttime ritual consisted of entering his bedroom cautiously, checking out the room, leaping onto his bed, and quickly burying himself under the covers.

Compounding Andy's difficulties was his tomboyish, talented, athletic sister, Arlene, three-and-a-half years his senior. Arlene possessed the qualities his father had longed for in a son. Arlene flaunted her athletic superiority over Andy and totally captured father's heart and mind to the total exclusion of Andy. In mother's absence, Andy clung to Arlene for comfort and support. She responded to his requests for protection by cruelly demanding that he watch frightening television programs and then teasing and tormenting him about how frightened he became. A repetitive game with Arlene was one in which she would play the father-husband and Andy would be the mother-wife.

The stage for the dramatization of this play was the parents' bed on those occasions when the parents were traveling and the children were cared for by their almost totally blind maternal grandmother.

Andy and Arlene bathed together until age seven, as mother found this more convenient and considered it the natural way to raise children. Following these baths, Andy was frequently observed attempting to push his penis inside of his body.

Mother rationalized Andy's feminine interests and seclusiveness as understandable for a boy with an older sister and a busy, preoccupied father. She was oblivious to the many ways that she not only actively encouraged and supported his femininity but also discouraged his separating and developing. Andy was her constant luncheon companion as well as her tasteful advisor at exclusive clothing boutiques. Although his attention to manners, his gourmet tastes, and his fastidious dress brought mother's admiration, any overt manifestation of anger on his part brought forth massive, crushing criticism from her. One time mother screamed, "I wish you would leave. Maybe you should be in a psychiatric hospital with the way that you act."

At school, Andy avoided the other boys and would sit only at the girls' lunch table. The other children disliked him because he seemed selfish, weird, and not willing to share in their activities. When he would occasionally have a boy classmate visit, he would be infuriated if anything in his room was disrupted. At those moments, his compliant façade was replaced by a dictatorial fury showing, like mother, no capacity to tolerate an initiative in play other than his own.

Andy's parents had an unusually difficult time recalling much about his history. Although his father had so much hoped for a boy, his mother exclaimed upon first seeing her newborn son, "Oh damn it, a boy. I don't know what to do with a boy." Andy was a cuddly, easy to manage infant, but after his birth, mother felt inordinately tired and became depressed. Because of his mother's unavailability for the first six weeks of his life, his maternal grandmother cared for him. Shortly thereafter, his grandmother developed a life-threatening episode of ulcerative colitis, which continued episodically for over a year. While mother did resume the care of Andy, she continued to be depressed and preoccupied with her own mother's illness.

Developmental milestones were recalled as being within normal limits with the possible exception of walking, which did not occur until sixteen months. Toilet training was completed by three years with both parents being surprised that they could not recall the details of his toilet training. His mother did recall that she very much wanted him toilet trained as young as possible and compensated for this by avoiding any coercion.

At two-and-a-half, Andy became preoccupied with vacuum cleaners, an implement in constant usage in his home. For long hours, he would follow mother around the house with his toy vacuum cleaner. Preceding this, Andy had been very frightened by the roar of mother's vacuum cleaner.

At three years of age, Andy developed an obsessive fascination with automobiles, amassing a large collection of toy cars and a precocious wealth of information about Mercedes, Rolls Royces and Lincoln Continentals. He avoided driving in father's battered Volkswagen beetle, but loved being driven by mother in her large Buick station wagon.

At age three, Andy had considerable difficulty adjusting to morning nursery school. He cried continuously for weeks, but was kept at the school until he settled down. At the same time, he developed night terrors. Father, naked, would come to his room to comfort him, frequently bringing him back to the parental bed.

Andy did have a slight speech impediment, which was corrected with speech therapy by age five. He sucked his thumb until age six when he stopped spontaneously.

It is reasonable to surmise that due to certain constitutional factors, Andy felt easily impinged upon. These factors included his acute sensoriperception, including hyperacusis and an inability to filter out much in the environment. His extreme malleability, integrative difficulties, passive inclinations, and concreteness were most likely significantly influenced by dispositional factors.

Andy's mother was a volatile, moody, physically attractive woman, whose ambivalence toward her son resulted in frequent vacillations between a desire to help her beloved unhappy son to hating and sadistically attacking him when he stepped out of line. Her compulsivity about cleanliness and orderliness at home was extreme. Brought up in an upper class family dominated by women, she had one sister two years younger and six female cousins. Her own mother was a dominant, narcissistic woman with whom she was in constant conflict.

Andy's father was an intelligent, dedicated lawyer, who spent many hours away from home, both out of professional necessity and as a way of avoiding the endless conflicts with his wife. A passive, verbally noncommunicative and emotionally restricted man, he was concerned and disappointed in his son's lack of interest in sports or any other boy activities. His father was not psychologically attuned and was skeptical about the scientific basis for psychoanalysis. He constantly inquired about the methodology for measuring his son's progress. Father's physical characteristics and body movements were subtly effeminate.

INTRODUCTION TO ANDY

When I first met Andy, his long flaxen hair, pretty face, and soft, delicate hesitant manners impressed me. He was obviously surprised and upset by his parents' sudden disapproval of his feminine behavior after the incident that brought him to treatment. He now steadfastly insisted that he only enjoyed boys' games and that he had only pretended that he had wanted to be a girl. Only when discussing his envy of his sister and his inability to successfully compete with her in sports and academics did he become less reticent. Andy desperately struggled to maintain a pleasing compliant façade, but his sadness and despair shone through.

At one point, he gingerly picked up a dragon hand puppet, which then devoured all of the other human and animal puppets. Carefully avoiding even touching a small toy gun, he made an angry crocodile attack a tank, pointing out to me how well the armor protected the tank. When I noted that if someone was worried about being hurt that they would feel safer in the tank, he quickly agreed and then told me that he was frightened at night when his parents would go out. He feared a robber would come and get him. He then told me that he felt foolish because his parents had assured him that nothing like that could possibly happen. When I told him that that was the way worries are, that sometimes you know you are safe, but you feel differently on the inside as if something awful is really going to happen, he smiled, agreed, and was peacefully silent.

COURSE OF THE ANALYSIS

The first year of the analysis focused on Andy's tenacious defensive compliance: his persistent need to present a pleasing façade in conformity with perceived maternal demands, while hiding those behaviors that he thought might be criticized. As Andy almost always agreed with my interventions, it took many months before I could differentiate a compliant "yes" from a more authentic, meaningful "yes." However, I quickly understood how terrified Andy was of displeasing his mother, whom he totally depended upon. In his play, he portrayed his mother as an all-powerful phallic witch who capriciously might turn on anyone or anything. Once unleashed, nothing could constrain her. The only way to avoid her wrath was to be just like her and to not do anything that might upset her.

Andy was very worried about the impact that the analysis might have upon him. Although he freely talked about his wish to be a girl, his love of cosmetics, hair styles, dresses, being with girls, and playing with Barbie dolls, he was fearful that our work together might take these interests from him and leave him only with his anxiety and more subject to his mother's wrath. Andy avoided any activity in which he thought he might suffer bodily injury. His feminine identifications defended against his fear of bodily injury. Andy relaxed when I told him that I wanted only to help him know who he wanted to be, not to make him into someone that he didn't want to be.

For over two years, Andy was preoccupied in his play with the theme of the powerful tyrannical woman, sometimes represented as a witch on a broomstick, or in a more benign way as a neighborhood woman driving a large station wagon. Andy imitated and wanted to be like this woman. In awe of her power and unpredictability, he became a supplicant and sought protection from her. At other times, he would regress further and want to become a part of her body by having her swallow him. As he recognized his rage, he became more organized in his attempts to destroy her. Furniture would be piled on her, powerful animals would attack her, but she could not be suppressed. Sadistically, he would beat her or be beaten by her. With excitement, he would flee from her and breathlessly have her pursue him. During this phase of the analysis, a powerful maternal transference dominated the hours. With great difficulty, Andy integrated his play with his feelings toward his mother, his sister, and myself. This took the form of his increasingly wanting me to protect him and intervene with his mother.

As Andy gradually began to perceive his mother as separate from himself, his disappointment in his father for not protecting him from her emerged. For the first time, he expressed the wish that he could fly like the witch on the broomstick and have his own source of power. Triumphantly, he would mount his broomstick, fly around the room, but then get scared that the broomstick would be taken from him and he would fall dead or injured to the ground. Andy needed my presence and reassurance in order to take his first tentative steps toward independence.

Andy carefully constructed a Lego car, which he named the "Contraption." It would get into repeated accidents but could always be rebuilt. It had a prominent hood adornment that wasn't functional, but could be easily damaged. For months, the Contraption traveled around my office getting into accidents and then being totally restored. I talked to Andy about how the "Contraption" could embark upon daring adventures because if damaged, it could be repaired, but that I thought he felt differently about himself. Andy agreed while holding his hand over his penis.

Coincident with this, Andy became more assertive at home. His mother thought that the analysis was making him worse because he was becoming more defiant and difficult to manage. Andy, however, felt protected by me and less needy and frightened of his mother.

One hour, at the beginning of his third year of analysis, Andy happily skipped into my office announcing that his problems were over because he had decided that he would be a queen and rule the earth. If he could rule the earth, he would never have to be frightened of being hurt or alone. He would finally be safe. During ensuing hours, Andy continued playing the queen who ruled the earth. At one point, I inquired as to what gave the queen her awesome powers. Andy didn't know but was determined to find out. He searched everywhere and one day made the momentous discovery that the power of the queen was derived from a treasured ruby found deep in a protected cave. Whoever possessed the ruby had all of the power. The momentous discovery of the ruby signified for Andy that the power of the queen was not inextricably linked to gender, but was transportable. When he had it, he had to deal with those who wanted it and would attack him, as he would attack them to obtain it. Simultaneously, Andy began to entertain the idea that it might be all right to be a boy as long as you had ways of protecting yourself and could choose what you wanted to do.

Andy one day presented with considerable flourish a proposal to me. He would be the person who would take care of my office. It would be our apartment. He would cook and clean for me. In exchange, I would earn money and protect him from the world outside of our apartment. Only when he chose to would he leave the apartment to do whatever he wanted. Andy also began to show interest in guns and shooting. At one dramatic moment, he aimed a toy gun at a bad witch, fired it, and broke her into small pieces. I noted how easily she fell apart. This led Andy to thoughts about his mother and how he had to be careful or he might do irreparable harm to her. For the first time, Andy understood that his mother was vulnerable and perhaps needed his protection. As he so poignantly indicated to me, "maybe she is worried about needing a psychiatric hospital for herself, not for me."

Andy gradually began to express disappointment in me. He had hoped that I would better protect him from his mother and that by seeing me I would convey the power he needed to be now "king of his own little kingdom" and "his own person." Under my protection and through my conveying to him my power, he would build his own life, construct a home of his own design, and decorate it with furniture of his own choosing. He also admitted to a fantasy of wanting to be a beautiful bird in a birdcage on my desk. He would sing to me all day and nothing else would be required of him. I related this wish to how he had been earlier with his mother, when he was her constant companion and admired by her and her friends and nothing else was asked of him. While Andy agreed, he was also insistent that he would prefer that I just take care of him instead of always talking in the way that I did. He didn't want to understand why he wanted me to take care of him; he just wanted me to do it!

During this time, Andy was making significant progress at school. He also told me that now he really did want to be a boy because a boy didn't just have to do boy things but could do some girl things. As the source of power was transportable, a boy could be as powerful as a woman. Also, he sadly said that he had been born a boy and there just wasn't anything that he could do about that but accept it.

Andy also confessed to me that there was something he had not told me: since the first year of analysis, he had two imaginary brothers, Stuart Harrington and Stuart R. The name Harrington derived from a television program about a young girl living with her cruel aunt. When fleeing from the aunt, the girl suffered a crippling accident that required her to be taken care of by the hated aunt. Her paralyzed legs took away choice and any possibility of leaving. In contrast, Stuart R. wanted to be and could be independent and accomplished, the master of his own destiny. Andy, with my assistance, came to understand how the two Stuarts represented two opposing aspects of his own feelings. Like Harrington, he felt as if he were a part of his mother's body, crippled and incapable of leaving her at the same time that he so much wanted to be like Stuart R.

During this phase of the analysis, Andy was even more frightened of being hurt. He experienced difficulty in terminating our appointments, which were now permeated by castration anxiety. When the Contraption broke, it no longer could be fixed. Andy brought in a mechanical lead pencil and demonstrated to me how easily the lead broke off when it stuck out and could write. When it was retracted and inside of the pencil, it was protected but nonfunctional. I related this to Andy's concerns about his body, especially his penis, and also his impression that women are not anatomically at risk the way men are. He responded by telling me that he no longer tries to push his penis inside of his body because that isn't where it belongs. The thought emerged and gradually consolidated that he could be safe if he acknowledged himself as a male and might even be able to accept his body and feel that his penis was not like the hood adornment on the "Contraption," so easily broken off.

Andy would regress and seek protection from me by being provocative and seductive. This was an enactment in the transference of how he had earlier felt teased, stimulated, and frustrated by both his mother and his sister. He wanted both to be captured and to get away. At first, he seemed to imitate me and then proceeded to more solid albeit transitory identifications with me. I was safer than mother in that I did not attack him or insist that he not separate if he felt he the need to be protected by me.

It was only after he felt more identified with and protected by me that he reluctantly admitted that part of his wish to be a beautiful woman was a fascination with beauty. He thought that beauty provided the power to be taken care of passively without doing anything other than attending to the details of proper grooming, which he so enjoyed anyway. It also seemed that one source of his preoccupation with the concrete details of being a beautiful woman was his way of holding onto his mother from early in life when she was depressed, self-preoccupied, and not available to hold and care for him. He could only take her in with his eyes at a time when he so longed for her touch.

New material emerged in which Andy was more assertive, insisting that he was now his own person. Many hours were consumed by his drawing elaborate, detailed floor plans. He wanted to be an architect and build things in the way in which he wanted them to be constructed. He expressed the wish to be a pilot, but was somewhat hesitant because the plane might get out of control and crash. He seemed increasingly comfortable in the world of men and even began to reach out to his uninvolved father. At times, he seemed delighted with his increasing independence and reduced conflict with being male.

In his play, he desperately wanted to both possess and protect from the loss the powerful jewel that would permit him to become the "boss man." If he was the boss man, he needed me to be a policeman to contain and control him. He feared that if he became too rich and powerful, like Midas, his greed might destroy him. Napoleon and Alexander the Great, both of who came close to conquering the

world, fascinated him. He also noted that neither of them totally succeeded. An ephemeral but powerful attraction to Hitler emerged,
but Andy was concerned that I would find that unacceptable, so he
quickly suppressed it.

Andy wanted to discuss with me only those ideas that he thought
would make me think more highly of him. As earlier with his mother,
it seemed necessary that we agreed about everything. To disagree
meant the loss of the special power and protection he derived from
our relationship and underscored his separateness and vulnerability.

As Andy became increasingly aggressive at home and openly expressed his desire to be bigger and more independent, his mother
became concerned about the effect of his analysis and sought a consultation in another city. Only after the consultant underscored the
criticalness of Andy's analysis for his optimizing his development did
mother back away and reduce her attacks on the analysis and her
son. This coincided with Andy's capacity to better differentiate the
penis as a source of power and pleasure, although previously he has
seen the source of power as being the ruby, which had been located
in the mother's body. If he saw me as a man who didn't attack but
protected him and also had power vis-à-vis his mother, he could be
safe from maternal attack and free to assert himself and his own phallic potency.

During his third year of analysis, Andy resolved and succeeded in
improving his academic performance. Simultaneously, he became
more regressed in our sessions, enacting repetitive scenes in which
he acknowledged his rage at his mother and his fear of her loss by beheading many women in his drawings and puppet play. He struggled
to reduce his aggression through compliance, but these efforts were
short lived. Andy reported a dream, "I was ice skating with my sister
when the ice cracked. There were houses around, but I couldn't tell
if they were attached or separate. Inside one house were three doll-
houses. They were weird and I couldn't tell what was wrong." His associations were to three children who had physical defects: one had
malformed teeth, another a crippled leg, and the third a nonfunctional arm. He spontaneously had the thought that he was skating on
thin ice and something awful would happen to him if he were too independent and distant from his mother.

Within several months, Andy was not just beheading his mother in
drawings. Rather, he began to speak up to her directly, expressing his
rage at her intrusiveness and unwillingness to tolerate his initiatives.

Andy perceived me as male, nurturing and powerful. Having previously perceived his father as ineffectual and unavailable and his mother as all-powerful, he gradually relinquished the need to grandiosely identify with his mother. Anticipating the possibility of giving up his treasured fantasy world, he once again feared that would be left with nothing and feared loss of control over his feelings of destructive greed. His ability to integrate, synthesize, and organize improved. His improvement was considerable, but he had little confidence that it would endure. He felt fragile, which seemed connected with his identification with mother's fragility.

Andy could identify with my maleness only after he ascertained that being male was not too dangerous. A period ensued in which there was considerable gender instability. States of acting like a boy or a girl would not be present simultaneously, but rather in sequence. He feared that as a boy he could be too destructive and also the object of other's destructiveness. At those times, it seemed safer to think of himself as a girl. At other times, he enjoyed his maleness, noting that even as a boy he didn't have to play football. He could play tennis and make other choices that were appropriate for boys or girls. His choices in life were less linked to gender.

Andy reported that when he was alone and would pretend to be a girl it was less satisfying. He couldn't push aside the reality of his own anatomy. He mourned the loss of the pleasurable and comforting aspects of his fantasies of being a girl.

In one session Andy excitedly told me about a transsexual who had given him a haircut at a unisex shop. His association to this "man-woman" was one of understanding, but also resignation that you have to be the way you are born. He added that he didn't want to be a person who was not admired and he thought that many people were critical of "gays" and transsexuals.

Anxious about the loss of his treasured and safe make-believe world of being a girl and insecure in his male identity, he drew a picture of three kingdoms: the kingdom of Dr. Zients, which he placed at the top of the pyramid; the kingdom of Andy, which he set in the middle of the pyramid; and the kingdom of his mother which formed the base of the pyramid. He used to worry that the kingdom of his mother would take over his kingdom, but now he thought that he might be pulled into the kingdom of Dr. Zients and the kingdom of Andy would vanish forever. Andy realized that he feared being taken over by me because he feared he would then cease to exist, but he also desired it because it meant safety and being totally taken care of. During this period, Andy benefited from my clarifying his thinking and verbalizing his conflicts. He acknowledged that I had helped him without his kingdom being invaded. That was possible because my help didn't demand compliance. He recognized that he felt inadequate when he compared himself to other boys. He was not a good athlete and feared contact sports. He realized that his preconception that all a girl needed was to be beautiful and the world would take care of her was false. Femininity had promised the power of being taken care of passively while he thought that only men had to go out and actively tackle problems. He realized that he had thought that his father would take better care of him, the way he did his sister, if he were a girl.

Andy was placed in an all-boys school at the end of his fourth year of analysis. The experience at the school helped him to further define himself as a male and to recognize the many alternative paths he could choose as a male. The dangers of maleness were lessened through his imitation and consolidating identifications with me. At first he just wanted to copy the other boys at school so that they would accept him, but he increasingly assumed a more comfortable individuated masculine identity.

In the fall of his fifth year of analysis, he returned from his summer vacation and told me that he wanted to stop treatment because then he would be more like the other boys at school who didn't see psychiatrists. He felt more accepted by his classmates and much more accepting of himself. His parents felt that he was "cured" and supported his wish to stop treatment. Most hours, he would discuss only the details of his homework and activities with his friends. He was doing well at school: there was little evidence of feminine behavior, and for the first time he had acceptable male friends. While his mother resented his independence, his willingness to participate in individual athletic activities such as tennis and swimming pleased his father.

During the four-month termination, Andy expressed some regrets at our not seeing each other anymore. Otherwise, he was resistant and focussed on detailing the events of each day. This was his way of separating from me and experiencing a greater sense of autonomy. He indicated that he would have to accept his mother and her limitations. "That's just the way she is. She's still my mother. I can't do anything about her, but I can decide what I am going to do about myself. That is my decision, not hers." Andy thought he might want to come back later to see me.

Three years later, Andy called me because he was in a panic while acting the role of an elegant dandyish English nobleman in a school play. He was unable to study and feared he would "disappear." While he was not motivated to return to analysis, I did see him weekly for several months. As a result of these consultations, he decided that he had enough difficulty being Andy and that he would not act in plays anymore, but would rather concentrate on his schoolwork and other activities. With this decision, he reported that he was doing well and stopped our appointments.

Andy contacted me during his freshman year at college because someone had called him "gay." During that contact, I was struck by how much his uses of language sounded like my ways of expressing myself. The homosexual worry was transient. He successfully completed college and married a wealthy opinionated woman, who he was able to stand up to and care about. Andy went on to have two children and has been successful as an art dealer. He has minimized his contact with his mother. Andy developed a life as a male that works for him.

DISCUSSION

Andy's difficulties derived not only from his drives but also from other constitutional difficulties in his capacity to integrate and synthesize that limited his ability to resolve conflict. The characteristics of his parents and their difficulties in providing optimal parenting fostered an environment that augmented his dispositional difficulties rather than optimizing his development. Although my interpretation of his gender-based defenses and conflicts was helpful to him, my construction of coherent narratives assisted him with his organizational difficulties. Also, our work with his anger and competitive conflicts freed him to form a more stable self-image and ego ideal. Andy gradually developed a more coherent and hopefully accurate intrapsychic and interpersonal understanding of himself. He had a better framework for thinking and problem solving. He used my various comments to establish an awareness of intrapsychic conflicts, to represent people in a meaningful way, and to create stories that were useful in putting together self and object. This narrative scaffolding was provided by my interpretations and by the full range of interactions between us, including empathy and my focus on verbalizing his subjective experience. His core wish was to possess those qualities, which would permit him to be taken care of—first by a woman and later by a man. Initially, he thought this was best accomplished by the power of physical beauty and only later acknowledged the importance of active efforts on his part. In the later years of his analysis, he derived considerable satisfaction from his own intellectual and physical accomplishments and understood that this did not preclude his being taken care of in a manner more appropriate to his age and level of development.

Femaleness was an important compromise formation for Andy in that it helped him cope with his rage and disappointment in his mother for her unavailability, her unremitting penetration of his boundaries, her refusal to recognize who he was, her extreme need for control, and her frequent cruel rejections of him. Femaleness provided protection for his penis by assisting him in his denial of its presence and perceived vulnerability. With the absence both psychologically and physically of his father and his perception that his mother was the source of all of the power, his identification with her femaleness helped him feel strong and effective rather than weak and helpless. Being female like his mother and not differentiating himself from her protected him from being the object of her aggression.

Andy was not able to organize his masculinity. He was too pulled by his mother to fulfill what she didn't complete in herself. We can speculate that mother was unable to feel separate and couldn't let her son go in his own independent direction. She attacked and suppressed his aggressiveness, which increased his difficulties in establishing his own separateness. Due to his special sensitivities, passivity, and psychological limitations, Andy felt his mother's message as an onslaught and a demand, and he couldn't tune her out. He shaped himself like her to gain her love, a feeling of safety and to protect his vulnerable self from her intrusions. By being female he could deny his own aggression and express his wish to be taken care of passively. His erotic life was conspicuous by its absence, swamped most likely by the extent of his aggression.

Initially, there were no indications of conflicts with father or observable father hunger. Since his father dismissed Andy because he didn't seem to have athletic abilities or other interests his father favored, Andy was pushed even more toward mother, despite her dangerousness. Mother was interested in him and needed him; father was not. Andy could fulfill what mother wanted; he couldn't satisfy his father. Father did not acknowledge or understand Andy's need for him to actively reach out and engage him. His father seemed to see Andy's passivity and feminine interests as rejecting and failed to see how he could have assisted his son. I also wondered if his father's own bisexual conflicts and passivity contributed to his not providing a contrasting and competing model for identification for Andy. His mother did not represent to Andy the opposite sex. Perhaps because his mother excluded maleness both in her and in Andy, both her feelings about a man in actuality and her possible inability to accept her own bisexuality contributed to Andy's attachment and ignorance about maleness.

Andy's gender confusion and ambiguity was part of his overall lack of a defined identity. As he grew more aware of his own psychological separateness, he began to coalesce his own interests and abilities. Initially, separation was experienced as annihilation, chaos, and destruction. As our work progressed, he began to fear punishment for doing well and separating. His vehicle for separation from his mother was an alignment with what he perceived to be my power because he needed structure, nurturance, and protection. His focus on the sensual concrete details of femininity was a way to hold onto his mother despite his intense ambivalence toward her. Through his analysis he gradually came to understand that he also viewed mother as explosive and fragile. As he felt safer in the analysis and found me more reliable, he was able to differentiate himself from his mother and gradually have less need for a feminine identification. Andy also appreciated that his mother needed him to take care of her and an impediment to his separation and further development was the guilt he felt for what he perceived as abandoning a fragile and dependent mother.

With his increasing capacity to tolerate his aggression toward his mother, his use of withdrawal and feminine identification to ward off his own destructive and voracious greed lessened as he grew more accepting of himself and less fearful of loss of control. Critical for this accomplishment was Andy's recognition of my own ability to contain his aggression and to not respond as mother had done by attacking him. Andy substantially progressed in his ability to differentiate masculine and feminine, his moods, his feelings toward his mother and father, and his sense of self and other. Previously powerful linkages between gender and passivity, power, beauty, accomplishment, and safety shifted. The powerful hidden jewel could belong to either a man or a woman, not just a woman. His aggression modulated and was available for adaptive purposes. While he mourned the loss of power through magical omnipotent merger, taming his primitive omnipotent wishes facilitated his increased capacity to deal with school, friends, and family. Initially, he wanted to be like me and later like the boys at school. Over time, he learned that he had feared acknowledging his own maleness because he thought that both his parents might reject and neglect him and that maleness was associated with unacceptable danger. He was convinced that he didn't possess the capacity to succeed as a boy because of his feminine identifications, the projection of his own aggression and misinformed conception of what it meant to be male. He was so frightened of aggression that he resorted to total withdrawal.

Andy attempted to use gender to resolve the dynamic conflicts that his equipmental difficulties had potentiated in such a painful way for him. During the analysis, he developed alternative organizational compromises, which facilitated better adaptations. While the source of later information about Andy is anecdotal and nonanalytic, my impression is that he has continued to consolidate the work of the analysis and is enjoying a satisfying life as a husband, father, and professional within the art world.

BIBLIOGRAPHY

Balsam, R. (2001). Integrating male and female elements in a woman's gender identity. *JAPA,* 49:1335–1360.

Coates, S. & Wolfe, S. (1995). Boyhood gender identity disorder: The interface of constitution and early experience. *Psychoanalytic Inquiry,* 51:6–38.

Olesker, W. (1990). Sex differences in early separation-individuation: Gender identity formation. *JAPA,* 38:325–346.

Silverman, M. & Bernstein, P. (1993). Gender identity disorders in boys. *JAPA,* 41:729–742.

Yanof, J. (2000). Barbie and the tree of life: The multiple functions of gender in development. *JAPA,* 48:1429–1465.

Zients, A. (1994). Gender identity disorders in boys. Presentation to the Boston Psychoanalytic Institute.

Margo and Me

Gender as a Cause and Solution to Unmet Needs

RONA KNIGHT, Ph.D.

This paper presents a six-year analytic treatment that began when Margo was five and a half years old. Unable to get the love and attention that her older brothers received, Margo sought repair by deciding to be both a boy and a girl. Before a solid gender identity could emerge, I needed to facilitate her development and help her obtain a cohesive sense of self that would include ego integration of feelings and object relationships. Margo's bi-gender solution crystallized a fundamental struggle and conflict with identity, and served to repair feelings of narcissistic injury, cope with extreme feelings of love and hate and good and bad objects, quell annihilation anxiety, and repair a sense of ego disintegration.

Assistant Professor of Pediatrics and Psychiatry, Boston University School of Medicine; Faculty, Adult and Child Psychoanalysis, Boston Psychoanalytic Society and Institute; Supervising Analyst, Massachusetts Institute of Psychoanalysis; Founding Member and Faculty, Berkshire Psychoanalytic Institute.

I would like to thank the members of the Study Group on Gender and its Clinical Manifestations, sponsored by the Psychoanalytic Research and Development Fund, whose thoughtful comments contributed to my thinking about development, gender, and my patient. Chair: Wendy Olesker; Members: Sam Abrams, Rosemary Balsam, Kirsten Dahl, Sidney Furst (deceased), Edward Hartmann, Theodore Jacobs, Nancy Kulish, Roy Lilleskov, Peter Neubauer, Mortimer Ostow, Rhonda Shaw, Anna Wolff, and Alan Zients. I would especially like to thank Wendy Olesker for her thoughtful editorial comments throughout the years, and Judith Yanof, who contributed to my understanding of this child.

Presenting Difficulties

MARGO WAS FIVE AND A HALF YEARS OLD WHEN HER PARENTS FIRST consulted with me because they were concerned about many aspects of her behavior that indicated difficulties in development. Her parents found her "hard to get close to" and noticed that she had difficulty playing with peers and interacting with adults. Margo had a very limited ability to regulate her affects. She had severe and rapid mood swings with an inability to control her anger. She was quick to hit people, threw chairs, wrote on the walls, and was generally uncontrollable when in an angry state. She often felt deprived, and mother reported that no matter how much attention she gave Margo it was never enough and nothing was satisfying, leaving mother feeling exhausted from all the time and attention Margo required. Her father did not spend much time with Margo. He spent what time he did have at home solely with her older brothers, feeling that Margo was her mother's child. Margo also refused to wear skirts, dresses, or girl's shoes; she wanted to be a boy.

History

From the very beginning of the consultation it was evident that Margo's parents were going to need my time and attention. These parents had carefully thought out a family history that went back several generations. They needed to have me listen to it and help them understand its complexity and how it affected their feelings about and management of Margo. A "Ghosts in the Nursery" (Fraiberg, 1975) story unfolded that made it clear that both parents' own insufficient parenting affected their ability to parent Margo. Mrs. P grew up in a large Italian family that valued men. She became a "tomboy" in her latency as a way to relate to her alcoholic father who was psychologically absent or abusive toward the females in his family, preferring to spend time with his sons. Her mother worked part-time and was overwhelmed with the care of her eight children. Mr. P's parents had divorced when he was a toddler, and he never saw his father again. His mother worked long hours to support her children, and he experienced her as exhausted most of the time. Both parents were firstborn children and resented having to help care for their younger siblings.

Mrs. P found her infant daughter difficult at birth. Margo could not be calmed, and Mrs. P became depressed. Margo was a temperamentally active baby who didn't sleep a lot, which further tired her mother, who also had two older, active sons to take care of. When Margo started to crawl at seven months "all hell broke out," and her parents reported that it was hard to connect with her—"it was more like just chasing." Mr. P complained that he always found Margo diffi-cult to engage—"I couldn't find anything in common with her."

Margo's history was riddled with loss and a lack of safety in rela-tionships. When Margo was one year old, Mrs. P returned to work. From ages one to five, Margo was placed in six different daycare and preschool settings and experienced both being picked on by the older children and the loss of many daycare workers in each of the settings. When she was at two and three years old, she had also been forgotten and "lost" on two different trips with her parents. Margo wanted to stay home with her mother whenever she could.

INITIAL PICTURE

When Margo first came to see me, her play and thoughts were frag-mented. A pretty, thin, wiry, and active child, she was quickly over-come with anxiety and had great difficulty keeping her attention on any task for very long. While she was clearly hungry for my attention, her play was devoid of any human interaction. Her drawing that first session told her version of her difficulty. She drew a little girl "who hates everything about herself and her mother and father because they don't spend any time and attention on her. Her mother will spend attention if the girl acts like a baby." She then told me that "the little girl doesn't like to do that but has to to get attention." The next session she drew "Rosemary Stupid Face." "Her mother named her that because she thinks that everything Rosemary does is stupid. Rosemary thinks that she is stupid, too. Rosemary hates people be-cause nobody will play with her," she told me.

I recommended twice-a-week psychotherapy for Margo, and once a week counseling for her parents. Margo was, in many ways, stuck at a toddler level of development. She had serious difficulties with her sense of self and agency, affect regulation, ego integration and orga-nization, gender orientation, and object relationships. Feeling de-prived, unloved, and unprotected in her relationships, her attach-ment to people appeared insecure and disorganized (Main, 1995; Main and Solomon, 1990). Margo's constant attempts to get and maintain her mother's attention, coupled with her father's lack of at-tention, made it difficult for her to go beyond dyadic relationships and enter into triadic relationships. Margo also seemed to be living out and making real her parents' feelings of insecurity. Mr. and Mrs.

P needed immediate help with parenting issues and their feelings
about Margo. I thought about analysis for this child from the very beginning, struggling with the issue of appropriate timing for Margo,
her family, and myself. While I felt that Margo would have loved to
meet with me every afternoon, I wasn't sure her parents would form
the necessary bond with me to sustain a long analysis at this point. I
told them early on that analysis might be necessary for Margo, but
that we would try therapy twice a week first.

During the one and a half years of therapy several themes emerged.
Margo, a very creative and imaginative child, loved to play pretend.
Hiding games expressed her feelings that she was not seen. Hot and
cold games communicated her extremes of feelings in which babies
are hungry and lions eat up people. She would change the thermo-
stat in the room so that I could literally experience the degrees of
change within her and how quickly they occurred. She had a great
desire to have me understand her affective states and what was causing them, often playing out a situation in which I was in her shoes
and made to feel how she felt. Typical of this was the "Time Machine
Game" in which I can't connect with a dog who keeps going to different places just as I am about to reach him. At times the dog is busy
reading his newspaper. This was a frantic game in which there is a
great deal of running around, with me chasing her in a desperate attempt to catch up to her. I would voice my feelings: how I long for the
dog and am desperate to play with it; how the dog is so tantalizingly
close, yet I can't get hold of it; how hungry/angry/lonely/sad I am,
depending on the play that day. Margo enjoyed this game as she experienced my understanding of her feelings, identified with the aggressor, and enjoyed the cruelty she could express in the play. I was
aware that this game also expressed her parents' description of always chasing Margo as a toddler.

Her doll house play featured a girl and boy who were totally out of
control. The children got hurt and lost, and the parents were completely ineffectual. Sometimes a magic dragon came and helped
them out of disastrous situations. Sometimes they were hurt so bad
that they had to go to the hospital and be taken care of by doctors
and nurses for long periods of time. I wondered with her about how
the children could feel safe and okay in this situation. I commented
on how the children needed the doctors and nurses to help them
feel better and protect them in the hospital. I was told that the children never wanted to leave the hospital because they got better care
there. Margo's problems with her parents and her feelings about it
were clear. In the transference I was the idealized, magic doctor who

would take good care of her. One day she covered a doll with red play make-up and told me that the doll was so sick and so hurt that even if she went to the doctor for years she might never be completely well. I told her that while the doll wanted the doctor to help her get better, she wasn't sure that all the hurt she felt could ever go away.

I saw her parents once a week for parent counseling. Neither of them knew how to respond to Margo in a way that was both loving and containing. While her father would not spend time with her, her mother was there but not there, feeling drained by her daughter's constant requests for more time and attention. Their parenting skills improved over time, and her father's positive relationship with me helped to foster a beginning relationship with his daughter. My experience in the chasing game allowed me to empathize with her father's feelings of rejection as he attempted to have a good relationship with his daughter and succeeded. Margo's mother formed a positive transference to me, seeing me as helping her to parent her daughter. I could understand her feeling drained by Margo's neediness and her need for another active adult to help her. She was also very much aware of Margo's psychological suffering and very much wanted her to be less pained. Although she could not really change her ability to be more available to Margo during her analysis, which lasted until Margo was eleven and a half years old, she always supported the treatment and took genuine delight in Margo's growth throughout the analysis and after, becoming a very responsive mother when Margo was a teenager.

At the beginning of the second year of therapy, Margo's body image/gender concerns surfaced in the treatment. She started to wear her "little guy" (a rabbit's tail, a key chain, etc.) clipped to the bottom of her shirts. Margo announced that she had a penis and didn't want to be a girl. Then He/She appeared in her play. He/She was both a boy and a girl who had everything and was great at school. He/She was perfection personified. I was given the role of speaking for all the boys and girls who weren't as good, who didn't have everything and felt stupid, neglected, angry, and sad. The children envied He/She, who had everything and was loved by his/her parents. They wished that they could have what He/She had so they could feel good about themselves. When she was seven years old Margo insisted that He/She had to choose one gender or the other. "Why does He/She have to choose?" I asked. "He/She just does!" she exclaimed. She broke off the play and began crying. The crying and screaming that followed lasted for two weeks, as she wailed about all that she didn't get. I talked with her about how badly I thought she felt about herself and how sad and angry she was because her brothers got more attention than she did. I wondered with her if she wished that she could be a boy as well as a girl so that she could be as smart as her older brothers and get what her brothers did.

The play in the office resumed, only this time the scenario was one of control in which she was the one giving the orders. She then started to call me every day, as the sessions could not provide enough containment for her feelings. One Friday evening Margo called and asked if she could have a Saturday session, knowing that I did not see people on the weekend. I gave her a time for the following morning. She came in, and in an angry, controlled, and methodical way proceeded to make a mess of my office. At no time during this session was she out of control, and she followed directions about what she could and couldn't mess in the room. Nothing was allowed to be broken or destroyed, although books and toys were all over the floor. I talked with her about the intensity of her feelings, how her sad and mad feelings could feel so big they sometimes just burst out of her. In the weeks that followed I limited her need to destroy to a specific place in the room as we explored her angry feelings toward me for not giving her enough time and attention and her angry feelings toward her parents for ignoring her and clearly preferring her brothers. While her destruction of my office may have also been an expression of her wish to destroy me, I did not feel this wish was near enough to her conscious experience to inquire about it at this time.

Her extended period of extreme sadness followed by her anger and making a mess of my office was a repetition of the same extreme behavior she used with her parents when she felt she needed more and was not getting it. It was part of her constitutional drive to get what she needed (either by action or fantasy) and protest when she didn't get it rather than confront the despair of a hopeless state. She needed more from me in my role as transference object, real object, and new developmental object. I felt that our work together was her attempt to find, in our relationship and in herself, what was bypassed or derailed in her development and to correct it.

At this point in the treatment I recommended analysis and her parents agreed. I felt that she was capable of an analysis because she was able to convey deep, painful feelings and relationships in her play, which was incredibly rich and imaginative. She had the capacity to see play as a form of speech and understood not playing as a way of avoiding talking about things that made her uncomfortable. She was incredibly insightful and intelligent, and she had an intense desire to be helped. Margo had the capacity to use the treatment modality and the analytic relationship as a platform from which she could create and engage in a narrative structure to put herself together differently that would allow her developmental potential to progress. At least this was what both she and I hoped for. I discussed coming four times a week with Margo, and she readily agreed.

THE ANALYSIS

Margo came to her first analytic session and kissed the floor, poignantly expressing her need and delight to have four sessions a week. I had not just understood her protest but had actually done what she was asking for; I had given her more time. From the very beginning of the analysis she could see that I was actively playing with her and talking with her about her needs and problems. She experienced my therapeutic actions as concretely giving her what she felt she needed. She looked into a crystal ball in my office, and I asked if she was wondering what it would be like now that we were meeting four times a week. She nodded yes. Her doll house play was about safety, and I said that perhaps she was worried about how safe she would be with me as we met more often. Several sessions later she asked if the pearls in my necklace were real. "Yes," I said, positioning myself as a real (genuine and not fake) person who would offer ideas and suggestions to help her understand and work out her thoughts and feelings. My countertransference wish to be able to provide her with what she had missed contributed to this stance as did my sense of urgency to help this child reach her appropriate developmental maturity as soon as possible. I felt that she immediately needed developmental assistance to help promote ego integration and a coherent sense of self and other. I thought that once she had achieved the latency level of ego functioning that she would need to manage in school and with peers, we would have the luxury of time—and her more integrated ego functioning—to explore the unconscious conflicts underlying her character development.

Our work together was often a recapitulation of her developmental relationships. The themes of not being properly cared for physically and emotionally were continuously worked on throughout the analysis as Margo felt incredibly sad and then angry about what she was not able to get from her parents. As a new object in her life, Margo was able to experience me as really there for her, which helped her identify her mother's preoccupied stance as well as cause her intense pain when she thought about what she was missing in her relationships with her mother and father. We did a lot of singing and dancing in the office, separately and together—"Somewhere Over the Rainbow" (from *The Wizard of Oz*) and "Someday" (from *Annie*) were her two favorite songs. This play was in many ways a repetition of an infant mirroring and fusing game in which I met her both vocally and physically, as well as an expression of her wishes. The centrality of the transference was her wish to have me be her mother, including her need to have me be the infant-mirroring mother, though I did not interpret this to her at this time. There were times when I watched her and she would notice the gleam in my eye and become pained and sad. I would sometimes comment about how hard it was to see how much I liked and appreciated her, and she would just nod yes.

Her lack of agency in relationships and her wish to be in control of people's coming and going was played out in a game called "Toll Booth." In this game Margo is the toll booth operator and I am the driver going through the tollbooth. I give her money and she tells me what stores to go to and what to buy in the stores. I commented on her wish to be in charge of my coming and going as a way to be sure of what would happen in our relationship. Her sense of deprivation in relationships and her need to recover the loss can be seen in the money part of this game. I give her money at the tollbooth and at the stores, which she has to keep because she needs more and more money. In another variation of this game she is a bank machine, and I have to put more and more money in the machine because she doesn't have enough. I said that the machine never seemed to have enough no matter how much money was deposited. She agreed.

In the first year of her analysis Margo would empty entire containers of Elmer's glue into a cardboard tray used for craft projects. The first time she emptied the entire container onto a craft tray, I wondered if she wished I had an endless supply of glue and toys so that she could use as much as she wanted. "Yes!" she said. "Do you have more?" I told her that I didn't that day, but that I would buy more glue. She looked sad. I said, "Sometimes people want more and more because they feel empty inside and feel like they never have enough. Do you ever feel that way?" "Yes," she said, as she noticed that there were holes in the cardboard that needed filling up with more glue. I wondered if she wished she could fill up the emptiness inside that she felt. She sadly said, "Yes." I said, "That's one of the reasons for the analysis, to help you feel less empty and to understand why you feel that way." She said, "That would really be very good." "Yes," I replied, "because with the empty feelings inside you, you feel so sad and angry." "Yes," she said, as she filled in all the holes and told me to leave it that way. Later in the session she drew a circle in my carpet and said, "The hole is a little more filled up." "Does feeling understood help with the empty feelings?" I asked. "Yes," she replied.

Each day I would have a new bottle of glue in the office and each day she would empty it on top of the dried glue, telling me that she needed to build a stronger and stronger base. She began to want more and more of me, noticing that I didn't work on the weekend, like her mother did. I asked if she particularly felt the emptiness over the weekend, when she didn't see me or as much of her mother as she wanted. She got angry and started putting the glue over herself and then on me. I noted her anger with me and wondered if she wanted to glue us together so that we didn't have to be separated over the weekend. She then asked me to tell her a story about He/She. In a stage whisper, I asked her what I should say. This is the story she dictated to me: He/She is in the second grade, knows all the languages, and has invented his/her own language. He/She reads the dictionary and the entire encyclopedia, writes in script, and is the best student in class. Although I thought that He/She might have been Margo's solution to her empty feelings at this time, I chose to not say this. I was concerned that it would prematurely foreclose this fantasy, and I wanted to give her the space to elaborate this defense.

As her eighth birthday was approaching, she asked me to buy her a birthday present, something I had not done for her before. When I asked her why she wanted one this year she said, "You buy your daughters birthday presents, don't you?" "Do you wish you were my daughter?" I asked. "No, I have a mother," she replied. As the weeks progressed she refused to further discuss the present issue and got angrier and angrier with me when I tried to explore it with her. I asked her if she was angry with me for not agreeing to get her a present and wondered if she felt she doesn't get enough of what she wants from me. She did not answer me and left the session angry, calling me a "scum sucking pig" as she walked out the door. The toll booth and bank games escalated to her needing more and more money. Each day more and more glue was used "to build a stronger base." She refused to elaborate about why she needed a stronger base, telling me that she just needed more glue. Then she drew two pictures: a hole that is a war zone and a volcano that is exploding.

The sequence of these analytic interactions is rich in meaning. As her analyst, I provided her with a structure for mentalization (Fonagy and Target, 1998), a narrative—as I understood her thinking—to help her begin to put words to and cognitively understand the emptiness that she felt from the deprivation and loss she experienced.

Margo was able to work with me on this narrative, which she expanded through the toll booth and bank games. Yet the emptiness was so hard to talk about at this point; it seemed that she just wanted to repair it and feel better, rather than experience the underlying feelings that lead to it. I thought that my words also were experienced as milk at this point in the analysis, as she conceived of me as the all-giving, idealized person who would fill all her holes (the white, milky glue) and meet all her needs—a transference that can only lead to an intensification of longing and ultimately disappointment.

Margo first experienced this when I would not see her over the weekend. Faced with her old unmet longing, anger, despair, and narcissistic injury, she invented the He/She gender solution in what I thought might be her attempt to defend against these upsetting feelings: If she is perfect and has everything, then she can get what she needs. When she could not get more time with me, she became enraged that I was not the all-giving, idealized analyst and then wanted some *thing* (a present) from me, which I thought was her attempt to help quell the longing and fill up the emptiness. Running parallel and alongside of all of this was Margo's need to provoke me in response to her anger. My countertransference need to be giving and understanding delayed but could not stop the inevitable enactment: I was disappointing her just like her mother—I gave but not enough. She was angry with me about that, and I thought that she was trying to provoke me.

The glue game continued through the first two years of the analysis, as she added more and more glue to the cardboard container, building a stronger and stronger base. Then Margo wanted it to become a tower, needing all the glue in the world to build the tallest tower. I wondered how having the tallest tower was going to help with the empty feeling and the hole feeling. She said, "It will get rid of it." Later in the analysis, as we worked through her gender identity, she would occasionally add decorations to the glue project, putting earrings, rings, and necklaces on the structure. I thought that the ongoing glue project had many developmental meanings: it represented early body formation; a way to fill up the emptiness she felt from not enough "good enough" parenting (Winnicott, 1969); a way to establish the secure attachment base that she felt she didn't have and needed; a way to cope with feelings of castration; a representation of the need to fill the hole that her feelings leak out of and deplete her; and a way to work out a female gender identity. He/She remained an active character in the office during this time. When she would be feeling particularly empty, worried about being able to do school work, or when I was about to leave for a vacation, He/She play would alternate with the glue project.

As her birthday neared she decided that she didn't want a present from me but would not tell me why she had changed her mind. Her play shifted to the dollhouse: The children are treated so badly by the parents that they die and are buried. The children come back to life and tell the parents that they had a nightmare in which they were treated poorly by the parents. The parents tell them it was no nightmare, it was *real*. The children get so angry that they kill the parents. Margo, who is the perfect parent, who gives them everything they want and protects them from harm, adopts them. At this point in the analysis, I thought that Margo experienced me as the real, depriving analyst who only saw her one session a day, didn't give her presents, and left her alone on the weekends. Later in the session I told her that it seemed to me that she was very angry at me for not seeing her on the weekend and not agreeing to give her a present; I wondered if she was trying to show me how a good person would act toward children. She agreed.

In the next session the dollhouse brother and sister wake up and discover that they each have both a penis and a vagina and can't figure out how to go to the bathroom. They go downstairs and tell their mother about their being both genders. Mother says, "That's nice," but basically is not really listening to them. Then the dolls switch gender roles; the boy becomes the sister and the girl becomes the brother. Margo says, "That doesn't solve anything." I wonder what it is that they are trying to solve. She answers, "Because they didn't get it." "What didn't they get?" I ask. Her response was to end the game and dictate a He/She story she wanted me to tell to her. It went like this: The children wish they could be as perfect as He/She because He/She can read and the other kids can't. Some kids had fathers that were not there, who spent too much time at work. Some had mothers who worked too much. Some had parents who didn't protect them. Some had parents who didn't feed them what they wanted. Then He/She invites the children to live with him/her. They all have their own room and the mother plays with them and cooks good food. I thought that Margo was using the He/She story to tell me about her sense of deprivation, her feeling abused and angry, and her fantasy solution. At this point I asked, "I wonder if you wish you could be perfect like He/She?" She beamed and said, "Yes!" Eventually I was able to talk with her about how her empty, longing feelings and the sadness and anger they produced were related to her feeling bad about herself and depleted. I suggested that she might wish that she could be perfect like He/She, who has everything and doesn't have to feel the empty, sad, mad, and not good enough feelings.

I thought that her play also suggested that she was beginning to see that her solution of being both genders didn't really solve the underlying problem of her sense of deprivation and anger at not getting what she needed. Her play suggested that she was polarized in her thinking about good and bad objects as well as love and hate. I thought she was using gender to try and work out this conundrum. I theorized that her polarized feelings of loving and hating made it necessary for her to maintain a split in her object representations. Her solution at this point was to protect and keep the idealized mother in the He/She story. On another level, I thought that she was also describing what was going on in her mind. The mind is bi-sexual (Freud, 1905), and she was trying to conceive of a bi-sexual mind that can have intellectual prowess, aggressive competitiveness, the ability to love and be loved, and have both maternal and paternal capacities while being only one gender on the outside of her body.

This period of play was soon disrupted by our summer vacations. When I returned, Margo was very angry. She told me that she was writing her feelings in her journal and was not going to share them with me. I asked, "Are you so angry with me about the vacation that you don't want to talk to me?" "Be quiet!" she ordered. "You are not going to get any answers." "Maybe you want to leave me out, the way I left you out over vacation," I replied. "You don't know anything. You think you are little miss perfect, but you're not nice," she retorted. "Not nice?" I asked. "The way you were born," she said. "I was born not nice?" I asked. "Right." she said. "Your parents didn't want you. They just wanted a child, but not you!" "I would feel pretty bad about myself if that were the case; so bad about myself I would want to be miss perfect," I responded.

That introduction led to four months of destruction of toys in the office and physical abuse toward me that I was not able to contain or control at times. It was the most challenging work I have ever done with a child, as I had to control the intense feelings of frustration and anger that Margo evoked in me. She threw toys at me when I was unaware, punched me during or while leaving sessions, and kicked me until I was black and blue on many occasions. When I would try and contain her physically she would just fight harder, very much enjoying hurting me and watching me control my intense anger at her. Eventually she was able to sustain a "time out" period in the waiting room, where she would often spend most of the session after I would physically remove her from the playroom.

During this period she said that she felt that she would never be happy again. She talked about how she hated her parents, her brothers, and me. She told me that no one paid any attention to her at home, even making her go to bed early so that her parents and brothers could play games together at night without her. In one of my attempts to keep some of these angry feelings in displacement, I gave her one of the dolls I keep for destruction. She cut up a doll and removed all the stuffing, as she attempted to play out what I experienced as the intensity of her murderous rage over not getting enough. The doll also represented my own children, whom she was intensely curious about and jealous of during this period. One day she came in and announced that she had read in the newspaper that my children had been murdered. But playing this out with dolls was not enough for Margo. She needed to work this out with me and on me.

During this time I felt that I was both the object and subject of her rage: the analyst/mother who did not give her enough of what she needed and that part of herself that she hated as she turned her anger against herself. She felt both guilty about and overly critical of her own rageful feelings. She wanted me to feel how she felt, and I did. I felt helpless, out of control, battered, bruised, and furious. No matter what I did it was wrong, and she took every opportunity to tell me about it. She experienced me as mean and hurting her as she projected the anger she couldn't stand within herself. I felt emotionally and physically depleted by her, much the way her mother experienced her and how, I thought, Margo felt inside herself. I had a very difficult time tolerating not just the abuse but the pleasure she got from hurting me. I frequently asked why she continually needed to be so mean and hurtful to me, what all of this behavior was about. "We just have to do it," she said each time I asked.

After I had learned a great deal about the shape and form of her anger, and she could be contained in the waiting room, I decided it was time to expand her thinking about her intense feelings. I thought this might help her gain some cognitive understanding that would hopefully provide more structure and mastery over her unregulated, uncontrolled, aggressive feelings. I met with her parents and suggested the idea of telling Margo about the events in her life that contributed to her angry feelings. Her parents agreed, and her mother asked to be there during that session. During this time her parents had been in and out of the play room as we all tried to help her contain her anger, so it was not out of the ordinary to have her mother there. I spoke with Margo about all the people in her life who had not been there enough for her, all the people who had actually left her, and how she had not been treated fairly with regard to her brothers. She cried as her mother corroborated what I was telling her with the actual facts of her life, which were heartbreaking.

During those months I became the container for her feelings. I was the identified horrible, angry person, as she needed to externalize those feelings within herself as well as have me understand her feelings. It also seemed to me that she was giving vent to all of her rage that she did not dare inflict on her mother because it would not have been safe. Margo feared the intensity of her own rage as well as her mother's. She and her mother had a similar temperament, and her mother was also capable of losing control when she was angry, which did not help Margo to feel safe with these feelings with her mother. To help Margo with this meant facing intense, angry feelings within myself, managing them in a way that was not hurtful to either of us, and talking about them with her. As we traversed this angry place, Margo very carefully watched me: my expression and description of my anger, my control of my anger, my ability to stay connected to her while we were both angry. My behavior represented a new and different model of affect regulation that she could identify with and begin to internalize. During this time Margo also learned that what she imagined she would or could do when she was enraged did not happen. As we traversed this experience, the platform that was being built with the building blocks of our relationship was, like the glue project, becoming more solid—solid enough to withstand her rage (and mine) and survive it. Contrary to her anxiety, no one died and no one was abandoned.

The therapeutic action permitted her to enter into the developmental process with me and identify with me as I modeled affect regulation strategies that I used to cope with my intense feelings. During those four very difficult months in analysis, Margo managed to continue to thrive in school and sports, developing considerable ego integration outside the office. A few weeks after the session with her mother present, Margo came in and announced that she had written down all the subjects that she wanted to talk about with me. The list included her parents, her brothers, and how I got my last name. She discussed the real problems she was having with her brothers and parents over: (1) time allotted to her brothers and not her; (2) how no matter how hard her mother tried she was not "really there" with her; and (3) how she wanted her father to read to her at night. We then got to my last name, which was really two questions: Was I married, and what was my husband like? She then put on my high heels and pranced around my office. When I asked her if she wanted to be in my shoes with my husband, she grinned.

She began to notice my jewelry, shoes, clothing, and hairstyle. Margo asked her mother if she could pierce her ears so that she could wear earrings, and bought girl's shoes and clothes for the first time, showing off her new outfits in the office. She was able to identify with me as a strong, aggressive woman who could also be feminine. As her female gender identity became more integrated, a heterosexual object choice crystallized. Her mother happily reported that Margo was flirting with her father, and that her father was thrilled and responsive.

Once she saw that we could both survive her rage, she seemed to shift into a more competitive stance. During this phase of our work, we played many competitive games of physical and mental skill. Margo's appointment time was at 6:30 in the morning, a time when she was often more physically awake than I was. We would play Spit, a very fast game of cards. We both gave it our all, and as she got older she won more and more. I had to work harder and harder to keep up with her as she got me to feel and act on the intensity of my competitive feelings, which were much like her own. One day she looked up at me and said, "You're just as competitive as I am; you want to win as much as I do." "How *is* that?" I asked. "It's okay. It feels even," she said. That day, as I said "See you tomorrow" at the door, she retorted, "No, *I'll* see *you.*"

Beauty parlor games then followed. She asked me to do her hair in fancy French-braid styles. She would then do my hair and make me look terrible, which she delighted in, as we would get ready to go to a party. "You look great and I look terrible," I said. "That's right! I'm prettier and thinner," she replied. "Then all the boys will dance just with you!" I complained. "That's right!" she said, smiling triumphantly. She began to include her father in our play. During the sessions when she made me look ridiculous in the make-up and hairstyles she fixed for me, she would insist on bringing her father in to see me, and she delighted in his humorous reaction to my appearance. Later she got suspicious of my relationship with her dad, not wanting me to talk with him in the waiting room before or after her session. "Why don't you want me to talk with him?" I asked. "He's MINE!" she quickly shot back at me.

As her oldest brother's high school graduation and party approached, Margo, age nine, got sad and angry, as themes of loss and inequality resurfaced. She was very angry with her parents for giving her brother so much attention and talked about wanting to destroy all the presents he got. By now she neither felt guilty about her anger over the unequal treatment nor responsible for it. "Anyone would feel this way," she said. I agreed. At this point in her life she was a star athlete, an excellent student, and had many close friends who wanted to spend time with her, all of which gave her a feeling that other people thought that she was a worthwhile person. She felt much more effective in her life outside the family and had a very good relationship with her father. She was beginning to feel worthwhile in her own right.

She decided it was time to tackle her mother's lack of attentiveness to her. She invited her mother into her sessions and told her all the ways in which she felt her mother was not present enough for her: reading to her at bedtime and then leaving in the middle to check on her brothers' homework, arranging for her to play with a friend or do an activity on the one afternoon mother had taken off to "be with Margo," interrupting time with her to make phone calls, etc. Her mother promised to remediate the behavior, but she was unable to sustain it for very long. Margo called her mother back in and told her how important it was to have some time with her. "I am not asking for very much," she said. "Most of the time I am in school, at sports, or with my friends." Her mother agreed, tried again, but couldn't do it.

When Margo realized that neither she nor I could change her mother, she became despairing and exhausted, crying a lot in her sessions. She wanted to be hospitalized for depression. I asked what she thought would happen in the hospital. "I would be able to just rest and sleep. I am so tired. And my mother would have to spend time with me." She then started to have suicidal thoughts. She wanted to see what it would be like to kill herself. I asked what killing herself would accomplish. "Being dead would be peaceful, and I wouldn't feel sad and disappointed anymore. I am so tired of working so hard. No matter how good I am, it doesn't change my mother," she said. I started to see her twice a day, before and after school. I was worried about the intensity of her suicidal feelings and thought that I could monitor her better if I saw her twice a day. I also hoped that seeing her more often would make her feel less alone with these very painful feelings and might help avoid needing to hospitalize her. In retrospect, I also think that hospitalization might have reinforced the regressive state that she longed for. We talked about how hard it was to realize that her mother was not going to change no matter how hard Margo tried to please her; how, without hope, she felt so sad and tired. I told her that these feelings would pass, and I would help her tolerate them. I also told her that while no one would ever take the place of her mother, she had many good friends, teachers, and me who did notice her and to whom she could talk and get help from. This was more comforting to me than to her at the time.

The suicidal ideation and crisis lasted a week. It was precipitated by her sense of hopelessness and despair about not getting what she felt she needed from her mother, as well as her strong feelings of frustration and anger. Her intense neediness returned, and she had a difficult time talking about it in a way that I could comprehend. One day, frustrated with my inability to understand her, she showed me how she felt. She took two pieces of clay and molded them together. "I get it," I said. "It would be so nice of we could be really, really close and always together, especially when you are feeling so bad about your mother right now." Games of longing and needing to get filled up followed, as we once more worked through this difficult set of feelings. This time we addressed her concern that it was her fault that she was so angry and had been treated so poorly.

Margo told me about a friend of hers "whose parents have no time for her and don't understand her." The girl felt it was her fault that she was treated so badly, though Margo knew that it wasn't. She suggested that the girl could see me. In fact, she could have Margo's hours. I thought that this was a test to see if I would abandon her because of her needy feelings that she couldn't stand in herself. I told her that her time with me was hers and no one could share it, acting on that interpretation at this point and staying within the displacement. She decided that she would help her friend, and she and I would figure out what to say to her. Over many sessions, we jointly discovered that the girl was sad and mad about how her parents were treating her, but that there was nothing to do about the situation with her parents. That was just the way they were. Acting mad didn't help and only made her feel bad about herself and her angry behavior. Talking to them about how she felt didn't change anything either, sad as that was. Margo decided she had to help the girl just feel sad about not getting all that she wanted from her parents. I agreed and suggested that the girl might also be feeling jealous and angry that other kids got what she didn't, and that Margo needed to explain to her friend that *all* these feelings were normal and right, given what the girl had missed and was missing. I told her that she needed to tell the girl that it was not wrong to have these feelings, although the girl might feel badly about herself for having them. Margo wondered how she could make her friend feel good about herself. I suggested that understanding these feelings and knowing they were okay to have would help, but that the friend also needed to find other people, like friends and teachers, and activities she liked to help her feel good about herself. Margo then decided that her friend needed a story about her future that "would give her some hope." (Throughout the treatment, I would often couch my interpretations in stories, which she greatly enjoyed.) I thought this was a very good idea and suggested she make one up. Here it is:

> Once upon a time there was a girl whose parents didn't understand and lived in a plain but nice house. The girl did well in school, in after-school activities, and had lots of friends. She worked hard in school and college and grew up to be a writer. She made lots of money and was able to buy herself lots of things and live in a really nice house. After that, she got married to a kind man who understands her and was really nice to her. They had lots of kids who the mother treated some of the way she wanted to be treated when she was a kid. The mother worked during the day and was home every afternoon when the kids got home from school, and she spent a lot of time with them and was understanding.

Margo had begun to make sense of her life with her parents, allowing herself to feel comfortable with and less guilty about a range of feelings that included sadness, anger, envy, and despair. Her story indicated that Margo had concluded that she, not her parents, would be the one to give her the things that she wanted and needed. She felt that she would have to work hard to do well in school to get what she wanted for herself. Yet she was not turning away from relationships in her independence. She wanted a husband who would be kind and understanding of her needs, and she hoped that by caring for her children in the ways that she had felt denied she could prevent/undo the pain she experienced.

With a sense of hope returning to her, she was able to once more look deeply within herself. When she was ten years old, she started to play out a pretend story that lasted for several months, incorporating all the previous themes that we had worked on for five years, and which led to the reconstruction, as she understood it, of her difficulties. The story starts with a family who has gone to New Hampshire on a vacation. She insists that I name the family. Thinking about the transference possibilities, I name them Gladys Knight and The Pips. The father has to leave and go on a business trip as soon as the vacation starts. They are a poor family, and while on vacation they win the New Hampshire Lottery and become rich. They buy a rich house in a gated community and stock up on lots of food and anything they want. There is a booth at the beginning of the entrance to the community where a very controlling guard watches to make sure that no robbers get in.

The scene then shifts to a lawyer's office. She is the judge and I am the secretary. Mr. Lawson is a lawyer who is defending Ronald McDonald, who is accused of having robbed the rich family's house. We spend a couple of weeks collecting information, making folders, and filing. It is very clear that she is well into latency behavior at this point and has developed intellectual and obsessional defenses. She is preparing for the trial and making up rules for the secretary's job: always be busy with work, never talk on the phone when there is work to do, never rest on the job, etc. I comment on how harsh and exacting the rules are. She says that the rules are only for this work, not for the rest of my life. As we learn more about the crime, it turns out that the robber held a gun to Gladys, killed two of the children, and ran off with the jewelry.

She asks me, the secretary, to tell her what I think of the case, "Is the person guilty or not?" I tell her, "You are the judge, and the judge has to make the decision after we hear all the facts of the case." The trial lasts many, many days. Witnesses are called to the stand and are asked to provide alibis. Ronald McDonald is grateful that Gladys has helped him change from a former robber to where he can now go to college and make something of himself. While he wished that he could steal some of her things, he didn't commit the crime. The judge finally concludes that it was Gladys who killed the children and was guilty of the crime. I ask, "Is it possible for a mother to want to murder her children?" "Of course," she replies, "You know the Smith case. There's a mother who put her children in the car and rolled them into the river." "Where did you hear about this?" I ask. "I watched it on TV," Margo answers. "That's very scary," I say. Margo shrugs and wants to continue the game.

Gladys insists that she is innocent and loves her children dearly. The judge continues to question her and eventually catches her in a mistake. Gladys confesses, but insists on telling her side of the story. She tells the judge about her terrible home life with a father that didn't treat her very kindly and a mother that was overworked with too many children. Gladys couldn't wait to leave home and married a man to leave her house. The husband worked all the time and wasn't home much. Gladys goes on to say that the first son was a difficult baby and kept her busy and exhausted all the time. Then the girl was born and she was a difficult baby, too. She was mainly home alone to take care of the children. Then Gladys had two more children and it was just too much for her and so she thought about killing them a lot. (It seemed to me that Margo was telling her own version of her mother's history, behavior, and feelings.) I wonder how the children felt during all of this. Margo tells me, "The children felt scared, not safe, not well taken care of. It made them sad and angry, and they felt not loved and terrible about themselves. It was a very unhappy house and made the children unhappy."

Then the judge asks Gladys if she drinks. She at first denies this, but eventually the judge accuses her of being a secret drinker. Gladys explains that her father was a drinker, that she got it from him, and that he treated her badly when he was drunk. The judge sentences Gladys to eight years in jail and tells her that she should have gone for counseling. Gladys says that she sent her husband and children for counseling. The judge is very stern and tells her that she should have gone a long time ago, but now will have counseling in jail.

The next day the judge calls the children to the stand. They are asked how they feel about what is happening, knowing that their mother is a murderer and a drunk. They feel scared for their own lives, they feel sad and mad, but they also love their mother—so they have a whole mix of feelings. They wonder if they are responsible for making her so tired and feel like killing her children. At this point she asks me what the judge should say. I say, "The judge needs to remind the children that they heard what a hard life their mother had, which made it difficult for her to manage at times, even before the last two kids were born. The judge needs to make sure they understand that they are not responsible for their mother's behavior and that their feelings are right, genuine and of course mixed. Also tell them that it is very scary to have a mother who is not in good control and can get so very angry." I then ask her to have the judge ask the kids how they feel about themselves, growing up in this family. Margo, speaking for the kids, tells the judge, "They felt bad about themselves a lot and wished that they could be different so that their mother would love them more." Gladys goes to jail where she attends AA—Analysis Anonymous.

At this point in the analysis Margo was able to use words to express the experiences in her life, and I could interpret her guilt and self-criticism, which she could also express. In this play sequence she put together her own narrative to help her understand her mother's behavior and her own feelings and sense of herself in relation to her parents. What she was able to convey is her understanding that children can feel there is no safety in relationships. That mothers can have murderous feelings toward their children and lose control, which can feel very scary. She was also aware of her own murderous and envious feelings and her need for tight control and a harsh superego so that she could manage in the world and keep her own robber-murderer feelings in check. While she still had a tendency to identify with the harsh aggressor, she didn't sentence her mother to death, but only eight years of analysis, still hoping that someone (me?) will be able to help her mother in the end.

Ronald McDonald represents the part of her that has developed from the analytic relationship: a person who used to be a robber and can acknowledge jealous feelings, but is also aware of and grateful for what she has been given in our relationship and how it has changed her sense of herself and her hope for her future. She also was able to understand that when something has been lost to her or taken away, it can not be made up with possessions; that the only hope for personal satisfaction that one can have is by making one's own life as productive and fruitful as possible. Her feelings became less polarized as she became aware of having mixed feelings of love and hate for people who have good and bad aspects to them. Her ability to contain these contrary feelings within herself helped make that possible.

Margo's analysis terminated when she was eleven and a half years old. Her parents' financial concerns were the driving force behind the ending and surfaced right after this last play sequence. In hindsight, Margo may have felt pressured to put her narrative together quickly at this time, knowing her time with me would be coming to an end. The eight years of analysis for Gladys may have been her wish for a longer time for us to work together. And the two children who are killed may have also represented her wish to kill my children and have me for herself forever. While we could have productively used more time, the ending of her analysis coincided with another normal phase of separation and autonomy. Because of the safety of our relationship, these separation issues were played out more directly with me than with her mother. I thought that this allowed her to enter into a good early adolescent, mother-daughter relationship.

During the termination phase of Margo's analysis, gender issues resurfaced as she once more confronted her intense sadness and murderous rage in the context of feeling the loss of me and the analysis, as I once again became the abandoning mother in the transference. In one pretend story during this phase, a teacher was found to have been eating little children from the elementary school. This was a regressive game she played on her toes; her toes being both he and she. I understood this game to both express and contain her anger over feelings of envy and loss. She was the child I was willing to let go while I kept my *other* two children. Once again she used externalization to cope with these strong feelings; it is the adult who is hungry and wants to eat up the children, not the other way around. However, I was now able to talk directly with her about these feelings toward me. "It's sad that we have to end sooner than we expected," I said. "I want to stop," Margo replied with anger in her voice. "Yes, but maybe this is another case of mixed feelings. You do want to leave, but maybe you also want to stay and are angry at me because I am allowing this to happen," I said. "Maybe," she said grudgingly. This was followed by play in which she and I wrote a magazine full of stories of destruction and loss and the feelings of intense sadness and anger such situations engender. In this play we both used sublimation to very thinly veil our feelings and communicate them to each other.

At the very end of the analysis Margo wrote a story in which a boy's best friend, a girl, dies. The boy feels a great deal of sadness and longing, which he is able to express through his writing. One night his friend returns to him, and they spend the night in the tree outside his house, enjoying the same wonderful relationship they always had together. In the morning his parents tell him it was a dream, but he knows that it was real. I didn't ask her or comment about the gender of the writer in the story, preferring to focus more on her feelings of loss over the very real relationship we had and will always have and her wish that we would see each other again in the future; however, I felt she may have used the male gender in the story to cope with the pain of our parting.

DISCUSSION

To what degree is the search for a needed object particularly important for gender identity differentiation? Margo concretely wanted a penis so that she could get the love and attention that her brothers were getting from her parents. She equated being a girl with being deprived and unloved and sought repair of her developmental situation through her wish to have a penis. She focused on gender as both the cause and solution of her sense of deprivation, thinking that the He/She solution would get her the love that she needed, eradicate her feelings of rage and despair, and repair her narcissistic injuries. She had a sense of herself as someone who was unwanted from the moment she was born, someone to be denigrated. If the only way to be loved is be someone and some way that you are not, then Margo's He/She solution crystallizes a fundamental struggle and conflict of identity: how to be some other person and still maintain the essence of who you are. If the root of this identity problem is the feeling of not being wanted, then Margo's He/She solution is also a defense against an anaclitic depression. Furthermore, if such an assault on the self comes in infancy and toddlerhood, when the ego is a body ego, then the solution has to have its origin in the concreteness of the early ego and sense of self and other.

In the course of Margo's development the concretized gender solution of having both a penis and vagina served many dynamic purposes. It was used to repair feelings of low self esteem, as a way of coping with polarized, extreme feelings of love and hate and good and bad objects, as a way to control feelings of envy and loss, to quell annihilation anxiety and repair a sense of ego disintegration. Margo used gender as a means to get all that she needed to help her development move forward: attention, protection, safety, love, and to be as able as her older brothers. At age seven her thinking matured, and she reached the limits of her cognitive capacity to solve her gender problem with a concrete solution. She was confronted with not really being able to be both male and female, a fantasy that had protected her against narcissistic injury and anxiety in the past. She turned to me, as both a real and developmental object, to get what she needed to repair her sense of self and other and to provide the developmental assistance she needed to attain normal development. I was also a transference object as she acted out the repetition compulsion of her early conflicts.

The concreteness with which Margo experienced her internal difficulties, the concreteness of her solutions, and the delay in her development raise interesting technical questions: To what degree do we need to alter standard analytic technique when we work with such a child? Does such concreteness around problems of identity and ego organization expressed in such concrete body solutions require a concreteness, or realness, of response that affects analytic technique? To what degree do we need to be both a real and developmental object that provides education, reality-oriented feedback, and a novel relationship throughout the body of the work when we are analyzing a child with disorganized attachment and serious difficulties with affect regulation?

My initial work with Margo was predominately reparative. My immediate concern was to help her develop aspects of ego organization that she lacked so that she could feel less fragmented and more organized in order for her to proceed with her development, which was predominately at a pre-oedipal level. By providing her with more and more glue, I gratified her wishes for an all-giving person rather than analyzing her defenses, allowing an idealized transference to continue while I helped her develop a sense of mindfulness of self and other (Fonagy and Target, 1998). I provided a beginning narrative that I hoped would stabilize her and enable her to establish a base for a secure attachment through the analytic relationship. I thought that by first establishing a real, positive, and secure relationship, the analysis might provide her a platform upon which to talk about and work through her rage and despair over not being wanted and not getting, which had led her to the dual-gender solution.

Margo lacked a solid inner capacity of affect regulation and a capacity to integrate polarities of feelings and object representations. Another early treatment priority was helping Margo develop these inner structures so that development could move forward with a capacity for a synthesis of feelings and experiences, which would lead to further development. Through the use of displacement and externalization, Margo was able to explore her longing, envy, despair, sadism, and murderous rage that resulted from her feeling deprived of the love and attention she needed from her parents. By making me feel and voice the range and intensity of her affects, Margo was able to feel understood by me while my behavior provided her with a new female model with which to identify and internalize a safer expression and regulation of affective states and a less polarized, safer sense of another person's feelings and actions. At later times in the analysis I also had to educate her about how to act when she had strong feelings, such as "You don't have to hit and throw things, you can tell me in words how you feel and I will hear you and respond to your feelings." Over time she also internalized my analyzing function and used it as an affect regulation strategy.

After Margo had worked through her murderous rage in our relationship, she was able to see that we had both survived the anger and could still care about each other. She was, through this process, able to feel more comfortable being a girl and was able to tolerate competitive feelings with me. Once she had achieved latency age cognition and defense strategies, I felt more comfortable using standard analytic techniques to analyze her defenses against and conflicts related to her longing, rage, despair, emptiness, depression, narcissistic injury, and fear of abandonment that led to her extreme self criticism, discomfort with her competitive and aggressive feelings, harsh superego, and her desire to be both a girl *and* a boy.

As we worked together on all of her myriad feelings and sense of herself and others using many different treatment techniques, Margo began to feel better about herself. She did very well in school and sports, had close and lasting friendships with girls, and eventually felt good about her aggressive, competitive feelings. Her self criticism lessened to the degree that she could hear what I was telling her about herself without becoming defensive or feel as if I was attacking her. She had established a good relationship with her father and remained hopeful of having a better relationship with her mother, which did happen in her early adolescence. Although vestiges of the He/She solution can be seen in her response to the loss of me in the termination phase, she left analysis with a coherent sense of self and other, happy to be a very smart, assertive, psychologically minded, determined pre-adolescent girl.

BIBLIOGRAPHY

Freud, S. (1905). Three essays on the theory of sexuality. *Standard Edition* 7:125–245.

Fonagy, P. & Target, M. (1998). Mentalization and the changing aims of child psychoanalysis. *Psychoanalytic Dialogues*, 8(1):87–114.

Fraiberg, S. (1975). Ghosts in the Nursery. *Journal of the American Academy of Child Psychiatry*, 14:387–421.

Main, M. (1995). Attachment: Overview, with implications for clinical work. In *Attachment Theory: Social, Developmental and Clinical Perspectives*, ed. S. Goldberg, R. Muir, & J. Kerr. Hillsdale, N.J.: Analytic Press, pp. 407–474.

Main, M. & Solomon, J. (1990). Procedures for identifying infants as disorganized/disoriented during the Ainsworth strange situation. In *Attachment in the Preschool Years: Theory, Research and Intervention*, ed. M. T. Greenberg, D. Cichetti, E. M. Cummings. Chicago: University of Chicago Press, pp. 121–160.

Winnicott, D. W. (1969). The mother-infant experience of mutuality. In *Psychoanalytic Exploration*, ed. C. Winnicott, R. Shepherd, & M. Davis. Cambridge, Mass.: Harvard University Press, 1989, pp. 251–260.

Conflicted Gender

The Case of a Woman Who Believed She Was Half Male and Half Female

NANCY KULISH, Ph.D.

The author presents the case of a middle-aged woman who had a fantasy that she was half male and half female, which did not emerge until she was well into her analysis. Initially, the analytic work focused on issues of attachment and trust, as the patient was mute and despairing, and unable to verbalize affects or put together a coherent story of her life. Gradually over the course of her analysis, a history of severe emotional neglect and trauma was pieced together—she had been left at the hospital as a newborn because her mother had not wanted a girl. It was only after the establishment of more comfortable and stable connection to the analyst that the conflicts around gender and the boy/girl fantasy came into focus. Two masturbation fantasies, a primitive, non-visualized sensation of sexual insatiability with abdominal throbbing, and a more traditional beating fantasy were also analyzed. The fantasy of being both male and female, which was conscious since childhood, was both a result of and a solution to more basic issues. It was a sign of problems in integration of internal parental identifications, a shaky maternal attachment, and difficulties in dealing with affect. The fantasy reflected a profound sense of being unwanted and unloved and became a narcissistic solution for these troubling feelings. The author details the interplay of constitutional,

---

Adjunct Professor of Psychology, University of Detroit/Mercy; Adjunct Assistant Professor, Department of Psychiatry, Wayne State Medical School; and Training and Supervising Analyst, Michigan Psychoanalytic Institute.

The Psychoanalytic Study of the Child 58, ed. Robert A. King, Peter B. Neubauer, Samuel Abrams, and A. Scott Dowling (Yale University Press, copyright © 2003 by Robert A. King, Peter B. Neubauer, Samuel Abrams, and A. Scott Dowling).

familial, and psychological factors that contributed to this solution.
Because issues of gender were highlighted in this case, their complex re-
lationship with other underlying factors could be appreciated.

PRESENTING COMPLAINT

MONA WAS A DIVORCED WOMAN WITH GROWN CHILDREN WHEN SHE
began analysis in her late fifties. Her reasons for doing this were
vague; she said only that she wanted to "try" a psychoanalytic approach after past experience with a variety of other treatments. But
Mona's appearance and demeanor spoke unmistakably of the problem; she struck me as profoundly depressed, like a dog that had lost
its master—mute, beaten, and lifeless. Initially she indicated no major concerns about gender, nor did she have a gender disorder per
se; Mona knew consciously that she was a female. But she had a long-
standing fantasy, which emerged in the course of her analysis, that
she was half male and half female. She did not speak of this fantasy
for some time.

Mona began psychotherapy on a once-a-week basis and increased
to twice a week after several months. She told me of her history and
her current concerns, but I had a hard time forming a coherent internalized picture of them for myself. This is not to say that she spoke
incoherently at the surface of the discourse, yet I strained for meaning; it was hard for me to put the people or incidents she mentioned
into a place or a frame. Retrospectively, I think that this was because
there was so little in her accounts of verbalized affect or of affective
connection of any kind, except for anxiety, and my sense of the heavy
presence of painful, silent depression. Later, after many years of
analysis, she said, "I never thought of myself as depressed."

Mona was soft-spoken and feminine-looking, and wore soft, arty
clothing. She was attractive but wore no make-up. She wore only
washable clothes, cottons and such, because she had a compulsion
for clean clothes. Everything worn in a given day had to be washed
immediately so that dirty laundry would not be left around.

What Mona spoke about in these early sessions was concern about
her relationships with her family. She had four grown sons who were
at the center of her life and of her conscious preoccupations. When
they did well, she felt better herself. The oldest son was recently married and the youngest still in college. Before she met her second husband, Mona had spent much time traveling and sharing outdoor
physical activities—camping, sailing, skiing, and mountain climbing

—with her sons, singly and all together. Mona did the climbing in a counter-phobic push, as she was deathly afraid of heights. She also once made herself stay in a remote cabin for a week by herself in an attempt to conquer her fear of being alone. Needless to say, these attempts resulted in very terrifying experiences, and over the course of her analysis she exhibited other behavior in which she put herself in actual bodily danger, even life-threatening situations.

A few weeks before she began treatment, Mona had quarreled with her oldest son and his wife. For some time before this, she had become uncomfortably aware of some resentment that the couple had been abusing her hospitality and taking advantage of her generosity by expecting to be treated as guests every weekend, for example. She and her other sons found it hard to warm to the daughter-in-law, a negative, hostile young woman. Yet it seemed apparent to me that the patient felt unconsciously jealous of the daughter-in-law's relationships with her son. Mona tried hard to avoid any confrontations, but her resentment toward her daughter-in-law was palpable. The ensuing quarrel, which erupted when Mona finally voiced a mild complaint to her son, was very, very painful to her.

She had a constant fear, which became a major theme in the analysis and in the transference, that she would drive away the people she loved. She wanted her sons with her for holidays, but their presence was also a huge strain, so great was her worry about offending them. Mona was tormented with concerns about doing or saying anything that might make someone feel angry or hurt, and feared that someday she would be left absolutely alone in the world. In her everyday life, she could not be comfortably at home alone. When alone, she filled up her time with housecleaning, working in the yard, or redecorating. It was hard for her to engage in solitary mental endeavors, such as reading.

It seemed to me that Mona was becoming quite attached in her therapy, although she did not verbalize this feeling, or in fact any affects. Her anxiety, sleeplessness, and depression—which were manifested in wordless crying—seemed to intensify on my breaks. I thought that Mona needed more consistency and more intensity to be able to manage and to understand the transference, but at the same time I hesitated about suggesting analysis, because of the depth and severity of the depression, which she did not yet even recognize. In retrospective, I wonder if this hesitation reflected a counter-transference worry that I could not bear the depth of her depression. I did suggest analysis, however, and Mona readily agreed. The analysis proved to be very difficult for the patient, but terminated successfully after eight years.

The patient could be characterized as having a masochistic, depressive character with problems in affect regulation and expression, some obsessive-compulsive symptoms and anxiety, and compulsive masturbation. In addition to a shaky sense of self and conflicts around gender was a problem of object constancy. Mona did not seem to have the comfort of a solid internal image of a safe and good mothering object. As I have said, a major theme in the analysis was her fear and expectation of abandonment. The fantasy of being a boy/girl was a major organizing fantasy and provided one way for this woman to cope with her problems.

HISTORY

In the beginning Mona provided the facts of her history in a flat voice, often with a bewildering sprinkling of names and events that she had apparently mentioned before. I struggled to put the pieces of her story together for myself and to keep it together. I worried about her flatness in speech and her inability to verbalize affects. Yet Mona seemed to have many girlfriends and male friends, some going all the way back to grade school. I speculated to myself that she must be more talkative and lively with them than she was with me, so I concluded that what I was seeing in the analysis was a deep regression and did not represent her everyday deportment.

Mona's maternal grandparents had been farmers. Her grandmother, the matriarch, plowed the fields early and then trudged off to teach in a one-room schoolhouse. Her mother went to college at sixteen as a musical prodigy. The grandparents sold their farm and moved to the college town to watch out for their daughter. Nonetheless, she soon got into trouble. She became pregnant by a man she was seeing (Mona's father), who was a few years older than she. The grandmother made her daughter have an abortion yet insisted that the couple marry after that. The father established a small business and speculated in real estate so that, by the time of his death, he was able to leave the patient a comfortable amount of money, which helped to finance her analysis.

The patient had a brother four years older than she. There was a major mystery surrounding her birth. The story (which has been verified) was told that her mother refused to keep her and left her at the hospital. She told the patient that she left her at the hospital because she had not wanted a girl. Finally after twelve days, the maternal grandmother came to get the baby. The father hired a woman to look after Mona for about eighteen months, as we were able to reconstruct it, while the mother was presumably refusing (or unable?) to care for her. However, as an adult, the patient tried to obtain her birth records from the hospital where she was supposedly born. There were none to be found under her mother's name—married, maiden, or otherwise.

The sense and the significance of this story first emerged in the following way. During the first months of the analysis a news story about "Baby Jessica" made national headlines. Baby Jessica was a two-year-old girl who had been adopted by a childless couple. The biological mother had given her up at birth but now wanted the baby back. A huge legal battle ensued; ultimately the biological parents won the child and a heart-breaking good-bye from the adopted parents appeared in public view. Mona was in agony about this event. It was difficult to observe her pain, which was written across her face as if a knife had been turned in her chest. She cried inconsolably and could not speak. Over some days of questioning, it became apparent that she was identifying with Jessica's adopted mother. How horrible, how unbearable it would be to let the child go, to worry about it, not to know how it was doing. I wondered aloud why she had not taken the child's vantage point. Haltingly and over several weeks an underlying source of her pain emerged. She again told me the story of her birth and somewhere in this context mentioned that she did not look anything like her father. Mona could not get words or feelings out easily at that stage in the analysis and especially at that moment. She wondered, "What if am not . . . not my . . . " She could not get the thought out, so I helped her to put into words the conclusion that she was fighting against thinking: "Not your father's child?"

During the patient's childhood and adolescence her mother had openly carried on a series of affairs. On several occasions, she left for short periods of time with a current lover. There were fights between the parents about this behavior, but for the most part the father put up with it and always took his wife back. He seemed hapless and helpless, a prisoner of the mother's control and allure. He defended the mother to the patient and seemed to idealize her. It seemed plausible to the patient that her mother had had an affair that culminated in her pregnancy with Mona; maybe there was another reason that she left the child at the hospital, besides just not wanting a girl. Later the patient speculated that her mother might have contemplated putting her up for adoption. Only toward the end of the treatment did the patient give up her search both in and outside the analysis to find out "the truth" of what might have happened at the time of her birth.

The trouble for Mona was that her father had been her only reliable parent, and the one on whom she depended and with whom she consciously could identify. If he were not really her father, then she would have lost the only real parent she felt she had. There were incestuous implications too of the father's not being the biological father, but these were obscure and were not addressed until years after the story of Baby Jessica emerged.

Mona's mother was an alcoholic. The father joined her in her partying and drinking, but he was not so severe a drinker. The mother made fun of "sober" and "church-going" people. A bitter and morose drunk, she bemoaned her fate, being married to her husband. Yet she was possessive and jealous of him, and openly resented any attention he paid his family—especially his daughter. She suffered from a variety of ailments and was, in the patient's view, hypochondriacal and complaining. The patient hated her mother's "negativity," which she feared she could recognize in herself. The mother died of alcoholism when the patient was in her late thirties. To the day of her death, the father denied her alcoholism. He himself died ten years later of a coronary, probably complicated by his drinking. His death was very difficult for the patient. She had an anniversary reaction to his death each year with a deepening of her depression, although it took several years for me to recognize this connection.

The mother very openly favored Mona's brother. He was scrawny and had reputedly been a sickly baby. Although the patient had absolutely no memories of her mother caring for her in any way, she remembered her mother making oatmeal for her brother and fussing over his health. From early on, the mother urged the brother to drink along with her. The patient described how, when he was in his twenties, he and her mother had hung out together. It seemed "creepy" to her and inappropriate. The brother, predictably, became an alcoholic, and died young of alcoholism.

The patient was closer to her father. She was "sturdy," and got his approval by working very hard at physical endeavors. He felt in contrast that his son was "lazy." He let her drive the family car at age twelve, although in retrospect Mona felt that this was "wrong," that is, neglectful. Her father gave her money, so that as a young adolescent she often ate out by herself.

Both children were frequently left to fend for themselves. The parents drank and went to parties, and very frequently and regularly went away on trips to warmer climates. Mona, in an early first expression of affect, told me how she was angry when they left her behind on their trips. She produced an early blurred memory of wandering terrified out of the house in her nightgown at the age of three when her mother was gone somewhere. There were other memories of panic at being alone in the house in a thunderstorm and of dashing out of the house on her bike in the drenching rain, crying into the wind.

Mona felt ashamed of her family and of the fact that she was so often alone, which she felt reflected badly on her. She felt that if she tried to act normal, people would not notice that anything was wrong. When a teacher or another parent voiced disapproval of her driving when so young or said something about her being left alone, she would be flooded with shame. When she was in grade school, the teachers' reports noted her silence and withdrawal.

There was, however, an African-American housekeeper, Hope, who came when the patient was six. Hope remembered how Mona barely spoke and would come home every day after school and ask, "Is my Mommy home?" Then without another word the girl would go to her room, and probably, as Mona speculated to me, masturbate to comfort herself. As the years passed, Mona began to talk more to Hope, first recounting the stories of movies or books she had read. She continued to remain close to Hope even through her adulthood, and I speculated that the patient's passionate housecleaning reflected her identification with Hope.

One of her earliest and most central memories pictured her father and herself when she was three. She remembered that he would rub her legs, presumably to help her with growing pains. This was sexually stimulating to her. He became aware of her excitement, she recalled, and perhaps his own, and pushed her away. From that moment, she believed, the rubbing stopped and he never touched her again, but told her that she was "too big" to be held or cuddled. She had other memories of consciously wishing her father would masturbate her. In the course of the analysis, I repeatedly interpreted that Mona felt that it was her sexual feelings that made her bad and unlovable. Indeed, her father frequently commented that Mona had been "over-sexed" from birth. He asserted that when she was a tiny infant, she would rub her blanket between her legs. And for as long as she could remember, Mona had masturbated compulsively.

Mona had two types of masturbation fantasies. The first was all bodily and without visual content. She experienced a painful something, an almost tangible substance, inside of her, like a kind of abdominal cramp. The most basic sensation was of insatiable sexual sensation that could not be filled or met, but which impelled her to masturbate to relieve the tension. She replicated this experience on many occasions in the early years of the analysis, writhing and rocking wordlessly on the couch. She had the fantasy that menstruation might help; blood flowing out would help; being rid of something inside would help.

A second more organized fantasy was a variant of a beating fantasy (Freud, 1919). A child, a boy, was being tormented and sexually stimulated. A group of other older youths or adults formed some kind of ring around him, the older ones behind the younger ones, and he was being tickled or masturbated without stop. There was always some ruse for this; the adults and very often one of the children's fathers knew but denied what was really going on. The patient's role was observer to the whole proceeding.

Her masturbation gave her only temporarily relief, and left her feeling frustration and pain at the belief that she could never be satiated. I interpreted the more bodily fantasy, especially as it came up in the transference, as an early longing to be fed, cared for, and contained by me as a longed-for mother. Different meanings of the second type of masturbation emerged later in the course of analysis. At some point it became clear that the patient was experiencing an exhibitionistic fantasy, both of my watching her and of her watching me. She admitted that she felt that I might be sexually excited listening to her and watching her. She remembered that she had repeatedly watched her mother "clean" her own genitals, and that she, the child, was excited, and perhaps her mother was as well.

This family in general had not observed sexual boundaries. The parents demanded that doors remain open, and nudity was habitual. The patient herself was not allowed to close the bathroom door, which after puberty she tried to do. She remembered her embarrassment at age sixteen when her brother, then in college, walked in with a boyfriend while she was taking a bath. Only when the friend became embarrassed did her brother retreat.

Many images in her dreams suggested the further experiences of the primal scene, and I wondered whether these might have included her mother and other men. From early on in the analysis, the patient wondered about sexual abuse. Part of this was stimulated by news reports and talk among friends about sexual abuse, but beyond that, she was aware of vague, but suggestive memories and dreams. She was at first terrified that her father would turn out to be the culprit, but no clear memories ever came up to confirm this idea.

There was some sex play with her brother. He invited her to masturbate him when she was around ten or eleven. She refused. She also remembered an exciting, and somehow sexual, game they played when they were younger of hanging balloons from the ceiling and sucking on them as if they were baby bottles. Aside from these moments, she said there was little interaction between the two of them. "It was as if we all were separate."

From the time she was a little girl the patient had the fantasy of having six boys when she grew up. Boys were better than girls; that was a fact not even questioned. This feeling went back through several generations. Her mother's brother had been adopted. Her grandfather had told her grandmother when she set off for the orphanage, "Don't be bringing back any girl." Males were valued and needed as help around the farm. The grandparents had preferred her brother over her. When asked in front of company and in the child's presence why she didn't like the patient, her grandmother replied crossly, "I just don't like her, and that's all." While she felt that her father liked her better than her brother, she believed, nevertheless, that the brother was more "important" and got more attention. Still a paradox was reflected in the family power dynamic; the maternal grandmother had all the power in the family, and the mother had the power in the parental pair. Mona's mother had also been the more "important" child to her own parents, as her brother, Mona's uncle, was wimpy and withdrawn.

As a child, Mona acted out her fantasy of having baby boys with life-size baby dolls that she dressed in real baby clothes and carried around with real baby bottles. Baby girls were out of the question. Until this attitude changed in the course of the analysis, Mona was repeatedly astonished at indications that others did not share her convictions: when, for example, they expressed happiness at the birth of a girl.

When she reached puberty, she denied her bodily changes. It was her brother who finally told her that she needed a bra. Her mother never once went shopping with her, and she felt bewildered about how to make herself presentable, what to wear when she began to date, and so on.

Mona got married shortly after she graduated from college to a man she did not love. She went through the motions, as she had done throughout her life, thinking a bungalow and children would make her "normal." The babies came—male babies, to her relief. With each of her four pregnancies, she was terrified that the baby would not be a boy. She was afraid that she could not love a girl and could not imagine bringing a girl home. She watched other women to see how they mothered their children. In spite of always having wanted babies, she had difficulty nursing and cuddling them. Her husband turned out to be a philanderer and a ne'er–do–well. When he made no efforts to conceal the fact that he had fathered a baby with a current girlfriend, Mona finally sought a divorce. Left with four young sons to support, she went to work. She was able to finish her education, buy herself a house, and put the boys through college. I felt that under the circumstances, this was extremely impressive, an indication of Mona's inner strengths.

There were also three brief homosexual episodes. One was a conscious, highly charged fantasy that preoccupied her for several days after a male lover turned away from her for another woman. Her initial despair was replaced with erotic thoughts of the rival. A second occurred when a neighbor woman made a play toward her, which Mona stopped after some abortive fondling. When homosexual material appeared in the transference in the middle phases of the analysis, Mona filled in the details of that episode, which was more extensive than she had first indicated. She also revealed another similar episode with the same woman.

PAST TREATMENTS

Mona began graduate school in education shortly before the breakup of her first marriage. She had sought marriage counseling with a man, with whom she continued in individual therapy after her husband refused to participate further. Shortly afterward, this counselor initiated a sexual relationship with Mona. In the first session in which this occurred, she performed fellatio on him. She described how the words, "Now it is truly hopeless," passed through her mind as she left. She went home and made a serious suicide attempt by taking many pills. A neighbor got her to the hospital. She was released after a couple of days and returned the next week to see the counselor. Neither of them spoke about the sex or connected the suicide attempt with what had happened in the previous session. She continued to see this man and have sex with him for several years, but finally was able to stop. It was only years later in the analysis when I first mentioned the word "abuse" that the patient was able to begin to think about this relationship in such terms. After it ended, she participated in therapy groups and saw several therapists individually, receiving some additional support.

We were able to link the incident with the counselor to the screen

memory of her sexual leg-rubbing experience with her father. The
sequence of events—the sexual encounter, the feeling of hopelessness, and the subsequent suicide attempt—seemed to parallel the
events at three. In Mona's mind, sexual activity led to the loss of her
father—he would never be close and cuddle her again.

COURSE OF THE ANALYSIS

Most of Mona's analysis was not particularly focused on issues of gender. In the initial and middle phases, the work concerned her problems with attachment and trust and her underlying depression and
rage. Her fantasies about being half boy and half girl were intertwined with all of this, but they were not unraveled until the very end
of the analysis, when the more basic problems had been resolved.

Initial phase: During the first several years of the analysis, the patient spent much time in mute miserable silence, with tears rolling
down her cheeks. I struggled to make sense of her life. I tried to put
her feelings, or what I thought were her feelings, into words, and also
tried to understand why she could not do so herself. What I conveyed
to her in those years was this: "You have had a sad and unhappy life;
this is why you are so miserable now, why you cannot know or speak
your feelings, and why you are struggling here with me." I did more
talking than I typically do, and was not at all sure what use Mona was
making of my communications. What she was able to say was that she
feared that when I went away, I might never return.

From early on, Mona began to bring in dreams—many, many
dreams. She put great stock in dreams, almost as if they were magic.
She could not associate easily in the first years of the analysis, except
to add elaborations, but she tried. I felt that she was attempting to
communicate with these dreams, but concretely, as if they were stone
tablets with unintelligible hieroglyphics carved into them, which I
could decipher, make some sense of, and then read back to her. I did
see repetitive themes in her dreams: over and over she dreamed of
lost baby boys who were in her care but whom she had through negli-
gence or accident let get lost or hurt. She dreamed of falling from
cliffs and great heights. She dreamed of being somewhere where she
should not have been and being caught. When I did make interpretations or interventions in the early years, I would often be met with silence, or intensified weeping which I took, rightly or wrongly, as
some kind of confirmation.

I think that she used dreams as she had used her stories about
movies that she had told to Hope, the housekeeper, as ways of mak-

ing contact and communicating something, anything. Hope encouraged the unhappy, almost mute child to talk to her. Her telling me dreams felt similar. It was a means of relating, in which whole dreams or whole narratives were handed over as gifts.

The following is a session from the fourth month of analysis. It illustrates a common rhythm of these earlier sessions, in which the analyst is trying to understand the patient's feeling and put it into words, and the patient was struggling with feelings of emptiness and anxiety. In this session there were several pauses and a very heavy feeling in the room, but she was less silent than usual. This is the session in which Mona first told me of her masturbation fantasies, and, through a dream, expressed fears that she might give way to her compulsion to masturbate on the couch. She had been to the funeral of a co-worker, an African-American teacher (which probably brought up feelings about her housekeeper, Hope).

"I was up all night. I don't know why. The funeral was harder than I thought. My remodeling is exciting, though. I had a dream. Was I asleep or was it like a fantasy? I got up at 2:00 am. I was on a bed in the woods. I had to masturbate. Just felt like I had to. There was a group of women who came along and then they went on. One woman stayed to see if I *didn't* masturbate. She was waiting for me. But then I was tied to a bed and masturbating, so I did it from the dream to a fantasy. I couldn't stop so I got up from bed. It felt like I had been masturbating. I'm all revved up and can't eat."

I asked what her thoughts were about the dream. She repeated the dream and added, "A middle-aged blonde stayed behind." I asked her about being tied down. She replied, "In fantasies. But it's never me." I asked for more details. She then told me some details of her typical masturbation fantasies. After a pause, she said: "In the dream there was a frog. A mist in the woods . . . My brother would baby-sit for me sometimes when I was about ten and my parents would go out. I would be afraid to be alone so I would go and stand by the door of his room. Finally he would say, 'OK,' I could go in. One time I got in bed with him and he masturbated. He never touched me, though . . . I wasn't afraid." She returned to thoughts about the funeral: "An open casket. It was sort of foreign to me."

I said, "I wonder if there is some part in this dream that comes from the funeral. You, a middle-aged blond woman, were looking down at the dead woman, laid out."

"Yes, I had thought about that. And you know what? I thought, if you're dead, you can't masturbate. When my brother was dying I was the only one there at the hospital. . . . [She was crying.] I wondered if

I should put his hand on his genitals, if that would make him feel better."

I said, "Another way to think about this is that when you masturbate you make sure you are not dead. When you masturbated as a child you felt so alone, you were left alone a lot. Then and now, you try to get relief from feeling so alone, frightened and deadened." I added that it sounded as if she was afraid she was going to die, like the rest of her family.

After a pause, she said, "My mother always said she was going to die. She told me once that I was going to die. [Another pause] I felt the same way last night. I'd get up to go urinate to see if it would relieve the tension. I can't lie down sometimes—like last night—without masturbating. When I was married and began graduate school, I couldn't study. Every time I started reading it was stimulating, or something."

I asked, "How so?" She replied, "I don't know. They were writing about feelings. There was one book about 'Man's Search for Meaning.' He said all those things in public. I couldn't believe it. I was disturbed, but in a good way."

I said, "The writer put feelings into words, instead of the body, which is how your feelings are expressed a lot. [She nodded, but was silent.] I understand something now. Perhaps you are afraid that you have the urge to masturbate here, as there is a repetition of that sort of experience. I put your feelings into words. This is what we are trying to do, understand your feelings, and that is stimulating, like when you were reading the book." [She nodded again.]

Here I addressed the issue of the patient's deadening of affect and her fear of dying like her mother. (In the weeks immediately preceding this session she had told me a chilling story of how her father had purchased four adjoining gravesites for their little family. This suggested to me that the father did not anticipate that she and her brother would move on to adulthood to establish their own families.) In this session I did not interpret her obvious fear of my dying and leaving her behind, a fear we addressed repeatedly throughout the analysis.

My initial worries about the depth of Mona's depression, however, did not return. Perhaps this was because in spite of the very painful and difficult process within the consulting room, Mona seemed to be getting gradually better in her external life. Three years after she began treatment, Mona was able to marry again, this time to a kind and supportive man, Leo. When she began analysis, she had worried that her relationship with Leo, like many of her past relationships with men, was without closeness or permanence. She complained that they did not communicate (which I readily could see) and that Leo was naturally reticent. She was worried that she could not love him or anyone. I had no clear picture of him. It took over a year for me to realize, by the bits and pieces of stories she told about him, that Leo was a very kind man, a very steady and solid one, who loved her.

This is the way it went in those early years. She would report the tangibles, and I would have to search for the feelings and the meanings for us both. The marriage seemed to be a consolidating one for her. She felt that in many respects Leo was like her father. We came to see that, with the exception of her first husband, there was also a strong maternal component to the men she picked.

Mona began to study the piano. She had been given an old one that had been in the family. Her mother, as I have said, had been a musician, but after her marriage she would have nothing more to do with music, and actively discouraged her daughter from studying it. In fact music was not allowed in the house, even in the form of a phonograph or radio. The patient was in the high school band briefly and enjoyed it, but she was ridiculed by her mother and brother and dropped out. With her characteristic compulsivity, Mona now took to her new lessons by practicing the piano a couple of hours a day. She was apparently quite talented and made rapid progress. More importantly, she was able to enjoy her playing and her progress.

Gradually also Mona became less silent and miserable in the sessions, more able to make sense herself of her history and her current relationships, more able to know her feelings. The initial positive and idealized transference seemed to reflect a wished-for, fantasized good mother and the care-taking father or Hope. Mona searched her mind and memories for any positive images of her mother. What she found instead were negative images or blankness, an empty spot. Longings for her mother were not acknowledged either.

Negative feelings toward me were fended off as she struggled to hold on to a positive image. For example, one bleak winter day she came in flustered after a sleepless night and a snowstorm that had made her late. She went on to talk about her sons' plans for a visit to Florida that were becoming complicated, and attributed angry feelings about this to her husband. I suggested that it was her own anger and annoyance that fueled her anxiety and that she projected her feelings onto others. She agreed, and began to voice more open feelings of jealousy about being left out of the plans. I said that it being Florida made it worse (that was where her parents had always gone without her on vacation, leaving her home when she was a child. She replied, "I thought when you started talking you were going to say that the weather made it worse.... I feel *hateful, hateful.* I walk around with all this stuff inside me. I don't want anybody to see. Dreams yesterday. I don't know what they were, but yesterday when you picked up your book at the end of the session I thought you'd tell me you would be gone.... I think of the avalanche in Canada. Those poor people who had lost their children. And the father can't even get in to the funeral. Why am I so upset?" I said, "The fear is that because of your anger, you will lose people, lose me."

Middle phases: It was only after two or three years, when she was able to hold an inner representation of me as a safe and stable object, and when she had gained a working language of feelings, that Mona began to be transformed into a more typical analytic patient—overly compliant, but no longer so mute, flat, and depressed. With much work on her resistances and fears, she was able to begin to speak about her angers and disappointments, and her criticisms of me. She became more able to associate to her dreams and to figure them out for herself. She gave up the search for the "truth" of her birth (although she remained curious) and for the confirmation of early sexual abuse.

Mona had tried to keep all sadistic angers at bay through an idealized transference and the splintering dialogue of the early phases of her analysis. As the idealization of me faded, I became the acknowledged object of more anger and jealousy, and insight into the split-off sides of the self became possible. In the following session from the fourth year of the analysis, we see that Mona was still dealing with feelings of being unliked and unlikable. Compared to the earlier sessions, however, she was more engaged, participatory, and able to make sense of her feelings herself. Here I linked her feelings of depression to her conflicts about being female.

"I ran into Joe again. [Joe, a friend who was also in analysis, had told her the previous week that my husband was an analyst. This thought had upset her.] He said actually your husband wasn't an analyst. So all day I kept thinking something good has happened." I said it was important for us to understand what those feelings—about my husband being an analyst—were all about.

"The thought seems scary. A little dangerous. But kooky. Where did that come from? Why feel that? Couples who are in the same profession get lopsided kind of. Depressing somehow. Heavy, gray. Is it like my parents somehow? They were the opposite, though, from two analysts; they never talked about feelings! My friends, the therapists who are married to each other, seem pretty happy. But it still feels gray and heavy, too serious. But why for me, why scary for me?"

Thinking to myself of primal scene, or that a couple whose identities are too fused might be frightening, I suggested that if I were married to an analyst, then my husband and I would be too similar a couple and she couldn't break into that. Crying now, she nodded and then said:

"The dream last night. It was about people not liking me. One woman was going to show me something and she said, 'I never did like you.' [I remembered that she reported her grandmother having said those exact words.] In another part, there was this ugly, skinny, little black woman. She had given me a silk scarf. I had on a silk scarf but not the one she had given me. She cried and she put her arms around my neck to be comforted, and I thought, I wish I had her scarf on, but at least she knew I wear scarves. [I was thinking that I wear a lot of scarves.] I was feeling not liked throughout."

I asked, "Is there a connection here with your feeling about my husband being an analyst?"

"Maybe something to do with the other dream we talked about. [In this dream, which had oedipal implications, she had Joe's baby, a boy. Her associations suggested jealousies and rivalries toward her daughter-in-law and Joe's wife.] Sometimes you do see people who are obnoxious and they don't realize what they're doing. I felt not being liked a lot. With one teacher I felt that."

"Saturday night I went to a party with my husband. All the women there were outgoing, vivacious, and talkative. I felt like I looked OK until I got there. I don't know if it's kind of a feeling of not being liked. I do or don't do something to affect people that I'm not aware of. In the neighborhood I lived when I was first married I was friendly. But I realized they didn't see me as one of them." I asked, "What makes you think that?" "They'd visit around with each other. One of them said I was really nice, but implied that they didn't see me as friendly. The feeling in the dream was not unusual [There was a tear running down her cheek]. Saturday night I had a headache when we got home. Probably from the feelings at the party. [This represented progress in that she herself could translate a bodily feeling into an emotion.] I got quieter around the people. They were talking, the women, like one was saying her mother was great and another one how she was so loved. I was aware that when I went home I looked in the mirror and my face looked bad, flat. [Crying]"

I said, "You feel that you are not liked because you aren't responsive, but the feeling of not being liked goes very deep. You feel I don't like you. You want desperately to be liked and accepted, but feel I don't because I know what is inside of you, and like your mother, I won't like you because you're a girl, or like your father because of your girl's sexual feelings."

She cried, nodded and became silent. Then she said very softly, "I didn't know why I was crying at first but the pain inside went away after you said that. At the party that feeling started right away. Maybe I withdrew. Didn't respond right away. My girlfriend was there and she was so alive and her face was alive. I thought about it. It seems like if your husband was an analyst, I don't know, what do I think . . . it went away . . . Hmmm . . . A flat face. It's like not having enough feeling. If I have something up here [she pointed to her neck] or hair over my face, then it would hide that. Yet I felt my expressions were ugly. I see now I *was* depressed. I didn't want to respond."

I remarked, "You can't win, either way—if you show your feelings or if you don't show your feelings."

"I remember in junior high I felt my teeth were too big and would put my hand in front of my mouth all of the time. . . ." [Worries about her oral aggression?]

The analytic exploration turned subsequently more and more to her guilt-ridden jealous and sadistic impulses, apparent in the above material, which were sources of her fears that people not be able to stand her and would leave her. As she became able to acknowledge these impulses, her fears of being abandoned and rejected lessened. She was able slowly to override her fears. For example, during one session she spoke of a women psychologist she knew: "I like her, but she irritates me. Maybe I want to be rude. Afraid of what I will say or do." When I suggested, "Afraid here of what you will do or say?" she laughed. Then, with good humor, she told a joke about a psychoanalyst and acknowledged that the hostile feelings were aimed at me.

At this time, she was able to acknowledge her jealousies toward her mother and her daughter-in-law as the rival women who got the men she loved and wanted for herself. She was also able to face her rage at her father who was weak, preferred her mother to her, and in many ways abandoned her. Jealousy toward her brother, who for many years in the analysis had been almost totally absent from her dreams and memories, was cloaked in guilt, as he too was a victim of early neglect. Her sadistic rage toward her own children was perhaps the hardest to recognize and work through.

In the fourth year of analysis, Mona had been talking about one source of her unhappiness with me. Like her mother during her adolescence, I was not helping her figure out how to be a woman. In this context, she was first able to admit, shamefully, to having sexual feelings about me, identical to feelings she had toward the woman in one of her past homosexual encounters. Her wishes were to fondle my breasts and genitals. She described her fantasy with the woman: "I wanted to touch her genitals to see what it felt like." I asked, "What do you mean?" She replied, "What a woman really feels like. I'm a woman. I've felt myself but I don't know what a woman feels like." Then she remembered a picture of herself as a young adolescent, in which she looked like a boy, "like part boy and part girl." Here her homosexual impulses reflected her wishes to be taught how it might feel to be a woman, in a concrete, literal, and bodily way: to *feel* or touch a woman would somehow almost magically teach her how a woman feels.

A turning point came about a year and a half before the end of analysis. After a stressful time struggling with her fear that I might hate her in reaction to her angry feelings, the patient came to a stark realization: "My mother hated me." Paradoxically, this realization was a major relief. The patient then could conclude that the hate arose from the mother's problems, and not because Mona was unlovable, ugly, female, over-sexed, or full of a terrible mess of evil, dirty, wrathful feelings. Perhaps the realization also relieved her of her guilt about her own hateful feelings.

GENDER ISSUES

For the purposes of this paper, I have distilled the gender-related issues that appeared as a leitmotiv throughout the material that Mona presented. Analysis revealed that she had the almost conscious fantasy that she was half boy and half girl. As she admitted, "sometimes I'm not sure whether I'm a boy or a girl." She dressed as a girl, but held the fantasy that underneath she was a boy. For example, she described a photo of herself as a young adolescent in which she was wearing her mother's suit; underneath was a red sweater—"that was the boy under the girl's clothing." Another fantasy she articulated was that the top half of her was the female; the bottom, the male.

There were also numerous representations and other manifestations of a fantasy of an inner penis and of a wish for a penis. She dreamed repeatedly of stolen statues, lost and then found baby boys, eight-inch long live dolls, and so on. In one dream a girl, with a red sore, was having a transplant. The sore brought to mind female genitals, body piercing. She fantasized that if she had a penis, she would be able to masturbate, finally, to a sense of completion and fulfilled orgasm. Having a penis would relieve the unbearable sexualized inner tension she felt: "If you had a penis you could get relief. Then it would be on the outside, not the inside, and the pressure wouldn't be there."

The more valued aspects of the self were masculine. The sturdy part of her, the athletic part that worked with her father, was a boy. "I liked being a boy. Thinking like that. I liked boys' bikes. Girls were bad." Her sense of herself as female seemed unarticulated, except for the feelings of ugliness and being out of control that she equated with being female. Her feeling that her face was ugly—too flat—was representative of her lack of affect, her wordlessness, and at the same time a defense against sexual feelings that might show, that she needed to flatten. Her face was ugly for other reasons connected to being female, too. One memory concerned her senior prom when she wore a strapless gown. That meant somehow that her face, her ugly face, was exposed. Her father, who had come home with her mother after going out, barged into the party in her basement after the prom. Flushed and slightly drunk, he demanded to dance with her. She was embarrassed in front of her friends and refused. He was hurt. The whole episode had sexual, incestuous meanings to her and brought back the trauma at age three when sexual feelings between her and her father led to rejection. Even as an adult, the patient liked to wear bangs and high collars so that her face would not be exposed. The face was a concrete representation of her ugly female genitalia. There were several periods during the analysis when Mona felt ashamed of her exposed face on the couch, and she took pains to wear high collars or turtle neck tops.

She consciously tried to throw off any identification with her mother. In the context of a dream about a wooden box, to which she related her "frozen genitals," she said, "I did not want to identify with her. It wasn't good to be a woman."

Yet she could not give up entirely the idea of being female. Being female also brought the possibility, short-lived, of being sexually special for her father, being "liked." "My dad liked girls. I think he liked me because I was a girl." Thus it was an insoluble dilemma. She did not want to be a woman like her mother, yet she did not want to give up the possibility of being liked by her father for being a girl.

Being female provided another solution to feeling unwanted. She could strive to become a mother herself, and give birth to wanted children, boys, with whom she could be close. Thus, she identified with the mother of the Jessica story, not the baby; this was her way of repairing the mother-infant dyad that in her own case had become disconnected. In this instance and throughout her life she identified with a mother who desperately loved her children and did not want to lose them. In this way, she constructed an identity for herself as the solution to her early abandonment. The identity was a mother-in-relation-to-a-child. In this fantasy the baby was male; she could not conceive of loving a female child. This too was a half-female/half-male entity—mother/male baby. At the same time, the lost, neglected, or damaged male babies that cluttered her dreams were manifestations of unconscious murderous and castrating impulses toward her brother, father, and all males.

On the other hand, being male meant that she could be the boy she felt her mother had wanted. That way, she would not be abandoned and might be loved. It meant trying to be a better son than her brother in her father's eyes. She was sturdier, a better student, and a harder worker than her brother—all qualities her father valued. The fantasy of having a penis meant to be in better control, less vulnerable sexually, and able to achieve sexual relief. To be male meant literal survival because boys were seen as sturdy, able to pull themselves out of danger. And after all, she was the only member of her family to have avoided the tragedy of alcoholism.

Being male and female both, therefore, was a narcissistic solution that quieted many fears and insured that she need not surrender conflicting wishes.

While Mona's avowed sexual orientation was heterosexual, the need to feel connected and wanted seemed to outweigh sexual preference or choice of object, so that in her conscious and unconscious fantasy life, and on rare occasions in reality, she had sexual urges toward females, as well.

The boy/girl fantasy signaled her problems in integration of internal parental identifications, her shaky attachment, and her difficulties in dealing with affect, especially depression and anger. These problems had to be worked out before the boy/girl fantasy could be fully analyzed.

RESOLUTION OF THE GENDER CONFLICT AND THE TERMINATION PHASE

Making sense of her history, finding a satisfactory narrative, owning up to and expressing her un-verbalized feelings, integrating major split-off parts of herself, gaining insight into the sources of her guilt and anxiety and, finally, accepting herself as she was, a female, comprised the major work of the analysis. Mona announced that she might be approaching termination with the following words: "I feel I'm lucky. How bad I felt for so many years and how different I feel now! People who have had bad childhoods never knew that it would be any different, or any way to get out of it. I felt there was no reason to be the way I was. It just was."

The termination phase was predictably very difficult for Mona. At first an affective flatness returned, as she tried to erase the painful feelings of loss and mourning for the disappointing abandoning objects of the past, and the loss of the analyst and the very real place the analyst had in her life. An important piece of work in the termination period concerned sorting out two different feelings associated with abandonment. One was the familiar deep, bodily depression associated with her mother's abandonment and rejection of her. These were the feelings, we had come to realize, that had been at play in her compulsive masturbation, the content-less abdominal pain and rocking—a sense of deep loneliness and badness which she needed to soothe and drain out of herself. But what also emerged in the termination phase were feelings of abandonment that had more form. Rather than a sense of a loss of something or somebody she had never had—a mother who wanted her—there was a painful fear of a loss of somebody she had had and had lost. Repeatedly she voiced the painful fear that I would disappear and not know any more about her or that she would not hear anything more of me. We were finally able to identify these as feelings about the caretaker that her father had hired to care for her in the first year and a half of her life: a person who had been important to her and had cared for her, but who had left mysteriously and never appeared again.

Besides working through losses from the past—caretaker, mother, father, brother—Mona experienced painful feelings of mourning and guilt about how she had lived her life. Looking back, and with the words she had finally found for her feelings, she talked about how desperately unhappy she had been throughout most of her life. She expressed intense guilt in her retrospective evaluation of herself as a mother. She now understood why she had not been able to actualize in herself the mother she longed for. Her unconscious rage and frozen yearnings had made her unable to assume the role she constructed for herself.

Major changes occurred in the female/male fantasy. Mona seemed to have given up the wish to be a male, and she accepted herself as a female. This change was clear in many different ways. Dreams that formerly were filled with only male children now included females: "Lots of little girls in dreams. Maybe I was adopting them. Dark, foreign girls. They were homely. And a little blonde girl who climbed up on my lap and went to sleep. Is the little blonde girl also me? Yes, I did wish for closeness." (For years such a thought would have been too painful and an anathema.) She was able to love her granddaughters. There was evidence that the fantasy of having a penis was fading. For example, there were many dreams of giving up male appendages. Hedging her bets, she dreamed of growing a very, very small penis, "an extra appendage." As she dreamed of losing or relinquishing her penis, there was a brief period of actually feeling physically weak, until she connected this experience with having given up the fantasy that she was armed with a male power. Yet shortly before she terminated, she interpreted a dream in which she had taken the masculine position with a somewhat unattractive woman "to have sex or something." She mused, "It's a solution to have a penis. In control, in charge. I think if I had a penis, I'd never be alone. I guess this is about my stopping. . . ."

Significantly, her beating masturbation fantasies changed. The fantasies were more fluid and variable. Now she identified herself in the fantasies as a girl, not always being forced into a situation, but choosing it. The girl was sometimes the one who was conducting the action on a boy, masturbating a male. Compulsive masturbation had abated by the end of the analysis. The other type of masturbation, the early bodily one, was gone completely.

She recounted how an interesting man flirted with her and tried to pick her up. He told her that she was a handsome woman. While she did not respond, inside herself she felt pleased and flattered. "It makes me feel good. Makes me feel feminine. What made me feel good was the word 'woman.' A grown woman. I like feeling like a mature woman. I think that for the first time now, inside myself, I like dressing like a woman and being a woman. Feeling attractive and feminine. I like to dress in dresses." In a dream the next night, she looked into a mirror to see that she had a face made up like a geisha's and she thought, "It looks pretty good." Her associations to geisha went to *Memoirs of a Geisha,* the novel she was reading. She had recently rediscovered her joy in reading. She found the story very moving. The geisha had a very troubled tough life, with which Mona identified and empathized. What she and the geisha shared, she felt, was that they found a way out of their backgrounds. (Since she commented on the fact that this novel was written by a man, we might speculate that she still harbored the unconscious fantasy of being a man, a man donning the mask of a geisha, authoring the tale.)

DISCUSSION

Given how the analysis unfolded, I believe that Mona's problems and conflicts around gender and sexuality reflected more basic, underlying problems of attachment, depression, and management of affects, especially anger. I felt that technically we would have to work on these more basic issues before her conflicts around her gender and sexuality could really be addressed. The focus in the initial years of the analysis was therefore on establishing first a sense of emotional safety, and secondarily a vocabulary for verbal communication. Terrified of abandonment and with an early history of trauma, Mona seemed to be an individual suffering from an insecure attachment, as described in recent research (Ainsworth, 1978; Main, 1995). Given her shaky attachment to a mother who did not want her, it took years for Mona to feel that she could trust me to be there with her and not to leave her. I repeatedly had to address her fears that I did not like her and that I would leave her. My steady presence had to be experienced and assimilated before she could feel secure. Moreover, Mona had no working vocabulary for feelings, and no cohesive sense of her own story or history. Thus, I felt that I had to be much more active in supplying words and connections for her than I usually am. One might wonder if Mona's problems might fit into the alexithymia category as described by Krystal (1982): that is, an arrest in affective and cognitive development. At the time, I thought of her problem not as arrest, but as a massive inhibition of affects and especially anger. Nevertheless, arrest or inhibition, the technique in working with her was in some way to supply for the patient what she was not able to supply for herself in terms of affect verbalization.

Early on, words in the analysis had concrete meanings for her, and served as a means of connection, without referents. At those times, my words probably were taken in as nourishment and containment as an infant might experience her mother's soothing voice. Later, words along with their meanings became a means of higher-level understandings, so that my interpretations about sexual conflicts could be appreciated and assimilated.

Once a more stable connection and image of me were established, which took years, more pointed work on her conflicts around gender became possible. Ultimately, Mona came to understand the meanings and functions of her fantasy of boy/girl. As we were able to understand this together, Mona's fantasy of being a boy/girl was both a result of problems in the family and a solution to them. The boy/girl fantasy was essential, because she felt she could not be who she was. Paradoxically, a half-and-half gender had to take the place of an integrated sense of self. Pieces of her experienced world—"male" bits and "female" bits—were taken in through identifications but could not be amalgamated into a cohesive sense of self. At the same time, because the trauma of abandonment and neglect came so early, Mona was overwhelmed by aggression that could not be managed. Thus, dangers from within (unmanageable aggression) and dangers from without (inevitable abandonment) remained very real throughout her life. The fantasy of being half male and half female helped to bolster her against an inner sense of weakness. It was noteworthy that she actually felt weak when she was relinquishing the fantasy at the end of the analysis.

Gender was highlighted in Mona's family. Males were privileged and preferred, but females seemed to grab the power. Her mother clearly had a troubled sense of her own femininity and sexuality, which she played out with her daughter, rejecting and ignoring her. The basic problem for this patient was her sense of being unloved, and her rage, depression, and fears of abandonment. Her solution was a narcissistic construction of her self as both male and female. Her need to be both sexes recalls Kubie's ideas (1974) about the importance of trying to integrate mutually irreconcilable, dual sexual identities. Both problem and solution reflected the family's idiosyncrasies.

That this solution was necessary and available for Mona came from several sources: constitutional, familial, and psychological. Constitutionally, she was indeed sturdy and athletic, and in that sense, like the boy in her fantasies. She was sturdy in other ways as well: made of strong psychological stuff, somehow. She was able to prevail over a troubled family life, as was the geisha in the novel. And she was the sole survivor of a family in which all the other members died before her. Alcoholism, depression, and affect intolerance all ran in the family. Mona's familial legacy and her early trauma left her prone from the beginning to depression. Fonagy (2000) has suggested that unresolved infantile trauma is associated with problems of mentalization and rigidity of thinking in later life. Mona's concreteness of thought was reflected in her belief in a literal fantasy of being half boy and half girl. Similarly, in order to know how a female felt, Mona fantasized that she had literally to touch or feel a female body.

Psychologically, Mona as a child came to believe that her gender and her sexuality were the causes of her being unloved, a belief perhaps less painful than other possibilities. Remember that a significant step forward came in the analysis when Mona finally became able to acknowledge that her mother hated her, and to recognize as well that the mother's hate was the product of self-hatred and being troubled herself.

Ultimately the fantasy of being half male and half female receded into the shadows of this woman's mind. Similarly, the rigidified gender roles that characterized her masturbation fantasies loosened. Issues of gender were highlighted in this case in a way that lets us appreciate their complex relationship with other underlying factors.

BIBLIOGRAPHY

AINSWORTH, M. D. S., BLEHAR, M. C., WATERS, E., & WALL, S., EDS. (1978). *Patterns of Attachment: A Psychological Study of the Strange Situation*. Hillsdale, N.Y.: Erlbaum.

FONAGY, P. (2000). Attachment and borderline personality disorder. *Journal of the American Psychoanalytic Association*, 48:1129–1146.

FREUD, S. (1919). A child is being beaten. *Standard Edition*, 17:175–204.

KRYSTAL, H. (1982). Alexithymia and the effectiveness of psychoanalytic treatment. *International Journal of Psychoanalytic Psychotherapy*, 9:353–388.

KUBIE, L. (1974). The drive to become both sexes. *Psychoanalytic Quarterly*, 43:349–426.

MAIN, M. (1995). Attachment: Overview, with implication for clinical work. In *Attachment Theory: Social, Developmental and Clinical Perspectives*, ed. S. Goldberg, P. Muir, & J. Kerr. Hillsdale, N.J.: Analytic Press, pp. 407–474.

DEVELOPMENT

Introduction

SAMUEL ABRAMS, M.D.

This section comprises the yield of a group of analysts studying developmental disorders in children. There are six contributions. One describes the clinical features of just such a child and the approaches used to overcome her many difficulties. A second presents an overview of the group process, the ways in which the participants struggled with concepts and sometimes with one another. A third paper outlines a point of view entirely different from the direction taken by most of the members of the study group; it proves to be of value on its own right and as a way of further clarifying some of the features described by other participants. Still another paper addresses in depth one of the major findings of the study group: the use of narrative building as a form of repair for such children. A fifth contribution reflects on future possible studies, natural outgrowths of the present one. Finally, the last of the papers summarizes the study group as a whole, paying particular attention to some informing theories of development while detailing observations and findings.

Each of the papers can be read individually or in a different sequence than the way they are presented. The intention of this section is to provide the reader with some of the excitement generated in a clinically based research study such as this. If this section were to provide a stimulus for further explorations into what is still unknown in our discipline, it will have served a major function.

The Psychoanalytic Study of the Child 58, ed. Robert A. King, Peter B. Neubauer, Samuel Abrams, and A. Scott Dowling (Yale University Press, copyright © 2003 by Robert A. King, Peter B. Neubauer, Samuel Abrams, and A. Scott Dowling).

An Analysis of a Developmentally Delayed Young Girl

Coordinating Analytic and Developmental Processes

WENDY OLESKER, Ph.D.

Clinical material is presented from a multi-year treatment of a five-year-old girl with a variety of developmental interferences, making it necessary to consider whether standard technique would suffice. History includes the fact that she was adopted five days after birth and told as early as possible about her adoption; she was placed in a restrictive brace from four months to twenty months because of congenital hip displasia. Sandy's ability to let in the outside world was limited by her intense denial, not looking, not taking in, and by her detachment. Her passivity—whether a defense (modeled on her experience of physical restraint) or an arrest—was a formidable obstacle to the development of active transference moments. I use this case as an opportunity to look at the role of developmental sequences in the context of the analytic process. While I consciously did not do anything different than I

Training and supervising analyst at the New York Psychoanalytic Institute; adjunct professor, New York University Postdoctoral Program in Psychoanalysis and Psychotherapy.

I wish to acknowledge and thank the members of the Study Group on Clinical Applications of Developmental Propositions, whose comments made a major contribution to my thinking and to the conduct of the treatment. Co-Chairmen: Sam Abrams and Al Solnit; Members: Alice Colonna, Karen Gilmore, Leon Hoffman, Nasir Ilahi, Rona Knight, Claudia Lament, Roy Lilleskov, Peter Neubauer, Mortimer Ostow, Noah Shaw, Judy Yanof.

The Psychoanalytic Study of the Child 58, ed. Robert A. King, Peter B. Neubauer, Samuel Abrams, and A. Scott Dowling (Yale University Press, copyright © 2003 by Robert A. King, Peter B. Neubauer, Samuel Abrams, and A. Scott Dowling).

would with any child analytic patient, I intuitively stressed certain kinds of interventions.

TO DEMONSTRATE MY ATTEMPT TO COORDINATE THE DEVELOPMENTAL process with the analytic process, I present here clinical material from a seven-year treatment of a five-year-old patient with a variety of developmental interferences, making it necessary to consider whether standard technique would suffice or whether other interventions might be necessary to facilitate progress. I use this case as an opportunity to look at the role of developmental sequences in the context of the analytic process. In Anna Freud's (1981) view the developmental process is an inherent blueprint of potential variations in sequential hierarchical growth that meet and interact with an object relational system and its availability, nature of stimulation, attunement, and attitude of the caregivers. In addition to differences in the caretaking environment, there may be inherent differences in forward-moving potential, in internal structuralization, in imbalances between the lines of development (A. Freud, 1965) and in the equipment, disposition, and constitution of the child.

While I consciously did not do anything different than I would with any child analytic patient, I intuitively stressed certain kinds of interventions, which were used in a somewhat different manner than intended. Sandy's ability to sample and let in the outside world was limited by her intense denial, not looking, not taking in, and by her detachment. Her passivity—whether a defense (modeled on her experience of physical restraint) or an arrest—was a formidable obstacle to the development of active transference moments. Specifically, my patient needed more than most help in the area of ego development: to create and stabilize psychic structures, particularly the development of object constancy, the signal function, and the control function, and aid in facilitating internalization and superego formation. Sandy externalized unacceptable parts of herself, particularly the "wild," "monster," "killing" parts of herself. She was able to find and reach me because I made myself affectively alive and engaging to her, and she identified with my ways of handling her externalized creations—not her "brace mother" way of coping but empathically anticipating her needs, verbalizing them, putting them in a historical context, accepting them—features about me that allowed her to face more honestly the nature of her inner world and eventually actualize more fully her oedipal-phase potential. Thus, at the outset her externalizations allowed for some coherence of self structure but in a very pathological way, where large aspects of herself had been split off and ejected. Careful delineation of her defensive maneuvers allowed her to integrate parts of herself that had been ejected. Our interactions helped to affirm and facilitate object seeking so as to help actualize newly emerging hierarchies and provided a model of a mutually constructed regulation pattern. Although one might question whether developmental facilitation might interfere with analysis, I hope to show that it provided assistance. Because this patient seldom used words to express her concerns, play helped set progressive and adaptational forces in motion, created the scaffolding for integration and organization, provided a window on internal conflicts, and created new perspectives on her inner world. It assisted nascent cognitive potential. Interpretations served the purpose of narrative building and enhancing expectable narrative development, a specific area of weakness in this patient. I helped link together thoughts and feelings to create narratives not only discovered and uncovered unconscious fantasies. Understanding her ways of defending against some of her anxieties allowed Sandy to be able to participate in building coherent narratives and create an organization stable enough to receive interpretations.

CASE MATERIAL

Presenting Problems: Sandy was an adopted, waif-like, pale, black-haired, blue-eyed, attractive five-year-old girl when I first saw her. She had an eighteen month older adopted sister. She was brought for treatment because, in addition to difficulties at school in expressive language, word-finding, and categorizing, she was very inhibited, prone to frantic rages when denied something, and seemed not to notice what was going on in the world around her, including dangers. Sandy's problems caused much conflict between the parents. Father, an East European immigrant who valued intelligence above all, felt disappointed in Sandy's lack of high or gifted intelligence and angry that she was allowed to get away with too much "because of her problems." Mother, a retired actress, a woman of action, sensitive, soft-spoken, with a narrow range of affect (possibility inhibited by guilt and ambivalence) tried to be firm with Sandy but was exhausted by her daughter's demandingness, especially for exclusivity. Mother saw Sandy as suffering from arrested development. "She went into the terrible two's late (around three) and has never come out."

Brief Family History: Sandy was a collicky baby with physical symptoms that later included frequent headaches and food allergies. Her
adoption was delayed five days because of her birth mother's ambivalence; being from the same middle class background as the birth
mother, Sandy's adoptive mother felt guilty as if she had stolen Sandy
and had no right to be her mother. Sandy was told as early as possible
about her adoption with storybooks and pictures, and she was placed
in a brace from four months to twenty months because of congenital
hip dysplasia. Once the brace was removed, she learned to walk very
quickly. She ate well, though ever since twenty months she was prone
to unexpected rages over being deprived of something she wanted,
especially sweets. Toilet training, eating, sleeping, all appeared to be
normal. She has had the same English-speaking though quiet baby-
sitter since birth, someone who has difficulty setting limits as does
mother. Mother never noticed any particular reaction to awareness
of anatomical differences and reported infrequent masturbation. Expressive language problems were picked up in preschool along with
word retrieval problems and difficulty using language effectively for
communication. Sandy lost confidence at school in the first grade
due to difficulty acquiring reading skills. She misheard words and got
angry quickly, sometimes thinking that someone was trying to trick
her. To this day she is very jealous of her older sister who is perceived
as getting more of everything, including parental love.

Testing at age eight confirmed that Sandy had a number of learning disabilities. Though of average intelligence (107 IQ), Sandy had
marked weakness, functioning in the retarded level on items tapping
her ability to concentrate on and take in information from the world
around her (she received a scaled score of 7 on information, picture
completion, and picture arrangement on the WPSSI). Furthermore,
her story memory was in the second percentile, her ability to delay
and plan ahead was in the retarded intellectual range, she had a
problem recognizing faces, and processing material auditorily. It was
noted that she needed help with organization of written work,
couldn't replicate narrative sequences (poor narrative memory) or
sequence material into a narrative structure. All these difficulties
seemed to contribute to a sense of something being wrong with her
and a sense of self as damaged. Projective testing suggested that she
wanted to hurt and bite yet feared being overwhelmed with the more
primitive aspects of her personality. Early trauma of abandonment
and restriction of physical movement seems to have increased her
anger and gave her little outlet for its expression and sublimation.

THE TREATMENT

The first issue to take center stage was just how limited Sandy's play was. She could present only simple one-step narratives. She had long exhibited her body skills (jumping off my couch, doing head stands), yet I could see that she could not elaborate a fantasy in words, and only a very limited one in action. She repetitively played out the theme of a girl being a leader and many other children following her every move. She got to go first; the activity was simply walking in a straight line with other children following. I tried to ask questions of the characters, what they were thinking or feeling, but she seemed not to know. It took some time for the sibling rivalry theme to emerge in some detail. When I tried to fill in feelings—how good it felt to be in the front of the line, how good it felt to be first and not last—she occasionally nodded but not much affect was forthcoming. Slowly I added more affect—that she had felt so small and helpless in the face of her older bigger stronger sister, and she could magically do away with those feelings by becoming the leader—she became more enlivened. Sandy confessed to me that she could never feel better because she could never be older than Kelly. She envied, admired, and wanted everything that Kelly had. According to mother, she was devastated when Kelly excluded her and worried that all people preferred Kelly to her (in fact both parents found Kelly easier and more pleasing than Sandy). I said that now it was clearer why she spent so much time in our early meetings making up to herself what she wasn't able to get in her life: being the leader not the lowly follower. Another theme followed: at a birthday party, Sandy was given all the presents, children sat around and watched. I said to her that it felt so good to be the center of attention and to have all the sweets and gifts she wanted that she couldn't get enough of it. She agreed.

By the second analytic year rage and competition toward her sister shifted to mother. She was angry at mother for having others in her life. Sandy told the following story: A black horse stamped on the mother horse for having too many others to take care of; a girl called to her mother angrily that she didn't want mother to go out. Then the story changed to the girl going out, moving into her own house all alone; the girl wanted to live there all by herself. Many play themes involved kids wanting to play on their own with no grown-ups around and having fun doing so. I said that the girl was so angry and hurt that her mother went out with others when she wanted her that the girl decided it was better not to want mother at all. But that was out of hurt, anger, and revenge that she wanted to live alone, not because she really wanted to. Sandy got more intense about cutting off the tie to mother, stating that she just wanted to be left alone. She liked people last: first she liked horses, then dogs, then apples, and then people. It came to light that Sandy had taken money from mother's pocketbook on a number of occasions. I suggested that when something hurts, like wanting mommy all to herself and not being able to get mommy all for herself or control mommy, she pretended she didn't care about mommy, or she just wanted mommy's things, not mommy. I added that when she was so angry at mommy, she felt she couldn't trust her so at least she could have her things. But that was out of anger and revenge, underneath she really did want mommy. But she also wanted to be the boss of all the supplies. To this her eyes lit up, and she heartily (for her) agreed.

Subsequently, fantasies of having two mothers emerged, first played out around the fantasy of having a dog who was given away to another family but then wanted to return to his first home. Many repetitive simple stories followed with themes of having two families, not being treated well by one and then finding another. A most poignant one involved a girl who wanted so much candy and food that the mother went to the supermarket and left her outside for hours. She was kidnapped and put with another family. When I suggested her confusion about having two mothers and her idea that she had been left by her first mother because her needs and wants were so great, she at first denied it—"I'm not confused because I never even met my first mother"—but then said she thought she wanted too much candy. I said she seemed to be testing her mother again and again—what would happen if she wanted more and more candy, would she be given away? At another point she turned the tables on adoption. A girl ran away from her family to a new family. Her parents came looking for her, begging her to come home but she hid, would not listen, and would never go back. Since Sandy's bland play had totally omitted the affective side and the underlying meaning, I said that she wanted revenge on her birth mother. She should come looking for her, want her terribly, and never be able to find her. Then she would be sorry. Sandy showed a slight flicker of recognition, and repeated the sequences with even more determination not to be found and to punish the original mother. Later a more elaborated theme added the dimension of aggression—horses were given away when they were too hungry, wild, angry, and couldn't be trained. She struggled with how to tame wild animals, first with violent discipline, with whips and guns. In many sessions she played out scenes of self-regulation, of being left or given away for being too wild and aggressive. I said she seemed to think the only way to teach self-control was by being harsh and cruel; part of her did not believe the horse could learn to control himself with affectionate, firm, kind support. This theme came up time and again with new additions. At many different points she brought in her own dog and would work on disciplining first in a harsh way and in a more kind and loving way over time, with patience, tolerance, and repetition.

Phallic conflicts, and identifying as a boy in order to solve a variety of issues, emerged during the third year of analysis. When most afraid of being unable to control her anger, she imagined herself as a boy to help her feel strong and invulnerable. She had the fantasy that she had a hidden phallus, the source of magical power (later she tried to get me to give her a special pen that seemed to confer on her the magical power). Hiding and stealing were regular play themes. She wanted revenge on the mother who she felt hid from her and did not really see her. Exhibitionistic play followed wherein a male teacher had his pupil sit on a table, playing the piano while all watched and applauded. It became clear that you got to choose whatever family you wanted if you were a boy, and you got rejected from a family if you were a girl—a girl was too greedy, too curious, too aggressive, or too damaged with a cut or a wound for which you hold a grudge. Feeling rejected by a first family upon learning of her adoption seemed interwoven with the idea of the superiority of the male who was seen as invulnerable to hurt, rejection, or stealing impulses. Many short, one-step play sequences involved the killing off of the male. At this time mother reported that Sandy continued to have nothing to do with father and would not let him come near her. Elaborate fantasies emerged suggesting the idea that one could change from being female to being male. These issues took a back seat for some time but reemerged in the seventh year of treatment when it was reported that Sandy had taken a pencil case from a child in school, and had stolen a toy horse from her sister. I suggested that there were two parts of Sandy, one that wanted to take things that seemed special, thinking it would make her feel so much better to have the "thing," and another part that didn't feel good about taking things that don't belong to her. She listened. We decided she would try to notice what was in her mind before she felt the urge to take something. A few days later she brought in a chart of how many times she felt like taking something, but nothing of her thoughts. She expected me to buy her a special pen as a reward. I said that seemed to be a new magical way to feel she had special power because it was hard to believe in her own abilities. It reminded me of a time awhile ago when she thought if she were a boy she would have special power. She told me emphatically that she didn't feel that way anymore.

In the fourth year of analysis when the adoption theme was being played out with the horse family a new element was added: the new family might think the young horse was a monster, so they taped him. Over a number of weeks she played taping horses again and again. She explained, "That protects him from people that don't like horses. The new family got him taped up because they really didn't like him. They kept him locked up." I brought up a time when she was very little and in a brace because her hips needed strengthening, which was like being all taped up. Maybe she thought she was being punished for something. She seemed to have the idea that someone is taped up or restrained because of "monster-like" feelings. Whatever the reason she didn't like it and it made her angry. She denied it all, saying "that never happened to me."

Sandy's readiness to shut down and regress was quite striking. She froze when she didn't like what I said. Once when she bumped her head in my office, she didn't cry but retreated to a fetal position for half the session, refusing any contact. Her reaction to trying to talk of the period in her life when she was in restraints was similarly intense in her continued refusal to allow anything in. Her shame was so great she would not allow acknowledgment of problems for a long time: over time I was able to tie together the angry feelings she felt at having to be taped up and at adoption to feeling frightened to be all alone with her violent feelings. Maybe when she was most scared of getting wildly angry, she rolled into a ball and didn't move at all. Slowly she began to talk more directly about her learning difficulties—saying "Sometimes it's hard to read fast," although she would freeze if I introduced the topic.

During the fifth analytic year Sandy became the proud owner of a fantasy pet store. She was gentle and kind with the animals who all loved her and wanted to come home with her. Some of the dogs were wild and had to be tied up tightly. I suggested that she wished she would be treated kindly, taken care of gently, helpfully not hurtfully, but sometimes when she was boss of the dog, she couldn't help getting strict. One dog decided he didn't like being covered so he could hardly move. The dad started to enter the play. He would be kind to the wild dogs and help contain them. The theme of restraint changed from being taped so that one couldn't move to being covered in a small cozy place and feeling safe. She emptied out my toy chest and climbed in, wanting me to put a blanket on her. I said she loved the cozy safe feeling in there, that the wild feelings could be covered and contained by being mixed with soft loving feelings, not with harsh punishing tape that wouldn't let you move. There was a shift from being totally taped or covered to wearing a mask and staying hidden. She slowly revealed her secret: she loved her father and wanted him, the father from the first family.

For a period Sandy showed good solid growth. She showed interest in feminine representatives of pop culture: the Olsen twins (in movies and TV shows) were replaced by the Spice Girls, she began to sew pocketbooks and skirts. In Sandy's outside life there were reports of improvement. The fourth grade teacher had established an excellent relationship with Sandy, who was able to stay focused and keep up her work as long as the teacher kept a careful supportive eye on her. Sandy was less inhibited in school, more willing to try classroom activities and put effort into her school work. The parents reported that Sandy was in a happier mood, seemed freer and less controlling with her mother, and much more affectionate and interested in her father. Sandy seemed more invested in her own activities and less ready to compare every aspect of herself with her sister. My working with the parents helped mother by giving her a place to air her guilt and anger, which allowed her to be more comfortably firm with Sandy and with father by facilitating his greater investment and involvement with Sandy.

Sandy's play, in the sixth analytic year, shifted to more typical latency activities such as games and away from doll play. Mother insisted that because of improvement, Sandy's treatment time should be cut back to three times per week in order to make room for outside afterschool activities. While some play with the animals continued, the theme of competition took center stage. Horse shows and horse races were very important, Sandy the constant winner of every race and every horse show. It emerged that her sister Kelly was always riding; Sandy would go to the barn but was actually afraid of getting on a horse. When I tried to approach her fear tactfully, she froze and refused to acknowledge any fear. Sandy concentrated on playing Clue and Parcheesi. She loved to play and wanted to win but seemed not to take in anything about strategies. I pointed out good moves when she made them, and some general guiding principles, but she seemed unable or uninterested in changing her ways. During the summer of her fifth grade year she went to sleep-away camp. She managed to handle the first week of camp but then felt so overwhelmed that the parents allowed her to come home.

Sandy's seventh year of treatment was difficult. Mother insisted on

cutting Sandy's treatment to twice per week. The school now instituted switching of teachers and classrooms for every subject area.
Sandy, who found it hard to stay organized anyway, was quite overwhelmed and regression set in: she became inhibited in her classes,
often incapable of keeping assignments straight or keeping up with
the homework. The parents hired outside tutors for her. She seemed
to know the work when at home, but froze on tests, unable to adapt
to questions in a different form. She whizzed through her work,
wanting to get people off her back rather than trying to understand
her assignments. She did not want to talk with me about the problems. When she showed me rubber bands on her braced teeth and
gradually admitted that they hurt, so she didn't like them and ended
up taking them off, I brought up things she had to do but didn't like,
especially homework. I said she sometimes showed her anger by just
not doing it (she smiled), and then by doing it as quickly as the could
(she smiled). I added that she could wear the rubber bands a little
longer and a little longer until she was used to them. I reminded her
of her play in which we counted how long she could stand on her
head: at first it was only for a minute, but with practice it was longer
and longer, then it became easier and easier. Maybe it could be like
that with homework too. She thereupon stood on her head, showing
me her excellent balance.

Old anxieties returned. Sandy had two near panic attacks, one
when she thought she was locked out of the apartment and another
when she thought the family left to see the Harry Potter movie without her. Although it was unusual for her, she could tell me how
scared she felt when locked out and how upset she was when she
thought she was all alone at home before the movie. I reminded her
of the game she used to play, in which I thought she was quite worried about being left, but in her play, she reversed it: The girl with
red hearts on her knees would always leave her family and say she
wanted to live alone, going to a little house in the middle of the
woods; she was not scared of being alone, she loved it and wanted it,
but, in fact it was one of the things she was most afraid of—being
alone especially feeling alone with angry feelings. She listened and
smiled, sort of acknowledging all that was being said. Following these
moments of recognition and connection Sandy showed renewed focus and an improved ability to play competitively. She negotiated a
change of rules in the Parcheesi game, not sending men back to
start. However, when it looked like I was going to win, she moved all
her men closer to the home base so she had a better chance. I said
that she hated to lose so at the last minute changed to "Sandy rules,"

magically letting herself feel she won. She loved magic. She smiled and invented a game that did away with competition. Each of us got one die and tried to move our men around the board as quickly as possible, a race among our men but not between us, which I pointed out to her. She agreed. After this discussion she played Parcheesi in a much more thoughtful and realistically competitive way, placing her home base ahead of mine to give her an advantage. I complimented her by saying that she figured out that she could block me better when she started in front of me. She instituted wise rules that allowed for only two missed turns when held back by a blockade instead of endless waiting. She was asserting herself more and in sensible ways.

At a point where the game playing seemed repetitive, I suggested that the game now was being used to help her clear her mind of any worries or thoughts, that the game had turned into a way of getting away from things that bothered her. She ignored me. I suggested that we could talk a few minutes and then play, and took the dice. She turned her hands into dice, pretending she was counting the numbers so she could move, and continued to ignore me. I told her I knew of a little girl who felt she had to build a fortress around herself. She really wanted to feel close to people but was too afraid. She felt she had to keep apart because she had a secret. Her secret was that she felt there was something wrong with her. She didn't want anyone to know. Slowly we talked about what she felt was wrong with her. She thought she wasn't smart. We learned that that wasn't true, that there were a few things she had trouble with, but actually she was a very smart girl and a good learner. Sandy didn't really listen to me, but after having some soup—a usual background feature of our work—she was enlivened. I said she could count on the food because it gave her comfort and didn't bother her with all this silly talk. She smiled though still very ready to ignore reality.

Shortly thereafter, mother called to say that Sandy had been to the doctor who noticed she had been biting her hands and was very concerned. Sandy was feeling very discouraged at school. She'd studied hard for a test and got a 68; the teacher asked, "Did you study for this?" She became frozen and did not defend herself. When Sandy came in and played Clue for a long while, I brought up that I had talked to her mother who said she was having a hard time. She went into a frozen stance, wouldn't play, talk to, or look at me. I told her about a little girl I once saw who used to feel so angry and frustrated at school because she found some of the work hard. She sometimes got so angry she would bite her feet, which didn't help. It just hurt her. When she found a teacher who taught her the right way, she had all the energy in the world and really got to work. But often that didn't happen. Some people thought she was lazy, but she wasn't. She just wasn't being taught the right way. She learned how to speak up after a while, but when she didn't understand the work, she felt small and awful. Sandy warmed up, her body relaxed, and she played Clue energetically, seeming to recover. She approached the doll-house and got out the girl with hearts on her knees (Amanda) that she always loved. She had the girl doing hand stands and splits; I admired all the things she could do with her body. She added to the play that Mother came in and told her to do her school work, or was it too hard? The girl said she wanted to go to a new school, Hogwarts for Witches and Wizards. The mother said "no" but the father said "yes." I said that when Sandy feels so small because she has a hard time with schoolwork, using magic helps her feel better; the only problem is that magic works only in movies, books, and the imagination. Sandy didn't want to leave the session. Play about magic school continued.

At this point I met with the school psychiatrist. Sandy was seen as being unable to integrate the material. She could give it back only exactly the way it was memorized. She had no real understanding of concepts, or only of the most concrete. The school felt that Sandy was unable to do the work and must transfer schools.

Christmas vacation followed. On her return Sandy brought her dog Patti in. She was uncommunicative, but when I talked through the dog, she grew responsive. Her first concern was about what food I had. We lovingly hugged Patti and told her that no matter how much she wanted, how hungry she felt, how strong her gobbly feelings were or how angry she felt, we loved her and would make sure she got enough of what she needed. Sandy relaxed. We ordered soup; she wanted me to surprise her, guess which kind she would want, and then she would guess what it was from the smell. (At a later point and after much repetition of this game, I said she liked me to know what she wanted without her telling me.) She smiled. The girl with hearts on her knees, Amanda, was riding on Patti. I said she felt scared (since I knew Sandy had gone to Dude Ranch and had a hard time): Patti is so big and Amanda's heart feels like it is beating very fast, those jumpy feelings inside. Sandy gave a big "yes." I told the girl that we would hold her hand until she felt safe. Sandy loved this. Then I told her to think of us holding her hand when Patti starts to go fast so she won't feel so scared and jumpy. Patti went off under the couch with Amanda. We talked to Amanda so she could remember us even though she couldn't see us. Sandy seemed back to feeling more comfortable with me.

The next session she was back to ordering soup, which we did. There was some talk of hating her classes, especially math. But she didn't want to change schools. Now Amanda had a pet lion and tiger, pretending to her family that they were just stuffed animals but in reality they were wild. Acting naive when father said they were wild, she went off and made them into robots with mechanical voices so they seemed not to be real. Amanda made a doll that looked like herself and put it in her bed so the family didn't know she was off with the wild animals training them in the steps of killing: "First you paw the ground, then you gnash your teeth, then you pounce, then you tear off the head." I said that I could see that they acted like robots to hide their killing feelings. She nodded, graphically having a lion bring back its prey, a chicken with the head off. The father was complimentary.

Much play continued with the wild animals disguised as robots. She showed father but kept a secret from mother. Finally she showed and accepted compliments from both. The gist of the play effort seemed to impress the parents and to use detachment to hide wildly aggressive feelings. The girl had her house look like it was flying, but it was held by wires. Then she was able to fly herself, kindly granted wings to the father and a tiny baby, possibly theirs. I said that the girl at first seemed to know that making a house fly wasn't really possible but she was so smart she figured out a way to make it look that way. Then she gave in to her wish for magic—she was able to fly and taught her father as well. She was above everyone else with her flying, not worried about school or learning but was the most able. I added that underneath the girl had very angry, killing feelings but thought her dad wouldn't like that, he would rather she act like a robot, not show feelings, but that's not very comfortable.

Knowing that Sandy didn't want to talk to me about the school issue, I pretended a stuffed dog was talking to Patti: sometimes people tell you things you don't want to hear or think about, like going to a different school. You don't like to go to a new place but it might be a place that could help you learn better. Then still talking through the stuffed dog to Patti I said, "You could look at the different schools and help decide which one you like." To my surprise, instead of freezing, Sandy participated: "I want to go to Julia's school. Maybe I could see her during lunch." Then she took out the Amanda doll and her father. They were able to enter Electrotonia because they made a great invention, bottled water. Haggard, the wizard, was impressed and welcomed them both. I said that Amanda felt she had to do something so grand to get her dad to admire her and maybe that too got her angry. I reminded her of how she used to be scared that her own dad would yell or criticize her like when she didn't know her math facts, but things were so different now. I added that Amanda really loved to have her dad with her and have him all to herself. Sometimes she might feel she needed special Electrotonia protection because she thought if mother knew she was with father, she might not like it. Sandy added, "Mom doesn't mind. Well, only once in a while." The theme of secrets from mother and closeness to father had continued. Amanda wanted to go to the woods by herself to build a special playhouse. She refused a friend's company. Her father was very impressed with her work. He promised to keep it a secret from the mother who might not like the idea. I added that she was able to impress her dad by doing just the kind of work he loved to do (he has a workshop in the woods at his country home) which was a good way to feel she was with him. She nodded.

The latest story to emerge in our work follows: Amanda got a new dog, Donnie, a Dalmatian who was extremely shy. Different members of the family tried to make contact with the dog, but none had any luck at all. The dog was so shy because he was given away by his original family so he didn't trust anybody. Amanda was sensitive to his fears. She felt she shouldn't push herself on him, but she also mustn't leave his side for a while. She told him, "I know you worry that I won't be able to give you what you need because your first family gave you away. I will listen very carefully to you, and you will see that you can trust me." She gave him very simple food. Later a lion tried to attack. She was unable to keep him away. Another lion came between them so her dog couldn't reach her. She was helpless. Amanda kept trying to talk to the dog and explain what was happening so he wouldn't be too scared. She told the dog, "I know you don't trust me yet because I couldn't protect you from the lions; you know you can count on the food but not yet on me. You will see I can't protect you from everything but I can do my best to keep you safe." A Superman-type figure came to save them. Amanda said, "You think the only thing you can count on is magic, but you can count on me. I will never give up trying to help you so come to me when you feel scared." Donnie was still afraid to rely on Amanda but trusted her a little bit more each day. Finally came the day when Donnie was totally calm, so much better due to Amanda's tender care and devoted attention.

DISCUSSION[1]

The old view that in analyzing conflicts the ego takes over has at times proved unworkable with some patients. We now address a range of ego/self experiences more directly in order to move both analytic process and development forward. Although conflict might move to the back burner, or a focus on the ego might mask the preconscious and unconscious conflicts, to my mind an analyst with an understanding of the developmental process is in the best position to coordinate these issues, and my focus on moments of transformation in this treatment is intended to discern them. At times Sandy could approach her instinctual side in a more direct way after being offered developmental help [*for example, after play with her dog facilitated a more solid sense that the object could stay loving despite aggression (object constancy), she approached a fuller expression of murderous impulses and her conflicts over them; after getting confirming appreciation for all she could do with her body, she approached her conflictual rivalrous wishes toward her sister*] and at other times analysis of conflict eased developmental moves forward [*for example, after linking the taped feeling to angry, monster-like feelings, she shifted from being totally taped to the idea of being hidden, ending the sequence with the revelation of a hidden secret—she loved her father and wanted him; after being reminded of her use of reversal, that behind wishing to be alone was her anger at feeling abandoned, she was better able to play latency games competitively*]—each transformational process (analysis and development) synergistically facilitating the other. As Sandy grew less frightened of her impulses, more able to put them into words, and integrate them in new ways instead of remaining so heavily defended, she could engage newly emerging phase-specific phallic and oedipal conflicts.

The Sandy who had refused to enter my office unless accompanied by mother presented as an ethereal five-year-old, self-contained, affectless, uninterested in the surround, intent on hiding and remaining remote, with little interest in engagement. It took much work to make sense of what was beneath this surface. Only slowly by trial and error did I find a way to enter Sandy's world and learn more about her. Sandy could not play symbolically at first but talked through action, demonstrating her feelings of inadequacy by their opposite, constantly emphasizing physical acts as great achievements, as if she had crossed an ocean. *I welcomed and admired her displays,* interpreting

---

1. Italized entries are examples from the case report that emphasize the way I used developmental facilitation.

their defensive elements only later while asking questions about how she or her representative was feeling and what she was thinking. This narrative scaffolding helped lay the groundwork for affective articulation and containment, combining developmental and analytic facilitation. It was striking, even in the beginning phases of our work, that Sandy would not allow me to add or impose elements on the story that did not tally with her inner experience. *Yet I helped her link the inchoate and the unthought elements of her inner world into a coherent structure. An early example that enriched and moved the analytic process along was her talk of anger at her sister and her sometimes seeing "blood"; when I helped fill in the thought that her angry rivalrous feelings toward her sister could lead to a fight that would draw blood, she confirmed this by having a boot representing her sister viciously kick the boot representing herself.*

Following are examples of how I worked with containment, establishment of regulatory structure, delay ability, basic trust, reaching the object, representing the object—elements of the work from the very first. At every step, however, developmental and analytic issues were commingled. I thought that the first order of business was to establish a sense of trust in men and a background of safety so that Sandy could approach her demons once I learned how anxious, unstable, and insecure she felt; but defenses made progress difficult as Sandy held dearly to her system of safety, leading to the analysis of defense. The intensity of Sandy's anger contributed to her difficulty with trust. Her defenses against the extent of her anger—a readiness to withdraw and inhibit herself which looked like passivity, her extreme use of denial (not looking), her avoidance, and detachment— made it particularly difficult to reach mother. *Since Sandy functioned on such a concrete, tangible level, I felt that giving her food was a tongue she could relate to: having saltines and soup seemed to mean that her needs could possibly be met.* Although she wished I could read her mind and know what she wanted without her having to use words, she played out clearly with me that she felt she couldn't count on people, only on tangible things. She wanted more than anything to be in control of supplies so she wouldn't have to ask anyone for anything, an example of her pseudoselfsufficiency. While interpretations were crucial and yet often could only be heard if made in displacement, so too was her feeling of safety and comfort derived from tangible nourishment with me as well. One did not replace the other, but taken together, Sandy's rigid defensive wall could be ameliorated. Although her weak impetus to move on to the next developmental level was in part constitutional, Sandy's rigid defenses contributed as well.

Interpretation of impulse and defense also aided synthesis and integration. Talking of her feelings and her defenses against them, such as detachment, and having them received in an empathically sensitive way helped shame to melt and led to better management of her feelings. While knowing she had two mothers may have added to Sandy's problem with integration and synthesis, throughout the analysis Sandy struggled with her sense that she was unlovable because of her aggression and had to get rid of it or somehow disown it. It informed her fantasies about why she was put up for adoption and why she was put in restraints (taped up). Much of our interpretive work centered on her fears of her parents' disapproval of her aggression and of her neediness: this first theme was played out through the girl abandoned by mother because she was too needy and hungry, then later with both mother and father as she revealed her murderous impulses through the animals who pretended to be robots who had learned the art of killing. She thought she had to be a robot, (an "as if" robotic type person) to please her parents. She struggled to explore whether it was possible for others (and for herself) to tolerate her aggression and stay loving. She learned of her many different ways of venting her aggression as when she wanted revenge on her birth mother by playing out running away to a new family and leaving her mother behind, when she bit her hands (directing the aggression at herself), when she passive aggressively refused to do her work or would do it quickly without thinking, when she wore her mother down by whining and demanding. *At times, with my descriptive accompaniment, and appreciation, she practiced the control function as when she became the owner of a pet store and took such careful care of the animals.* However, her cruel handling of the animals at times got the upper hand. Father entered the play as someone who could be kind to wild dogs. *Sandy literally found containment by climbing into my toy chest and letting herself feel covered and contained by me as I helped her in and put a cover over her, helping to temper her angry feelings by getting in touch with soft loving feelings.* She linked the intense anger in part to feeling "totally taped." The loving feelings toward the one who could affectionately restrain, her father, helped her temper and contain her anger. *Our work in displacement, through our loving care of the dog Patti also helped her feel there was a way to temper and channel her anger and remain loving.* Interpretation, engaging in containing interactions, and narrative construction facilitated organization while at the same time allowed for affective containment through self understanding and understanding of others. Sandy could slowly appreciate that mothers can't always protect their children, that life events place limits so that everything is not mother's fault, that people are born with certain strengths and certain weaknesses, that realistic help can be found.

Focused work on object constancy occurred after a Christmas vacation when Sandy brought her dog, Patti, in. Closed off, Sandy could best be reached not directly but by talking through displacement to the dog. *When she couldn't see me any more (the dog and doll had disappeared under the couch) with my articulation she could imagine holding my hand and our being together, all the things we did, so she could feel safe even if I wasn't there.* Sandy loved this and played it over and over. Some of our work seemed to have become internalized as demonstrated by her last story to me. *Together we constructed the narrative in which she turned passive to active adaptively by creating a story where Amanda got a new dog, Donnie, who was scared because he was given away by his original family. She stayed by his side until he felt safe, she fed him and protected him; slowly he began to trust her and feel calm.*

The importance of facilitating synthesis and integration was core through the use of narrative construction with its accompanying affective containment, interpretation, literal containment, and understanding and integration of loving and hating feelings. Woven throughout the work was Sandy's ability to tolerate and accept my help in articulating and linking affects with her slowly constructed narratives, different from uncovering unconscious fantasies. At first the narratives were simple one-step stories—for example, a child gets birthday presents and children watch, a girl goes to live alone in the woods. *Yet over time I was able to add the intense affective component in these stories and elaborate them into more complex themes (e.g., A girl felt deprived and rejected by learning of her adoption. She needed to feel wanted and given to with presents and sweets, not deprived and rejected. She tested her mother over and over to see if she would be rejecting, and whether she could take her constant wants. A girl went to live in the woods alone in order to express her rage and hurt that her mother had so many others and that she had a birth mother who gave her away. The girl didn't want anyone; she wanted to be alone out of revenge and hurt). The narrative construction and the affective linking were central to our work* and helped Sandy integrate and own her overwhelmingly aggressive feelings with loving feelings. Furthermore, she lived through being with me in an affectively rich, alive way. As Fonagy (1999) suggests, "Psychoanalysis is more than the creation of a narrative, it is the active construction of a new way of experiencing self with other."

Following are specific examples of how I worked with facilitation of delay ability and self regulation. Sandy's ability to tolerate delay was seriously challenged by life's exigencies. She felt she had suffered enough—adoption, restraints, being the youngest—and she was owed. Her anger made her want to grab things, things that were tangible so she could count on them. She had stolen money from mother, so much did she not want to have to depend on anyone and so much did she want to be in charge of the supplies. She also took what didn't belong to her—phallic representatives such as a pencil case, a small toy horse of her sister's—when she thought that maleness would give her power and invulnerability. She hoped I would provide phallic power for her through a special pen. She turned to the quickest, easiest, and most immediate solution—magic. *Careful discussion about her learning problems (acknowledging that she had a hard time remembering a story, sometimes she couldn't find the right word, sometimes she needed to write things down to remember them) led to our talk of her need to be taught the right way. When her shame could be overcome (often only by talking in displacement) we talked about the need to make efforts (applying the same energy to schoolwork that she did to head stands) and about practicing a little at a time, which led to a hopeful sense that there were other solutions than magic. Repetitive play that involved training wild dogs and horses with patience, availability, and affectionate support rather than whips allowed a sense of mastery, delay, and modulation through identification with my attitude toward wild creatures and her own experimentation and practice.* Linking cruel training methods to the "brace" mother experience and then to the "brace mother" in herself began to be accepted though at first only acknowledged in relation to the braces on her teeth that hurt. When I helped her reality test some of her ideas, especially around her use of detachment—that father wanted a robotic person rather than to know of her angry side—she felt that with the naming and understanding of her feelings and with a sense of empathy for why she had to turn away from people, she could begin to give up magic and try other solutions. Slowly Sandy is taking more risks, such as taking an active part in finding a school she liked, letting herself invest in reality, and giving up her denial and quick turn to magic. She slowly moved closer to her own inner aggressivity and showed greater tolerance for examining it.

Central to her acceptance of reality was the indirect work in the transference. At first Sandy could accept me only if I were in effect a part object, under her control. *I went along with her wishes and did her bidding, not calling attention to our separateness. It was important for her to feel together with me (some form of communion, not communication [Stern, 1998]), doing the same activities—eating together, playing together.* For some time I think she thought of me as her twin. I only gradually intervened, pointing out her denial with empathy for her reasons. I had to titrate the dose of interventions because of her readiness to freeze, be overwhelmed, withdraw, and regress. At times she used me for organization (developmental object) instead of projecting onto me aspects of her past relationships (transference object). *I found that interpreting in displacement, which was only slightly jarring—that is, "a little girl I knew" or talking to the dog Patti as if she had Sandy's issues, or through the dolls—helped her take in what I had to say.* At times shame and her cognitive limitations slowed the pace at which we could put things together. Her attempt to keep me unimportant alternated with counting the days until a vacation separation, after we spent many hours of playing and being together at her pace. Presenting this case material to a group of analysts helped energize me to take chances with disrupting her omnipotent control in order to keep the work moving. In the end I vacillated between providing developmental help when her anxiety was too great to be approached and interpreting conflict when the situation presented itself and the time was ripe (Olesker, 1999).

By addressing both the developmental process issues and analytic process issues, Sandy has moved into a fuller experience of the oedipal phase, though bits and pieces of anxieties and concerns from different phases of development were present by the end of the third analytic year. A more cohesive, integrated experience of oedipal dynamics has been slowly building, replete with intense rivalry toward mother. Father emerged as the accepting, containing parent who could remain loving despite anger. He was constructed by her as the father she wanted him to be, as admiring her ingenuity, supporting her alternative ways of learning, accepting her desires (to go to magic school) while mother was critical. Sandy remembered with me when he was not that way and how frightened she was of him. Now she could imagine going off to a special place with him, building a family together, taking on his ways to be with him and to impress him (building a house in the woods). The bits of excitement with father are being woven into a more solid cohesive experience of oedipal dynamics. All this has followed on the developmental and analytic achievements described above. Transformations have taken place both through interpretation and through the outcome of interactions leading to an ego that could tolerate anxiety and rivalry. I welcomed, esteemed, and valued her developmental moves and achievements.

In summary, Sandy presented with a variety of developmental interferences and neurotic conflicts, multiply-determined. She was born with a readiness to anxiety, and a somewhat low stimulus barrier (ready to get anxious quickly), congenital hip dysplasia, adopted five days after birth—these unpleasurable life circumstances imposing a limit on ego development and what she was able to extract from the environment and contributing to a low investment in the outside world. Both being put in restraints and told so early about adoption were externally generated events, but she came to these experiences with weak mental representations to begin with due to her weak capacities (a difficulty taking in from the outside world), making it hard to hold in mind an integrated picture of the caretaking ones, especially when angry; it is easier to detach if you are not too connected in the first place. Having been put in restraints so early may have affected her overall sense of safety, anxiety, and alertness as well as her choice of defense—her own tendency then to put herself in restraints, to inhibit, to deny (in effect closing her eyes to incoming stimuli), to avoid and to detach, also in part built on certain cognitive weaknesses, leading to withdrawal and regression. Her parents each had their own issues, but overweighting parental shortcomings would be incorrect; mother's limited range of affect and guilt and ambivalence over "stealing" Sandy from her birth mother perhaps limited the amount of stimulation she could provide, and father was brusque and disappointed over Sandy's limitations and demandingness of mother. But Sandy's low sending power and low level of engagement did not easily give reassuring feedback to the parents. The limited pull forward seemed an additional factor as well as the unevennesses in Sandy's different capacities, especially her problematic verbal memory and difficulty sequencing and forming narrative structures. Furthermore, it was hard to keep Sandy engaged in part due to her limited ability to extract, her constitutional passivity, and in part because her ego, traumatized so early, habitually shut down quickly. The combination of forces here seemed quite daunting.

Sandy's final story captures some of her gains: she provided a helpless puppy with what it needed to feel safe, she built a sense of trust and presented herself as a reliable object for the puppy but allowed that there were limits to her power (the power of the caretaker) in providing for safety—a healthy recognition of reality. Sandy could understand her core defensive stance of denial and reversal in the service of mastery of feelings of inadequacy. Mastery and acceptance of her anger for all its many sources was a central part of the work, especially work on the use of detachment to hide the "killing" feelings. Further work has yet to be done on reconstruction—one aspect of which is the relation between her rageful feelings and the experience of the harsh, constricting "brace" mother she envisioned as a result of her year-and-a-half in restraints. Her wish for special protection (Electrotonia or a broom that could knock down any enemies) was gradually replaced by a sense that she could assert herself and have her wishes and needs considered. She grew able to tolerate conflict—part of her wanted to take what she wanted, yet another part of her did not feel good about doing so—a sign of internalization and superego development.

There are ways to extend the analytic frame with a developmentally challenged child yet allow for both development and analysis to progress. With awareness of pathological developmental issues, the analyst highlights activities that address such pathological features in addition to paying attention to conflict. Interpretation could be broadened to include not just an understanding of unconscious conflict and addressing maladaptive defenses but unconscious elements outside conflict—features that touch on establishing basic trust, delay capacity, self-regulatory functions, signal function, the construction of self and object, and superego development. I helped Sandy enter a particular phase conflict in an appropriate fashion, in this case the oedipal phase, not just find appropriate compromise formations afterward. Building ego capacities and consolidating structures was an important focus. Sandy required some time to take in and integrate what we were doing and her affective tolerance only gradually increased; building narrative structures and living out with me experiences of sharing and containment was important in helping her to understand and contain her impulses, giving the inchoate aspects room to be sorted out and put into place. I was a reliable object she could use for structure formation, emotionally responsive to her affective life. For some time she fought growing and fought attachment as she feared it was a destructive process, as she so feared her own destructiveness and the possible destructiveness of others. Regression had to be carefully monitored. Of equal importance was holding Sandy in my mind at many different levels and attempting to convey this view to her (Fonagy et al., 1993; Mayes & Cohen, 1996), which resulted in her more cohesive view of herself as a thinking feeling person with her own mind.

BIBLIOGRAPHY

FONAGY, P., STEELE, M., MORAN, G., STEELE, H., & HIGGITT, A. (1993). Measuring the Ghost in the Nursery: An Empirical Study of the Relation Between Parents' Mental Representations of Childhood Experiences and Their Infants' Security of Attachment, *JAPA*, 41:4, 957–989.

FONAGY, P. (1999). Memory and Therapeutic Action, *Int. J. Psycho-anal.* 80, 215–223.

FREUD, A. (1965). *Normality and Pathology in Childhood: Assessments of Development.* New York: IUP.

—— (1981). *The Writings of Anna Freud,* Vol. VIII, 1970–1980, New York: IUP.

MAYES, L., & COHEN, D. (1996). Children's Developing Theory of Mind, *JAPA*, 44, 1:117–142.

OLESKER, W. (1999). Treatment of a Boy with Atypical Ego Development, *Psychoanalytic Study of the Child.* New Haven: Yale University Press.

STERN, D. (1998). The Process of Therapeutic Change Involving Implicit Knowledge: Some Implications of Developmental Observations for Adult Psychotherapy, *Infant Mental Health Journal,* Vol. 19, No. 3, Fall, pp. 300–308.

The Many Dimensions of Group Process

A Discussion of the Treatment of Sandy

CLAUDIA LAMENT, Phd.

*What is presented is a summary of the study group's discussion of Dr.
Olesker's work with her patient Sandy. A spotlight was thrown on the
group process with an emphasis on the organic nature of how this
group of psychoanalysts came to grips with the nature of Sandy's inner
world. One central issue which challenged the group was how to conceptualize the structure of her mind: Was she a child whose mental life
could best be described as compromised by a fundamental biological
frailty so that a primary emptiness or inchoate quality of mental contents reigned? If so, technical interventions which turned on narrative
building were viewed as the principal therapeutic action. On the other
hand, if her difficulties were perceived as stemming primarily from
primitive psychological anxieties of annihilation and separateness, a
dynamic approach was agreed upon as the preferred mode of treatment. Other issues regarding the transformational potentialities in the
developmental process and the use of the analyst as a transformational object were also highlighted.*

*Lastly, I offered my own perspective as to what I imagined occurred
between Dr. Olesker and Sandy over the course of her treatment which
enabled Sandy to change.*

Assistant Clinical Professor, Department of Psychiatry, The New York University
School of Medicine; faculty, The Psychoanalytic Institute, The New York University
School of Medicine.

The Psychoanalytic Study of the Child 58, ed. Robert A. King, Peter B. Neubauer,
Samuel Abrams, and A. Scott Dowling (Yale University Press, copyright © 2003 by
Robert A. King, Peter B. Neubauer, Samuel Abrams, and A. Scott Dowling).

IN THIS SUMMARY, I WILL PRESENT A SCAFFOLDING FOR THE IDEAS presented in the meetings of our group which focused on Sandy's treatment. I note the word "scaffolding" as this summation will reflect only what I considered to be the highlights of our discussions and may not do justice to each viewpoint expressed. I also elected, for the most part, to put together Sandy's material as it developed *in statu nascendi* as I think this method best demonstrates the organic ebb and flow of the group's thinking, and the natural way in which ideas were put together, challenged, revised, re-constructed or co-constructed or sometimes discarded altogether only to resurface at later moments.

Dr. Olesker's presentation of Sandy's historical data was remarkable for its illustration of the problem with which the group is grappling, namely, how to treat a child who falls outside the normative range of neurotic difficulties. A five-year-old adopted child when Dr. Olesker began to treat her, she is now approaching the age of twelve. The first years of Sandy's life were noteworthy for her limitations in her ability to use language to communicate with others. As the years marched on, this problem grew to encompass a more generalized constriction in language, as evidenced by her marked difficulty in forming narrative structure, even in creating fantasy stories. Impaired with regard to particular memory functions as well, Sandy has always been burdened by a deficit in verbal remembering which has compromised her capacity to process information of all sorts. Compounding these cognitive deficiencies, Sandy's body was also born without hip sockets. To correct this problem, she was harnessed between four and twenty months of age; she was also braced between twelve and twenty months, preventing her from moving and crawling.

In addition, Sandy's family situation did little to lighten the heavy loading of her physical and cognitive problems. The father's high powered and wealthy family valued intellectual endeavors and achievements above all else. These the father subscribed to with a fierce tenacity and so it was not surprising that he could not rest comfortably with having a child who had such challenges. With this background, Sandy behaved in the initial phase of her treatment as a child who was opaque, detached and difficult to reach emotionally.

Her dramatic history and presentation invited the following points of inquiry:

Was her pathology largely the culmination of a defensive inhibition against aggressive impulses or was it the result of a lackluster thrust forward, a deficient impetus in her blueprint for the "pull toward the object" as well as a fault in the equipment that determines the unfolding of hierarchical phases? Dr. Neubauer first drew our attention to her apparent inability to reach out for the other—"which she cannot capture enough" and "to make something, an internal representation with the object." I found Dr. Neubauer's use of the word "capture" in these remarks to have at once illuminated, rather poetically, the painful quality of Sandy's detachment and the group's evolving hypothesis of a dispositional deficit in this aspect. Perhaps, too, Sandy was moving toward the inanimate as a transitional space before she could safely attach to the human world. But before foreclosing on other possibilities, one could also formulate an opposing argument, namely, was this so-called inability to connect actually the outcome of a defensive maneuver that would point to one or more dynamic motivations such as a fear of her aggression or engulfment by the object? To add to the ever-widening complexity, the group wondered further whether both were possible; namely, that these two processes, the faulty dispositional blueprint and the impaired object relational dynamic, were both active and simultaneous. In an aside, the overlapping and interweaving nature of these processes was called into view, an enmeshment that taxed our capacities to parse them. As well, never far from view was Sandy's inclination, when hurt or frightened, to tumble down a steep slope of regression where she could land in a state of semi-withdrawal from human contact.

Dr. Olesker's reporting of Sandy's extreme reaction to having bumped her head prompted the group's interest in the origins of Sandy's fragile sense of self, one that may have been partially borne of a narrative created by the parents as opposed to Sandy's having a genuine dispositional frailty: Does Sandy really feel the pea at the bottom of all those mattresses or was she simply perceived as such a child and the perception as such begot the creation of this story, which was mistakenly laid down as if it were fact? Might the notion of extraction as a method of tracking those elements that have influenced a child's experience: to wit, what might Sandy have extracted from such a narrative and what could have informed that extraction?

The discussion thus far spurred some to consider the term "narcissistic vulnerability" and some queried whether thinking about Sandy in this way might bridge the issue of dynamic versus dispositional.

Others' reading of Sandy's material prompted us to wonder about Sandy's difficulty in distinguishing between her internal life and external exigencies—emanating in part from the brace—and the impact such blurring would make on the unfolding of her mental structures and the separation-individuation processes.

One individual drew a red ring around Sandy's fraught self-esteem. She is painfully aware of not living up to the expectations of her family. By way of an adult patient of his, this participant threw light on the myriad ways in which Sandy might conceive of herself.

While some participants grappled with putting together the constitutional variants with a dynamic grasp of Sandy's history, one member introduced his view that underscored a dynamic approach. He drew the conclusion that Sandy was primarily preoccupied with the dearth of emotional nutrients in her environment, especially with a mother who was described as "too old" to have children of her own. Might it be, he hypothesized, given Sandy's interest in Dr. Olesker's saltines and her ordering of soups and cakes in her treatment sessions, that she is concerned about whether her analyst has ample psychological supplies? Secondly, he argued, as Sandy could never replace her older sister's special access to mother, she yearns deeply for an exclusive attachment to the mother. This analyst would try to find access to these hypotheses in the transference, which for him, would be indispensable for the treatment to have meaning. A rough draft of how this might work in the consulting room would be something like: "perhaps you are wondering whether it is possible to grow here, that there will be enough food for you. . . ."

Dr. Olesker demurred. Her sense was that such a statement would be too direct for Sandy. In fact, "any talking about what we are doing, or about here, even if I'm not in it . . ." would be met with clamped ears. Her feeling was that Sandy worked more productively in the realm of displacement via play.

One member took the group on a different tack by his articulation of an implicit theory in Wendy's remarks about the mother: that her relative lackluster emotional expression was a key feature in Sandy's developmental disturbance. He preferred to keep this theory qua theory as opposed to treating it as data. In fact, in a larger way, it seemed to some that the group reacted to the in extremis quality of Sandy's story with rapid-fire constructions and theories about her development that could slide too easily down the slippery slope of hypothesis-making into fact-discovering. Like a watchman who sees a runaway train, one member cautioned against a too-quick theory-building program within the group process. Indeed, there are many stories one could tell about the origins of Sandy's problems, but to her, the salient question to ask would be what parts of the stories that we have been told about Sandy's life were most important to her? Circling back to the earlier mentioned notion of extraction as a way of handling this issue enabled the group to feel more easy about how to sift through the multitude of impinging elements: What has Sandy extracted from her environment, from her faulty blueprint, from her low impetus in forward movement, from her language delays? Another member extended the length of this Ariadne thread, and asked, What has informed what she has extracted, and secondly, what is the range of her capability to extract? If her limited environment was coupled with an equally limited ability to extract whatever salubrious elements were present, we are surely confronted by a double curse.

In addition, are we witness to a child—so easily overwhelmed by emotions in general—with a deficient stimulus barrier? The group drew a deep breath at the enormity of the problem.

As our meetings continued, it was clear that Sandy's material lent itself to one of the central challenges of our group: Is our established psychoanalytic framework sufficient to both grasp and treat developmentally challenged children like her? Must we extend analytic concepts beyond dynamic and object-relations models, beyond compromise-formation and interpretation? An extension of the classical view of interpretation would include the necessity of helping such a child access more of the unconscious world than that part which is relegated to conflicts. As the developmentally challenged child's unconscious world is not merely filled with representable conflicts and object relations, the analyst must arguably extend her locus of attention with a child like Sandy to include facilitating Sandy's recognition of those unrecognized features of her structures that are not fully formed. The analyst's assisting in the constructions of narratives or stories, based on the inchoate fragments that the child expresses, may be one way of meeting this need.

It appeared to some that the narrative building which Dr. Olesker and Sandy created in the treatment was the measure of the slowly evolving structure building that was beginning to take hold in Sandy's mental world. Directly discussing Sandy's monster like feelings would fall on deaf ears, but using the displacement of the dog was a vehicle by which Dr. Olesker could point out her monster-like feelings and then experiment with ways to anticipate the fears surrounding such feelings so that Sandy could take considered action to manage them. This appeared to help Sandy feel more at ease with these and other forbidden feelings, albeit in a displaced venue. This method also appeared to have paved the way for a broadening and gradual integration and regulation of these feelings within Sandy's constricted framework. One participant resonated strongly with this view by placing the accent on the intensity of Sandy's self-criticism.

This, she felt, would act as an obstruction to an approach that would directly confront her with her aggression, as she would hear only such remarks as the analyst's chastisement. This point taken, she poised the query as to whether Dr. Olesker's and Sandy's narratives operated as containers for her forbidden feelings within which the shard-like fragments of whatever has been psychically represented can be embellished, elaborated upon, and sorted out.

A different group member took a step back from our focus on Sandy and offered an observation about our use of theoretical constructs such as structure building, ego integration, affect regulation, cognitive processes, and the like which were conceived for the purposes of clarification. He pointed to an inherent paradox: as our definitions lean upon our theoretical biases do they ultimately cloud more than clarify what occurs in the mind of the child? The group concurred that this contradiction is an artifact of our work. Even if we might attempt a remedy that would include a phenomenological approach—a close reading of the child's behavior—there still remains a wide latitude for inexactitude and inference.

In another's associations and remarks, there was a prefiguring and bridge to what would become Dr. Neubauer's focus in the meetings to come: Were we witness to the facilitation of structure formation or the movement toward effecting developmental transformations?

As one participant listened, he observed a tendency in the group to place the issue of biological features on a secondary plane. To even this bias, he put into sharp relief his emphasis on the importance of tending to the biological elements of a child's mind, as their impact on the capacity to create mental representations is absolutely fundamental. He felt this must take pride of place, as to trivialize or lose sight altogether of the enormity of this aspect is to chance setting off on a course of treatment that could well come to naught.

While another member agreed with this view in the abstract, his perspective in the consulting room is different. He feels that given the absence of a litmus test that can determine how much of a child's disturbance can be traced back to biological frailty, our best recourse is to set our sights on a dynamic course which necessarily invokes the interpretive method. The first participant in this dialogue replied that indeed, culling evidence for either position is "very difficult to state" but for him what was of singular importance was where one's starting block is: Does the analyst start by considering the biological givens? or does she put that to one side as an unknowable and turn instead to considerations regarding her dynamic unconscious?

The delineation of these opposing perspectives was a flashpoint for a rich exchange among the group members. The view was argued that the material Sandy presented was largely representable, albeit quite primitive. As this participant saw it, Dr. Olesker's work has been an anodyne of soups and cakes, but has avoided tackling Sandy's splintered self. He thought that the use of narratives obfuscated Sandy's primitive anxieties of annihilation and separateness. He suggested that if she were to use a theoretical framework which considers very primitive object relations, Sandy would feel understood, or at least, one could see how far one could get. This would be his starting position.

In contradistinction, another group member thought that her primary anxiety might reflect something even more basic: a recognition of a fundamental emptiness or absence of psychic structure and content—an inner chaotic quality which is of a different order from a more concretely defined psychological danger like annihilation or separation. One would have to create some semblance of coherence via narrative building in order to conceive of a mental world that would be made up of more than merely liminal contours.

With the setting apart of these two positions, the question of therapeutic action locked easily into place. If the analyst decides that the child does not have the basic, ordinary foundations of mind, the task for that analyst is to help in the co-creating or co-invention of such foundations. The idea put forward was that narratives can accomplish this aim; this, then, would define the therapeutic action. If, on the other hand, one feels that dynamic considerations are the operating theater, the analytic task is to discover, or co-discover what has been there all along, but repressed. This therapeutic action rests on the belief that there is a good-enough foundation populated with good-enough textured representations to discover.

Dr. Olesker felt that Sandy shut down with any mention of her primitive anxieties. "Unless she has some more coherent structure . . . some sense of the object as reliable . . . she can't even go near" [primitive anxieties]. As evidence for this perspective, we were reminded of the step-by-step evolution of the theme of wildness in Sandy's play which eventually lead to the revelation of the animals' full-blooded murderousness: it was not until Sandy relinquished partial control to Dr. Olesker as guarantor of protection against her warded-off sadism and murderousness (granted, this sense of Dr. Olesker as protector was never wholly secure, but was enough to off-set terror) that ground was taken. She began, finally, to relax her inner guard and made a boundary crossing into the new frontier of her violent imaginings.

The use of narratives for Sandy was also valued in the following way: in the consulting room, the analyst hopes for the proper titration with respect to the patient's regressive capacity. Too much regression can make for an enterprise that lists dangerously in one direction so as to threaten the optimal balance one needs to effect a steady-enough therapeutic engagement. It was also brought to our attention that the fact of her having two mothers, a feature of adoption which would explain Sandy's readiness to split off her feelings, added another level of complexity to the transference and to sorting out the optimal therapeutic tack.

Still another participant reflected mixed feelings about working with such a child primarily in the mode of displacement. While honoring the value of narrative building, she couldn't help but wonder if what is truly mutative is the work that is accomplished in the interactions with the analyst. Are we deluding ourselves in thinking that Sandy will be able to take responsibility for her inner life if these issues stay only within the displaced narrative? One member ventured the idea that Dr. Olesker created a pastiche of narrative building and interpretation. The former was offered in the context of Dr. Olesker allowing herself to be used by Sandy as a part-object, akin to a twinship of sorts. However, at moments when Dr. Olesker intuited that Sandy could withstand a dynamic intervention, she took a half step above that part-object level. With this set-up, Dr. Olesker could experiment with interpretations that successfully "jarred" their union just enough to penetrate Sandy's defensive wall without demolishing it.

Leaving the issue of therapeutic action for a moment, Dr. Neubauer looped back to an earlier question: Had Sandy actually achieved a developmental transformation? If Sandy had truly proceeded from basic trust and security toward a new developmental position with respect "to facing new ways of looking at her own individuation . . . Where do you place her in connection with development and in connection with structure formation?" There was a general consensus in the group that the treatment assisted in the consolidation of core structures that had been absent, but did narratives provide a stimulus for the ushering in of fresh developmental processes with their underlying transformational potential? The spotlight was also thrown on Sandy's extraordinary passivity which was tethered to the position of constitutional frailty—a yawning emptiness within her which she yearns to have filled up by her analyst. Might this emptiness work against transformational potentialities?

Deepening this inquiry, the group pondered the distinction between transformational potentiality which occurs organically from the blue-print of hierarchical growth from transformations which also engage psychic conflict. Psychoanalysts must look to the transformation of psychic conflict as the touchstone for what makes the treatment endeavor a truly analytic one. And for Sandy, has this been accomplished? If so, might we say that Dr. Olesker served as a developmental object for her? That is, did Sandy use her analyst to effect transformations and reorganizations of her past and present conflicts? Dr. Neubauer was intrigued by Sandy's apparent affective shift, which was evidenced in her smiling responses. Did this mean that she could "accept the pleasant object but that she could also accept herself as a pleasant object"? If this change occurred in the sense that Sandy could transform her robotic self into a more emotionally enriched human child, such a change would be of great moment. If, however, she simply returns to Dr. Olesker as the source of nutrients or as the robot, one would see development that remained in irons. An ancillary issue that arose from this quandary was whether the construction of a more stable organization was the sine qua non for the transformational capacity to take hold?

Another participant argued that "even an unstable organization can undergo reorganization of that disorganization." He also stated his ease with the notion that Sandy had progressed with respect to having solidified certain psychic structures such as the formation and elaboration of the "brace mother" within Sandy, but was dubious that developmental and transformational progression had taken place. He then piqued the group's curiosity about the fresh appearance of the father in Sandy's material. Though it was unlikely to reflect true oedipal interest, might this herald a new developmental platform with elements of the oedipal within it? Another wondered too if her interest in small creatures mirrored something similar.

One participant relayed his uncertainty about Sandy's capacity to bind and neutralize anxiety and upended a conjecture of the group's: perhaps it was true that Sandy became anxious and withdrew when Dr. Olesker "got it wrong" but are we so sure that she doesn't become anxious when Dr. Olesker "gets it right"?

There was also a view expressed that Dr. Olesker's therapeutic activities provided a better synthesis of libidinal and aggressive wishes. Using the model of Piaget, this participant understood that Dr. Olesker set the stage for assimilative processes to take hold. This then, set the stage for transformations as the natural outgrowth of her ability to accommodate to her newly evolving structures.

What happened between Dr. Olesker and Sandy? Sandy got better, but how? Would we define her problem largely as one in which her mind was inhabited by shard-like fragments of barely representable structures? Or, on the other hand, were we witness to an impenetrable defensive wall, a metallic armature not unlike her robotic inventions which compartmentalized and split off Sandy's awareness of her deepest feelings and anxieties? My own view is that the hypothesis of biological frailty is paramount and the evidence for this, while never absolute, was convincing. Her severe limitations in language, in narrative-building and sequencing, her formidable auditory processing and memory problems were testimony to this perspective. Yet, I also believe that whatever bits and pieces of representability were there in her mental world in the beginning were cast in a primitive mold as measured by the gradual unveiling of the quality of Sandy's murderous fantasies and the near vertical scree of regression when she was confronted with unexpected separations or with the slightest knock to her body.

Given this picture, what I found remarkable in this analytic journey was how Sandy came to develop the inchoate remnants of her mind into the textured weave and fabric of her doppelganger Amanda, whose adventures with Ellie, the scary dog; or with her wild horses who had to be trained in the steps of killing; or with her broken heart as she could never possess the very all of her beloved mother, filled the hours. Year by year what seemed to come were stories and imaginings which breathed with human frailty and feeling and spoke of the risks of experiencing fears and murderousness, and the wishes for impossible transformations into magical solutions.

I think that what was vital for Sandy's awakening was the penumbra-like existence of her analyst—a light which surrounded the dark edges of Sandy's phantoms. In those early days, Dr. Olesker allowed herself to become an inseparable other for Sandy, as Dr. Neubauer once put it—drawing from Shakespeare—a "selfsame." It was Dr. Olesker's acceptance of this paradox, to be joined with her in the same breath that she was also "other"—a bearing of a divided consciousness between existing in Sandy's world of shade and shadow but at the same time helping her to take a step and a step and a step until she finally crossed the border into the land of the living—which enabled Sandy to grow at her own pace, in her own time.

When I speak of a divided consciousness for the analyst, I am referring to Dr. Olesker's ability to exist as a part of Sandy and to let Sandy cleave onto her without needing to press for separateness; in silent concert with this twin-like existence, Dr. Olesker held onto her analytic function as an ever present observer and witness, an Echo to Sandy's Narcissus. In this mode, Dr. Olesker felt for openings, for moments between them that breathed with life. Dr. Olesker's narrative-making that occurred in such moments provided just the proper words for Sandy's silent experiences. When Dr. Olesker noted Amanda's fear of the big dog Ellie, who made her feel so little and small, Sandy lit up: "Oh, yes!" Responding to Sandy's excitement, Dr. Olesker was moved to elaborate and made the offering that Sandy help Amanda feel safe: "Perhaps we can hold onto Amanda's hand," said Dr. Olesker. "Oh, yes!" cried Sandy, and begged to play it again, and again and again. To my ears, this is the yes of trust, the yes of aliveness—the building blocks of self which had to be laid down before any other work could be accomplished.

Once Sandy had dug a toe-hold into a more multi-dimensional existence, Dr. Olesker's technique shifted to a series of alternating switchbacks between the continuation of narrative building and the work of interpretation. It appeared to me that as the work of the narratives replaced the ghostly inhabitants of Sandy's world with three dimensional forms that there came to be textured material to work with and to analyze. Before, Sandy's fears could not be adequately articulated with the vocabulary of the dynamic unconscious; nor, given her lack of stability and cohesiveness at the beginning of her treatment would I imagine her making good use of such an approach. Now, with a self that could meet the winds of change, of anger, of sadness, of separations, and dare I add, the possibility of oedipal love with all its listing passions and still stay afloat, interpretations became possible.

Lastly, what are we to make of the most recent incarnation of Sandy's play, this time about Donnie, the frightened dog, undoubtedly the long ago version of Sandy's muted self who is healed by the devoted and ever-faithful Amanda? Is this not a heartrending re-charting of her journey with Dr. Olesker? "I will listen very carefully to you," says Amanda to the trembling, frightened Donnie, "and I think you will see that you can trust me. I can't protect you from everything, but I can do my best to keep you safe. You think you can only count on magic, but you can count on me. I will never give up trying to help you." What is a better or more tender proof of the coming of age of a developmental transformation, or of the analyst as a developmental object?

Comments to the Discussion Group

Clinical Applications of Developmental Propositions

M. NASIR ILAHI

*This note summarizes some of the areas of difference between the au-
thor's views, rooted as they are in the contributions of Freud, Klein,
Winnicott, Bion and certain other British theorists, and those of the
various American schools influenced by ego psychology, as they pertain
to developmental propositions and their application in clinical work.
The areas of differences in understanding touched upon relate to,* in-
ter alia, *how early development of the ego is conceptualized; the role of
the infant's objects, actual and phantasied; the factors that inhibit or
promote such development; and the implications of these ideas for clinical work and for the aims of analytic therapy.*

AT THE CONCLUSION OF THE WORK OF THE DISCUSSION GROUP ON
Clinical Applications of Developmental Propositions it was requested
that I provide some overall comments on development and on the
vast topic of this group from my perspective. This is a daunting task
as there is such a wide gulf that separates my approach to psychoanalysis (rooted in Freud, Klein, Bion, Winnicott, and a number of

Practicing Psychoanalyst; Clinical Assistant Professor, Department of Psychiatry,
New York University Medical School; Faculty, NYU Psychoanalytic Institute; Visiting
Lecturer, New York Psychoanalytic Institute; Visiting Teaching Analyst, Baltimore-
Washington Psychoanalytic Institute; Member, British Psychoanalytic Society.

The Psychoanalytic Study of the Child 58, ed. Robert A. King, Peter B. Neubauer,
Samuel Abrams, and A. Scott Dowling (Yale University Press, copyright © 2003 by
Robert A. King, Peter B. Neubauer, Samuel Abrams, and A. Scott Dowling).

others working in these traditions, mainly in the United Kingdom and, to some extent, in France, where of course there has also been the influence of Lacan) and those of others in the Group, belonging to the various American schools. Consequently, I cannot take for granted a basic familiarity with the theories and techniques deriving from these traditions from across the Atlantic. I am thus necessarily apprehensive about the wisdom of even attempting such a task within the confines of a few pages, and thereby risk sowing the seeds for yet more confusion rather than shedding light on our different perspectives. Against this, however, is the shared experience of some useful discussions in the Group (in a congenial atmosphere) where some of these issues have been broached, even though only in a necessarily cursory manner. Rashly or otherwise, I decided to take a plunge.

Clearly, summarizing the developmental and structural propositions of the authors that have influenced me and their application to clinical work covers almost the whole of psychoanalysis and cannot be undertaken here. There is a vast and evolving literature in this area to which reference can be made by those who wish to pursue these further. Nor would it be possible to make a comprehensive statement about how my understanding of developmental propositions, and their applicability to clinical work, differs from that of the various American schools. I will therefore restrict myself to highlighting below certain very broad themes in an attempt to bring out *some* of the areas of difference between my thinking on this topic and that of other group members, as they emerged during our discussions.

SOME OVERALL COMMENTS ON DEVELOPMENT

(1) Psychological development comprises various aspects: (a) physiological maturation; (b) libidinal development, consisting of transformations of sexual and aggressive drives; (c) the reality principle; (d) the development of object relations; (e) development of the ego; and (f) the sequence of anxiety situations. (Hinshelwood, 1991; Rycroft, 1968).

(2) Without entering into detail on any of the above aspects and remaining at a general level, the first point to note is that, influenced by the contributions of Melanie Klein, a considerable majority of contemporary British analysts, irrespective of the school they belong to, see development of the mind as taking place in close conjunction with objects (both internal and external) from the outset. While the mind also unfolds in a natural epigenetic way, just as the physical body does, and the physical directly underlies the psychological—in

that it sets the phases of the libido; determines certain ego characteristics; and sets a balance between the sexual and aggressive instincts
(Hinshelwood, 1991); nevertheless the development of the mind in
an integrated sense (and thus including functions such as thinking,
symbolization, memory, perception, language, etc.) takes place in
close connection to object relationships. This is in sharp contrast to
the position of all American schools, where this process is seen as occurring relatively autonomously.

(3) Klein initially opened the way for a recognition that it was insufficient to think of the human mental apparatus, and of the ego, in
a mechanistic way whereby the development of personality and of
"ego strengths" are seen as due to successful defense against instinctual drives and to adaptation to social realities. This is the view of ego
psychology and is a development of one strand of Freud's thinking in
The Ego and the Id. However, Freud also held in the same book that
ego as personality developed by the internalization of love relationships that had been given up ("abandoned object cathexes"), which
meant that it was not possible to clearly distinguish between the ego
and its objects with which it has identified. Klein and other British
theorists have attempted to develop this latter line of thinking in
great detail.

(4) To elaborate further, in the Kleinian framework, for instance,
the mental representation[1] of an instinct includes the (internal) object as a component and this takes place from birth onwards. The object is, at first, an emotional one based in the infant's bodily *sensations*
of pleasure or pain before going through further elaboration and development. While there are complex differences between the various
theorists (Freud, Klein, Winnicott, Bick, and Bion, for instance) on
the manner in which the internal world of objects is elaborated or
"created," the fact that all this happens in intimately close connection with external object relationships which provide "containment"
and "holding" from the outset is widely accepted by these British analysts. This is clearly too vast a topic, concerned with many subtle and
micro stages of early development, to be considered here.

(5) Thus, in the view of these analysts, the development of the
mind and, indeed, psychic structure itself—that is, the capacity to
think and have a mind of one's own that adequately resides in the
soma, or, in the words of the French analyst J. Kristeva, the develop-

---

1. "Representation" is being used in an extended sense to take into account the registering of internal and external events in all sorts of archaic forms, both psychic and
somatic.

ment of "thought-sexuality"—is a developmental achievement, with genetic origins in the interaction of inherited disposition and experience from birth onwards. For instance, for Bion, a form of early interchange takes place between mother and infant whereby the role of the mother's "thinking ability" (her "alpha function") is to "contain," process and "metabolize" the "unthinkable" anxieties and sensations of the infant (the "beta elements") and give them back to the infant in the form of manageable and "digestible" feelings who will, it is hoped, thereafter be able to use them for the formation of his own "thinking apparatus," thoughts and memory.

(6) Note that in the above view, the process of maturation and development depends to a considerable extent on the progressive modification of anxiety which is brought about by the environment functioning as a container. This enables the introjection of an object that can tolerate and make sense of anxiety. A corollary of this is the particular attention paid by the analyst to what is most urgent in the patient's material and to the nature and *content* of the anxieties that are being communicated, consciously and unconsciously, and the defenses against them.

(7) Thus all development, including the building and consolidation of inner psychic structure itself, takes place within the intimate social context of child and mother/environment. To put it in terms of Winnicott, the mother's "good enough" presence (here *quality* of this relationship is being invoked) fosters the infant's capacity to increasingly "hold her in mind" and thus to keep an inner emotional picture of her in her absences, provided, of course, that these are not for a duration longer than what can be tolerated. Only from such a process can a "potential space" be realized and the infant become able to begin separating the me from not-me.

(8) When there is a failure in this process, either because of an insufficient capacity in the infant to tolerate frustration or the mother's failure to make an appropriately receptive emotional attunement, then, according to Bion, the infant resorts to increasingly forceful attempts to project into mother and this can lead to the development of "the apparatus for ridding the psyche of bad internal objects," rather than of an integrated mind and self that can hold itself together. An impairment in the capacity to think and have memory will thus be a failure of the original context. Note here that *thinking* is being differentiated from a split-off *intellect*.

(9) An essential feature of this complex phenomenon of the "facilitating environment" (which plays such a crucial role in enabling the infant's inherited potential to mature and which requires a detailed

study in its own right) is that it has a growth and development of its own, being adapted to the changing needs of the growing individual (Winnicott).

(10) Note that in these accounts the emphasis is on *emotional development*, which is common to the major British analysts. As Green (2000, p. 72) puts it "Winnicott and Bion place emotional development and emotional experience at the beginning . . . or at the center, depending upon whether you are developmentally or structurally minded." This is very different from the classical approach, as Meltzer (1983) points out, where emotionality is only seen in a Darwinian way as a relic of primitive forms of communication. For Freud emotion was "—an indicator of mental functioning rather than—a function itself, much like a noise-in-the-machine" (Meltzer, 1983).

(11) Further, it will be noted from some of the comments made above that development of the ego (and its relationship with objects) is conceived by these analysts as moving from an ego or self state that is relatively unintegrated at the beginning to a gradual movement toward integration.[2] Following the influence of Klein and Fairbairn, the various British analysts referred to above have, in their different ways, given up the idea of the mind being an integral entity. Thus, instead of assuming the existence of an id, ego, and super ego that form part of an inter-related structure, the gaining of integrity of the mind, and therefore the formation of such a structure, is in itself seen as a *developmental achievement*. By integration it is not meant that different parts of the self acquire uniformity. On the contrary, what is being referred to is a greater flexibility in the choice of different aspects of the self, or freedom and flexibility in the capacity to identify with the objects that have been assimilated in the make up of the self.

(12) The British analysts have worked out in considerable detail these issues, the complex developmental processes that are involved and the problems that the individual encounters in his/her attempts to achieve greater internal cohesion. While the differences between these analysts in how they conceptualize development at the micro levels are very important, leading to considerable differences in their clinical approaches, nevertheless they all share the notion of there being a precursor stage of some sort of unintegratedness from where there is a journey toward integration. For Klein, there are two "posi-

---

2. Freud, too, was concerned with the issue of greater integration, for instance between ego and drive, love and hate, ego and super-ego, in various ways at different stages in his work though, on the whole, not at this underlying level that is being referred to here.

tions" (by which she meant a configuration of early impulses, defenses, anxieties, and relationships to objects) which she called the "paranoid-schizoid" and the "depressive" positions. To describe these in a necessarily schematic way, in the paranoid-schizoid she saw that the individual, or infant, attempts to deal with early anxiety situations, caused by painful, conflicting feelings, by splitting them off along with parts of the self and via projection placing them (in phantasy) into other objects, thereby relieving himself of them. She considers this to be part of normal development in the young infant and the child's feelings and perceptions about itself and others are then affected by this mental state. It is also important to note here that, for Klein, the way in which the infant then experiences objects is crucial to the way in which he takes them back into his inner world (introjection), to the building of his ego and his super-ego and the way he relates to others. Only after some further maturation has taken place over the next few months, including that of cognitive capacities, that splitting and projection lessen and there is a beginning of awareness that these different impulses are his own, and love and hate can be tolerated toward the same person at the same time. This is the onset of the depressive position. The infant's perceptions of others becomes more human and more grounded, the balance shifts toward introjection and thus new objects can be taken in and identified with in a more realistic manner. Klein and her followers emphasize that the movement from the paranoid-schizoid position to the depressive is not a linear one; small series of steps are involved, with backward and forward movement, leading to greater capacity to tolerate love and hate. All this contributes to a spurt in development resulting in an increasingly enriched internal world. Concern and guilt emerge as does the capacity to feel for and repairing the object that may have been damaged in phantasy. This leads to a deepening of emotional life and relations with others.

(13) Winnicott approaches these early developmental issues in a somewhat different manner from Klein. I will not attempt to summarize his unique and very complex views with their fundamental emphasis on "mutuality" within a "facilitating environment." As previously stated, like Klein and certain other British analysts, Winnicott too focused in his own way on how "integration of the unit self" is achieved starting from an "unintegrated" state. Thus, all these analysts in their different ways profoundly challenged the classical notion (subscribed to by all the American schools) that the normal ego is a unified entity, and maintained that dissociation processes were abundant in ordinary child development. Further, these analysts in

their different ways, see such processes as of great value in understanding adult schizoid phenomena and disturbances.

(14) Another point to note is that for Klein psychic reality is treated in a concrete way as an *internal world,* a *place* and a life-space "—where relationships are taking place and where the meaning of life was generated for deployment into the outside world—" (Meltzer, 1983). This is a very different emphasis on internal life, compared to Freud, who while having a concept of internalization and the super-ego, did not quite come to this "geographical notion of an internal world, restricted, perhaps, by his need to keep reconciling his theories with his basic neuro-anatomical model (Meltzer, 1983).

(15) A clarification needs to be made at this point about my use of the notion of unconscious phantasy to which several references have been made above. Following the influence of Klein, Kleinian and many independent analysts in the United Kingdom consider unconscious phantasies to be ubiquitous and underlying all of mental life, including the expression of internal object relations in the analytic situation. As Spillius (2001) points out, this is a much more inclusive definition of phantasy than Freud's, especially his "central usage" of the term where phantasies are activities of the ego and conceived as consciously or preconsciously imagined fulfillments of frustrated wishes, formed according to the principles of the secondary process. Further, I agree with her (Spillius, 2001) when she observes that

> less attention has been paid to manifestations of unconscious phantasy or of the unconscious in general in American psychoanalysis than in British and Continental analysis . . . I think this neglect is perhaps encouraged by the structural model of id/ego/superego, which focuses attention on the conflict between the three conceptualized agencies of the mind and on the defenses and adaptations of the ego. The two distinctions of conscious/unconscious and primary/secondary process which cut across each other and which are so important in Freud's characterizing of different types of phantasy, also cut across the id/ego/superego classification, which does not provide a "natural" home for unconscious phantasy . . . [T]he decreasing focus on unconscious phantasy is even more apparent among self-psychologists, intersubjectivists and relational analysts than among other sorts of American psychoanalysts."[3]

3. In this context, it is interesting to note that the notion of "primal phantasies" which Freud (1916) refers to, that have been "unconscious all along" (Spillius, 2001), and which have an important place in French analytic thinking, and are not that dissimilar to certain ideas about inherent knowledge in Klein, Bion, and Winnicott have

(16) Also, from my descriptions of the approaches of these British analysts, it will be noted that their emphasis is on the *genetic continuities* in development of inner psychic structure, and psychic organization as a whole, with early antecedents, rather than seeing such structures, and organization, as suddenly arriving on the scene, in a discontinuous manner.

(17) It is also worth noting that in these British approaches a great deal of attention is paid to the earliest interaction between eros and the aggressive drive (death drive for Klein and certain others) including the role of the latter in either promoting or inhibiting development. Inhibitions can take the form of either regression in libidinal development or promoting too rapid a progress leading to precocity and "premature ego development." As several aspects of cognitive development are seen as intrinsically linked with emotional development, these too can therefore be significantly inhibited or even stopped. On the positive side, Winnicott, more than anyone else, has shown how aggression is necessary to discover the external world, and it is a condition for achievement of the reality of the object as separate from the self.[4] Note that this view of aggression broadens our understanding of it as it is not limited to negative themes such as anger, frustration, envy, etc.

(18) The aim of psychoanalytic therapy itself diverges radically between the American approaches (all influenced in one way or another by ego psychology) and those of the British schools influenced by Klein. Broadly speaking, in the British approaches the aim is to bring together aspects of the personality which are unconsciously disassociated from each other or which are in significant conflict with each other. This is quite different from the aim (in ego psychology, for instance) of releasing the inherent and natural unfolding of a normative adaptation to the social world through a mature and conflict-free alliance with the patient (Hinshelwood, 1991).

(19) Further, the understanding of transference and countertransference issues is necessarily very different in these British approaches compared to the American schools, given their divergent conceptualizations in many respects. In the former compared to the latter, there is, as stated earlier, far greater attention paid to unconscious

---

not found much resonance with analysts belonging to the various American schools. Could this be a consequence of a belief in the New World of an individual's ability to make a fresh beginning unencumbered by (pre)historical constraints?

4. Freud (1915) had already posited that the object is discovered in hate, a statement which has led to many different readings.

phantasies, anxieties and defenses and these may be communicated by the more disturbed patient, such as Sandy (see Olesker, this volume, "Development" paper), symbolically (or, more accurately, often proto symbolically) to us via a variety of means, including enactments in the transference of split off relations between parts of the self and objects, gaps, somatizations, concretizations, projective identifications, corporeal and emotional behavior, nonverbal gestures, and so forth. The analyst needs to be able to decode these so that "silent phantasies" and "memories in feelings" (Klein) can be helped to evolve and gradually thought about in the space of the transference. While this, of course, requires scrupulous attention to, and respect for, the patient's *language* and pre-conscious, it is also the diverse *semiology of his/her affects* that need to be taken into account. This, necessarily, also requires that the analyst be sufficiently free to have access to his/her own affective states at multiple levels, and the shifting patterns of these be carefully attended to in the context of the patient's material. This is an enormous topic in its own right which, again, cannot be detailed here.

(20) In the absence of such an approach, I believe we can remain only on the outside of our patients, at their more mature verbal levels, engaging them in a more educational/intellectual manner. Perhaps it is with the latter approaches that, when faced with disturbances that are more than the neurotic, certain colleagues in the discussion group additionally proposed resorting to measures such as non-dynamic and directive "developmental assist" or "narrative building" by the telling of stories, or encouraging the development of some sort of an interactive, non-verbal, generally benign and well meaning, relationship. This is suggested just as much with adults as with children. With all these essentially non-dynamic measures, it is hoped, that somehow the penny will drop and the child or adult patient will resume those aspects of his or her development, at the more verbal or oedipal level, whose "blue print" has thus far not unfolded or been thwarted. From all that I have said, it should be clear that my clinical experience and understanding of psychoanalysis has not endorsed such more optimistic approaches of colleagues from the American schools. These latter approaches have not taken into account how projective identificatory processes work in the clinical situation, which make it crucial for the analyst not to act out in response to unconsciously determined pressures from the patient. The projected aspects of the patient have to be accepted and understood, and the gradual conveying back of these to the patient is needed if one is to engage, in any manner that is lasting, those areas in patients

such as Sandy (see Olesker, this Volume, "Development" paper) where help is most needed.

(21) To summarize for the purposes of the group, while in addition to the physiological and the biological, psychological maturation also unfolds, the various American schools (whether based in ego psychology, self psychology, or some version of relational orientations), and the British ones differ widely in their understanding of at least (a) the *content* of what unfolds, beginning from the outset, (b) the *manner* in, and the *conditions* under, which this, and further development, takes place, and (c) the nature of the *methodological approach* to be adopted in learning about both (a) and (b).

BIBLIOGRAPHY

FREUD, S. (1915). *Instincts and their Vicissitudes. S.E.* 14.

——— (1916). *Introductory Lectures on Psycho-Analysis. S.E.* 16.

GREEN A. (2000). The posthumous Winnicott: On *Human Nature.* In *Andre Green at the Squiggle Foundation,* ed. J. Abram. London: Karnac Books.

HINSHELWOOD, R. D. (1991). *A Dictionary of Kleinian Thought.* London: Free Associations.

MELTZER, D. (1983). Dream Life: A Re-Examination of the Psychoanalytical Theory and Technique. London: Clunie Press.

RYCROFT, C. (1968). *A Critical Dictionary of Psychoanalysis.* London: Nelson.

SPILLIUS, E. BOTT (2001). Freud and Klein on the concept of phantasy. *Int. J. Psychoanal.,* 82:361–373.

Margo and Me II

The Role of Narrative Building in Child Analytic Technique*

RONA KNIGHT, Ph.D.

Winner of the Albert J. Solnit Award, 2003

Practicing child and adolescent psychoanalysis requires an under-standing of the interdependence of analytic and developmental pro-cesses. Child analysts work with children whose organizing and regu-lating systems are still developing, allowing the analyst and her patient to tap the child's transformational potential as new hierarchies evolve and consolidate in the course of an analysis. The use of the nar-rative building technique is helpful to that process and is informed by and makes clinically applicable recent research data in development and therapeutic process. Narrative building can help the child develop phase specific organization that has been impeded by conflictual and non-conflictual elements in the child's inner and outer world, promote the developmental process, provide more flexible regulatory systems for emotional and cognitive development, lead to innovative views of peo-ple and relationships, and facilitate the organization of emerging structures necessary for progressive development.

I would like to thank the members of the Study Group on Clinical Applications of Developmental Propositions, sponsored by the Psychoanalytic Research and Develop-ment Fund, whose thoughtful comments about development and therapeutic action inspired this paper. Co-Chairmen: Sam Abrams and Al Solnit; Members: Alice Co-lonna, Karen Gilmore, Leon Hoffman, Nasir Ilahi, Claudia Lament, Roy Lilleskov, Pe-ter Neubauer, Wendy Olesker, Mortimer Ostow, Noah Shaw, and Judy Yanof. I would especially like to thank Sam Abrams for his ideas, help, and encouragement during the preparation of this paper.

The Psychoanalytic Study of the Child 58, ed. Robert A. King, Peter B. Neubauer, Samuel Abrams, and A. Scott Dowling (Yale University Press, copyright © 2003 by Robert A. King, Peter B. Neubauer, Samuel Abrams, and A. Scott Dowling).

RESEARCH IN THE AREAS OF PSYCHOSOMATICS, INFANCY DEVELOP-
ment, attachment, cognition, biology, physics, nonlinear statistical
models, and therapeutic process, have greatly added to our understanding of development, the developmental process, and therapeutic action in psychoanalysis. Psychoanalysts interested in child development and therapeutic action (Abrams, 1980, 1987, 1988, 1989,
1990, 1993, 1999; Neubauer, 1994, 1996, 2001; Solnit, 1998; Mayes,
1999, 2001; Fajardo, 1998; Jacobs, 1986, 1990, 1994, 2001abc, 2002;
Beebe et al., 1997a, 1997b; Pine, 1995; Galatzer-Levy, 1995; Yanof,
1996; Fonagy, 1999a, 1999c, among others) have been trying to make
sense of all the new data and theories that suggest that within each
human being, and within each analysis, there are coordinated, interacting elements that constitute regulating systems that make order
out of chaos, which contributes to development, psychoanalytic
process, and therapeutic action.

Unlike adult analysis, child analysis has the added advantage of
working with organizing and regulating systems as they are developing. Working with children and adolescents, the child analyst can tap
the transformational potential that occurs as new hierarchies consolidate, allowing us to help the child develop *phase specific* organizational
systems that make order out of chaos and aid in the maturational
change in those systems over time. In this paper I will: (1) discuss the
research and ideas mentioned above; (2) briefly consider the use of
the narrative in psychoanalytic work; (3) show how the use of narrative building in child analytic work is informed by and makes clinically
applicable the discussed recent research and ideas about human development and analytic process; (4) suggest that the use of narrative
building helps to explicate and resolve conflict as well as pull together
various non-conflictual elements from the child's inner and outer
world—both of which are necessary for organizing systems to evolve;
and (5) explain why I think narrative building promotes the developmental process and fosters therapeutic change in child analysis.

DEVELOPMENTAL CONSIDERATIONS

Children and adolescents are still growing and developing. Evaluating a child or adolescent for age-appropriate levels of development is
essential for anyone working with children and teenagers. Child analysts always have to keep the developmental process in mind and be
attuned to where our patients are along that process in the course of
an analysis. To be able to do this, the child analyst must have a good
understanding of all the complex processes that underlie develop-

ment as well as understanding the deficits and defects in each child's development. Both levels of understanding inform our diagnosis, therapeutic goals, and treatment for each individual patient (Abrams and Solnit, 1998).

Development, as we currently understand it, is both continuous and discontinuous (Abrams and Solnit, 1998). It emerges through an assimilative and accommodative process (Piaget, 1952) in which children take in bits of information (Miller, 1956) from all sensory pathways, both conscious and unconscious (Freud, 1915; Bucci, 2001), and assimilate them to already existing, hereditary biological structures and systems inherent in both the brain and the body (Hofer, 1981). This new sensory input effects changes in the developing structures; having to accommodate to the new information, these structures are subtly transformed. In this manner, the infant and child begin to make order out of the chaos of incoming sensory stimuli through the continuing changing and developing neuro-biological systems that were genetically programmed to establish organizational and regulatory structures and systems. Abrams (2002) defines developmental bedrock as the "progressive transformations into new psychological organization guided by an inherent blueprint in each child." These transformations result from the tension between assimilation and accommodation. Neubauer (1996) makes a similar point, suggesting that the developmental process requires a transformation of old structures into new ones as the child grows biologically and processes new affective and cognitive information.

Edelman (1987), working in the area of genetics and memory, proposed that there are genetically defined regulatory systems within human development. These regulatory systems make order out of the chaos of incoming stimuli and are both synchronic and interactive. A very complex interaction between these internal processing and regulating systems already exists at birth. Meltzoff and Borton (1979) demonstrated that babies who explored objects by touch alone could then recognize those objects visually, suggesting that there is some reciprocal assimilation and accommodation of information in the visual and motor systems. Thus, change in one organizational system can also modify other organizational systems, indicating that the infant is already biologically wired to organize and abstract the chaos of incoming stimuli.

This complex interaction between biological structures also exists between biological and psychological structures. The extensive literature in psychosomatic research has and continues to delineate the interrelated effects of psychological structures, behavior, and the body's biochemistry. Recent advances in non-linear statistical models (Scharfstein, 1996) have given us the mathematical tools to study the multiple forces that influence the changing patterns in these structures as well as their coordination, greatly enhancing our ability to understand the development of both the individual and interacting organizational and regulatory systems. This dynamic systems approach to development (Sander, 2002; Mayes, 2001; Galatzer-Levy, 1995; Tyson, 2002) informs our understanding of linear and non-linear human development as well as individual differences in development. Linda Mayes (2001) has written a well thought out integration of these ideas and suggests that we "study the symphony as an orchestrated whole as well as the behavior of its individual parts, for when the individual parts are brought together, their behavior as a whole might be different" (p. 153).

Anna Freud (1965) cautioned not to put therapeutic limits on our analytic work with children:

> Only in child analysis proper is the whole range of therapeutic possibilities kept available to the patient, and all parts of him are given the chance on the one hand to reveal and on the other to cure themselves . . . We need to be absolutely certain of the classification of a given case before taking the choice of therapeutic element away from the patient and into our own hands, i.e., before limiting the chances of therapy to one single factor. As our skill in assessment stands today, however, such accuracy of diagnostic judgement seems to me an ideal to be realized not in our present state of knowledge but in the distant future (vol. 6, pp. 234–235).

Since that time, research in development and analytic process has moved us toward that distant future. While we are not yet at the ideal state of knowing, we are at least a significant step along the way. Understanding the interdependence of analytic and developmental processes enhances our ability to help the children we treat (Abrams, 1999; Hurry, 1998; Settlage, 1993).

Infant development research has gone a long way toward understanding the interactions in the infant-caregiver dyad that promote or inhibit development. Some analytic process research has confirmed that what we do as analysts is similar to what parents do with children. Many child and adult analysts have understood and written about the clinical use of the infant research findings in their work with patients, particularly through the lens of the developmental relationship (Emde, 1988; Osofsky, 1988; Stern, 1995; Lachmann and Beebe, 1996; Morgan, 1997; Stern et al., 1998). Other analysts have cautioned us to be careful of just providing a "corrective emotional experience" (Alexander and French, 1946), without addressing the conflicts that interfere with development (Neubauer, 1996). Both sides of this controversy have valid points. It is impossible to separate out normal and pathological conflict within a developmental process, and both must be addressed.

RESEARCH IN DEVELOPMENT

Piaget (1952, 1965, 1981), a biologist studying cognitive, affective, and moral development in the infant and child, elaborated a theory of development that is based on the child's assimilating external stimuli of all kinds into genetically predetermined biological structures, which then are transformed in the process of accommodating the new information.

Stern (1977, 1985) investigated the processes of engagement in the infant-caregiver dyad. He found engagement to have four different states: initiating, maintaining, terminating, and avoiding contact in the dyad, and has proposed an interactive regulatory system that starts in the beginning of infancy and continues in a pattern of engagement through the first two years of life. Sander (1980, 2002) studied the mutual regulation system in the mother-infant dyad. In such a system both self and mutual regulation must be integrated. Hofer, studying mother rats with their infant pups, found that the mother-infant regulation system had profound effects on the biological regulatory systems of the pups, influencing such basic functioning as heart rates, respiration, hormonal output and inhibition, temperature, sleep, stomach acidity, and behavior (Hofer and Reiser, 1969; Hofer and Weiner, 1971, 1975; Hofer et al., 1972; Hofer, 1981, 1984, 1996).

Tronick (Tronick, 1989; Tronick and Cohen, 1989), studying the interaction of the mother-infant dyad, found that the dyadic interaction was not a smooth one; there were frequent times of disruptions in the interaction system that then had to be repaired. It was the success of the repairs that determined how robust and healthy the developing relationship, and the infant within that relationship, would become. Fraiberg (Fraiberg et al., 1975), working with mother-infant pairs, observed how much a mother's effect on her infant determined normal and pathological psychological development. Other researchers have found that the successes or failures in the infant-mother dyadic interaction can determine affect regulation (Emde, 1983, 1988) and cognitive and social functioning in the toddler (Trevarthan, 1980; Malatesta et al., 1989).

Bowlby (1969, 1973), working within an ethological framework, viewed the infant/child-caregiver relationship from an attachment and loss perspective. Bowlby's attachment theory of development inspired further research that delineated different types of attachment models (Ainsworth et al., 1978; Main et al., 1985; Fonagy, 1993a; Fonagy and Target, 2000) that aided or impeded a child's developmental process. Working first within attachment theory and then looking at the child/caregiver interaction and applying it to cognitive and affective development, Fonagy and Target have defined a process of mentalization in which the infant and child develops a sense of her own and another's mind through the continual development of the reflective function (Fonagy and Target, 1996b, 1998, 2000; Mayes and Cohen, 1996).

RESEARCH IN THERAPEUTIC PROCESS

Bucci (1997, 2001), researching therapeutic action, developed a multiple code theory of emotional communication that includes processing emotional and cognitive information on three levels: the subsymbolic, the symbolic nonverbal, and the symbolic verbal mode. Building on the work of earlier researchers and theorists (see Bucci, 2001), she postulates that all three modes of processing emotional information can occur both within and outside of conscious awareness. While Piaget organized cognitive development in terms of cognitive schemas, Bucci applies the idea of schemas to emotional development. She considers emotional schemas as organizers of our interpersonal interactions. Formed by our repeated interactions with people, particularly the infant's and child's early caregivers (see Lachmann and Beebe, 1996, for a discussion of infancy research in this area), emotional schemas "determine what we expect from others, how we perceive them, and how we act toward them" (Bucci, 2001, p. 50). They act like cognitive schemas, in that they work through the same assimilative and accommodative processes outlined by Piaget. Her subsymbolic mode is similar to Piaget's preverbal sensory motor stage of cognitive functioning that remains in all later stages of cognition (like driving a car). The difference is that Bucci assumes a *dominance* of subsymbolic elements, wherein "actions and sensory and visceral reactions . . . constitute the schema's 'affective core'" (p. 50). Subsymbolic processes often operate outside of awareness, are often expressed in nonverbal form, and can be brought into consciousness through a referential process in which the analyst, reflecting on the nonverbal cues (such as action or imagery), creates a *verbal narrative* to bring the subsymbolic elements of the affective core into conscious awareness. Bucci has demonstrated this multiple code process through computer analysis of analytic process material in adult analyses.

Bucci's model nicely explains how the narrative building technique helps make unrecognized thoughts and feelings both conscious and understandable in our work with children. However, Bucci's theoretical model is only one of many process research models that look at both individual and interactive verbal and nonverbal affective and mental schemas in the analytic dyad. Using both audio and video tapes of analytic sessions, researchers in the United States, Germany, Great Britain, and South America are collaborating in the micro-study of the analytic process through various computer generated models looking at individual sessions. Fonagy (Fonagy et al., 1999) and Wallerstein (2001) have written extensive reviews of the process research being done worldwide.

Analysis of nonverbal and verbal interactions in the analytic dyad has also been extensively thought about by clinicians doing psychoanalysis (Jacobs, 1986, 1994, 2002; Kantrowitz, 1999, 2001; Ogden, 1997, 1998, 1999; Arlow, 1993, 1995). All of them, in one way or another, have discussed the need to work with the patient to construct a narrative that makes unrecognized thoughts and feelings conscious through some verbal narrative that may have reconstructive elements in it, but more importantly describes the patient's present thoughts and feelings as they are expressed in interactions in the analytic dyad. In child analysis, bringing subsymbolic and nonverbal, unrecognized thoughts and feelings into awareness can be done by the analyst's understanding and making inferences from the child's play, actions and verbalizations and/or by the analyst's inferring the child's feelings through understanding her own affective states resulting from the processes of projective identification, role responsiveness, or role assignment. In addition, the patient may be able to develop her own narrative once she has expressed in imagery or action aspects of her own subsymbolic and nonverbal affective core.

ANALYTIC APPLICATIONS OF DEVELOPMENTAL RESEARCH

Child and adult analysts have applied the interactive, regulatory systems described by the researchers in development and biology, and the parental functions necessary for the development of those structures and systems, to the analytic dyad, engendering a more relational view of analysis than was initially proposed by classical Freudian theory. Their ideas include Winnicott's (1965) concept of the holding environment, Sandler's (1987) ideas about safety in the analytic relationship and role responsiveness, and Loewald's (1960) formulations of the analytic relationship and therapeutic action.

Using the caregiver-infant interaction models proposed by infant researchers and applying those models to the analyst-patient interaction, Lachmann and Beebe (1996) have posited a model of therapeutic action that includes: (1) ongoing regulations that express a pattern of repeated interactions in the treatment situation; (2) disruption and repair; and (3) heightened affective moments (Pine, 1985). They consider these "three principles of salience" as relevant to and mediating all therapeutic action. Fajardo (1998) makes the point that "observations of the mother-child dyad are not merely metaphors for the psychoanalytic dyad; rather, both are highly conditional and different instances of the same mutually organizing phenomena" (p. 204). Hurry (1998), while clearly delineating the many parenting functions that are part of our analytic work with children, cautions us to more clearly distinguish between parental functions that belong in analysis and those that should only be the purview of parents. Osofsky (1988), in an overview of attachment research and theory, suggests that part of the therapeutic task of both adult and child analysis is "to help the patient discover that not everyone in the world is as unreliable as the models of parental figures they have built and come to expect as a result of their experience. When the patient is able to develop some degree of basic trust in the analyst, progression can occur" (p. 166).

Thinking about therapeutic action in child analysis, Abrams and Solnit (1998) discuss how the therapeutic action in our work with children is a coordination of the developmental process with the analytic process. They define the developmental process as the "step-by-step changes from infancy to adulthood [that] are informed by an inherent maturational blueprint or timetable of potential steps in organization that becomes realized in the form of a progressive sequence of developmental hierarchies. Each new organizational configuration builds on antecedents (continuities) while bringing in novel structures and functions unavailable in earlier forms (discontinuities). In effect, psychological development unfolds in a series of systems of 'minds,' each containing new, drive-related experiences as well as innovative defenses, affects, adaptive strategies, and object-relating and -representing capacities. Under optimal conditions, the constituents are harmoniously brought together at each level of sequential organization" (pp. 89–90). They point out that the steps in the sequence may overlap, interweave, co-mingle, or be sharply demarcated from one another. External experience "codetermines the timing, patterning, and coherence of the organizational hierarchies" (p. 91). They understand the therapeutic action of child and adolescent psychoanalysis as resulting from the coordination of the past (understanding the transference relationship), the present (facilitation of a new way of knowing about the past and understanding the present), and the future (the analyst as new developmental object assisting progressive development through the child's new and novel relationship with the analyst). The developmental process promotes organization and the psychoanalytic process facilitates integration. They make the important point that at different times in the treatment, and with careful attention to the particular developmental disorders of each child, the child analyst may choose to focus on "ways of redressing disharmonies, deviations, and impairments to impetus, rather than toward reviving features of the past" (p. 101). When a child is in need of a developmental assist (Neubauer, 2001), focusing on interventions that help promote forward growth becomes a priority.

Fonagy and Target (1996a) think of developmental intervention as pertaining to "the pathologies traditionally defined as residing in the ego, labeled as developmental disturbances, and thought to relate to ego functions and self and object representations" (p. 61). They list 13 aspects of the analytic interaction that address developmental intervention:

> (1) ego functions (mental processes) via self and object representations; (2) the verbalization of internal states and differentiation of affects; (3) the breaking down of unmanageable affects (anxiety) into smaller manageable entities which the child can master; (4) the development of internal representations of affects so that the child can master his own feelings; (5) the facilitation of thinking by reducing anxiety and making links between different aspects of thought processes; (6) facilitation of thinking about cause and effect, particularly within relationships; (7) helping the child separate internal from external, real from unreal, fantasy from reality; (8) setting limits and offering explanations for the limits provided; (9) facilitating the creation of internal representations of self and other; (10) establishing reciprocity; (11) developing the capacity to delay gratification; (12) helping the child to develop an "as if" attitude, and the encouragement of fantasy; (13) gradually confronting the child with opposing ideas, for example, the possibility of hatred and dependence on the same person (p. 61).

I would point out that all of the items on their list are also functions performed by parents in the normal course of their children's development.

THE NARRATIVE IN PSYCHOANALYSIS

In the 1980's Donald Spence (1982) and Roy Schafer (1983a, 1983b, 1985), thinking within a hermeneutic perspective, introduced the use of the narrative in adult psychoanalysis. Spence focused on narrative rather than historical truth, preferring construction to reconstruction. He recommended the co-construction of truth in the past and in the present based on the mutual agreement of patient and analyst as a narrative unfolded. The co-constructed narrative then leads to a coherence that aids the patient in the present and in the future. Schafer proposed that the analysand's story held more personal meaning than established fact. He suggested that if we privilege psychic reality over historical fact, the patient then becomes a more reliable narrator and responsible partner in the analytic endeavor. The analyst must listen more closely to the uniqueness of the patient's story and be less influenced by metapsychological theories, resulting in a less compromised, tailor-made analysis for each patient. Using the idea of action language, which includes behavior, thought and fantasy, Shafer has advocated making action the central focus of analysis and the transference interaction the primary mode of understanding.

This hermeneutic approach to psychoanalysis occurred at the same time infant development research was becoming well known. Work and discussion in these two areas led to a major sea change in the way contemporary analysts formulate analytic theory and practice analysis, a topic beyond the scope of this paper. However, the research and ideas of that time also changed the way we view development within contemporary analytic theory and technique. Abrams (1999) has applied the present-day theory of mind to the idea of the narrative in child analytic work. He writes: "Developmental hierarchies define increasingly differentiated 'minds' through childhood and adolescence into early adult life. . . . Each emerging mind frequently coalesces about binding individual narratives, narratives that convert the ongoing biological and the interactive into personal meanings" (p. 6). He notes that unlike adult analysts, whose patients have completed the biological growth of their brain functions, child analysts must always look forward to the construction and organization of the potential development of their child patients. Thus child analysts must not only deconstruct the present narratives but also help the child develop a more felicitous narrative in the present analytic relationship that acts as a corrective substitute for an already formed narrative that is impeding development. The transformational process of accommodation necessary for the creation of a newly developed narrative in the mind of the child will lead, hopefully, to the further development of new cognitive and emotional functioning, which then creates the possibility of subsequent emerging narratives that have the potential to promote continued development in the growing child.

NARRATIVE BUILDING AS DEVELOPMENTAL ASSIST

The use of narrative building is a technique well suited to the child and adolescent. Children are used to hearing and reading stories as a way to express and understand their feelings, relationships, and the world around them. Pretend fantasy play, the child's own use of narrative to help them express and master their own feelings, starts in toddlerhood (First, 1994) and becomes a major defense in the latency age child. I learned this from my very first child patient, a five year old girl who was playing out a story using a dollhouse. We met for several therapy sessions before my first meeting with my supervisor. My anxiety about telling my first child supervisor that I had *just* been playing with my patient led me to say to this little girl that we couldn't just play; we had to talk about what was worrying her. She looked at me with a dumbfounded expression and said, "We *are* talking about it."

Play as a means of narrative expression, both the child's and mine, can explain the past and present, promote symbolization and metaphor, and signify developmental progress through progressively hierarchically ordered stories. Co-constructing narratives helps the child feel understood, promoting the self-reflective function involved in understanding one's own mind and the mind of the other. Abrams (1999) points out that play also promotes organization of unconscious thoughts, feelings, and conflict and aids in the reorganization and transformation of cognitive and affective schemas that lead to innovative new narratives. These narratives provide more flexible regulatory systems for emotional and cognitive development and innovative views of people and object interactions.

When I play with a child I engage in not just talking but in action, which takes the issue of the analyst's disclosure to a whole other level. Playing with children inevitably means that the child analyst must express aspects of her own psyche. If I am assigned the roles of playing out extreme sadness or murderous rage, I can't just put that expression into words; it also must be there in my tone of voice, my expressions, and in the actions I perform in the play with the toys I am using. Sometimes there are no toys and just action between the therapist and the child that is used to express and work through feelings (Frankel, 1998). In addition, the child analyst must also keep in mind the developmental level of the child, who often is guiding the actions of the analyst. This awareness requires me to get in touch with my childhood ways of expressing feelings, if I am to genuinely meet my patient at her developmental level as she attempts to tell me her story about her worries. At the same time, I am also the adult helping the child weave together all the thoughts and feelings expressed in the play to put together a narrative that helps the child understand not only her present thoughts, feelings, and conflicts but also an understanding of events and relationships in the child's past that have led up to the present narrative. And as the adult, I am also helping the child in the functioning delineated by Fonagy and Target (1996a) as I co-construct her narrative.

In this kind of action-interaction, the child is able to express subsymbolic and nonverbal feelings and patterns of interaction that are not yet symbolized and within the conscious, cognitive awareness of the child. It then becomes my job, together with my patient, to put the myriad feelings and interactions into a verbal narrative that the child can then use to understand both what is happening in her environment and within herself that is making her so unhappy, angry, worried, scared, and so forth. This helps bring the subsymbolic and nonverbal thoughts and feelings into awareness so that they can be further expressed and worked through. It also provides a mentalization interaction: the child feels that her thoughts and feelings are understood, and she has the chance to understand the mind of the analyst through the analyst's expression of herself in the play. Feeling understood by the analyst and understanding the analyst assists in the organization of confused feelings and thoughts. Feeling understood also provides a new level of relational and intrapsychic integration as the child assimilates the understanding of new thoughts and feelings within the analytic dyad and the co-constructed narrative. Old patterns of thinking, feeling, and relating are transformed by the new information, which leads to further development through structure building. Therefore helping a child construct a narrative encourages the development of reflective functioning, facilitating the understanding, organization, and internal representation of self and other.

Part of the interaction system of the analytic dyad involves the relationship-building tools of object constancy, mirroring, mutually regulating stimulation and affect, teaching more flexible ways of coping with and regulating affects, repairing disruptions in the relationship, helping the child synthesize oppositional feelings like loving and hating within the relationship, lending ego functions that the child does not yet have, to mention just a few of the relational processes and tasks that make up the analytic relationship with children. By doing all of the above and more, both with and for the child in the process of narrative building, the analyst helps the child develop a sense of cohesiveness and reorganizes the self-object system in ways that move development forward.

The child analyst needs to understand and address both normal and pathological conflicts embedded in the child's development. The narrative building technique provides the analyst with a format to help the child understand the conflicts and defenses that are constricting and/or preventing further development. When we interpret, we address the assimilative tendencies of the child in the hope that the child will accommodate the information and transform the psychic structures we are trying to address and further develop. While our interpretations are often in the form of language, we often make interpretations through our actions with children (Ablon, 2001). Nonverbal aspects of conflicts also get played out and actualized in the analytic environment (Frankel, 1998; Abrams and Solnit, 1998; Emde, 1986) and the concreteness of children's thinking sometimes requires the analyst to show and do the conflict resolution with the child or adolescent.

In the working through process we help development move forward by resolving the embedded conflicts that are impeding development. Narratives become a way of understanding and resolving conflicts while helping the child attain higher level and less rigid and constricted defenses, promoting a more flexible and less harsh intrapsychic structure. The success of the working through process can be measured by the hierarchical development of the continuing narrative. The analytic relationship employed in the creation of new narratives engages the intrapsychic structures of id, ego, and superego, the self and object interaction system, and the integrative elements within and between these structures, and promotes a cohesiveness, synthesis, and organization of these structures within a central story.

There are different levels of operation in the construction of a narrative. A distinction needs to be made between *co-discovering*, in which the patient and analyst access thoughts, feelings, fantasies, and experiences that are out of conscious awareness and are causing problems, and *co-creating*, in which the child analyst helps her patient assimilate new experiences (which include new ways of thinking and feeling about self and other) in the analytic dyad which creates innovative organizations that further aid in the consolidation of new, hierarchical intrapsychic and interpersonal structures. By uncovering unrecognized thoughts, feelings, and interactions related to the past and the present, understanding how they impede present functioning and interactions, and helping the patient discover new ways of thinking, feeling, and interacting, we can help adult patients change by *co-constructing* a more functional narrative, accessing alternative affective, cognitive, and interactional functions *that are existing elements within their fully developed organizational systems.* The child analyst has the additional function of *co-creating,* a process of facilitating the organization and integration of both present and *emerging* structures that are necessary for the continued progressive development of the child's mind.

This complex process requires us to fulfill many roles for the child. As a *transference object* we are assigned the task of helping the child become aware of thoughts, feelings, and interactions from the past. In this capacity, we also help the child understand how her unconscious conflicts and previous ways of reacting to or coping with old feelings about self and other interfere with her being happy and more functional in the present. As a *real object* we are kind, caring and provide general nutrients (sometimes concretely), as well as bring our own temperament and relational style into the developing analytic relationship. In our roles as transference and real object, we also promote development in the ways defined by Fonagy and Target, the infant researchers and the process researchers. As a *developmental object* we accept the assignment of a new person in the child's life who will assist them in creating new, hierarchical, phase specific development. The functions of the analyst who promotes development and the functions of the analyst as a developmental object are complementary. Promoting development allows for an assimilation-accommodation process that produces new organizations in the child's self and interactional structures that *allow* a hierarchical transformational process to occur in which we are assigned a role in the creation and consolidation of a new phase of development.

Narratives also help the child understand the strengths and weaknesses in their constitutional make-up. As analysts, we help the child shore up what is possible and understand what is not possible, furthering a child's capacity to understand themselves and helping them learn to manage with both the positive and dysfunctional aspects embedded in their biological blueprint. In this respect, it may be important to distinguish between primary developmental disorders (retardation, learning disorders, low impetus, among others) and secondary developmental disorders (developmental delay caused by early unconscious conflicts, limitations in parenting, trauma, among others). Some primary disorders are amenable to developmental remediation, but they are not necessarily capable of developmental transformation. Learning disabilities and true attentional disorders are typical of this; they can be remediated at each progressive stage of cognitive development, but they are wired in as part of the neurological blueprint that remains throughout the lifespan. In a normal child with a learning disability, the hierarchical development of cognition will move forward from concrete thinking to a formal level of thinking without any external intervention. We can help the child with her reaction to her learning problem at each new level of cognitive development, we can help with remediation and/or medication, but we can't eliminate the disorder in succeeding developmental transformations. Secondary developmental disorders, in which the developmental blueprint has been derailed because of external situations that have impacted the child's developing structural organization, are more amenable to developmental assistance through the relationship with the analyst and the narrative building technique. It then becomes important for the child analyst to assess which aspects of the child's development are amenable to change and which are not.

To provide the child with a more propitious narrative in the analytic dyad is often not enough. The child lives within a family system that has helped form a narrative that has impeded development in the past. These narratives include: (1) the child's own constitutional strengths and weaknesses, temperament, and inherent genetic blueprint; (2) those of the other family members; and (3) the interactions of the family members based on both of the above. I find it equally important to meet regularly with the parents of the child I am treating to help them gain a better understanding of their own minds and the mind of their child. Helping the child transform old self and object schemas into higher level and more flexible structures requires a change in the family system to accommodate the change in the child's development, and often parents need help understanding how to do that. Alternately, if the internal structures of the child go too far awry, we also have to intercede with medication, educational measures, and other treatments to best help the child's assimilative functioning.

CLINICAL ILLUSTRATION

In "Margo and Me I," published in this volume, I focused on Margo's use of gender as a solution to unmet needs (Knight, 2003). In this paper I will focus on the verbal and nonverbal interactions within the analytic relationship that led to the progressive hierarchical development of narratives that promoted Margo's forward development.

The games Margo played in the first one and one-half years of twice a week therapy elaborated her early narrative. Hiding games expressed her feelings that she was not seen. I was always able to find her, which established that I was a person who would consistently make an effort to "find out" where she was with me. She would not feel lost with me, and I was someone who would play with her. As we played, I would talk about her feelings and actions, placing the nonverbal into a verbal context. This play provided the possibility of a changing narrative of object interaction for her. In the Time Machine Game I was assigned her feelings, and she could see how well I understood them as well as how I expressed such feelings within myself. When she could count on me to most often understand her feelings and not lose her in direct interaction with me, there was some indication that she had assimilated the many processes that contributed to this new interaction and made the necessary accommodation in her self-organization. She was able to shift into more sophisticated, displaced, symbolic doll house play to express herself, indicating the beginning formation of a more developmentally advanced cognitive structure to manage her thoughts and feelings.

In Margo's early narrative, covering ages five and one-half to seven years old, her self representation and affective core was stupid, lonely, sad, damaged, and hateful, with little control over her intense feelings; she had little hope for repairing the hurt she felt. Her interaction system suggested that she felt neglected by her parents and unsafe in relationships. As Abrams (1999) would say, this was not a felicitous narrative to optimize progressive development on any level. I recommended analytic treatment for this child.

Margo experienced the increased number of sessions as concretely giving her what she felt she needed and had been asking for. When she asked if the pearls I wore were real, and I told her they were, I positioned myself as a real person who could provide warmth, caring, and general nutrients for growth and as a differentiated person who would provide the interactional functions that both the infant development and therapeutic process researchers regard as necessary to promote development. As a real person I provided the functions Fonagy and Target outlined to assist her flagging development. I also provided some of the mirroring and fusing functions that she had not experienced with her parents. We sang and danced, and I matched her both vocally and physically throughout the analysis. She would perform stunts on a balance beam, and I would admire her. We were building a new relationship in which she felt understood, loved, appreciated, and emotionally and physically mirrored in the analytic dyad.

Acquisition games in which she needed more and more money and objects were played. The glue project was started. When I felt I had deduced enough information from her play, the feelings she assigned to me, and her need for more and more materials, I constructed a narrative about her metaphorical inner sense of emptiness and her desperate desire to have that filled up. I suggested that the analysis would help her understand why she felt so empty, which made her want more and more things. As we talked about this, she drew a circle in my carpet and said, "The hole is a little more filled up," which I interpreted to mean that feeling understood by me helped fill the emptiness. Both concretely giving to her and constructing this narrative with her not only provided her with a conscious, verbal understanding of her subsymbolic feeling of inner emptiness, it also made her feel that I understood and responded to the emptiness she felt from the deprivation and loss she had experienced. This interplay provided a novel relationship interaction to be assimilated and accommodated within her self-and-other relational system.

When I returned after summer vacation, Margo, now eight years old, was very angry and didn't want to talk to me. As we discussed her feelings about me she said, "You don't know anything. You think you are little miss perfect, but you're not nice. . . . Your parents didn't want you. They just wanted a child, but not you!" In this extension of her narrative, she tried to understand what happened in her past that made her feel empty, angry, and "not nice," deciding that she wasn't the child that her parents wanted. I interpreted her wanting to be perfect to defend against feeling angry, unwanted, and stupid. Both her anger at my leaving her and the construction of this narrative led to her giving full expression to her rage, which was intense and out of control. Once again, she wanted me to feel how she felt, and she succeeded. I felt helpless, out of control, battered, bruised, furious, and guilty. I felt emotionally and physically depleted by her, much the way her mother sometimes experienced her and how, I thought, Margo felt inside herself. I had a very difficult time tolerating the abuse and frequently asked why she needed to be so mean and hurtful to me, what all of this behavior was about. "We just have to do it," she said each time I asked. To help Margo with this meant facing intense, angry feelings within myself and managing them in a way that was not hurtful to either of us. As we traversed this angry place, Margo very carefully watched me. My behavior represented a new and different model of affect regulation with which she could identify and begin to internalize. New strategies for managing rage within herself and between people were being worked on. A new narrative was being constructed in which people could live through periods of intense rage, stay connected, and still care about each other. This new relationship narrative contradicted aspects of her earlier narrative in which anger was thought to cause death or abandonment.

Once she saw that we could both survive her rage, she shifted into a more competitive stance, which I understood as an indication that she had traversed a toddler level of developmental organization that had originally not included enough affect regulation and safety in relationships to establish structures that would lead to a higher level of triadic functioning. During this phase of our work, we played many competitive games of physical and mental skill. When she could see that I felt the same competitive feelings that she did and that I did not mind her wanting to be better than me, she felt safe enough to include her father in our triadic play. The analytic relationship and play was helping to change her narrative of self and other. Envy and competition could be expressed without being dampened by fear and guilt, as I allowed, encouraged, and participated in the playing out of this part of the narrative. It was also apparent that she was learning about my mind as well as hers, accompanied by the important realization that the difficult feelings we were working on were not hers alone but are human within all of us.

As we constructed a narrative that allowed her to rework dyadic and triadic feelings and conflicts that had interfered with more flexible and expansive psychological growth during earlier phases of development, she was then able to use me as a *developmental object* who could assist her in the pull forward and usher in new developmental phase functioning in the latency age stage of differentiation and autonomy. Margo was then able to engage more fully in the world outside her family. By the time she was nine years old she was a star athlete, an excellent student, and had many close friends. She was beginning to feel more autonomous and worthwhile in her own right.

Feeling better about herself, she decided it was time to tackle her mother's lack of consistent attentiveness to her. When Margo realized that neither she nor I could change her mother she became despairing, exhausted, hopeless, and suicidal. During this time she told me that she felt it was her fault that she had been treated so badly. If she had been less angry things would be different. As we addressed the guilt related to her despair and hopelessness, a new version of her family narrative was constructed. Margo told me about a friend of hers "whose parents have no time for her and don't understand her." As we talked about this girlfriend we discovered that the girl was sad and mad about how her parents were treating her, but that there was nothing to do about her parents. That was just the way they were. Acting mad didn't help and only made her feel bad about herself and her angry behavior. Talking to them about how she felt didn't change anything either, sad as that was. In this sequence of the analysis Margo and I addressed her despair, hopelessness, guilt, her self representation as bad for having these feelings, and her feeling responsible for her mother's lack of consistent attentive behavior. I normalized the feelings, interpreted her conflict and guilt, and provided suggestions to help her move out in the world, fostering latency age separation and autonomy. I encouraged her to find other relationships that would duplicate the relationship she and I had, relationships that would engender further development after the analysis was over.

Margo then created a narrative to provide her hope for the future. In this latest version of her narrative, Margo showed a more mature understanding of her relationship with her mother. She could allow feelings of sadness with a quiet acceptance into her affective repertoire. She understood that she would have to provide for herself and was confident that she could do that. The hope that she could develop a relationship with a kind, caring person developed from her relationship with me and the change in her relationship with her father. In this narrative, hope has replaced her despair of never getting better. She can allow feelings of separation and envision a time when she will no longer be living with her parents, a necessary step in the early latency phase of separation-individuation (Knight, 1998). Following this analytic work, Margo decided she wanted to go to a sleepaway summer camp and was able to separate from her family for an extended time.

Several months later, toward the end of a session Margo, now ten years old, picked up the crystal ball I have in my office. I wonder if she wants to tell the future. She tells me that she is going to tell me my future: I am going to have another baby soon. I wonder if I am too old to have a new baby. She then puts down the crystal ball and picks up the beanbags, juggling them for several minutes, and then starts throwing them at me. I tell her she can't hit me and notice that it seemed that what I said made her angry. She denies this and puts a clearly fake, happy expression on her face. I tell her that I know her well by now and putting on a happy face does not hide the fact that she is angry. She hits me in the face with the beanbag. I tell her that she has to stop hitting me, that she is too old for this behavior and can now contain it and talk about it. "*I'm* too old? *You're* the one who is too old!" she shouts at me. It is the end of her session, and she leaves, with me not yet understanding the enactment. That night she left a message on my answering machine telling me she was very angry about what I had said and that she didn't want to talk about it in her next session.

I started the next session by saying, "I got your message, and we do have to talk about what happened. Just like you, I also thought about what happened and why you got so mad. I think it was because I wouldn't go along with the crystal ball game and me having another baby. I hurt your feelings and you got angry, but I couldn't understand *why* so fast. If you could have told me, instead of hitting me, I would have understood immediately that I had hurt your feelings and I could have apologized, because I am sorry." "What was I supposed to say?" Margo asks. "You could have said, 'You jerk! I wanted to play this game and you didn't and it hurt my feelings,'" I reply. Margo answers, "I prefer to be polite." We are now back in territory she and I have gone over many times before as we analyzed her conflict between her anger and her fear of retaliation and/or rejection. I say, "Your polite side doesn't let the angry feelings out when they are still small enough to talk about, so they build up and get bigger and bigger until they burst out and you have to act on them. It would feel better to talk about them when they are small and can get settled, instead of letting them build up and then feel badly about having acted on them." "Okay, okay," she says, "let's play." She then looks at me and says, "I know *you* a long time, and you look angry." I stopped and thought for a minute, unaware that I looked angry, and then said, "Well you're right, I am still angry about your hitting me in the face yesterday." "I'm sorry about that," she says. I tell her again that I am also sorry that I hurt her feelings yesterday. She then instructs me in my role in her play in which I, as a robber, am going to have a baby that I am going to raise very differently from the way I was raised. The new mother is going to give the baby plenty of attention and love it very much and never play favorites.

In this sequence there was clearly a disruption in need of repair. I had enacted her worst thoughts and feelings: a mother who does not want her baby. But we had already experienced many disruptions and repairs, and she knew that we would work it out together. Her telephone message indicated that she now had the ability to reflect on what had happened and put her anger into words. She protested talking about it because she knew that I would have thought about it as well and would insist on discussing it the next day. She knew my mind, and she counted on my figuring out hers. I felt truly awful about what I had done, and I knew I could count on her to understand that from my tone of voice when I apologized. She was empathic enough to accept my apology and not make me feel worse about it. She also allowed me to make up for it by having us play out the game in another arena, while letting me know that the disruption had brought her robber feelings to the fore again. While I interpreted her conflict about her anger, I thought it tactful not to mention her robber feelings, or her wish that she be my child, and just allow her to get on with the game, which was working on a better narrative for the future. Both the robber feelings and her wishes had been interpreted many times before, and I knew she knew what they meant when she brought them into the session.

Margo was also able to know me well enough to see something on my face that I was not aware of at the time—my preverbal anger. She could now do for me what I had helped her to do many times before: bring the preverbal affect into verbal awareness. She could also trust that I would take her observations seriously and validate them, which I did. Our relationship had progressed to a real give and take of two minds working together, and I am sure she could see from my facial expression that I was proud of her accomplishment. This very real exchange between us was assimilated and led to a final narrative that illuminated her understanding and integration of her own feelings and conflicts and demonstrated her empathic understanding of her mother's feelings and behavior. The crime trial narrative illustrates Margo's development of organizational abilities to see cause and effect, confront and manage opposing feelings and ideas, understand mental processes in herself and others, and understand the concept of consequences for actions.

Margo and I terminated her analysis about a year later. We made a magazine filled with stories about how mad and sad we were to leave each other. My feelings mirrored hers; we were in this together to the end. I could let her leave me, we could both feel terribly sad and mad about it, and we would still love each other. She left at another developmental period of separation and independence that occurs between ages ten and eleven years in girls (Knight, 1998), using me as the developmental object to assist her achieving this new phase of separation. In Margo's early adolescence, her mother was finally able to become the mother Margo always wanted her to be. They had a very close and loving relationship that also included the normal mother-daughter tensions of adolescence, creating an adolescent narrative that would allow her to develop both attachment and independence in this next phase of development.

In her senior year of high school Margo returned for a brief period of psychotherapy. She wanted my help in understanding what was getting in the way of her succeeding at a school subject that was important to her. I privately wondered about the significance of her coming back to work with me in her last year of high school, when separation once again looms large for the adolescent and her family. I had been the developmental object that had assisted her in achieving earlier levels of separation and autonomy, and I wondered if she sought me out to be the person who would assist this next developmental milestone. I could help her understand her concerns about her mother's welfare while Margo was away at college (a normal developmental conflict in the separation-individuation phase), encourage her separating without any conflictual feelings of my own about her leaving, allow her to be bristly with me as we engaged in this process without the normal parental reaction of hurt and anger, talk with her about how to manage her learning difficulties at college without the normal regressive pull that talking with her parents about this issue engendered, and underline all of her many strengths that would be available to her once she was on her own.

DISCUSSION

When I work with children, development is always in the room, often in a variety of shifting appearances. I feel that my child patient and I are in a race with it. The parents are in the bleachers; sometimes they are cheering us on, from time to time they are ignoring the race because they are too distracted by talking with other parents, now and then they don't show up at all. Sometimes development feels like my opponent. The child's actual age is in the lead and we are running as fast as we can to help the child's emotional and cognitive abilities catch up so that a tie can occur at the finish line. Sometimes development feels like our teammate, something we can count on to help us keep up a fast enough pace to foster the child's psychological development so that the child can catch up to his actual age for a tie finish. Sometimes development feels like a gust of wind that suddenly appears as the child and I are slogging along in our lane and whooshes the child to a tie at the finish line, while I am left in the dust wondering how the hell that happened. And sometimes, when the child has inborn limitations, I have to accept that there will never be a tie finish and the goal becomes helping the child run as much of the track as he is capable of, knowing that development will help us along the way.

Child analysts are always in training for this analytic meet, learning as much as we can about the bio-social-psychological aspects of human development and the techniques that can foster its progression. In the beginning of this paper I discussed some of the contemporary theory and research in development and therapeutic process that has influenced my recent analytic work with children, particularly the use of narrative building. My work with Margo demonstrates some of the many interactional processes that help a narrative evolve over the course of an analysis and how the narrative building technique can aid the developmental process in our analytic work with children.

In my role as a real object I did many things that parents do to aid their child's development. In addition to the interventions that Fonagy and Target delineate as aiding a child's development, I also repaired frequent disruptions in the analytic relationship, which Tronick suggests is an essential part of the development of an interactional system in the developing child. And I did something that all "good enough" parents do and that Freud understood as aiding transformation—I loved, appreciated, and believed in Margo and communicated that to her in language and many nonverbal gestures throughout the analysis.

I also performed many functions as an analyst that parents do not do. I helped her co-discover and co-construct an increasingly elaborated narrative about her past and present. These narratives helped her understand her feelings, conflicts, and defenses that had developed out of her experiences in the past, and showed her how they were now operating to hinder her self representation and interfere with relationships in the present. I did this through the standard analytic technique of following her associative thoughts and feelings in her play and in her relationship with me. I gently pointed out and interpreted her conflicts and the defenses she used to manage the feelings within herself and in our relationship. I also facilitated her forward psychological growth by suggesting alternative ways to think and feel about herself and her reactions as we continually evolved a narrative about her past. I was a transference object who allowed old thoughts, feelings, and interactions to occur in the analytic relationship, promoting an understanding about herself and her parents. As a real object I provided a new, safe relationship within which she could risk testing out and practicing novel ways of thinking about herself and being in a relationship, which allowed her to create new narratives about self and other that increasingly helped her attain age appropriate developmental structures and functioning. And as a developmental object I facilitated the creation of new, hierarchical latency age development (a tie finish).

Although there was a lowered level of discontinuous change in Margo's developing narrative about her relationship with her parents, I believe there were changes in her relationship with me that informed discontinuities and led to the appearance of a transformed mind over time. I think that there are dual narratives in child analysis, one constructed and one created. While Margo and I worked on co-discovering and co-constructing a narrative about herself in the past and in the present with regard to her parents that allowed her to come to terms with her life during the analysis, we also *co-created* a parallel narrative in our relationship that fostered new development.

In all my different object assignments, I first provided her with a feeling of safety in a relationship, a sense that someone could understand her thoughts and feelings and not lose sight of her. She and I created a solid base for our relationship that allowed her to develop trust, a sense of consistency, and mutuality in loving. As we worked on constructing her narrative about her past and present, we were fashioning a novel relationship and establishing new hierarchical narratives about self and other interaction that were being acted out and spoken about. As Margo assimilated this new relationship into her internal structures of self and other, she could then rework an early phase of separation and differentiation in which she could express the rage inherent in the toddler separation-individuation process between mothers and daughters (Mahler, 1981), a necessary developmental precondition to further oedipal development and the triangulation of the mind. Using me as a transference object, she could then act out and feel dyadic competitive feelings with me and then triadic competition with me in relation to her father. This was a hierarchical, developmental progression that was not fully available to her in the first couple of years of our relationship. In this respect, I stood in for her mother, helping her try a new way to work through an earlier phase of development.

Like my very first child patient, Margo understood something about therapeutic action and development that I did not yet fully understand. When we were traversing that difficult period of intense anger, Margo said, "We just have to do it." What she understood better than I was that she needed me to provide her with a different experience that would allow for the assimilation of novel interactions that her old organization could then accommodate, laying down a different structural base that would allow her developmental process to move foreword. My successful fulfillment of this object assignment permitted Margo to then utilize our relationship to help her achieve a reorganization of old intrapsychic and interpersonal structures. Once her psychological development caught up to her appropriate age, she was then able to make use of our relationship to assist her in the creation of latency age development. All this required a balancing act of old, real, and developmental object assignments in my analytic role responsiveness. While the biologically driven developmental process occurs with or without our help, I have no doubt Margo's development would have been significantly hampered without an analysis. I think our mutual desire and energy necessary to create new, more felicitous narratives in our relationship helped facilitate a more robust developmental process.

Abrams and Solnit (1998) define therapeutic action as "those psychological changes that occur once the split-off components of the pathological past are integrated into the prevailing organizational hierarchy. In child analysis, the freed 'old' does more than introduce a new knowing. By simultaneously facilitating novel emotional development, child analysis also promotes a new *way* of knowing old issues; hence the advance is both organizational and integrative. Because future organizations are less burdened, the freeing of the 'old' also assures that the normal developmental progression can resume" (p. 96). It is at those crucial times that child analysts become developmental objects. Once we have paved the way for developmental progression to happen, the child can then make use of us in the novel analytic relationship to reach for and attain the next level of developmental functioning.

The practice of child and adolescent psychoanalysis will continue to benefit from more research in child and adolescent development. We know about the development of psychosexual structures, we are learning about the development of self and object structures in infancy and early childhood, we know about the early separation-individuation process, we are learning about the development of the reflective function, to mention just a few areas of developmental research, but we have yet to map out the intricate internal processes that are involved in the phase specific organization in all of the above. For instance, looking at the process of separation, differentiation and autonomy in normal latency children, I could distinguish many different components of that process that had to be integrated at different ages in latency (Knight, 1998). In a lagging latency development one way to promote development would be to help with the emergence and integration of the new components embedded in the larger separation-individuation structure.

Until we have a better understanding of the layering that occurs in each phase of development, it becomes difficult for me, at times, to distinguish between fostering development, consolidating organizations, and assisting in the pull forward. Also, the lens through which we think about development will determine what we see as necessary preconditions for those transformations to occur, the hierarchy of those transformations, and additional elements that might be necessary in narrative building to promote development. We have come a long way in our understanding of development but, as Anna Freud said, future research will hopefully provide better and better answers to help us nurture and foster the development of our child and adolescent patients.

BIBLIOGRAPHY

ABLON, S. (2001). The work of transformation. *Psychoanal. Study Child,* 56:27–38.

ABRAMS, S. (1980). Therapeutic action and ways of knowing. *J. Amer. Psychoanal. Assn.,* 28:291–308.

——— (1987). The psychoanalytic process: A schematic model. *Int. J. Psychoanal.,* 68:441–452.

——— (1988). The psychoanalytic process in adults and children. *Psychoanal. Study Child,* 43:245–262.

——— (1989). Therapeutic processes: A longitudinal view. *Psychoanal. Study Child,* 44:43–56.

——— (1990). Psychoanalytic process: The developmental and the integrative. *Psychoanal. Q.,* 59:650–677.

——— (1993). How people get better. *Psychoanal. Study Child,* 48:3–8.

——— (1996). Offerings and acceptances: Technique and therapeutic action. *Psychoanal. Study Child,* 51:71–86.

——— (1999). How child and adult analysis inform and misinform one another. *Annual Psychoanal.,* 26:3–22.

———— (2002). Personal Communication.

———— & SOLNIT, A. (1998). Coordinating developmental and psychoanalytic processes. *J. Amer. Psychoanal. Assn.*, 46:85–104.

ABRAMS, S., ET AL. (1999). Coordinating the developmental and psychoanalytic processes: Case reports. *Psychoanal. Study Child*, 54:87–92.

AINSWORTH, M. S., BLEHAR, M. C., WATERS, E., & WALL, S. (1978). *Patterns of Attachment*. Hillsdale, N.J.: Lawrence Erlbaum.

ALEXANDER, F., & FRENCH, T. (1946). *Psychoanalytic Therapy*. New York: The Ronald Press Co.

ARLOW, J. (1993). *Psychoanalysis: Clinical Theory and Practice*. New York: Int. Univ. Press.

———— (1995). Stilted listening: Psychoanalysis as discourse. *Psychoanal. Q.*, 64:215–233.

BEEBE, B., LACHMANN, F., & JAFFE, J. (1997). A transformational model of presymbolic representations: Reply. *Psychoanal. Dialogues*, 7:215–224.

———— (1997). Mother-infant structures interaction, presymbolic self and object. *Psychoanal. Dialogues*, 7:133–182.

BEEBE, B., & LACHMANN, F. (1998). Co-constructing inner and relational processes: Infant & adult. *Psychoanal. Psychol.*, 15:480–516.

BOWLBY, J. (1969). *Attachment and Loss. Vol. I Attachment*. London: Hogarth Press.

———— (1973). *Attachment and Loss: Vol. II. Separation*. London: Hogarth Press.

BUCCI, W. (1997). *Psychoanalysis and Cognitive Science. A Multiple Code Theory*. New York: Guilford Press.

———— (2001). Pathways of emotional communication. *Psychoanal. Inquiry*, 21:40–70.

COHEN, P. M., & SOLNIT, A. J. (1993). Play and therapeutic action. *Psychoanal. Study Child*, 48:49–66.

EDELMAN, G. (1987). *Neural Darwinism: The Theory of Neuronal Group Selection*. New York: Basic Books.

EMDE, R. N. (1983). Pre-representational self and its affective core. *Psychoanal. Study Child*, 38:165–192.

———— (1988a). Development terminable and interminable: Innate and motivational factors. *Int. J. Psychoanal.*, 69:23–42.

———— (1988b). Development terminable and interminable. Considerations for theory and therapy. *Int. J. Psychoanal.*, 69:283–296.

FAJARDO, B. (1998). A new view of developmental research for psychoanalysts. *J. Amer. Psychoanal. Assn.*, 46:185–208.

FIRST, E. (1994). The leaving game, or I'll play you and you play me: The emergence of dramatic role play in 2-year-olds. In Slade, A. & Wolf, D. P. (Eds.) *Children at Play*. New York: Oxford University Press, 111–132.

FONAGY, P. (1999a). Memory and therapeutic action. *Int. J. Psychoanal.*, 80:215–224.

———— (1999b). Process and outcome in mental health care delivery: Treatment. *Bull. Menninger Clin.*, 63:288–304.

———— (1999c). The process of remembering: Recovery and discovery. *Int. J. Psychoanal.*, 80:961–978.

FONAGY, P., KACHELE, H., KRAUSE, R., JONES, E., & PERRON, R. (1999). *An open door review of outcome studies in psychoanalysis: Report prepared by the Research Committee of the IPA at the request of the President.* London: University College London.

FONAGY, P., & TARGET, M. (1996a). Outcome predictors in child psychoanalysis: 763 cases at the Anna Freud Centre., *J. Amer. Psychoanal. Assn.*, 44:27–78.

———— (1996b). Playing with reality I. *Int. J. Psychoanal.*, 77:217–234.

———— (1998a). Mentalization and the changing aims of child psychoanalysis. *Psychoanal. Dialogues*, 8:87–114.

———— (1998b). An interpersonal view of the infant. In Hurry, A. (Ed.) *Psychoanalysis and Developmental Theory.* London: Karnac Books, 3–31.

———— (2000). Playing and reality III. Dual psychic reality in borderline. *Int. J. Psychoanal.*, 81:853–874.

FONAGY, P., ET AL. (1993a). Mental representations and processes in therapeutic action. *Psychoanal. Study Child*, 48:9–48.

———— (1993b). Relationship of parents' representations of childhood and infants' attachment security. *J. Amer. Psychoanal. Assn.*, 41:957–990.

FRAIBERG, S., ADELSON, E., & SHAPIRO, V. (1975). Ghosts in the nursery: A psychoanalytic approach to the problems of impaired infant-mother relationships. *Journal of the American Academy of Child Psychiatry*, 14:387–422.

FRANKEL, J. B. (1998). Play's the thing: Processes of therapy are seen clearly in child psychotherapy. *Psychoanal. Dialogues*, 8:149–182.

FREUD, A. (1965). *The Writings of Anna Freud, Vol. VI.* New York: Int. Univ. Press.

FREUD, S. (1915). The unconscious. *Standard Edition, Vol. XIV.* London: Hogarth Press.

GALATZER-LEVY, R. M. (1995). Psychoanalysis and dynamical system theory: Prediction and self similarity. *J. Amer. Psychoanal. Assn.*, 43:1085–1114.

HOFER, M. (1981). *The Roots of Human Behavior. An Introduction to the Psychobiology of Early Development.* San Francisco: W. H. Freeman.

———— (1984). Relationships as regulators: A psychobiologic perspective on bereavement. *Psychosom. Med.*, 46:183–197.

———— (1996). On the nature and consequences of early loss. *Psychosom. Med.*, 58:570–581.

HOFER, M., & REISER, M. (1969). The development of cardiac rate regulation in preweaning rats. *Psychosom. Med.*, 31:372–388.

HOFER, M., & WEINER, H. (1971). Development and mechanisms of cardiorespiratory responses to maternal deprivation in rat pups. *Psychosom. Med.*, 33:353–362.

———— (1975). Physiological mechanisms for cardiac control by nutritional intake after early maternal separation in the young rat. *Psychosom. Med.*, 37:8–24.

HOFER, M., WOLFF, C., FRIEDMAN, S., & MASON, J. (1972). A psychoendocrine study of bereavement. II. Observations on the process of mourning in relation to adrenocortical function. *Psychosom. Med.*, 34:492–504.

HURRY, A. (1998). Psychoanalysis and developmental theory. In Hurry, A. (Ed.) *Psychoanalysis and Developmental Theory.* London: Karnac Books, 32–73.

JACOBS, T. J. (1986). On countertransference enactments. *J. Amer. Psychoanal. Assn.,* 34:289–308.

——— (1990). The corrective emotional experience: Place in current technique. *Psychoanal. Inquiry,* 10:433–454.

——— (1994). Nonverbal communications in analytic process and analytic education. *J. Amer. Psychoanal. Assn.,* 42:741–762.

——— (2001a). Misreading & misleading patients: Countertransference enactments. *Int. J. Psychoanal.,* 82:653–670.

——— (2001b). On the goals of psychoanalysis, the psychoanalytic process and change. *Psychoanal. Q.,* 70:149–182.

——— (2001c). On unconscious communications & covert enactments. *Psychoanal. Inquiry,* 21:4–23.

——— (2002). Secondary revision: On rethinking the analytic process and analytic technique. *Psychoanalytic Inquiry,* 22:3–38.

JONES, E. (1997). Modes of therapeutic action. *Int. J. Psychoanal.,* 78:1135–1150.

KANTROWITZ, J. (1999). The role of the preconscious in psychoanalysis., *J. Amer. Psychoanal. Assn.,* 47:65–90.

——— (2001). The analysis of preconscious phenomena and its communication. *Psychoanal. Inquiry,* 21:24–39.

KNIGHT, R. (1998). The Process of Separation and Independence in Latency: A longitudinal study. Paper presented at the Beata Rank Lecture, The Boston Psychoanalytic Society and Institute, Boston, Massachusetts, May 14, 1998.

——— (2003). Margo and Me: Gender as a cause and solution to unmet needs. *Psychoanal. Study Child,* 58:35–59.

LACHMANN, F., & BEEBE, B. (1996). Three principles of salience in the patient-analyst interaction. *Psychoanal. Psychol.,* 13:1–22.

LOEWALD, H. (1960). On the therapeutic action of psychoanalysis. Int. J. Psychoanal., 41:16–33.

MAHLER, M. (1981). Aggression re separation-individuation: mother-daughter. *Psychoanal. Q.,* 50:625–638.

MAHLER, M., PINE, F., & BERGMAN, A. (1975). *The Psychological Birth of the Human Infant.* New York: Basic Books.

MAIN, M. (2000). The organized categories of infant, child and adult attachment. *J. Amer. Psychoanal. Assn.,* 48:1055–1127.

MAIN, M., KAPLAN, K., & CASSIDY, J. (1985). Security in infancy, childhood and adulthood: A move to the level of representation. In Bretherton, I., & Waters, E. (Eds.), *Growing Points in Attachment Theory and Research. Monograph of the Society for Research in Child Development,* 50:1–2, Serial No. 209, 276–297.

MALATESTA, C., CULVER, C., TESMAN, J., & SHEPARD, B. (1989). *The Development of Emotion Expression During the First Two Years of Life. Monographs of the Society for Research in Child Development*, 54:1–2, Serial No. 219.

MAYES, L. (1999). Clocks, engines, quarks-love, dreams, genes: What makes development. *Psychoanal. Study Child*, 54:169–192.

—— (2001). The twin poles of order and chaos. *Psychoanal. Study Child*, 56:137–170.

MAYES, L. C., & COHEN, D. J. (1992). Development of capacity for imagination in early childhood. *Psychoanal. Study Child*, 47:23–48.

—— (1996a). Anna Freud and developmental psychoanalytic psychology. *Psychoanal. Study Child*, 51:117–141.

—— (1996b). Children's developing theory of mind. *J. Amer. Psychoanal. Assn.*, 44:117–142.

MAYES, L. C., & SPENCE, D. P. (1994). Therapeutic action in the analytic situation: Developmental metaphor. *J. Amer. Psychoanal. Assn.*, 42:789–818.

MELTZOFF, A. N., & BORTON, W. (1979). Intermodal matching by human neonates. *Nature*, 282:403–404.

MEYERSON, P. (1981). Transactions in other than classical analysis. *Int. Rev. Psychoanal.*, 8:173–190.

MILLER, G. A. (1956). The magical number seven, plus or minus two. *Psychol. Rev.*, 63:81–97.

MORGAN, A. (1997). Application of infant research to psychoanalytic theory and therapy, *Psychoanal. Psychol.*, 14:315–336.

NEUBAUER, P. B. (1994). The role of displacement in psychoanalysis. *Psychoanal. Study Child*, 49:107–119.

—— (1996). Current issues in psychoanalytic child development. *Psychoanal. Study Child*, 51:35–45.

—— (2001). Emerging issues: Some observations about changes in technique in child analysis. *Psychoanal. Study Child*, 56:16–26.

OGDEN, T. (1997). Reverie and metaphor: Thoughts on how I work as a psychoanalyst. *Int. J. Psychoanal.*, 78:719–732.

—— (1998). A question of voice in poetry and psychoanalysis. *Psychoanal. Q.*, 67:426–448.

—— (1999). 'The music of what happens' in poetry and psychoanalysis. *Int. J. Psychoanal.*, 80:979–994.

OSOFSKY, J. D. (1988). Attachment theory, research, and the psychoanalytic process. *Psychoanal. Psychol.*, 5:159–178.

PIAGET, J. (1952). *The Origins of Intelligence in Children*. New York: W. W. Norton & Co., Inc.

—— (1965). *The Moral Judgement of the Child*. New York: The Free Press.

—— (1981). *Intelligence and Affectivity: The Relationship During Child Development*. Palo Alto: Annual Reviews, Inc.

PINE, F. (1985). *Developmental Theory and Clinical Process*. New Haven: Yale University Press.

SANDER, L. (1980). Investigation of the infant and its caregiving environment as a biological system. In *The Course of Life: Vol. 1. Infancy and Early Childhood*. (Ed.) Greenspan, S. I., & Pollock, G. H. Publication No. (ADM)80-786. Washington, DC: DHHS, pp. 177–201.

SANDER, L. (2002). Thinking differently: Principles of process in living systems and the specificity of being known. *Psychoanalytic Dialogues*, 12:11–42.

SANDLER, J. (1987). *From Safety to Superego*. New York, London: Guilford Press.

SCHAFER, R. (1983a). Construction of the psychoanalytic narrative: Introduction. *Psychoanal. Contemp. Thought*, 6:403–404.

——— (1983b). *The Analytic Attitude*. New York: Basic Books.

——— (1985). Interpretation, psychic reality, developmental influences, unconscious. Communication. *J. Amer. Psychoanal. Assn.*, 33:537–554.

SCHARFSTEIN, D. O. (1996). Semiparametric efficiency: Implications for the design and analysis of group sequential studies. Doctoral Dissertation, Harvard University, Boston.

SETTLAGE, C. F. (1980). Psychoanalytic developmental thinking: Current, historical perspective. *Psychoanal. Contemp. Thought*, 3:139–170.

——— (1993). Therapeutic process and developmental process in the restructuring of object and self constancy. *J. Amer. Psychoanal. Assn.*, 41:473–492.

SOLNIT, A. (1998). Beyond play and playfulness. *Psychoanal. Study Child*, 53:102–112.

SPENCE, D. (1982). *Narrative Truth and Historical Truth. Meaning and Interpretation in Psychoanalysis*. New York: W. W. Norton & Co.

STERN, D. (1977). *The First Relationship*. Cambridge, MA: Harvard Univ. Press.

——— (1985). *The Interpersonal World of the Infant*. New York: Basic Books.

——— (1995). *The Motherhood Constellation: A Unified View of Parent-Infant Psychotherapy*. New York: Basic Books.

STERN, D., ET AL. (1998). Non-interpretive mechanisms in psychoanalytic therapy. *Int. J. Psychoanal.*, 79:903–922.

TARGET, M., & FONAGY, P. (1996). Playing with reality II. *Int. J. Psychoanal.*, 77:459–480.

TREVARTHAN, C. (1980). The foundations of intersubjectivity: Development of interpersonal cooperative understanding in infants. In Olsen, D. R. (Ed.). *The Social Foundation of Language and Thought: Essays in Honor of Jerome Bruner*. New York: Norton.

TRONICK, E. (1989). Emotions and emotional communication in infants. *American Psychologist*, 44:112–119.

TRONICK, E., & COHEN, J. (1989). Infant-mother face-to-face interaction: Age and gender differences in coordination and miscoordination. *Child Development*, 59:85–92.

TYSON, P. (2002). Challenges of developmental theory. *J. Amer. Psychoanal. Assn.*, 50:19–52.

WALLERSTEIN, R. (2001). The generations of psychotherapy research: An overview. *Psychoanal. Psychol.*, 18:243–267.

WALLERSTEIN, R., & FONAGY, P. (1999). Psychoanalytic research and the IPA: History, present status, future potential. *Int. J. Psychoanal.*, 80:91–110.

WINNICOTT, D. W. (1965). *The Maturation Process and the Facilitating Environment.* London: Hogarth Press.

YANOF, J. (1996). Language, communication, and transference in child analysis. *J. Amer. Psychoanal. Assn.*, 44:79–116.

Some Notes on the Role of Development in Psychoanalytic Assistance, Differentiation, and Regression

PETER B. NEUBAUER, M.D.

This paper outlines the role of development assistance as a therapeutic measure within the normal psychoanalytic technique. Freud's definition of assistance "that the analyst gives the patient . . . the conscious anticipatory idea to grasp the unconscious material." This proposal is elaborated in the context of developmental differentiation and regression.

THE DISCUSSION ARISING FROM OUR STUDY GROUP HAS LED ME TO further explore my views of the concept of "developmental assistance" and to consider some components of development not previously reviewed.

Our group was alerted to the complexity of the developmental and maturational processes. Proceeding beyond the well-known lines of development, we considered the variations of the developmental blueprint—that is, accelerated or retarded, discrete or overlapping phase emergence, the coexistence of conflicts, and unevenness during various stages of development. We agreed on categorizing developmental disorders as primary and secondary. Primary disorders are those anchored to impairments of the biological blueprint, and sec-

Clinical Professor of Psychiatry, New York University; Editor of *The Psychoanalytic Study of the Child;* Former President of The Association of Child and Adolescent Psychoanalysis.

The Psychoanalytic Study of the Child 58, ed. Robert A. King, Peter B. Neubauer, Samuel Abrams, and A. Scott Dowling (Yale University Press, copyright © 2003 by Robert A. King, Peter B. Neubauer, Samuel Abrams, and A. Scott Dowling).

ondary disorders arise from many sources, for example, the consequences of deviations within the ego apparatuses, or impoverishment or excesses in the environment, products of the two, or dynamic conflicts that are of such a nature that they constrain rather than promote the expected progression.

Analysts are accustomed to looking back upon the origin of disorders: they trace the line of continuity from an earlier time to the current one. The child analyst is also required to look forward, a far more complex task. Freud (1920) recognized this need:

> So long as we trace the chain of development from its final outcome backwards, the chain of events appears continuous, and we feel we have gained an insight which is completely satisfactory or even exhaustive. But if we proceed in the reverse way, if we start from the premises inferred from the analysis and try to follow these up to results, then we no longer get the impression of an inevitable sequence of events which could not have been otherwise determined.... But we never know beforehand which of the determining factors will prove the weaker or the stronger. We only say at the end that those which succeeded must have been stronger. Hence the chain of causation can always be recognized with certainty if we follow the line of analysis, whereas to predict it along the line of synthesis is impossible. (pp. 167–168)

When Freud speaks of the determining factors that will prove the weaker or the stronger, he refers to the biologically determined influences, to the strengths of the ego, or to vulnerabilities based upon environmental conditions. He also implies that these various determinants can never be known at one particular past period, but rather will reveal themselves through development as it proceeds in a *discontinuous* fashion.

It is this latter point that is so often absent in some presentations of the psychoanalytic treatment of children. We find references in case reports about the child's age-related conflicts, but what also is required is the focus on the developmental transformation of pathology or the various points of fixation, or an assessment of the normal discontinuities along with the continuities, of the strength or weakness of the developmental pull forward, and so on. An additional glaring contemporary clinical deficiency is the tendency to assign all pathology to the earliest mother/child dyad, attributing to it the inevitable core of lasting malfunction. This might be called the "continuity fallacy." Uncorrectable early pathology is well known, but this cannot be so readily generalized while ignoring so many of the complexities or variations in ego development, transformations, and the effect of discontinuities on development.

Assistance: What is the role of assistance in the area of developmental pathology? I have used the term in a broad sense, relying on the way Freud approached the issue of technique. Freud (1912) notes,

> In a psycho-analysis the physician always gives his patient (sometimes to a greater and sometimes to a lesser extent) the conscious anticipatory ideas by the help of which he is put in a position to recognize and to grasp the unconscious material. For there are some patients who need more of such assistance and some who need less; but there are none who get through without some of it. Slight disorders may perhaps be brought to an end by the subject's unaided efforts, but never a neurosis—a thing which has set itself up against the ego as an element alien to it. To get the better of such an element another person must be brought in, and in so far as that other person be of assistance the neurosis will be curable.

The assistance Freud refers to here requires the analyst's ability to anticipate the unfolding dynamics, his knowing what is likely to come. Such assistance is offered in preparation for the interpretation of the associated experience.

This readily extends itself to the treatment of children. A child analyst is required to anticipate the influence of the developmental features that affect growth. The task is not only to reconstruct the pathogenic past but to be aware of the child's active construction of the future, that is, the analyst must be alert to both analysis and synthesis. This knowledge establishes him in the position to be of assistance to the move forward, analogous to assisting a patient in preparation for an appropriate interpretation. In a sense, knowledge of the developmental components must be a component of every child and adolescent analysis because such factors are so prominent. Perhaps they play a role in the components of adults as well. No doubt there are some children, perhaps Little Hans was one of them, who may benefit principally by providing the assistance needed to overcome the neurosis through interpretation, without the necessity of also facilitating other faulty features of development. Nevertheless, even in such circumstances, a child analyst must be fully aware of the many features of progressive development that are active within the patient as the neurotic conflict is resolved to fully leverage the resultant freedom to thrive.

Invariably, when confronted with developmental disorders, we require additional technical interventions to provide some assistance to overcome those other factors that constrain the progression. Sometimes these extra efforts require the analyst to see to it that certain deficiencies in the ego apparatuses acquire remedial help, or to intervene where the environment does not permit an appropriate unfolding or to try ways to achieve balance when there is unevenness in development. These and other factors can secondarily impair development in addition to the neuroses.

The concept of assistance to development is especially necessary in those instances where the usual psychoanalytic technique is insufficient to free development to proceed. Assisting development is a complex technical activity, involving first and foremost an intimate knowledge of the various features of the growing mind and particularly the influences of the discontinuous processes upon them. As Freud noted, only by anticipating what is to come is it possible to render the appropriate technical tool, interpretation in the instance of the repressed unconscious, a variety of other interventions in the instance of developmental pathology.

DIFFERENTIATION AND REGRESSION

Two components of development are also immediately connected to our topic of techniques that render assistance to development.

Differentiation: All theories of development accept the finding that development proceeds from global organizations and responses to more differentiated ones, whether in cognition or affect, or object relations. Differentiation influences all the components of growth. It is therefore surprising that little attention is given to the role of developmental sequences in the course of growth in spite of Anna Freud's "lines of development," which is, after all, nothing more nor less, than a guide along the path of progressive differentiation. There is considerable emphasis today on the role of the synthesizing, integrating, and organizing functions. Object relations theory, for example, stresses the interactive experience between mother and child, ways in which the affective and cognitive influences of the mother establish the cohesive self of the child. These theories propose "that insecure attachments confer vulnerability because they fail to offer children interpersonal experiences that foster an integrative self-organizational process." However, such a proposition excludes the role of developmentally determined processes of differentiation. The recognition of the significance of differentiation gains importance because there are children who maintain a basic undifferentiated self-state, but are able to coordinate and organize their functions, and there are those where highly differentiated mental conditions cannot be integrated into a stable organization. Integration can accomplish a sense of coherence among a wide variety of multiple differentiated conditions. Viewed from this perspective, Mahler's work on separation-individuation, her outline of the many steps to achieve the evolvement of a cohesive self, is clearly based on the activities of differentiation. In her view, the establishment of autonomy is the result of a process that differentiates the object from the self. However, attachment leads not only to integration but demands differentiation. Mother's role of pleasure and comfort-giving provides the child with the capacity to become himself. New states of differentiation lead to new integration and autonomy formation. It is revealing that Mahler did not propose these as steps of progressive attachment, but regarded her work to be an investigation into separation and individuation.

Whether they are aware of it or not, analysts contribute to the differentiating progression. They do that in a variety of ways. The analysis of the transference invariably aids in the differentiation between the repetition of the past as it distorts present reality, while the analysis of wishful thinking or past fears is more and more measured by secondary process thinking as differentiating interventions and interpretations have their impact. This is also valid for the analytic contribution of the differentiation of affect from basic, global pain-pleasure experiences to the more differentiated affect modulation.

I give attention to this topic because I believe that a careful examination of the analytic role in promoting differentiation will give us new insight into the pivotal role this plays in achieving optimal developmental progression. The process of psychoanalysis is to undo distortions and points of developmental fixation in order to free the developmental differentiation. Only then can new stages of integration and organization be established.

Regression: Earlier, I referred to the innate timetable that determines the accelerated pull or delay in progression.

There are those children with developmental characteristics who seem to avoid the regressive move and there are children who seem to possess an elasticity in the forward or backward developmental movement. Further, neither the progression nor the regression or fixation necessarily occurs across the developmental organization as a whole. It may affect only one component, either aggression or libidinal expressions, for example, or one or more of the factors of the ego apparatus—language, motility, or reality assessment. Unless the regression leads to points of fixation, regressive activities may not be pathological on their own, in fact they may facilitate development. They do so by permitting a return to earlier non-conflictual or conflictual stages in order to overcome those unresolved conflicts and other impediments so that development may proceed.

I am leaning on a term coined by Ernst Kris: *controlled regression of the ego* (1934). He addressed the question of how the ego is able to keep control as it gives up what has been achieved, some of the higher differentiated and organizing functions. Often this phenomenon is referred to as regression in the service of the ego. The inability to regress may at times be a sign of disorder. We know, for example, of the regressive period during adolescence where the revival of the preoedipal conditions offers a new chance to correct earlier pathology in order to move toward a new cohesion of the self or to a secondary individuation. This regression facilitates development, by allowing the evolvement of a new autonomy by reducing the idealization of the primary objects.

One can also observe regression under the influence of trauma when latent fears are triggered to become manifest. During the posttraumatic stage there may be a loosening of the defenses that offers the opportunity to analyze unresolved and until then repressed conflicts. These regressive movements may increase the need for the therapist to be a real person in whose presence there is safety. Thereby certain resistances to analysis may be given up. As Freud (1912) states, "Psycho-analytic work shows us every day that translations of this kind (from unconscious to the conscious) is possible. In order that this should come about, the person under analysis must overcome certain resistances, the same resistances as those which earlier made the material concerned into something repressed by rejecting it from the conscious."

From a developmental point of view, regression is another attempt to overcome these "resistances" and opens the opportunity to resolve the old problems. Analysts who are unfamiliar with such components of development may be inclined to simply view regression as inimical to analytic progress rather than being, at times, an assist of it.

In his paper, "The Function of Regression in Clinical Situations," Schlesinger emphasized that regressive phenomena are "always with us," and are inextricably linked with intrapsychic conflicts. He views regressive phenomena as the expectable result of proper analyzing and considers that "they are indeed necessary for the patient."

Contemporary brain research affirms these views of these essential components of development. Allan Schore (1998) writes, "the organization of brain systems does not involve a simple pattern of increments but rather large changes in organization. Development, the process of self assembly, thus involves both progressive and regressive phenomena, and is best characterized as a sequence of processes of organization, disorganization and reorganization." Here he confirms the discontinuities in development. As psychoanalysts we usually speak of developmental hierarchical reorganization and he adds that disorganization is part of a 'normal' developmental process. It may be fruitful to include this in our formulations.

I look forward to future studies of children committed to observing more carefully the progressive and regressive developmental balances during treatment, thereby introducing additional opportunities for more effective interventions that will assist the progression.

BIBLIOGRAPHY

FREUD, S. (1912). Analysis of a phobia in a 5-year-old boy. *S.E.* 10:14. In Levy, Donald, *Freud among the Philosophers* (1996). New Haven: Yale University Press.

FREUD, S. (1914). The unconscious. *S.E.* 14:156.

FREUD, S. (1920). The psychogenesis of a case of homosexuality in a woman. *S.E.* 18:147–72. In *Jrnl of A. Psa. A.* 47, 4. Fall 1999 p. 1056.

KRIS, E. (1934). *The Psychology of Character.* Selected Essays (1975). New Haven: Yale University Press.

SCHLESINGER, S. In GOLDBERG S. (1999). "Regression: Essential clinical condition or latrogenic phenomena?" *Jrnl. A. Psa. A.* 47/4, p. 1170.

SCHORE, A. (1998). Brain and values. In Siegel, D. *The Developing Mind.* New York: Guilford Press, pp. 337–338.

SIEGEL, D. (1999). *The Developing Mind,* New York: Guilford Press, p. 314.

Looking Forwards and Backwards

SAMUEL ABRAMS, M.D.

A study group examines ways of clinically integrating the developmental process with the psychoanalytic process. The intentions of the group are described along with the degree to which its aims are realized. The capacity to bring together the expectations of the future and the pathogenic impact upon the past proves to be a challenging endeavor for the child clinician. Some obstacles are confronted and a variety of ways of overcoming them are regarded.

INTRODUCTION

FOR SOME YEARS, THE PSYCHOANALYTIC RESEARCH AND DEVELOPment Fund has been sponsoring study groups on the treatment of children. Many of these were informed by an interest in coordinating the requirements of the naturally evolving developmental process with the therapeutically created analytic one. This report summarizes the activities of the latest of these study groups.[1] It was specifically constituted to address the practical task of adding tools to the analyst's technical repertoire that could optimize the potential of the unrealized future without interfering with engaging the pathogenic

---

1. The group was composed of Samuel Abrams and Albert J. Solnit, who acted as co-chairmen, and Alice Colonna, Karen Gilmore, Leon Hoffman, Nasir Ilahi, Rona Knight, Claudia Lament, Roy K. Lilleskov, Peter B. Neubauer, Wendy Olesker, Mortimer Ostow, Noah Shaw, and Judy Yanof.

Training and supervising psychoanalyst, adult and child sections, The Psychoanalytic Institute at the New York University School of Medicine; Clinical Professor, Department of Psychiatry, New York University School of Medicine.

The Psychoanalytic Study of the Child 58, ed. Robert A. King, Peter B. Neubauer, Samuel Abrams, and A. Scott Dowling (Yale University Press, copyright © 2003 by Robert A. King, Peter B. Neubauer, Samuel Abrams, and A. Scott Dowling).

past, or, in other words, to help child analysts fruitfully look forwards and backwards at the same time.

The object of this paper is to summarize the group's experiences. What concrete proposals were forthcoming to broaden how child analysts think about their work? How do these additional ways of thinking translate into new ways of acting? What were the useful findings and where did the research fall short? And what future studies might be entertained to enhance the yield?

Quite early during the group's deliberations, it was demonstrated that there was at least one circumstance in which the analyst could incorporate the developmental features rather easily because the progression was relatively unfettered. Two participants offered brief presentations illustrating their analytically informed treatment of two pre-pubescent girls. Each girl established a "best friend" scenario with her analyst. Within the setting of confiding to her very best friend—a typical style for pre-adolescent girls as they move forward—many past conflicts and features of disordered structures were successfully addressed. Both treatments went well.

This outcome led to a hypothesis: where the developmental process is otherwise *unimpaired,* the analytic alliance can be constructed with children in an object-related style that arises naturally from their prevailing hierarchical organization. Within this freshly constructed interaction, the untoward past may then be more effectively addressed even as the future is being actualized. From the standpoint of adding to the analyst's customary ways of thinking and acting, all that would be required is the ability to accept being appropriately costumed for the drama. When development is moving along its expectable steps, child analysts need only be flexible enough to employ their customary approach within newly framed role assignments. It is not necessary to consider particular ways to facilitate or assist development.

This initial observation and hypothesis led to differentiating the various features of the child analytic relationship. The pre-pubescent girls illustrated how analysts may become "new" objects, "new" in the sense that the accepted assignment was derived from the specific object need of the freshly emerging hierarchy. Within this conceptual model, analysts may successively be extracted as needed Oedipal actors, as aiding the repression in latency, as very best friends, as comrades in adolescence, and as sources of object removal in early adulthood. Such "new" objects can occur alongside of the analyst being actual or "real" objects, real in the sense of possessing and providing noticeable traits that may be used for growth through identification.

For example, the analyst's behavior can include being "cool" under fire, that is, tolerating affective storms and being reflective while illustrating the logical thinking that moves from observations to conclusions. Identifications with these "real" aspects of the analyst are part of every treatment action, with adults as well as children. These real features may also be viewed descriptively as "new" offerings for those children who have not been exposed to adults with such traits. It seemed useful to some of the participants to take this descriptive "new" and differentiate the conceptual "real" and "new" subsumed within it, while others had little difficulty holding on to the distinctions with the same term. And, finally, every analyst anticipates being experienced as an object from the patient's past as the unconscious pathogens are revived and confronted. This mixing of the past, the real, and the new can prove to be confusing and cumbersome to both patient and analyst, yet successfully differentiating and balancing them may prove necessary for optimally coordinating the analytic process with the developmental. The cases of the pre-pubescent girls reflect an ease of balance because the developmental process was relatively unencumbered.

The discussion put another conceptual proposal into play. Instead of thinking of the analytic interaction in the global term, *transference,* it might be helpful to differentiate what features the child was extracting from the transaction moment to moment.

Additional goals sprung quickly from these promising beginnings. The pre-pubescent girls were not unusually challenging because the expectable sequences of growth were in place. But, what if the developmental process was compromised? The focus turned to consider children where the move forward is clearly burdened. Over the course of the study, quite a few patients were described, often briefly to illustrate a point of view, while two cases were examined with greater depth so that the elements of the treatment process could be tracked more closely. Eight monthly meetings were scheduled. A transcript of each meeting was made available to all members prior to the next one to insure accuracy and promote clarity.

The search was on for further conceptual proposals, fresh ways to think about clinical data. It encountered several major obstacles that have been met before in similar study groups. These included: (1) how to add something new to previously preferred positions; (2) what to add in the face of definitional differences about the process of development; (3) finding suitable words that can convey the additions; and (4) assessing the compatibility of balancing such different domains as development and analysis.

OBSTACLES

The first obstacle. Everyone agreed on the necessity of attending to clinical data, but differences in preferred orientations surfaced quickly, affecting the observational yield. It is difficult to look upon the ambiguities that abound in clinical settings without some organizing perspective. In Piagetian terms—and his name appeared often during the meetings (see especially Knight, 2003)—intellectual growth proceeds within the dialectic of assimilative and accommodative forces. Consequently, data are invariably extracted from clinical observations informed by one preferred way of thinking or another. Organizing perspectives are necessary for taking information in, but rigidly adhered to perspectives limit what can be seen. Science can advance only when some observations succeed in modifying informing theories enough so that they can be used to find something different during subsequent research. With this in mind, the group turned to trying to introduce propositions of development into the mix of perspectives and study the yield.

What might those additions be?

The second obstacle. Regrettably, the developmental process does not enjoy definitional consensus. It is a subject that is mired in both controversy and confusion. In the broadest of strokes, some developmental theorists are rooted in *continuity*. They focus on the earliest times of growth, assuming that the foundation that is laid down in the first months or years will leave an indelible mark on the course of growth thereafter. In addition, many who are analytically trained are inclined to attend almost exclusively to dynamics and object-related encounters. For such theorists, no additional orienting perspective is seen as necessary to understand development; in fact some believe that additions only obfuscate the analytic encounter. In our group, their voices provided a useful counterpoint to what engaged many of the others.

The group centered on a set of propositions that acknowledges continuity but also recognizes that development is *discontinuous,* occurring within a series of progressively differentiated hierarchical psychological organizations that arise over time. These propositions have a distinguished psychoanalytic history. They first appeared in the literature in the early writings of Freud. They were further elaborated in the works of Anna Freud, and, elaborated further still by a variety of highly regarded theorists.[2] One of those is Peter B.

2. See, for example, Olesker (2003), Knight (2003), and Neubauer (2003).

Neubauer, a member of the study group who has been, and continues to be, a steady guide for these research endeavors.

This psychoanalytic theory of the developmental process entails several hypotheses: (1) there exists an inherent biologically determined maturational program that informs a potential sequence of hierarchically ordered steps; (2) the steps become actualized in the form of new organizations as emerging internal structures interact with stimuli in the surround; (3) each succeeding organization has a transformational impact upon development as each ushers in novel ways of thinking, feeling, and behaving.

What could be done to persuade child analysts to think about the presence of this inherent program as they evaluate and treat children?

The task is made more arduous because the process is subject to variations, not to mention deviations. The *impetus* that fuels the pull forward may vary widely, ultimately impacting upon the potential for consolidation. The *style* of the emerging sequence, balanced between progressive and regressive swings, may vary as well, for example, in some instances, new organizations may entirely replace pre-existing ones, in others, later organizations may interweave with some earlier ones, or overlap, intersect, and so on. Sometimes the pull forward may crest in an earlier step, rather than in the expectable later ones. In addition, some of the emerging internal realms such as those that guide instinctual development, ego development, and the representation of objects may not arise at appropriately equivalent times, casting the additional burden of *unevenness* upon the progression. Furthermore, some necessary structures or functions may be limited by virtue of disposition, thereby additionally hampering growth by saddling integrative efforts. And finally, since appropriate persons and stimuli arising from the environment are essential for the inevitable organizational yield, different qualities of nutrients need to be available often from the same pool of persons in the child's surround over long periods of time.

The third obstacle. Different theories, different definitions are problematic enough. There is also a language problem. The conversation of psychoanalysis is filled with a language dominated by dynamic and object-related phrases. Analysts readily observe conflicts, comfortably make inferences about drives and defenses. The impact of relationships is tangible and, with children, immediate. Patients usually introduce their experiences within descriptions of encounters and dilemmas. But what language is available to define the influences of such covert developmental influences as impetus? What does an impaired impetus look like and how would a patient record its effect or distinguish the ongoing sensations from experiences derived from other sources? As for the variations in the progressive unfolding of organizations, many analysts think of psychological organizations as discretely differentiated entities, earlier ones being re-organized into later ones or earlier ones being so dominant that later ones fail to surface. What would overlap or interweave look like? We require a new language to begin to bring such silent processes into awareness.

Even with the use of a limited language, however, many members of the group were prepared to accept the idea that deviations within the program itself introduce a class of disturbances that may be designated as primary developmental disorders. Those members felt that it would be useful to incorporate these concepts into the clinician's thinking to facilitate the tasks of appraising and treating children. Amongst other things, attending to dispositional variations induces analysts to explore the way children can create their parents, that is, perceive them, extract certain features over others, incorporate them, just as attention to historical details and dynamics has always helped explain how parents create children.

The subordinate psychoanalytic realms of instincts, ego, and objects may also saddle the developmental process—*secondarily*. Unlike the more silent influences, drives, ego functions, and object representations noisily engage the attention of analysts. It is well known that unresolved dynamic conflicts can secondarily interfere with development. When a neurotic disorder constrains the developmental progression, analysis becomes the treatment of choice. Ego and object deficiencies may also induce a disturbance, secondarily. A dispositional impairment that cramps a crucial ego function such as appears in autism invariably interferes with the developmental progression. This requires the application of very different tools than an analyst is generally familiar with. A serious deficiency in the environmental stimuli may require the child analyst to consider some form of intervention with parents to make the surround more congenial for growth. At least one analyst in the group expressed the idea that this is almost always necessary with developmentally challenged children, whatever the etiology.

These considerations immediately lead to a useful classification of developmental disorders: primary developmental disorders, derived from deviations within the biologically inspired program itself, and secondary developmental disorders, arising from dynamic, dispositional or environmental impoverishments or excesses that saddle the process—even when the inherent program remains intact. (See also

Neubauer, 2003). However, to be able to do something about such disorders requires that analysts first acquire a language to think about them.

The fourth obstacle. A nagging question surfaced throughout the year's study. For some of the participants it was a central question and for a few never satisfactorily resolved. While it might be helpful to address children with these additional perspectives, is thinking about them in this way compatible with working with them analytically altogether? The answers were, regrettably, yes and no.

Developmental deviations can produce unusual symptoms and signs. Is analysis possible altogether for such children? As far as method is concerned, *no,* if analysis means using an interpretative approach that leads to the discovery of a patient's hidden world of pathogenic object relations and dynamic conflicts; *yes,* if analysis can be stretched to also mean helping patients co-create their inevitable conflicts and move them toward resolution.

As far as aim in concerned, *no,* analysis is not possible, if analysis means principally discovering the unconscious, that is, the dynamically repressed; *yes,* analysis is possible, if interpretation can be extended to include the bringing into awareness of unrecognized configurations of structures and processes as well as fantasies, that is, addressing the unrecognized—unrecognizable until is acquires language linkages—as well as the unconscious.

As for focus of interest, *yes,* analysis is possible independent of the difficulties in development, if the treatment ultimately attends to the influence of early mother-child interactions and oedipal conflicts; *no,* such a view privileges one feature of the mind over another, thereby interfering with new discoveries. Analysis should always allow for the prospect of discoveries.

As for the analytic scope, *yes,* the developmental additions are analytic if propositions of development can be included along with object-relations and conflicts as treatable through psychological means; *no,* such a treatment could not fall into the analytic domain, if developmental propositions are to be regarded as a different order of pathogenesis, requiring other forms of therapeutic activity.

And what of the mode of therapeutic action? Can the analytic process and the developmental process ever be truly integrated or is their treatment action so different that only degrees of co-ordination are possible? The most valued yields of the developmental process and the analytic process are transformations. However that yield derives from different sources. In development, transformations are an outgrowth of consolidating new organizations. This occurrence is readily observed at all stages of development, although how this happens is steeped in mystery. Analytic success is also measured by its transformational yield—this means something more than simply new compromise-formations. The transformations are hypothesized to occur when the components of unconscious conflicts and impaired object relations are discovered, taken apart, and put back together in a different way. Why this new mix of old components sometimes has a transformational yield is equally mysterious.

When analysts help development move forward they hope for the transformational yield arising from the crystallizing fresh organizational step. When they promote an analysis, they hope for the yield arising from new integrations often experienced as insights. Are these different transformational yields compatible with one another? Theoretically, at first blush, there seems to be no conflict. The difficulties mostly arise from the analyst being required to attend to shifting object seeking as the developmental and the analytic intersect in the treatment. So, *yes,* adding developmental concepts lies within the domain of analysis, since the aim of transformations is the same; *no,* it does not lie within the domain of analysis, because the transformations that occur arise from very different sources, more organizational rather than integrative.

Can you incorporate developmental concepts into your thinking and still practice analysis? The question remains open but concerns that the answer might be "no" may constrain some child analysts from trying.

CLINICAL DATA

These obstacles were concretely engaged during the extensive discussion of the case of a girl named Sandy. A detailed description is included in this volume (Olesker, 2003).

Sandy showed signs of a delayed and derailed development. She had many presenting difficulties that hampered her capacities for engagement. She had problems in sequencing, in connecting feelings with ideas, and in pulling together the ordinary kinds of stories that children create as they try to make some sense of themselves and the world around them. Her history included a physical disability that limited her motility in the early years of life. Olesker, the analyst who treated her, judged the parenting as adequate, although, some participants in the group were prone to find limitations. Sandy was anxious, confused, angry, and sad. Many, including Olesker, had the impression that the earlier expectable phase organizations were held together rather weakly. Consequently, it was hypothesized that a low impetus for the progression, that is, a primary developmental disorder, could account for some of the presenting difficulties.

However, it was also evident that there existed unsettled conflicts, ego deficiencies, and impaired personal relationships. Was it the failure of the process that burdened these areas or were burdensome areas the cause of the failing process, that is, was the more fundamental diagnosis a primary or a secondary developmental disorder?

Armed with her broader view of a child's mind, Sandy's analyst moved vigorously to do something about these problematic terrains. She applied herself to the conflicts, using transference models. She took note of the ego weaknesses and assisted Sandy in naming, in connecting and containing feelings, and in creating narratives to help bring coherence into Sandy's world. She buttressed the noticeably limited integrative capacities and, by her real behavior, illustrated ways of tolerating poorly regulated affects. She also tried to ally herself with the emerging needs of new phases. In short she tapped the therapeutic virtues of being a past, real, and new object at different times and sometimes, it seemed, all at once. However, at least one group participant, Nasir Ilahi, took issue with the entire approach (Ilahi, 2003). He held to the position that Sandy's development was possibly derailed because of deficiencies arising principally from early (and continuing) difficulties within Sandy's relationships with her caretakers, compounded by her considerable early physical tribulations. Acknowledging the inevitable role of biological and dispositional factors in growth, he argued that the boundary between the biological and psychological was being too narrowly drawn in this case. Within the ambiguous setting of the clinical situation, he is disposed to look closely first to the patient's *internal* dynamics, as they unfold in the transference relationship, before being in a position to comment on dispositional determinants. In fact, he suggested that premature attention to a hypothetical biologically determined inherent program or to ego apparatuses could be distracting. In the case illustration, a broader view encompassing developmental propositions was unnecessary in order to understand what was transpiring. Early development, he argued from a different orienting perspective, occurs in close conjunction with object relationships, whereby the unintegrated aspects of the infant's self are enabled to come together through the "holding" and "containment" provided by effective parenting. He emphasized the continuing effects of this early dynamic on all that follows. For him, Sandy's clinical picture suggested a failure within the mother/child dyad, leaving her with considerable anxieties and dissociated aspects of herself that she lived out in the treatment and her relationships. Often he demonstrated his position through line-by-line analysis of transcript. By focusing on the transference, he went on, and especially the way Sandy's unbearable destructive aspects were deployed through projective identifications within the interaction, it was possible to perhaps gradually enable Sandy to bring together these split off and unbearable feelings, and aspects of herself, so that they could become thinkable and thus create conditions under which development could take place. For him, the only technical tool necessary was the time-honored one of appropriately attuned interpretation of these issues in the transference. This "interpretation" not only meant discovering, it also meant the analyst's ability to help Sandy in gathering together the various split off parts of herself, liberating the thinking capacities of the child.

Ilahi's conceptualization of development had the advantage of parsimony. Since it echoed long-honored postulates, it coordinated readily with analytic views of treatment action, the influences of the past, and the value of interpretations. It put aside the need to try to balance the features of two very different domains by merging the one into the other.

However, his point of view was disputed on a variety of grounds. For some participants, it seemed as if he was too heavily influenced by a pre-existing theoretical formulation. For others, it appeared that the clinical picture could not be so readily explained by such proposed concepts. The mind of a developing child is far more complex than Ilahi's reconstructions implied. They believed that it was simply not possible to rely on continuities alone to account for all that transpires as the mature mind emerges. It says something about the limits of group process that neither Ilahi nor those who disputed him were to change their views very much despite protracted discussions.

The search turned toward understanding the technical novelties that appeared to have assisted Sandy's flagging development. These included the buttressing of failing functions, attending to problems in affect regulation, and frankly supportive actions designed to limit disorganizing tendencies. It also included using the person of the analyst not only to revive the past but as a real backup for failing current functions. And the analyst was also assigned to be a new object that could be used to meet the requirements of the developmental phase that was surfacing, however limiting the pull forward might have been.

As the treatment moved forward it was clear that Sandy was better put together and the world about her was more comprehensible. It

seemed to many members of the group that she had particularly benefited from a technique that was dominated by what came to be
called the co-constructing of narratives. The stories that were created
during the treatment served many functions. Sometimes, the analyst
would supply words to object encounters and chaotic feelings that
the patient could not locate on her own. Sometimes, the new stories
provided containers for affects that threatened the patient's coherence, thus acquiring a regulating function. They also had the effect
of permitting the patient a series of explanations for her difficulties
that she could comprehend. The narratives helped her to locate herself and others in some tangible space. This seemed to be true
whether the constructions were entirely accurate or not so long as
they made some sort of sense. Co-constructing narratives is a form of
intervention in itself, quite aside from its influence upon other path-
ologic areas.

The group also wondered if co-constructing narratives was also a
way of facilitating the developmental process in a more primary way,
not merely by buttressing the faltering functions that were necessary
for development to move forward. New organizations often organize
around the kernels of coherent narratives that promote the consolidation of freshly surfacing phases. The psychoanalytic model for this
is the way that the oedipal conflict promotes the consolidation of the
oedipal organization and leaves the structural yield of the superego
in its wake. The integrity of the developmental process assures the
transformations that occur in the march toward maturity, transformations that often are abetted as narratives move on to structures. If
such necessary narratives could be enabled in the work with children, perhaps with the analyst herself briefly extracted as a *new* object
for the fresh drama, could this effectively provide assistance for a
progression otherwise saddled by a weak impetus (a primary developmental disorder), and thereby help actualize the transformational
potential? The question was asked but could not be answered, because the narratives provided assistance for Sandy for so many other
functions that it was difficult to see if the program that guided the developmental process was also served in a more direct fashion.

Narrative building became an important subject for the group.
Rona Knight (2003) prepared a comprehensive paper on the subject.
In her paper, she usefully differentiates co-creating and co-discovering, co-creating serving just as significant a function for developmental disorders as co-discovering does for neurotic ones.

Another case presentation demonstrated a different technical strategy that might arise if developmental propositions are added to the orientating mix.

In this second case presented as process notes over time, a young boy struggled with feelings of helplessness in terms that reflected an angry conflict with an early mother—too engulfing or too remote. This struggle was also apparent in terms of phallic assertion, exerting the power of masculinity as a triumph of separateness and conquest. The participants in the group seemed divided about ways of addressing the data. Some were inclined to take the position that treatment action depended upon dealing with the earlier mother/child conflict, arguing that the later phallic elements were merely displaced expressions of the more fundamental earlier conflict. Others viewed it the other way around, that is, the phallic conflict was surfacing and only metaphorically being re-enacted in "oral" terms. Did the clinical picture represent a regressive expression of a later stage or the persistence of an earlier one because of a fixation? How an analyst thinks about that influences the kind of action she is likely to take.

However, awareness of the developmental propositions offered a third possibility. Phases do not necessarily swing forward and backward in sharply differentiated ways. They can also overlap or interweave. Perhaps this child's particular unfolding psychological configuration that features overlap could account for the clinical picture. If so, the analyst would be required to attend to both conflicts. To privilege either one would be surrendering to a theoretical point of view about developmental styles that fails to engage the many possibilities.

DISCUSSION

What were the accomplishments of the study group and what else might still be done? These questions were specifically addressed as the meetings came to a close.

For some members, the achievements were viewed as modest, little more than the adding of different words and phrases to describe ways they've practiced all along. To others, it was seen as having a more radical impact upon their work with children. For this latter group, the yield could be divided into conceptual ones—additional ways of thinking—and practical ones—additional ways of intervening.

The study posits the view that there are many psychological illnesses in children that require evaluative perspectives that go beyond conventional analytically informed approaches. It may be useful to expand the customary perspectives for the sake of a large group of developmentally challenged children.

Often overlooked, are the hypotheses that inform the developmental process. However, introducing a developmental perspective requires analysts to overcome a variety of obstacles that they are somewhat reluctant to confront. The group addressed different definitions of the developmental process and considered the prospects implicit in two of them. A useful conceptualization of the process may prove necessary for the clinician, but for many analysts some of the propositions raised in the course of the study appeared either too cumbersome, inconsequential, or irrelevant. One participant thought that even the word "assistance" seemed to trivialize a therapeutic endeavor dominated by such substantive interventions as interpretation and reconstruction. One aim of future studies would be to more effectively demonstrate the clinical applications of propositions such as these, dignifying the act of differentiating how, where, and when to intervene with "assistance."

Conceptual proposals about classification and treatment action were also introduced. This study suggests that it may be important to differentiate a primary from a secondary developmental disorder. It may also be useful to distinguish transformations accruing from the developmental progression from those that occur with customary analytic work. Can one be leveraged to support the other or does each remain fundamentally outside of the other? Only future clinical research can provide answers to these questions.

Additional studies, leveraged by such concepts, might clear up other clinical matters as well. Will symptoms and signs of illness be looked upon differently? Are there new formulations waiting to inform those symptoms and signs more usefully? And finally the domain issue: what falls inside and what is outside of the analytic domain? And why is that so urgent an issue for some analysts?

Another conceptual contribution was the differentiating of features of the therapeutic interaction. Some members thought it would be beneficial if the global term "transference" were to give way to a differentiation of the objects embedded in that term. Old, real, and new objects were proposed as possible starting points for that differentiation. At times the term "developmental object" surfaced, sometimes used descriptively to mean the different ways that analysts help development, at other times used technically to specifically describe the "new" object feature that occurs in child analysis. There were moments when the term "developmental object" threatened to challenge the term "transference" in its diffuseness.

If modes of therapeutic action entail transformational processes, it should also prove useful to distinguish the transformations that occur in successful development from those that occur in successful analyses. This was also raised as a future subject for study.

In addition to these conceptual issues, several technical proposals arose in the group. In one it was noted that narrative building is useful to overcome disorders of development, certainly when development is derailed secondarily because of aberrant apparatuses or impaired object-relations and possibly in some primary disorders where the narratives may promote the consolidation of the new hierarchies. A second technical addition addressed the style of the progression. Guided by knowledge of the consequences of different styles, analysts may be able to view clinical data in a fashion that will have a beneficial yield for their work. For example, the concept of overlapping or interweaving progressive organizations may prove useful for dealing with conflict resolution as well as developmental burdens.

The different forms of progressions may also help explain the different ways in which adult minds are configured. Perhaps someday analysts will become accustomed to adding developmental reconstructions to their explanatory repertoire, in addition to genetic (historical) ones. How else might these developmental propositions assist analysts more directly in their work with adults? When raised, this question evoked an active and even somewhat heated exchange, thereby guaranteeing that it would be earmarked for a future study group.

Neubauer (2003) came up with additional topics for inquiry. Experience has shown, he said, that sometimes a forward spurt in development intensifies pathological conflicts rather than reducing them. Studying how and when that occurs should be fruitful. He also said that while we have been preoccupied with the progressive side of the progressive/regressive swings, some attention might also be directed to the regressive component. Growth is a more assured outcome when regressive re-visiting and re-organization is easily activated. What can analysts do to keep the regressive potential alive, to avoid fixations that might constrain proper growth? The defined topic was, regression in the service of development.

As the meeting came to a close, methodological considerations were raised. What are preferred ways to study these propositions further? Some suggested child research studies, others more active involvement in clinical work. Many felt that how the analyst thinks would be an important addition to the so-called empirical observations.

186 *Samuel Abrams*

However, the most important yield of the study may be that psychoanalysts are still at the beginning of tapping the potential of therapeutic work rather than near the end of that effort. Technical gains may reside in urging colleagues to try on additional ways of thinking and testing the yield of such added perspectives. The propositions of the developmental process represent one prospective set of such thoughts; surely there are others.

BIBLIOGRAPHY

ILAHI, N. (2003). Comments to the discussion group: Clinical applications of Developmental Propositions, in this volume, pp. 123–132.

KNIGHT, R. (2003). Margo and Me II: The role of narrative building in child analytic technique, in this volume, pp. 133–164.

LAMENT, C. (2003). The many dimensions of group process: A discussion of the Treatment of Sandy, in this volume, pp. 112–122.

OLESKER, W. (2003). An analysis of a developmentally delayed young girl: Coordinating analytic and developmental processes, in this volume, pp. 89–111.

NEUBAUER, P. (2003). Some notes on the role of development in psychoanalytic assistance, differentiation, and regression, in this volume, pp. 165–185.

INTEGRATING THEORY AND
CLINICAL PRACTICE

Dimensions of the Child Analyst's Role as a Developmental Object

Affect Regulation and Limit Setting

ALAN SUGARMAN, Ph.D.

This paper will attempt to explain certain dimensions of the child ana-lyst's role as a developmental object in an effort to better clarify the na-ture of that function as well as demonstrate that it is an important part of most child analyses. A review of the literature reveals a bias to-ward differentiating this function from that of promoting insight with the belief that these two functions determine different treatment modal-ities. Therefore, many authors suggest that being a developmental ob-ject is necessary only in the treatment of seriously disturbed children and/or those whose familial histories require a departure from a "gen-uinely" analytic stance. A case of a prelatency boy is presented to dem-onstrate the child analyst's need to serve as a developmental object in regard to setting limits in order to promote affect regulation. Closer scrutiny of these interventions raises the possibility that they may sim-ply have been transference of defense interpretations at a concrete level commensurate with the child's level of cognitive development. This pos-sibility is highlighted as an area for further study.

Training and Supervising Child, Adolescent, and Adult Analyst, San Diego Psycho-analytic Society and Institute; Clinical Professor, University of California San Diego, Department of Psychiatry.

The author wishes to thank Drs. Stephen Silk and Judy Yanof for their helpful com-ments on earlier drafts of this manuscript.

The Psychoanalytic Study of the Child 58, ed. Robert A. King, Peter B. Neubauer, Samuel Abrams, and A. Scott Dowling (Yale University Press, copyright © 2003 by Robert A. King, Peter B. Neubauer, Samuel Abrams, and A. Scott Dowling).

ESPECIALLY IMPORTANT IN DISCUSSIONS OF CHILD ANALYTIC TECH-
nique is the need to consider both insight and the analytic relationship with the analyst. This perspective has led child analysts to be cognizant of what has been traditionally viewed as the non-transferential
nature of their relationships with the child patient from the earliest
days of child analysis. Thus, Anna Freud (1965) in her earliest writings about child analytic technique emphasized the need to form a
positive relationship with the child to better prepare him or her for a
proper analytic experience. Recently the provision of developmental
help rather than insight has been found to be crucial in successful
outcomes when treating very seriously disturbed children (Fonagy
and Target 1996a).

Despite this awareness that many aspects of the analytic relationship and frame contribute to the ultimate therapeutic benefit of
child analysis (Ferro 1999; Smirnoff 1971), there continues to be a
surprising degree of ambivalence over the degree to which various
interactions other than interpretations should be acknowledged as
being part of the analytic process rather than parameters (Hurry
1998). Most child analysts are taught that just the regularity of sched-
uling, the analyst's emotional equanimity, the putting words to emotions and behavior are all mutative in their own rights. Similarly, it is
increasingly accepted that the act of playing with children in analysis
promotes important ego functions and facilitates structural change
even when interpretive activity is minimized or virtually absent (Scott
1998; Mayes and Cohen 1993a; Cohen and Solnit 1993; Frankel
1998). The above-described activities of the child analyst, traditionally considered as outside the scope of insight work, may be alterna-
tively viewed as vehicles for the analysis of structural factors in the
young child's life, while remaining cognizant of the limited capacity
for symbolizing and verbalizing possessed by the young child. Such
developmental immaturities may require that various confronta-
tions/clarifications of ego/superego functioning involve concrete,
behavioral interventions rather than or in addition to verbal interpretation. We know that interpretation does more than promote insight into unconscious processes that impede development (Sugarman 1994). Analysands, both adult and children, may choose to
experience interpretations as an affirmation and acceptance of previously disavowed aspects of the self-representation in addition to
providing cognitive and conscious awareness of previously defended
aspects of themselves. Such affirmation can promote greater integration within the self-representation (Ornstein and Ornstein 1994).

Given this seeming acceptance of factors beyond verbal interpretation as mutative by child analysts, it is striking how much confusion and ambivalence about including such dimensions as part of the analytic process with children continues to exist. Recently, Hurry (1998) has found it necessary to remind us that such aspects of the treatment frame (what she calls developmental therapy) need to be both accepted as a legitimate component of the child analytic process and to be integrated theoretically rather than seen as parameters. "Child analysts have always used such techniques as helping a child to be able to play, to name feelings, to control wishes and impulses rather than be driven to enact them, to relate to others, and to think of and see others as thinking and feeling. They have done such work intuitively, and at times, lacking a fully developed theoretical framework in which to view it, they have undervalued and sometimes failed to record it" (Hurry 1998, p. 37).

The need for the child analyst to be a developmental object as well as a provider of insight appears often in the child analytic literature (Chused 1982; Sandler, Kennedy, and Tyson 1980) and is a staple in seminars and presentations of work with children. How it should be implemented or integrated with our theory of technique remains an obstacle to its clear definition, however. For example, the aspects of child analytic technique described above by Hurry have been called a different technical approach than traditional child analysis, which in turn gives rise to a different process. Fonagy and Target (1996b) introduced the term "psychodynamic developmental therapy" while Greenspan (1997) wrote about "developmentally based psychotherapy." These differences in terminology are based on the belief that techniques aimed at addressing developmental deviations require a treatment approach going beyond the promotion of insight into unconscious conflict as they define it, and thus qualitatively distinct from it. Fonagy and Target (1996b) explicitly differentiate the use of the relationship with the therapist as the primary vehicle of therapeutic change from their definition of standard child analytic practice with interpretation being the primary mutative vehicle despite their finding that both factors occurred in successful child analyses (Fonagy and Target 1996a). They believe that the different approaches are relevant for different types of psychopathology and that sicker children need developmental therapy while healthier children can be treated primarily with standard analytic technique (i.e., verbal interpretation). This position is congruent with Fonagy et al.'s (1993) distinction between patients who suffer from distorted or repudiated feelings and ideas and those who have inhibited prominent mental processes leading to deviant development. Greenspan concurs that the different approaches are applicable to different types of children when he argues that children with less developed egos need a developmentally based psychotherapy that relies more on the relationship with the analyst for change.

Other child analysts emphasize that the meaning of the analyst to the child changes because of the developmental process paralleling the course of the analysis (Abrams 1988). This meaning is also affected by the stage of the analysis and the nature of the child's conflicts (Lilleskov 1971; Neubauer 1971). For example, adolescents look for new objects as they modify their superego identifications, leading them to regard the analyst as a love object, an ego ideal, etc. (Abrams 2001; Abrams and Solnit 1998; Scharfman 1971). This perspective implies that the child analyst will function as a developmental object for all children with regard to specific developmental issues. Yanof (1996) demonstrated this point beautifully in her treatment of a boy with elective mutism.

Thus, it seems likely that functioning as a developmental object is an essential component in child analysis. This paper attempts to contribute some clarity to this important concept by describing certain aspects of being a developmental object—limit setting and affect regulation. Bringing specificity to some dimensions of being a developmental object should hopefully integrate this concept into our theory of child analytic technique and improve our understanding of the child analytic process. In a different context, Busch (1999) pointed to a tendency within psychoanalysis to nurture certain myths when conceptualizing the psychoanalytic method. He said that the result of such myths was a developmental lag (Gray 1994) with regard to certain technical areas while other areas hypertrophy. The child analyst's role as a developmental object seems to be one such myth. Most child analysts believe that the necessity to function as one is so basic that we understand its importance as well as its dimensions, although the literature on child analytic technique suggests otherwise. Ordinary clinical wisdom does not appear to be integrated into our professional literature in a way that promotes its articulation or evaluation. Thus, we run the risk of believing that we have integrated the child analyst's need to help the child master developmental tasks into our definition and theory of technique. Such a false belief compromises our ability to study and improve the process of child analysis.

Vignettes from the analysis of a two-and-one-half-year-old boy for whom my function as a developmental object was significant will be presented to clarify my point. Traditionally defined interpretations of conflict were also an important part of the analysis (Sugarman

1999). But I will focus primarily on interventions in which I functioned as a developmental object for heuristic reasons. The complex subject of how to formulate the interaction between these two functions of the child analyst (promoter of insight and developmental object) will be examined separately (Sugarman, 2003). The focus here will be on conceptually clarifying two dimensions of the developmental object function—limit setting and affect regulation.

BOBBY

Bobby was a two-and-a-half-year-old boy when his parents sought consultation about his extreme regression following minor outpatient surgery for chronic otitis several months earlier. Bobby had been prepared for the surgery with a straightforward discussion, reading of age-appropriate books about hospitals, and attending the widely acclaimed orientation program of the local children's hospital.

Consequently his parents were surprised and dismayed when his behavior changed three to four days after the surgery. Bobby became seriously aggressive and oppositional; his anger and defiance continued unabated at the time of his consultation four months later. Physical attacks on his parents and brother (four years his senior) when angered began several days after surgery along with hitting and throwing things at glass doors and windows in defiance of parental prohibition. Bobby's toilet training regressed, and he also grabbed toys from his brother's friends while accusing them angrily of being "bad." A sleep disturbance wherein Bobby repeatedly awoke and entered the parents' bedroom had also developed. At times he would allow one of his parents to return him to his room where he would fall asleep again, and other times he would repeatedly return to his parents' bedroom until his father spanked him. At that point he would remain in his bed and fall back asleep. Bobby's parents agreed to five-session weekly analysis after all environmental manipulation and behavior modification techniques had failed.

RELEVANT HISTORY

Bobby was the second of two sons born to a professional family. His four year older brother, T., was constantly presented to me as the easy and good son in contrast to Bobby, who, almost from conception, was experienced by his parents as being difficult. They reported noticing that he had even been more active in utero than his brother. After birth he was perceived to have been noticeably louder and more active than his brother. Their emotional tone when describing this greater activity expressed their disapproval and dismay.

Significant feeding problems characterized Bobby's first three months. Crying and refusing to suck despite being hungry predominated those early months until his mother isolated the problem to her ingestion of spicy foods. Bobby's eating became normal once she removed them from her diet. However, his first three months of attachment and affect regulation had been significantly disrupted.

Bobby's early temperament was loud and active; his parents were upset by his tendency to screech whenever placed in the car seat during his first four months. Developmental milestones were normal except for poor speech articulation caused by severe ear infections and hearing difficulties which had improved by the time Bobby was two. At approximately 20 months of age, a possibility arose that he had *accidentally* eaten poison mushrooms. This incident heralded a distinct pattern that became clearer when the analysis began wherein his parents repeatedly demonstrated an inability to anticipate Bobby's actions and to protect him from his own impulses. His mother administered medication to make him vomit; she interpreted its failure to work immediately as evidence of Bobby's *stubborn* refusal. Angrily she took him to the emergency room only to have him vomit as he was removed from the car.

Negativism began at 18 months but direct anger was notably lacking until after Bobby's surgery. Prior to the surgery, mild irritation when others could not understand his speech or when he could not keep up with his brother were the only manifest evidence of anger. In contrast he had been notably resistant to discipline, refusing to behave even before the surgery. Bobby would defy a rule immediately after it had been established and neither scoldings nor spankings altered his oppositionalism. When provoked in play group, he would fall asleep rather than react angrily. Although he could play with other children by age two, Bobby's favorite game was to knock down things that others had built. He also enjoyed building things and then knocking down his own creations. Thus, modulation of aggression had gone awry by age two so that Bobby inhibited direct expressions of anger while being severely oppositional.

ANXIETY OVER AN INABILITY TO SELF REGULATE

Bobby began analysis by regressing swiftly and extremely at home. He persistently defied parental edicts, created huge messes, and broke things far more than he had done prior to beginning treatment. Random urinary incontinence returned while fecal incontinence remained. Both parents seemed at their wits' end about such behavior as well as Bobby's darting suddenly and unexpectedly into the street or a parking lot. Bobby continually surprised his parents by running into hazardous situations as they invariably failed to keep a tight grip on his hand. I was struck by their difficulty with anticipating such conduct and thought how unsafe Bobby must feel in their company.

Bobby's early sessions were characterized by emotional inhibition, facial impassivity, and minimal manifest connectedness with me. Furthermore, his play was far less verbal and lacked the degree of fantasy elaboration that would be expected for a child his age. Bobby's play included creating huge messes or running wildly around the office, and the few constricted themes that he did verbalize always involved aggression. He seemed excited and out-of-control as he climbed over furniture, rattled doors, and tried to break or throw things. Therefore, I suspected that his newfound regression at home spoke to an inability to contain the anxiety generated in sessions by my failure to set limits on his play and messes. In my efforts to be empathic and neutral, I suspected that I had been drawn into an enactment. I thought that Bobby might interpret the absence of limits as a failure to keep him safe from his poorly controlled impulses in the same manner that his parents failed to defend him. I felt far more confused and bewildered than usual during these early sessions with Bobby, as he failed to respond, either with words or apparent shifts in play, to any of my interpretations.

Bobby's discomfort with aggressive impulses became apparent in his regular tendency to return to his mother in the waiting room, climb into her lap, and suck his thumb whenever he became angry with me or uncomfortable with the aggressive tone of his play. For example, he tried to rip apart the box of a puzzle that he had been unable to put together. I set a limit on his ripping and Bobby ran to the waiting room where he crawled into his mother's lap and sucked his thumb. I interpreted that Bobby did not want to be angry and so sat on his mommy's lap and sucked his thumb to make his scary, angry feelings toward me go away. He agreed but refused to leave her lap.

Two repetitive themes of dumping things on top of each other or crashing things into each other were Bobby's early rudimentary attempts to express his anger. Otherwise, Bobby's play was quite inhibited. Before I realized the need to address his wish to have me help him to feel safe with his aggression I often interpreted that the dumping and messing play had to do with his feelings about his poops or his anger. These content or impulse interpretations, not surprisingly, made Bobby anxious and he fled to his mother. Bobby responded to one such interpretation by trying to throw things, then fled to his mother in fear of his poorly controlled aggressive impulses or of my fantasied response. Other times I interpreted that Bobby's expression of aggression in the play had to do with wanting help with his wild running and messing feelings because they felt scary. But even these interpretations of defense failed to attenuate his anxiety. Finally I realized that Bobby's defenses were simply too weak to control his impulses and anxiety that were being generated in our sessions. It seemed to me that he either lacked or inhibited the ability to represent his internal states and to think about them abstractly so that verbal interpretations were of little help in organizing his behavior. Therefore, I decided that I would have to act as an auxiliary ego until his defenses were strengthened. I instituted a variety of behavioral limits including encouraging him to help me clean up the office at the end of sessions. I hypothesized that Bobby needed me to demonstrate that I could help him contain his impulses which he could not control himself. As the analysis progressed it became clear that he also wanted me to demonstrate that unlike his parents I could make him feel safe from his impulses. Only in retrospect did I realize that Bobby may also have needed me to demonstrate concretely that his impulses and aggression were actually limited and not as powerful as he feared.

Bobby did tolerate his anger in the analysis better by the end of the first month as I became more adept at providing behavioral controls. For example, I limited the degree of dumping he was doing one session. Bobby responded by heading for the door to the waiting room until I interpreted his wish to flee from his anger at me because he was afraid that he could not be the boss of his angry feelings. For the first time Bobby stopped his flight and returned to playing as though he no longer felt overwhelmed by anxiety. I understood this increased affect tolerance to indicate an identification with my improved ability to help him contain his aggressive impulses. It also seemed that my limit setting had alleviated his anxiety over his presumed omnipotent impulses making him feel safe enough that he could begin hearing my interpretations and use them to gain some control over his affects and impulses.

My weekly meetings with Mrs. T. further clarified Bobby's need to use me to protect his safety. It soon became clear that throughout Bobby's short life both parents had failed to anticipate his impulsive behavior: for example, various sudden forays into the street or parking lot. Mrs. T. recalled an episode wherein nine-month-old Bobby had choked so severely on something he had ingested that she called 911. Bobby's bringing up spontaneously "falling in a lake" at the end of one session, and at home, prompted his parents to remember a family trip when his father turned his back "for a split second" and Bobby fell in a lake one month prior to the surgery. A picture of parental benign neglect gradually emerged, highlighting Bobby's need for me to help him to learn to regulate his affects and impulses so that he remained safe and not anxious.

SUPEREGO REACTIONS TO DIFFICULTIES
WITH REGULATING AGGRESSION

Following my first vacation Bobby tested me to see whether I could control his affects and impulses and keep him safe. He seemed to court disaster with his defiance at home while his parents continued to show remarkable difficulty in helping him control his behavior. While I was away Bobby burnt his finger on a hot iron, lay down in front of cars, ran impulsively into the street and through parking lots, and ran wildly up and down bleacher seats at a rodeo. His anxiety about losing my help in coping with his affects and impulses was striking. Upon my return, he balked at attending our sessions, fell asleep in the car on the way to them, and complained to his mother that he hated me; reactions which I interpreted as due to his feelings about my having left him for a week. During one session wherein Bobby had been shooting me, he ran out suddenly to his mother and started kicking her, seemingly illustrating that I was his mother in terms of his angry transference, and that my *abandonment* of him had been experienced from this perspective. During another session Bobby played at having the baby monkey hit the mother monkey and vice versa. Then the baby monkey started to hit another toy upon which Bobby conferred my name. His reported references to *bad guys* during such play sequences seemed to indicate that his guilt over his anger at me and his mother was lowering his self-esteem and making him feel like a *bad guy*. Bobby's renewed need to bring his mother into our sessions suggested that this conflict was making him anxious about object loss, and I suspected that his magical thinking and omnipotence led him to assume that I had left him because he was angry and bad. I chose to interpret his anxiety about affect regulation, saying that he wondered whether I would let his *bad guy* feelings get out of control which made him feel unsafe.

I again reinstituted limits on Bobby's messes and impulse expressions in an effort to reduce his anxiety. Such limits included cleaning up at the end of sessions so that he could see that his *messes* did not have to be permanent. He tested these limits by climbing on my bookcases. I forbade all climbing and interpreted his fear that I could not be the boss of his angry feelings. Whenever he started to test this limit I grabbed him and repeated variations of this interpretation. He would respond "fine" and snuggle into me while he had me read him a story. Bobby also tried to break toys at this stage of the analysis. I set limits on the breaking and said that I thought he was trying to figure out what was safe to do in my office. I explained that he would not feel safe from his breaking feelings if I allowed him to break things. Bobby also requested to *borrow* certain favored toys from me. In contrast to my usual practice, I allowed him to do so at this stage while interpreting his wish to feel that I liked him so that he could take those feelings with him. They made him feel I would keep him safe, and help him to be the boss of his feelings. Bobby also began to refuse to help me to clean up his messes at the end of our sessions, and became even more wild when I tried to clean up. This time, he seemed to experience my cleaning up as an emotional withdrawal characteristic of his parents' lapses in attentiveness that allowed his many accidents to happen. This sort of limit was no longer as reassuring as it had been at the beginning of the analysis. I decided to postpone cleaning until Bobby left because of his need at this point of the analysis to feel that he had my undivided attention. Within a few sessions he stopped his struggles about attending sessions and seemed eager and happy to see me.

ANALYSIS OF AGGRESSION

Continued analysis allowed Bobby's development to get back on track as he engaged phallic issues more clearly in the second year of the analysis. For example, he carried a long stick between his legs, hitting the door and ceiling of the office. Bobby said that he was not big like his father but he would get big and strong if he drank milk, adding a seeming nonsequitur that babies get thrown in the water and sharks eat them up. I said that he must want to be big and strong so as not to have to worry about that and he agreed. To myself I thought that this statement probably had something to do with the time he had fallen into the lake.

The lake incident soon became a preoccupation in sessions and at home. He told his mother that he feared he would drown when he fell in the lake. He told me that he had been afraid that a shark would eat him up so that he was all gone, and that this would make

his "mommy and daddy mad." This working through led Bobby to remember a time that his father had gotten mad at his defiance and
started the car to scare him out from under it. In one session Bobby
had a *good* policeman chase a *bad* policeman. Then the *good* policeman's Jeep needed to be fixed. It began to drive away while the man
was underneath fixing it. I said that the car was driving with the man
still under it, and Bobby replied that cars did not do that. I commented on how glad that must make him; he then said that sometimes cars do do that. I then recalled out loud how his daddy had
started the car when he was under it. Bobby agreed that his daddy
had done so but refused to discuss his feelings about it. In yet another session Bobby wanted me to play at running a car over him and
then tried to wrap the venetian blinds cord around his neck. I
stopped him and interpreted that he felt that he was bad and should
be punished for his angry feelings about his daddy starting the car
when he was under it; I added that he seemed to want me to help
him be the boss of his punishing feelings because they were so scary.

Bobby's mother's resolve was soon tested by an upsurge in Bobby's
explicit expression of anger toward her. Much of his anger was expressed verbally, and for the most part seemed like normal assertiveness. For example, one day Bobby told his mother that he was going
to run away because she and his daddy were so mean to him. Angrily
she told him to go ahead and he went to the neighbor's house. In this
way his magical worries about the power of his impulses were heightened. Even verbal expressions of anger were dangerous for Bobby,
carrying with them the dual dangers of object loss and loss of love.

Bobby's ability to express verbal fantasy improved markedly as conflicts over his own aggression remained central in the analysis. During one session Bobby wrapped his hand in a cord and said that it was
in jail because it had thrown things at people. I reminded him that
recently he had thrown a toy telephone at his mother in the waiting
room, making him feel as if he was a bad guy. I added that he was
telling me that his hand was in jail because he seemed still to want me
to help him not do things like throw rocks that made him feel like a
bad guy and unsafe. I suggested he was afraid that his angry feelings
would hurt somebody or he would be punished. Self-directed anger
remained evident; after I set a limit on his behavior in one session,
Bobby turned the toy gun on himself. I then interpreted the defense
against his anger at me; his angry feelings made him lose his good
feelings about me, making him feel unsafe, so he shot himself instead. Bobby's anger remained directed at his mother also. For example, a *bad guy* said that he hated his mom and then fell down, and was

injured. I said that the guy felt so bad for hating his mom that he punished himself by falling down. Bobby's response allowed me to add that his angry feelings at his mom made his good feelings about her go away, and then he felt he had lost her. He expanded the theme to his mother being lost and taken by burglars, spelling out his fear that his anger led to abandonment. In another session a *bad guy* lost his mommy and went looking for her.

Over a number of sessions revolving around his reactions to his father's temper, anger toward his father began to appear, and Bobby told me that he wanted to kill his daddy when he grew up because he hated him. Rapid regression after these expressions of anger followed. Bobby would fall asleep in his mother's lap in the waiting room prior to sessions, refusing to leave her. Interpreting his regressive behavior as a defense against his anger had no effect. During a session in which Bobby sucked his thumb, I reminded him how a few weeks before he had enjoyed showing me what a big guy he was; I recalled out loud his fear that he would no longer be babied if he were big. I then interpreted that he was afraid that his mommy might stop babying him if he acted like a big boy who showed anger toward his dad. Bobby confirmed this interpretation by returning to phallic play themes and ceasing to fall asleep on his mother's lap.

REGAINING DEVELOPMENTAL MOMENTUM

Soon we loaded our guns while Bobby had a *bigger gun* than mine that would kill me. We sailed off to sea together to shoot monsters. But Bobby decided that he wanted my ship, so he killed me. His immediate retreat to his mother in the waiting room was followed by a request to come trick-or-treating at my house, demonstrating how much Bobby still feared his anger. The subsequent play theme in which a horse fell in the lake and was bitten by a shark suggested that castration anxiety was replacing earlier anxieties as a feared consequence of phallic, aggressive strivings.

Continued working through these anxieties led Bobby to become more verbal about wanting my help with his bad guy feelings. Conflict expression was increasingly confined to sessions, and the T.'s seemed far more comfortable with his episodic aggression at home. Bobby stopped his more flagrant misbehavior and regained bowel and urinary control. Oedipal themes became predominant in his play during sessions. Consequently a brief regression to messing and defiant behavior in sessions seemed related directly to the phallic, aggressive material. Exploration led first to Bobby's anxiety about my allowing him to *borrow* toys from my office. This parameter had come to represent a lack of limits over his aggressive wishes to steal my valuables. Bobby's exquisite sensitivity and wish to feel that the environment was both attuned and regulating of his omnipotently experienced affects and impulses became clear. I interpreted and stopped allowing him to take toys home. But the alternation between phallic-oedipal themes and messing-defiant regression continued. I finally interpreted to Bobby that he had been wanting to take my things— my toys, my ship, and probably my penis. I said that he was acting once again like the little boy who used to make messes, and was not following rules because he was afraid that his big boy *taking feelings* would make me angry; therefore I would try to take his penis away from him just as he feared his daddy might.

Bobby confirmed this interpretation by asking me to read him a story about a boy who was eaten by sharks, and then to tell a story about a baseball player who chased sharks away with his bat. I wove into the story an interpretation that the little boy wished that he could have a big bat like the baseball player. Bobby interrupted me excitedly to talk about the little boy getting a big bat and beating up the shark on his own. Bobby appeared at the next session wearing toy glasses, seemingly an identification with me.

Repeatedly themes of people being punished by falling off ships, or falling into water after *being bad* began to occur. In one session after shooting our guns we were constantly knocked off our boat by a storm. I wondered if we were being punished for shooting. Bobby first said no but then added that we had shot our moms. Then he remembered falling in the lake on his family's vacation. I suggested he thought it had happened because he had been bad and had angry feelings. Bobby admitted that this was so, and mumbled something about his father which I could not understand, and which he would not repeat. Later in the play I had my action figure express anger that his father had allowed him to fall in the lake. Bobby's figure responded that his daddy had pushed him into the lake one time because his daddy was mad at him. Our figures commiserated with each other about how angry they felt toward their dads for such behavior.

Soon Bobby elaborated directly in the play his fantasy that he had been pushed into the lake by his dad to punish him for his angry feelings toward his mother. In another play sequence a baby threw its mother into the mud after sticking its fingers in her face. Then the baby fell into the mud also. I interpreted that the baby was being punished just as Bobby had felt punished by his dad, and Bobby agreed. His behavior continued to improve at home, and his flirting with danger seemed a thing of the past.

Oedipal themes became overt in the transference as Bobby cheated at board games with me, and then created obsessive rules that made it difficult for him to win. Or, after winning, he would declare that I had won also. I interpreted that Bobby felt bad if he defeated me. He agreed and asked if it was time to stop. I said that I thought he wanted to leave in order not to think about winning so much. His winning feelings made him feel like a bad guy who hurt me and who might get punished. Bobby resumed his competitive play, this time with action figures, and shot off the various body parts of mine, culminating in shooting off my figure's penis. He actually swaggered around the room after doing so. The analysis seemed to be progressing well. At this point I end my discussion of Bobby's analysis. Rather than providing an overview of the entire analysis of this interesting little boy, I will use the clinical material presented to elaborate further my function as a developmental object for him.

CONCLUSION

In these clinical vignettes I have attempted to describe a psychoanalytic process with a prelatency child wherein my role as a developmental object was a significant contributor. I hope that the vignette was sufficiently detailed to demonstrate that I also promoted insight, and tried to work within the transference as much as seemed clinically indicated. However, the immaturity of Bobby's ego and his representational world wherein his parents failed to help him regulate his drives and related affects, as well as the parents' actual problems in meeting these needs and stimulating his aggression required that I do more than solely promote verbal insight.

This became evident quite early in the analysis when I realized that my attempts to be neutral and empathic were experienced by Bobby as a failure to help him control his impulses and feel safe, just as he experienced his parents to be deficient in that area. His resumed out-of-control, flirting-with-danger behavior at home, as well as his chaotic behavior during our early sessions, were regressive expressions of anxiety that he found difficult to put into words or to modulate symbolically. At this stage of the analysis my words were insufficient to bind his anxiety about the omnipotent power of his affects which he seemed unable to use as signals to elicit defenses and inner control (Tyson 1996). When I put his anger into words prematurely, even when I put his fear of anger into words, he became more anxious. Therefore, I instituted a variety of behavioral limits including the un-usual-for-me requirement to help clean up his messes at the end of each session. By doing this I was functioning as an auxiliary ego and demonstrating to him that his affects and impulses were not as om-nipotently powerful as he feared. Furthermore, I interpreted and explained that Bobby felt unsafe about his inability to be the boss of his feelings; he needed me to help him be the boss in order to feel safe.

Bobby's history revealed a parental discomfort with handling ag-gression. His parents' disapproval of his aggressive tendencies began in utero, where his greater activity was interpreted as less desirable than his brother's passivity. They seemed unable to experience Bob-by's aggression as the positive force in development that child ana-lysts have found it to be (Downey 1984; Mayes and Cohen 1993b). It seems likely that Bobby's early feeding difficulties also intensified his aggression as a reaction to serious frustration and discomfort. From his mother's account it sounded as though Bobby's experience dur-ing his first several months was dominated by pain, unpleasure, and an inability to be gratified. Attachment difficulties would be ex-pected. Only after that time could Bobby find any comfort or safety in his interactions with his mother. It appeared that his mother as well as his father found those early months so distressing that they implicitly experienced him as a bad seed in comparison to his quiet older brother. Thus, several of the risk factors for negative affect and general arousal that undermine affect regulation and cause psycho-pathology were present (Bradley 2000).

Developmental research has shown that the first 12 to 18 months of life determine whether aggression feels adaptive, essential, and positive or scary and dreadful (Mayes and Cohen 1993b). By the time that Bobby entered rapprochement, he had learned that ag-gressive impulses were unmanageable, frightening, and distasteful. Thus, psychic representations that are built up gradually through aggressive stimulation and discharge led to a representational world colored by frightening attacks and punishment. This translated to behavior wherein direct expressions of anger were notably inhibited by the age of two while oppositionality and negativism were far more extreme than is typical.

By the time of his first consultation the degree to which Bobby's parents and his early somatic traumas (feeding difficulties, ear pain) had overstimulated his anger while not helping him modulate it was already undermining his development. Furthermore, his parents had difficulty in helping Bobby to internalize regulatory functions. Children become increasingly independent and individualized as they gain the ability for self-regulation through good enough parenting (Sugarman and Jaffe 1990). Bobby's parents' own conflicts about regulating their anger or tolerating frustration left toddlerhood an insurmountable obstacle for Bobby.

AFFECT REGULATION AND DEVELOPMENT

A major role of the parents of the toddler involves helping him or her to master three developmental necessities: (1) the differentiation and integration of self and object representations; (2) the regulation of drives and related affects; and (3) the maturation of autonomous ego functions, in particular reality testing and secondary process thinking. That is, the parents of the toddler provide key functions that allow for solid establishment and development of the psychic apparatus by serving as auxiliary egos at this stage and, hence, promoting internalization of key ego functions. In large part they do this through facilitating the development of object constancy (Tyson 1996). "Predictable emotional involvement on the part of the mother seems to facilitate the rich unfolding of the toddler's thought processes, reality testing, and coping behavior by the end of the second or the beginning of the third year" (Mahler et al. 1975, p. 79). Mentalization or reflective function develops, allowing the toddler to label and find his internal experiences meaningful (Coates 1998; Fonagy and Target 1998). In this way he learns to distinguish between his own inner wishes and interests and those of the mother, while also learning to regulate affects, control impulses, and experience self-agency. Internal conflict (Nagera 1966) arises and must be mastered for the representation of the beloved parent(s) to be internalized as a source of sustenance, comfort, and love (Mahler and Furer 1968). The parents must tolerate the child's mood swings and control battles while not getting so angry that they withdraw and/or respond in a critical or controlling manner. Bobby's mother found it difficult to tolerate verbal defiance while his father's rage over control battles made Bobby feel in danger (i.e., starting the car while Bobby was under it).

Aggression, in particular, must be regulated and modulated for the toddler's ego functions to expand. "Aggression more than the internalization of consistent nurturing fosters individuation, self-other differentiation, and the young child's recognition of object permanence and an external reality shared with the parent" (Mayes and

Cohen 1993b, p. 152). Ambivalence threatens to destroy the object whom he needs too much at this stage. Parental responding in a soothing and regulating manner with gentle but firm limits that are explained with words help the child to experience emotions that are not overwhelming or excessively frightening. Frustration tolerance and self-coping are taught when words are used to modulate intense affects. Identification with the parent and internalization of these regulatory functions allow the toddler to use affects as signals for actions (Tyson 1996). Such improved self-regulation promotes the development of mental mechanisms to delay immediate discharge. These delay and detour mechanisms are crucial for the ascendency of secondary process thinking. They allow thinking to become relatively independent from intense drives and affects. Segal (1978) traces the capacity for abstract thinking to the mother's labeling of the toddler's internal states. It is the internalization of the mother's soothing that promotes cognitive development and improves reality testing by teaching the toddler to evaluate external reality in a more objective, less affectively biased fashion. Bobby's excessive concreteness at the beginning of the analysis suggests that he had not felt soothed.

TREATING AGGRESSION IN CHILDREN

Bobby's difficulties in tolerating or modulating his aggressive impulses and affects demonstrate how much the child analyst must step out of the neutral role with such disturbances (Maenchen 1984). It is impossible for children to use interpretations of affect or impulse and to gain insight into their anger when they feel overwhelmed by what they experience as omnipotently powerful states. Furthermore, children such as Bobby do not allow us the luxury to gain an understanding of the motives for their aggressive behavior in the relaxed and gradual manner implicit in standard discussions of the use of insight with children. "Aggression can be simple discharge, reaction to frustration, a defense, resistance, provocation of punishment because of superego anxiety, and it can be predominantly sadistic" (Maenchen 1984, p. 402). Therefore, the child analyst must find a way for both him or her as well as the child to survive and to feel safe while trying to determine which of these alternatives is most relevant. Some child analysts argue that physical activity such as my holding Bobby to contain his climbing are parameters that can interfere with analysis of the transference (Weiss 1964). Countertransference is thought to be the culprit in such instances (Kohrman et al. 1971).

Most modern child analysts would agree that this view of transference may be appropriate for adults but not for children. It is commonly accepted that the child analyst must set limits to keep both partners safe in order to allay the child's anxiety that his or her feelings can destroy (Maenchen 1984; Olesker 1999; Scott 1998; Yanof 1996). Limits must be set—otherwise children such as Bobby become so anxious about losing control of their destructive feelings and impulses that they cannot use interpretations. By way of the behavioral enactments with the analyst, the child concretely represents the structural contributions to his anxieties. These can only become progressively more interpretable by verbal means as the analyst's limit setting helps the child understand the limits of his power and facilitates his ability to use mental structures to modulate his impulses (Sugarman, 2003).

Recent reports in the literature emphasize the analyst's need to serve first as a developmental object in helping children to regulate affects before being able to work in a more classically interpretive fashion (Olesker 1999; Yanof 1996). The articulation of emotions, transition of visual imagery into feelings and helping to modulate, delay, and channel the child's affects promote self-regulation, a sense of mastery, and a reduction in punitive defenses that allow for deeper interpretations about internal conflicts (Olesker 1999). Likewise, helping the child to lower his level of stimulation and to become self-regulating establishes an emotional dialogue with the child that promotes sustaining and regulating affects (Yanof 1996). Such interventions do not appear to hinder the development of transference or the analysis of it.

My work with Bobby was guided by a similar formulation. In part, I saw myself as behaving like the practicing-rapprochement mother whose predictable emotional involvement is necessary to facilitate the development of the toddler's thinking, reality testing, and coping skills. It seemed obvious that Bobby's intense rage toward both parents left him terrified that he would destroy his mother, his father, and/or himself. Thus, I tried to provide the gentle but firm limits that were necessary while providing a rationale in words so he could learn to tolerate frustration of impulse and to modulate his affects with words. I was containing him, articulating his internal states, and conveying the message that they were manageable, bearable, and understandable. In this way Bobby gained a perception of himself in my mind, facilitating the formation of a representational world of a self-interacting with others for comprehensible reasons (Fonagy and Target 1998). By the end of the first month of the analysis, Bobby seemed to be identifying with my improved ability to control his impulses just as such maternal behavior helps the toddler learn to use affects as signals. Bobby's regressive symptoms began to abate, and he seemed to regain some of the mental development and capacity to delay immediate discharge that he had exhibited prior to his surgery. As this occurred his capacity for fantasy and verbal affect expression improved.

In my role as a developmental object I helped Bobby's internal world develop in other ways. His strikingly affectless demeanor at the beginning of the analysis combined with his almost inability to engage in symbolic play was unusual for a child his age. It appeared that his poorly modulated aggression toward both parents along with their own emotional reactions to him led Bobby's early superego introjects to be unusually harsh and restrictive. Thus, he seemed to be trying to control affects and fantasies as much as his young, immature ego would permit at the time of the consultation. He was demonstrating the degree to which important mental processes can be defensively inhibited by early conflict (Fonagy et al. 1993). In a sense my limiting more extreme regressions of affect and impulse, while at the same time accepting his affects and impulses without reacting angrily or punitively, allowed my interventions (both verbal and behavioral) to have a mutative impact on Bobby's developing superego (Strachey 1934). He became more tolerant of his affects and fantasies as he found that I insured his and my survival in the face of them, and as he identified with my interest, curiosity, and acceptance of his internal world as well as my benign superego.

TRANSFERENCE OR DEVELOPMENTAL OBJECT

It is important to emphasize that this role as a developmental object was done largely through focusing on the patient-analyst relationship. Most of the interventions which I view as involving my function as a developmental object to Bobby revolved around interactions between us. This is consistent with Fonagy and Target's (1998) notions about how to promote mentalization in children. "Work takes place strictly in the analyst-patient relationship and focuses on the mental states of patient and analyst. Interpretations are not global summaries, but rather attempts at placing affect into a causal chain of concurrent mental experiences" (p. 109). A definitional question of whether to regard such work as working within the transference arises. Cohen and Solnit (1993) take pains to differentiate this work from analysis of transference. "Paradoxically, in the context of treating developmentally deviant children, the analyst as a new or real person gained an importance in fueling the therapeutic process, while the analyst as a transference object, never insignificant, became less central in providing therapeutic change" (p. 60). In contrast Yanof (1996) opts for a wider definition of transference that seems to include our function as a developmental object. Thus, she emphasizes the central place of work in the transference in child analysis while describing a broader meaning of transference. "Work in the transference, I mean addressing the whole process that takes shape between patient and analyst . . . part of this process includes other aspects of the analytic relationship (the analyst as new, real, or developmental object)" (p. 105).

Ultimately the questions revolve around how to define transference. At the beginning of the analysis my functioning as a developmental object occurred while I puzzled over what possible transferential meaning it might have; I believed that Bobby needed my help in containing impulses and emotions because he felt unable to control them himself while I remained uncertain about possible unconscious wishes associated with his actions. Therefore, I instituted a variety of limits while acting as a role model for identification. I hoped that identifying with my capacity to regulate his impulses and emotions through both behavior and words would promote some internalization of these regulatory functions—something that his parents had been unable to facilitate in him. I focused on the precipitant of his anxiety over losing control of his behavior or emotions as well as his defensive efforts to cope with his anxiety within the interactions between us. For example, I interpreted his fleeing to his mother's lap and sucking his thumb early on as an effort to eliminate angry feelings at me that he found frightening. Although I considered that his anger might be associated with some fantasy about me, it seemed more important to demonstrate his defenses against his transferential affects. Similar interpretations were made when I set limits on messing, breaking, throwing, etc. At that point in the analysis I saw myself as attempting to enhance Bobby's reflective processes and teach him that his behavior and mine had meaning (Fonagy and Target 1996b, 1998). Some might argue for adding to the interpretation, even at this early stage of analysis, a comment such as "You're trying to show me you want me to help you be the boss of your feelings." Such an interpretation would suggest a transference wish based on the assumption that Bobby's out of control behavior at home was fueled by a similar wish. However, such an interpretation would have seemed too far "out of the neighborhood" and not at Bobby's workable clinical surface (Busch 1993). As greater evidence for it developed, I was soon able to address Bobby's transference wish to have me help him to control his anger.

This transference wish became more clearly evident in Bobby's striking regression around my first vacation, a few months into the analysis. My absence stirred up anxiety about both the loss of my ability to help him control his aggressive feelings and the fantasy that I had left him because he was so angry and bad. At that point I chose to make the first interpretation—to emphasize his anxiety about losing me as a developmental object who would help him control his angry feelings. Most child analysts would consider this a transference interpretation despite its emphasis on my developmental object function. By this point in the analysis it seemed clear that Bobby did not feel secure that his parents could protect him from himself. His misbehavior at home seemed to be a defensive externalization and attempt to provoke them into protecting him, something at which they repeatedly failed. My vacation had made me seem as unreliable to him as his parents. Interpreting his behavior in this way allowed me to make increasingly specific transference interpretations as the analysis progressed—eventually interpreting his anxiety that I would be as irate and punitive over his phallic anger as his father seemed.

But even this latter phase wherein transference interpretations were specific and direct continued to require me to function as a developmental object. Even at these times Bobby generally needed me to help him to regulate his anxiety with limiting behavior as well as with words. His parents' own difficulties with modulating their impulses or with helping him with his seemed to require that I continue to serve as a figure for identification while promoting his greater insightfulness into the meaning of his own behavior. In other words, being a developmental object was coexisting with my function as a promoter of insight, something that I believe is common in child analysis.

The question becomes whether being a developmental object or a provider of interpretations is truly different. If one adheres to a narrow definition of transference as the projection and/or displacement of primary object relational paradigms onto the analyst, it make sense to distinguish the two functions as clearly as possible (e.g. Chused 1988). This is clearly the definition used by those who argue that developmental object functions are parameters that should be minimized at all costs (e.g. Weiss 1964). "If the child's psychology is in the past, if it is structuralized, then it can be analyzed in the transference. If the psychology is of the present, and is a continuum of the past, that aspect which is current and *not a transference* onto the parents cannot be analyzed at that time" (p. 593, my italics). But if one adopts a broader definition of transference as the externalization of aspects of the analysand's internal structure into the analytic relationship, that is, transference of defense (A. Freud 1936), one must question how separate the two functions truly are. The limit setting and affect regulation that I provided to Bobby could be viewed as interpretations in the form of concrete, behavioral interventions appropriate to the concrete and egocentric nature of his thinking. Thus, the defensive omnipotence surrounding his aggressive impulses as well as the superego issues generated by them were externalized and enacted in our relationship. In this way, my setting limits was a confrontation and interpretation of his omnipotence and a concrete demonstration that his aggressive impulses were not as powerful or as dangerous as he believed. To the degree that his omnipotence also involved a wish for a gratification, my limit setting could be viewed as an interpretation of his omnipotent wish to do anything he wanted to with me. It was the only way that he could hear such an interpretation. Certainly Bobby's developmental history and analytic material provide ample evidence of enough early internal structure and conflict to believe that his seemingly out of control behavior involved conflict induced regression, and not simply developmental deficit. Therefore, interpretation via limit setting would be an appropriate intervention for an ego capable of conflict and defensive regression.

In summary, I have attempted to delineate my function as a developmental object in Bobby's analysis in an effort to help define the concept better. But close examination of the developmental object functions that I provided leaves open the question of how distinct this facet of our role as a child analyst may be. The behaviors which I limited and the affects which I helped regulate were expressions of structural factors and conflicts in Bobby's inner life. And my limits, in essence, could be viewed as concrete interpretations of the aspects of ego and superego structure that Bobby used as resistances to the awareness of unconscious conflict and transference. From this perspective, interpreting concretely at a behavioral level commensurate with his developmental level may be simply a parallel to the way in which we interpret such resistances verbally with our adult patients.

It will take further study and careful attention to the way in which we work with child patients before this question can be answered definitively. Bobby's analytic material does seem to indicate that we do the field of child analysis a disservice if we cling to the notion that neurotic children can be analyzed with only the provision of verbal interpretations. Interventions need to be provided in a way that takes into account the child's developmental limitations. For many children, functioning as a developmental object is an essential aspect of the analytic process. The analyst's behavior can be as important as his or her words in facilitating the child's ability for self-reflection and self-regulation. "Language is less often a useful vehicle for promoting insight than behavioral enactments. That is, insight in a child may sometimes arise more from doing and perceiving something in a new way within the session than from new cognitive awareness" (Sugarman 1994, p. 331).

BIBLIOGRAPHY

ABRAMS, S. (1988). The psychoanalytic process in adults and children. *Psychoanalytic Study of the Child* 43:245–261.

ABRAMS, S. (2001). Summation—unrealized possibilities: Comments on Anna Freud's normality and pathology in childhood. *Psychoanalytic Study of the Child,* 56:105–119.

ABRAMS, S. & SOLNIT, A. J. (1998). Coordinating developmental and psychoanalytic processes: Conceptualizing technique. *JAPA* 46:85–103.

BRADLEY, S. J. (2000). *Affect Regulation and the Development of Psychopathology.* New York: Guilford Press.

BUSCH, F. (1993). In the neighborhood: Aspects of a good interpretation and its relationship to a "developmental lag" in ego psychology. *JAPA* 41: 151–178.

BUSCH, F. (1999). *Rethinking Clinical Technique.* Northvale, N.J.: Aronson.

CHUSED, J. F. (1982). The role of analytic neutrality in the use of the child analyst as a new object. *JAPA* 30:3–28.

CHUSED, J. F. (1988). The transference neurosis in child analysis. *Psychoanalytic Study of the Child* 43:51–81.

COHEN, P. M. & SOLNIT, A. J. (1993). Play and therapeutic action. *Psychoanalytic Study of the Child* 48:49–63.

COATES, S. W. (1998). Having a mind of one's own and holding the other in mind: Commentary on paper by Peter Fonagy and Mary Target. *Psychoanalytic Dialogues* 8:115–148.

DOWNEY, T. W. (1984). Within the pleasure principle: Child analytic perspectives on aggression. *Psychoanalytic Study of the Child* 39:101–136.

FERRO, A. (1999). *The Bi-Personal Field. Experiences in Child Analysis.* London: Routledge.

FONAGY, P. & TARGET, M. (1996a). Predictors of outcome in child psychoanalysis: A retrospective study of 763 cases at the Anna Freud Centre. *JAPA* 44:27–77.

FONAGY, P. & TARGET, M. (1996b). A contemporary psychoanalytical perspective: Psychodynamic developmental therapy. In *Psychosocial Treatments for Child and Adolescent Disorders,* ed. E. D. Hibbs & P. S. Jensen. Washington, D.C.: American Psychological Association, pp. 619–638.

FONAGY, P. & TARGET, M. (1998). Mentalization and the changing aims of child psychoanalysis. *Psychoanalytic Dialogues* 8:87–114.

FONAGY, P., MORAN, G. S., EDGECUMBE, R., KENNEDY, H., & TARGET, M. (1993). The roles of mental representations and mental processes in therapeutic action. *Psychoanalytic Study of the Child,* 48:9–48.

FRANKEL, J. B. (1998). The play's the thing. How the essential processes of therapy are seen most clearly in child therapy. *Psychoanalytic Dialogues* 8:149–182.

FREUD, A. (1936). *The Ego and the Mechanisms of Defense.* New York: International Universities Press.

FREUD, A. (1965). *Normality and Pathology in Childhood.* New York: International Universities Press.

GRAY, P. (1994). *The Ego and the Analysis of Defense.* Northvale, N.J.: Aronson.

GREENSPAN, S. (1997). *Developmentally Based Psychotherapy.* Madison, Conn.: International Universities Press.

HURRY, A. (1998). Psychoanalysis and developmental therapy. In *Psychoanalysis and Developmental Therapy,* ed. A. Hurry. Madison, Conn.: International Universities Press, pp. 32–73.

KOHRMAN, R., FINEBERG, H., GELMAN, R. & WEISS, S. (1971). Techniques of child analysis: Problems of countertransference. *Internat. J. Psycho-Anal.* 52:487–497.

LILLESKOV, R. K. (1971). Transference and transference neurosis in child analysis. In *The Unconscious Today: Essays in Honor of Max Schur,* ed. M. Kanzer. New York: International Universities Press, pp. 400–408.

MAENCHEN, A. (1984). The handling of overt aggression in child psychoanalysis. *Psychoanalytic Study of the Child,* 39:393–405.

MAHLER, M. & FURER, E. (1968). *Infantile Psychosis. Vol. I. on Human Symbiosis and the Vicissitudes of Individuation.* New York: International Universities Press.

MAHLER, M., PINE, F., & BERGMAN, A. (1975). *The Psychological Birth of the Human Infant.* New York: Basic Books.

MAYES, L. & COHEN, D. J. (1993a). Playing and therapeutic action in child analysis. *International Journal of Psycho-Analysis,* 74:1225–1244.

MAYES, L. & COHEN, D. J. (1993b). The social matrix of aggression. *Psychoanalytic Study of the Child,* 48:145–169.

NAGERA, H. (1966). *Early Childhood Disturbances, the Infantile Neurosis, and the Adult Disturbances.* New York: International Universities Press.

NEUBAUER, P. B. (1971). Transference in childhood: A review of special issues. In *The Unconscious Today: Essays in Honor of Max Schur,* ed. M. Kanzer. New York: International Universities Press, pp. 452–455.

OLESKER, W. (1999). Treatment of a boy with atypical ego development. *Psychoanalytic Study of the Child*, 54:25–46.

ORNSTEIN, A. & ORNSTEIN, P. (1994). On the conceptualization of clinical facts in psychoanalysis. *International Journal of Psycho-Analysis*, 75:977–994.

SANDLER, J., KENNEDY, H., & TYSON, R. L. (1980). *The Technique of Child Psychoanalysis: Discussions with Anna Freud*. Cambridge: Harvard University Press.

SCHARFMAN, M. A. (1971). Transference phenomena in adolescent analysis. In *The Unconscious Today: Essays in Honor of Max Schur*, ed. M. Kanzer. New York: International Universities Press, pp. 422–435.

SCOTT, M. (1998). Play and therapeutic action. Multiple perspectives. *Psychoanalytic Study of the Child*, 53:94–101.

SEGAL, H. (1978). On symbolism. *Internat. J. Psycho-Anal.* 59:315–319.

SMIRNOFF, V. (1971). *The Scope of Child Analysis*. New York: International Universities Press.

SPIEGEL, S. (1996). *An Interpersonal Approach to Child and Adolescent Psychotherapy*. Northvale, N.J.: Aronson.

STRACHEY, J. (1934). The nature of the therapeutic action of psychoanalysis. *Internat. J. Psycho-Anal.* 15:127–159.

SUGARMAN, A. (1994). Helping child analysands observe mental functioning. *Psychoanalytic Psychology* 11:329–339.

SUGARMAN, A. (1999). The boy in the iron mask: Superego issues in the analysis of a 2-year-old encopretic boy. *Psychoanalytic Quarterly*, 58:497–519.

SUGARMAN, A. (2003). A new model for conceptualizing insightfulness in the psychoanalysis of young children. *Psychoanalytic Quarterly*, 72:325–355.

SUGARMAN, A. & JAFFE, L. S. (1990). Toward a developmental understanding of the self schema. *Psychoanalysis and Contemporary Thought* 13:117–138.

TYSON, P. (1996). Object relations, affect management, and psychic structure formation: The concept of object constancy. *Psychoanalytic Study of the Child*, 51:172–189.

WEISS, S. (1964). Parameters in child analysis. *JAPA* 12:587–599.

YANOF, J. (1996). Language, communication and transference in child analysis. 1. Selective mutism: The medium is the message. 2. Is child analysis really analysis? *JAPA* 44:79–116.

The "Sweet and Sour" of Being Lonely and Alone

LUCILLE SPIRA, CSW, Ph.D., and
ARLENE KRAMER RICHARDS, Ed. D.

*This paper explores the question of why some lonely people seem to for-
get what goes on in their treatment when they are away from the analyst's presence. The authors look at loneliness from the perspective of a
female patient using the transference to attempt to undo a childhood
trauma of early abandonment and neglect. This woman appeared
child-like and helpless while she resisted using insight. A dream highlights the unconscious wishes and fantasies that fueled her stance in
treatment. The premise is that by not allowing herself to use her insights when out of the analyst's presence, she was maintaining herself
as the lonely abandoned child that she had been. Using her treatment
in this way seemed to assuage her pain while she waited for the father
of her fantasy. The price she paid for waiting was loneliness, loss of
self-esteem, and a life with few adult pleasures. Her fantasy of cure followed a sequence from a deficit model, to a model of internalization of
bad objects, to a conflict model. The authors believe that sequencing the
view of her troubles in this way had a therapeutic effect.*

Lucille Spira is a member of NYSPP and co-chair, with Arlene Kramer Richards, of
the Apsaa Discussion Group, "Towards an Understanding of Loneliness and Aloneness in Women." Arlene Kramer Richards is a Fellow of IPTAR and Supervisor and
Training analyst of the New York Freudian Society and of the IPA; and a member of
the American Psychoanalytic Association.

The patient was treated by Lucille Spira. The discussion is a collaboration between
the authors. We wish to thank Doctors Martin Widzer and Jane Kupersmidt, and
members of the discussion group of the American Psychoanalytic Association "Towards an Understanding of Loneliness and Aloneness in Women" for generously
sharing ideas and clinical material that has enriched our understanding.

The Psychoanalytic Study of the Child 58, ed. Robert A. King, Peter B. Neubauer,
Samuel Abrams, and A. Scott Dowling (Yale University Press, copyright © 2003 by
Robert A. King, Peter B. Neubauer, Samuel Abrams, and A. Scott Dowling).

WHAT MAKES SOME LONELY PATIENTS ACT AS IF THEY DO NOT REMEM-
ber what went on in sessions after they leave the office? One such patient, Ms. A, maintained continuity from one session to the next, but
recalled her insights only vaguely, and only when she was with her analyst. Having arrived in New York from the South a year before, Ms. A
was in her late twenties when she began treatment. Dissatisfied with
her office temp job, she could not see her way to a career that might
satisfy her. Worried, and neglectful of her appearance, she seemed
like a fearful and fragile teenager who was large and overweight. To
soothe herself she would overeat or smoke. She was lonely and without friends, which she attributed to her large size, lack of sophistica-
tion, and a chronic rheumatoid condition. While she reported being
unhappy about being alone, she avoided potential friendships as she
held on to a belief that no one whom she would value would be interested in her.

Almost everything made her anxious and advocating for herself
aroused intense anxiety. When she began treatment, she said that she
wanted to feel less anxious and in better control of her eating. She
also wanted a college degree and a career. Later, we came to see that
she wanted something else even more; she wanted to be the favorite
child of her father. After years of treatment we came to believe that
keeping herself alone preserved her fantasy of becoming her father's
favorite as she had imagined herself being as a little girl.

The following vignette typified her behavior. She had not been
given her recent paycheck because the woman who usually gave her
the check had been absent. Although she needed the money, she
could not ask her male department manager for it because she
feared that he might be annoyed by such a request or think that
she was rude. She said that she would die if the manager reacted toward her as she imagined that he might. I asked if she were scared to
ask him for her check because he was a man. She said that she
thought his age and position intimidated her. I said that fear might
be related to other experiences when she had asked something from
an older powerful person. We could not understand why her fear was
so intense. Because I thought that she wanted me to confirm or dis-
confirm her belief about what might happen with the manager, I told
her that while I could not guarantee how he would react if she asked
for her check, I would be available to help her with her feelings,
whatever might happen. She decided to wait for her check rather
than chance the result that she feared. She waited several days. Over
the years she kept longing ineffectually for most of what she wanted.

Ms. A acted as if she had all the time in the world. The issue of time came up while trying to understand one of her self-abusive behaviors. She was surprised that I thought it had been a long time, adding that she herself had not thought about time, since she did not know how long treatment should take. Then she had been in treatment for about nine years.

Ms. A's History

Ms. A is a middle child; she has a sister two years older and another two years younger. She was subject to a number of traumas and misfortunes, which included her mother leaving home for a year when Ms. A was three. Ms. A has no memories of having missed her mother during that time. She did not blame her problems on her mother's leaving. During her mother's absence, a nanny, with whom Ms. A became embroiled in a struggle over bowel habits, cared for the children. As Ms. A reports it, the nanny believed that her failure to defecate on schedule meant that she was withholding her feces; Ms. A believes that the nanny punished her by isolating her.

Ms. A was criticized for her weight since she was four years old and offered bribes to reduce. She was messy in her appearance and with her belongings throughout childhood. Her mother had the task of seeing to it that she met the father's standards for attractiveness and neatness. The fact that Ms. A did not in fact conform in these ways caused her father to criticize her mother; Ms. A later decided that she was guilty of causing the breakup of the marriage during her own adolescence.

Ms. A also suffered from her mother's alcoholism. Ms. A said her mother constantly criticized her unfairly, did not love her, and was meaner when she was drunk. Her successful father worked long hours. The care of the children was provided by a series of nannies and maids who her mother told her disliked her because she was loud and messy. But mostly she and her sisters were left to their own devices. Ms. A idealized her father and believed that she was his favorite because he granted her requests for toys and other things. Her sisters too saw her as the favorite, as they felt that they received even less of his attention than she did. Her requests seemed to have been few. She did not report having taken care of her mother or siblings, nor did she describe herself as a pseudo-companion to her father. She was the child who mirrored his tastes and interests, that is, for particular foods and music. She tried to live up to his wish for her to be a singer despite a sense of hopelessness about her ability.

While she remembered being lonely and scared in childhood, the painful reality of her life had not kept Ms. A from having friends at school. In adolescence, she felt less a part of the group because she tried to avoid dating; so scared was she of the pressures that she saw went with it. She avoided being admired by boys by making herself obese.

When she was about 14, her father separated from her mother and took up residence with a woman reputed to have been his mistress. Eventually they married and moved out of her home state. No one in her family had had any inkling that her father was leaving; she remembered being scared when he did not show up for a week. As a college senior she transferred to a school in his new community, losing credits in the process. She felt humiliated when he showed little interest in her. But because her sisters had not been offered this "opportunity," to live near her father, she concluded that she was the favorite; this perception evoked guilt as it had in her childhood.

Ms. A had her first sexual encounter when she was in her early twenties. She allowed a handyman to seduce her, only to have him leave her when his previous lover returned. Shortly after this brief affair, she became ill with a rheumatoid condition that she learned would be chronic. For years she believed that her illness was caused by her relationship with the man. She saw her condition also as a punishment for choosing someone of so much less status than her father. The illness clinched her belief that she could never be a performer. If she were not to be a singer, however, she wondered how she would be able to recapture even her father's lukewarm interest.

TREATMENT

Her symptoms were persistent and witnessing her suffering was painful for the analyst. Each of her traumatic experiences contributed to her fear of failure and frequent claims of being the victim of other people's rudeness or inconsistencies. The analyst told her that she was neglectful toward herself not only because she was unsophisticated, as she claimed, but also because she was treating herself as she had been treated, turning passive experience into active. Rather than complain about the loss of her mother, her concern was to hold onto her *father's* love.

Through many years of treatment Ms. A avoided opportunities that might have provided her with comfort or pleasure despite her wishes. For years she resisted buying a comfortable bed. She did not complain enough to her doctor to receive adequate pain management. Despite her suffering, she was rarely tearful when discussing her history or current situation. Her empathy toward others did not extend to herself.

She did not alienate her peers at work, nor did she report not liking them. She once generously gave a peer a computer for his child; she gave to collections for office parties. She reported waiting to be asked to join peers at lunch; she did not take social initiatives like asking to join social groups at work. Thus her loneliness was due to her passivity rather than exclusion by others.

She believed that she was greedy and messy because she could not be any different. The small steps she took toward her career goal led to modest successes, although she did not feel empowered, nor did she seem to build on these successes. For example, she would get her hair cut so that it was neat, but then not cut it again for a year so that she looked increasingly messy again. When her boss criticized her messy desk, she cleaned it up, but did not keep it clean. In therapy she made an effort to be what she thought of as a good patient: never missing sessions, always paying her bill on time, and being polite. The greediness she reported as part of her history and her current life was absent. She never criticized the analyst. Characterized as "bad," she acted "good" in treatment. At work she enacted her mother's view of her, so that her bosses experienced her oppositional characteristics.

She had first insisted her troubles were due to personal deficit, then accepted that neglect had a role, and about ten years into treatment, we saw how conflict played a role in her compromises. Remarking that the only job she was fit for was to be a street cleaner, she stated that this was a job for an "ex-con." This self-perception contributed to her slow progress. While she berated herself for past "crimes" like her overeating, which she saw as greed, we eventually came to see that she had other reasons for her guilt. Previously, her taking responsibility for all that was bad had been understood as a way to defend against helplessness by defensive omnipotence. Fantasies of revenge were persistent, in the form of fears that someone she knew might be killed in a transit accident. It was always someone with whom she had been angry. Eventually, she connected this fear to one she had had in childhood of her mother dying in a car crash. Later she was able to talk about her fear that my plane might crash when I left for vacation. In this way we began to talk about present feelings and fantasies that might be contributing to her guilt, rather than only those from the past.

Oedipal interpretations resonated with Ms. A since she could connect with feeling envious, fearing envy, and being angry when she thought she was being excluded. Her long-held guilt for stealing sweets and thus depriving her mother and sisters was eventually interpreted as a displacement of her fear of having stolen her father from her mother and sisters. She expressed fear that her mother would envy her if she were to have a richer life.

Her fear of being envied showed up in the transference as well. Once she kept her raincoat on during a session just before she was to meet her father. Her step-mother was not going to be there. Under the coat was a nice dress. The analyst interpreted her fear of the analyst's envy. Her usual messy teenager-like style functioned as a compromise that allowed her to hold on to her father while not exciting the envy of other women. Following that interpretation she adopted a less messy but plain style.

Eventually, we were able to understand what made it so difficult for her to use their collaboration when they were not together. She related a very dramatic fantasy that illustrated how her relationship to her father sustained her isolation of her insights. She reported feeling frustrated by spending endless weekends alone in her apartment. She added that it was particularly uncomfortable when it was warm because she could not open her windows because she did not want a pigeon to fly in and hurt her. When she was about nine she had left the kitchen door open and a bird flew into the oven. Her father was called home to handle the "crisis." She remembered that he told her afterward to keep the door closed, because if birds fly in, she could get hurt. This memory seemed to be not only a screen memory but also the kernel of an organizing principle by which Ms. A tried to lead her life, a magical solution for safety. Being open and taking anything in is dangerous. This fantasy might explain why she was not open to the interpretations that came from her treatment. While this idea did not work magic, it did open a dialogue in which we could consider how she was allowing her father to impact her life.

Ms. A's idealization of her father had been maintained in the face of constant disappointments. Several events occurred that resulted in her father being idealized less. She came to trust her analyst. Once her father set her up with a date by giving her phone number to a man from New York who had visited his country club in the South. Ms. A fantasized that the man was the "one." She felt humiliated when they met because the man seemed shocked that she was ten years older than he. She felt hurt by her father had set her up for rejection. Before this date, the analyst had opened up the possibility that the man might not be what she imagined. Later, she told me that our discussion had, to some degree cushioned the pain that would have resulted had she gone in cold. She began to consider that her father could be sadistic and withholding.

Seeing some of her father's negative traits seemed to increase her investment in herself. She began to see the analyst as more connected to her and to her reality than her father was. While she still wanted him to see her as mirroring him, she began to see her own ideas as valid. She also overvalued the analyst.

About two years ago and after many years of treatment, a poignant moment allowed her to consider how she might be overvaluing our relationship at her own expense. On returning from vacation, the analyst noticed that she had laryngitis, and wondered if she had been neglecting her health. When asked how long she had been suffering with the chest cold and laryngitis, she tearfully said that when the analyst is away she has no need for her real voice, the one that talks about her feelings; it was as if she herself were not reason enough to take care of herself. It was the first time she had cried about anything that occurred between them. The theme of others denying her voice began to appear when she believed that she was being excluded. When she imagines others to be more powerful than herself she narrows the range of her voice by excluding the part that tells her to take care of herself.

Now we return to the question: Why do some lonely patients act as if what went on in therapy does not exist for them outside of the therapeutic relationship? Thus far, we have touched on a number of factors that we understood as contributing to the way that she used her treatment: the early history which likely made it difficult for her to trust, the anal aspects of her character, her guilt over her wishes, and her relationship with her father, both real and fantasied. These factors kept her locked alone in her past. A dream she had after thirteen years of treatment added to our understanding of why she seemed to forget the therapy collaboration when she was alone. It suggests that Ms. A consciously wished to be a baby with her father as she unconsciously wished to be my favorite baby.

Ms. A's Dream

Patient: I had a dream. You were in it. We went on a trip together—but it was to my family, dad and Mary [step-mother]. Dad was playing with a baby [Her father and Mary do not have children]. I said to myself: I feel so jealous. Then we had to do this presentation. Yours was really good, and it was amazing how you put it together with very little effort—colors and miniature figures. It was really good. Then, we are leaving and you are going on your way. You left carrying your portfolio with you. That's it.

Analyst: What do you make of it?

Patient: In the beginning we met and you had to persuade me to go, in a neutral way. Maybe in the dream you are helping me to get to another someplace. But, I'm not doing well, just an observer—watching it all—not participating. I brought you to meet my dad because maybe I wanted you to see how many problems I have because of my family. Dad was playing with the baby. I said to myself I wish I could be that baby, that's why I was jealous, I wanted to be the baby. I was bringing you to the root of my problems. I have been worried that I can't job hunt well. You might think I'm not doing everything I can.

Analyst: Is there something that I did that makes you feel that way?

Patient: No, I think I wish I could report more progress. I want to be doing everything I can. I want to get on with things. I may also want you to think I'm the best patient. But, instead I think: all these years, and I throw things out. I'm quick to avoid what I can't easily do. I take things in from here, but I take the far road to get there. It feels like a long wooded forest and I get lost sometimes and I forget about reality a little bit; space out denying myself and punishing myself. Sometimes I think I forget that when I think I am indulging myself I may actually be denying myself something else. When we talk about it here, I get it but, when I'm alone and have to think it out, I think it's a struggle. I have to make decisions by myself; that's why we went on the journey so I could do that, it's hard. The presentation in the dream, it was weird. I was surprised how good it was pulling a rabbit out of a hat. It was as if you were performing magic, but I knew it wasn't magic. I was impressed and confused. There was a slanted board you could display pictures on it like panoramas. You were in it and shrunk down walking across it. I said oh my god and you used lighting also, wow cool then over.

Analyst: Is there a fantasy about what I do?

Patient: I think you have a perfect but difficult job. Perfect because no boss, you are your own boss, nice setting the hard part is always having to deal with the human elements instead of like with paper work that I do. You don't know what they will bring to the table. You met my father in the dream, weird but you didn't really since there was no interacting. Mary was peripherally there on the side, some others too but can't figure that out. I wished I could be that baby, but that's a sweet and sour wish. What are the chances of my father being able to do better? Very very iffy, and I'd have to grow up and that wouldn't be so good either. No new beginning. This dream was different, but the same too as some of those dreams that have a supernatural quality, those are where evil things are out to get me. But not this dream, but I knew it might be lurking in the background, never really safe. I'm go-

ing to get working on my job hunt. I didn't need to take time out to
go to Janet's get-together, would not have made a bit of difference if I
had not shown up. I used the party as an excuse not to work on my
stuff.

Analyst: Does the dream say anything about that?

Patient: Tells me I avoid, wishing someone else could do it for me. That's
a wish in the dream: if I could follow someone, not have to think for
myself, you know like a baby. I think I have a wish to recreate the past
and have it come out so I would feel better. When I stop being active I
fall back. I hang on to staying passive. Being active takes me a universe
away from the possibility of the fantasy. I need a magician, give you
that job.

Analyst: Maybe you want me to know not only how painful it was when
your sister was born, since it felt like you lost your dad, but how you
try to avoid the painful reality that you can't get him back by giving all
the awe to me. Maybe I fall into it, and that doesn't leave you confident.

This dream was her story of her treatment. I was the one in awe reversing the dream—since she had not reported many dreams nor
had she taken an active role in analyzing her productions. She was
newly willing to recognize what she had achieved in her treatment.
Beyond the two degrees and her six-figure salary, she had learned to
use a process that enabled her to feel in touch with herself, rather
than lost. She now understands her defenses and why she needed to
take the "far" road. She was demonstrating that she could hold on to
her insights.

After she told me the dream, I chose to let her take charge rather
than to refocus her on each dream element. What's new here is her
readiness to mourn the fact that "you can't go home again." Her use
of the metaphor "sweet and sour" shows that she is recognizing the
conflict inherent in her wish. In other words, if you act like you know
how to get along in the world, you have to give up on the idea that
you can still get the family that you never had in childhood. As we
can see from Ms. A's resolutions, it may be that you can only let go of
the wish in tiny stages, as you come to realize bit by bit that it was a
fantasy maintained at the price of self-esteem and adult gratifica-
tions. Interestingly, "sweet and sour" also refers to a favorite dish she
and her father enjoyed together.

Since Ms. A's parents had never acknowledged their role in her difficulties, I said that I was doing *too* much. I could see how I overwhelmed her, which left her feeling misunderstood and alone. The
painful affect in the dream is represented by her standing in my
shadow. It is also represented in the form of the lurking danger. This

danger is superego anxiety: punishment for rivalrous feelings toward the baby, toward Mary, (perhaps standing in for her mother), and less consciously toward me.

Over a year later Ms. A told me that when she doesn't stay on her track, she is choosing to ignore what we have done. She is aware that she can call upon her inner resources if she so chooses. After 15 years Ms. A, now over 40, has become able to make more favorable compromises that allow her friendships and more pleasure. She has her career and an advanced degree, has traveled, given up smoking, and controls her eating. She allows herself pleasure from a pet. Most importantly, however, she can own her skills and accept the fact that conflict plays a role in her life. How does she use our collaboration when we are not together? Recently, she put a world map in her office to symbolize that she never has to feel lost again. At an office event she recalled my idea that she overeats when angry with herself. Although she was not sure if she were in fact angry, she decided not to binge in case she was. Later, we could explore what she had been feeling. Her thoughts about her treatment? She has told me that I cannot retire for at least five years. We have yet to understand how she arrived at that time frame.

DISCUSSION

The following formulations derive from discussion by the authors. The ideas developed as we analyzed the clinical material and from our reading and experience with other lonely patients. To return to our original question: Why do people act as if what went on in therapy does not exist for them outside of the therapeutic relationship?

Abend (1979) showed how a patient's unconscious fantasy, as it interweaves with his/her theory of cure, can act as a resistance in treatment. He believes that it is important to analyze a patient's fantasy of cure as early as possible. In this case understanding the many layers of fantasy has taken many years and still goes on.

Ms. A's original goals were: to control her overeating (weight); position herself for a career; and reduce the anxiety that made such goals seem impossible. These wishes were associated with getting her father's love. While she was telling her analyst what she wanted, she was enacting something else; her theory of cure—to be re-parented by her analyst. We believe that her wish for her analyst to see her as good prevented her from using her treatment outside of her sessions. She had to be the obedient little girl and get praise more than she needed adult success. To rely on her insights outside of her sessions, even when they derived from her therapy, was in conflict with this wish to be a good girl. Using her mind on her own would mean being assertive. She equated assertiveness with greed, aggressiveness, and being bad. To act more adult by relying on her inner resources would mean giving up the hope of regaining her father—the father of her fantasy, where there were no rivals. Her wish to be loved had to be disguised as a wish to be a baby because it was less anxiety provoking for her to imagine being her father's baby than being his lover.

By trying to acquire what she missed in childhood, Ms. A was avoiding mourning. Her reluctance to use her insights reinforced her sense of helplessness as it determined her need for her analyst. This was a paternal transference; in the past she had made her father too important, now she needed her analyst for the same thing. The fact that her esteem suffered by her adherence to remaining child-like meant less to her than the fantasy that she could return to and correct her past.

Paradoxically, when Ms. A persisted in depending on her analyst's presence, she created her scenario of loneliness. Our understanding of this dynamic differs from that of Silverman (1998), who believed that her patient held on to his negative objects to *avoid* loneliness and from that of M. V. Bergmann (1985), who believed that her patients avoided marriage and children so as not to repeat the relationship with the draining helpless mothers of childhood. Her self-neglect and her compulsive eating was an identification with her neglectful alcoholic mother (Anna Freud, 1946). She numbed anxiety by compulsive eating just as her mother had numbed her feelings by drinking. Like many neglected children (Jarvis 1965), she had used compulsive behaviors to mitigate loneliness. The sequence we hypothesized was the wish for closeness and being loved, the prohibition of this wish when it caused loss of her mother's love, turning to father for this love and defensive turning toward compulsive eating to soothe her anxiety and depression. In her adult life this pattern cut her off from other people because it made her fat and unattractive and because it sapped the energies she would otherwise have had available to engage with them.

The major way in which Ms. A had attempted to deal with the loss of her mother and of her mother's love was to turn to her father for maternal nurturance. It was only later when she got into analysis that she experienced the analyst as nurturant in a dependable way that she could understand her loneliness as a child and see that her current loneliness was a recreation of a fantasy characterized by manic overoptimism (Klein 1963) in which her father would come to rescue, nurture, and admire her. This, in turn, allowed her to attempt to get something from her current environment that made her feel loved.

By understanding her loneliness as a longing for a specific lost object (Brenner 1974), she was enabled to assuage it with people in her current life. This differs from Fromm-Reichmann's (1959) formulation that those with "real" loneliness forget past objects and do not believe that there will be others in the future. By her forgetting the therapeutic relationship, Ms. A created a fantasy that mother was absent and father would have to rescue her. It allowed her to mute her analyst or abandon her for not being omnipresent, as she herself been abandoned. That she put her analyst in suspension only when she was not with her, and acted engaged in her presence, may explain why her analyst did not feel alone when she was with her, as others have found who work with some isolated patients (Greene and Kaplan 1978; Cohen 1982; Schafer 1995.) By forgetting her analyst, was she imagining that she was lonely when away from the patient (Anna Freud 1967)?

Her current reluctance to pursue a mate seems designed to protect her from being hurt as she had been in the past (Kohut and Wolf 1986). She fears humiliation from a man as she had it from her father. If she were to seek out a man, it is not clear to what degree social factors like being overweight in a culture that values slimness (Hirschmann and Munter 1988) and the scarcity of suitable men (Lieberman 1991; Rucker 1993) prevent her finding a mate.

Despite Ms. A's conflict about moving on with her life, and the fact that her analyst did not fully understand the depth of what was being enacted in treatment, Ms. A has been able to form new compromises that are more compatible with her adult ambitions, ones that leave her in less pain. What helped? We think it was a sequence of the analyst's hope, her initial acceptance of Ms. A's view of herself as a victim, her interest in listening to her feelings, and her understanding the defensive value of Ms. A's oppositional erasing of the interpretations. She needed to gradually become stronger, less guilty, and more sure about her analyst so that she could mourn the loss of her fantasy. The analyst's patiently waiting for Ms. A to establish her own schedule that finally allowed her to use the analyst's formulations to change her view of the world so that she could exercise her own power to form new relationships outside the analytic one.

Many analytic contributions helped in understanding this patient: the idea of fantasy formation (Freud 1907); the unconscious fantasy (Arlow 1991) as the discovery that leads to freedom from the unsatisfactory compromise formations (Brenner 1983); a developmental perspective including the way one symptom can reflect conflict from more than one psychosexual stage (A. Freud 1965); the various routes through which masochism can be traced through development (Novick and Novick 1996). M. S. Bergmann's (1966) idea of the dream as a communication led to focusing on what might be new in the patient's dreams and associations. Like D. J. Cohen (1990) we found that the patient who had suffered early loss could not sustain a sense of personal value. Our case corroborates his idea that for such patients the relationship with the analyst, although it is resisted, is necessary for the acquisition of such a sense of personal value.

BIBLIOGRAPHY

ABEND, S. (1979). Unconscious fantasy and theories of cure. *J. Amer. Psychoanal. Assn.* 27:579–596.

ARLOW, J., WITH DAVID BERES. Fantasy and identification in empathy, 217–234. In *Psychoanalysis.* J. Arlow. Madison, Conn. IUP.

BERGMANN, M. S. (1966). Intrapsychic and communicative aspects of the dream. *Int. J. Psychoanal.* 47:356–363.

BERGMANN, M. V. (1985). Effect of role reversal on delayed marriage and maternity. *Psychoanal. Study Child.* 40:197–219.

BRENNER, C. (1974). On the nature and development of affects: A unified theory. *Psychoanal. Quarterly.* 43:532–556.

―――― (1983). *The Mind in Conflict.* New York. IUP.

COHEN, D. J. (1990). Enduring sadness: Early loss, vulnerability and the shaping of character. *Psychoanal. Study Child.* 45:357–375. New Haven: Yale.

COHEN, N. A. (1982). On loneliness and the ageing process. *Int. J. Psychoanal.* 63:149–155.

FREUD, A. (1946). *The Ego and the Mechanisms of Defense.* New York: IUP.

―――― (1965). *Normality and Pathology in Childhood: Assessments of Development.* New York: IUP.

―――― (1967). About losing and being lost. *Psychoanal. Study Child.* 22:9–19.

FREUD, S. (1907[1906]). Delusions and dreams in Jensen's Gradiva. *Standard Edition* 9:3–95.

FROMM-REICHMANN, F. (1959). Loneliness. *Psychiatry.* 22:1–15.

GREENE, M. & KAPLAN, B. L. (1978). Aspect of loneliness in the therapeutic situation. *Int. Review. Psycho-anal.* 5:321–330.

HIRSCHMANN, J. R. & MUNTER, C. H. (1988). *Overcoming Overeating.* New York: Addison Wesley.

JARVIS, V. (1965). Loneliness and compulsion. *J. Amer. Psychoanal. Assn.* 13:122–158.

KLEIN, M. (1963). On the sense of loneliness. In *Writings of Melanie Klein 1946–1963*. (1984). New York: The New Library of Psychoanalysis.

KOHUT, H. & WOLF, E. S. (1986). The disorders of the self and their treatment: An outline. In *Essential Papers on Narcissism*. ed. A. P. Morrison. New York: IUP, 175–196.

LIEBERMAN, J. S. (1991). Issues in the psychoanalytic treatment of single females over thirty. *Psychoanal. Review* 78 (2):176–198.

NOVICK, J. & NOVICK, K. K. (1996). *Fearful Symmetry: The Development and Treatment of Sadomasochism*. Northvale, New Jersey: Jason Aronson Inc.

RUCKER, N. (1993). Cupid's misses: relational vicissitudes in the analyses of single women. *Psychoanalytic Psychology* 10 (3):377–391.

SCHAFER, R. (1995). Aloneness in the countertransference. *Psychoanalytic Quarterly* 64:496–516.

SILVERMAN, D. K. (1998). The tie that binds: Affect regulation, attachment, and psychoanalysis. *Psychoanalytic Psychology* 15(2):187–212.

Signs of Connection

Working with Deaf Parents and Hearing Children in a Nursery Setting

SARA ZAREM, PH.D.

When deaf adults find themselves the parents of a hearing child, a cycle of disrupted communication and attachment may ensue between the parent and child. Not only may the parent-child bond be compromised, but the social-emotional development of the child and the parents' feelings of empowerment may be at risk as well. This paper details a psychoanalytically-informed approach to working with mixed deaf and hearing parent-child relationships in a nursery setting where the goal is to prevent such potential disruptions and derailments.

THIS PAPER IS AN EXPLORATION OF A PSYCHOANALYTIC, PREVENTATIVE approach that has been developed to work with mixed deaf and hearing parent-child dyads in a nursery setting. Deaf parents and their hearing children (birth to three) meet with a (hearing) therapist for an hour and fifteen minutes twice a week. Usually just the mother attends but sometimes father joins or the parents alternate sessions. Meetings are held in a large nursery, with a variety of age-appropriate

Supervising psychologist at the Lexington Center for Mental Health Services, Inc., and in private practice in New York City.

The author would like to acknowledge the contribution of Diana Silber, M.S.W., and Asher Rosenberg, M.D., in developing the nursery model on which this paper is based. Thanks are also due to Dee Brodbar, M.A., Arlene Richards, Ed.D., Louis Aron, Ph.D., Shelia Blechner, M.S.W., Linda Larkin, Ph.D., and Jerome Levin, Ph.D., for their careful reading of and thoughtful feedback on this paper.

The Psychoanalytic Study of the Child 58, ed. Robert A. King, Peter B. Neubauer, Samuel Abrams, and A. Scott Dowling (Yale University Press, copyright © 2003 by Robert A. King, Peter B. Neubauer, Samuel Abrams, and A. Scott Dowling).

toys available for the child. Parents are encouraged to be both observers of and participants in their child's play. In addition to deafness, much of our parent population struggles with issues of poverty and domestic violence. Many have immigrated to the United States from other countries and have learned English and/or American Sign Language as their second language. While all the children are hearing, the deaf parents do not all have the same degree of hearing loss. Some are profoundly deaf, others hard-of-hearing.[1] It is not the hearing loss as an audiological phenomenon that is significant, so much as the impact the loss has had on the individual's significant relationships. With that in mind, our goals are to strengthen the parent-child bond, attend to the parents' own social-emotional needs and the ways in which they impact on the relationship with their child, and facilitate age-appropriate social-emotional development in the child. Each of these goals is uniquely influenced and created by both real and psychic meanings of deafness and hearing.

Working preventatively in a nursery setting is not a new idea. Selma Fraiberg (1980) brought psychoanalytic thinking into the nursery with her pioneering infant-psychotherapy work:

> In treatment we examine with the parents the past and the present in order to free them and their baby from old "ghosts" who have invaded the nursery, and then we must make meaningful links between the past and the present through interpretations that lead to insight. At the same time . . . we maintain the focus on the baby through the provision of developmental information and discussion. We move back and forth, between present and past, parent and baby, but we always return to the baby. (p. 61)

---

1. "Deafness is, itself, a heterogeneous category and as used here refers to an audiological condition. Deafness is generally divided into four classifications depending upon the degree of decibel loss: profound, severe, moderate, and mild. Some people are born with a hearing loss due to genetic factors or maternal illness; others become deafened by childhood illnesses or reactions to drugs. Some people have progressive losses, which worsen over their lifespan and/or develop later in life due to aging. There is not always a synchrony between the degree of objective loss and the person's subjective experience of their deafness. Thus, some people classified as hard-of-hearing may consider themselves "Deaf" and prefer to use sign rather than spoken language. Not all people who have a hearing loss choose to wear hearing aids and/or to use their voice and not all profoundly deaf persons choose to use ASL exclusively or even partially. When Deafness is spelled with an upper-case "D" it refers to much more than an audiological loss. Rather, it refers to a group of deaf people who share a language—ASL and a culture mediated through that language. Deafness, with a capital "D" is thus no longer defined as a *lack* of hearing so much as a *presence* of a unique language and culture (Padden and Humphries, 1988).

She was followed by many other important analytic researcher/clinicians such as Beatrice Beebe (Beebe and Lachmann, 1988), Alicia Lieberman (Lieberman et al., 2000), and Daniel Stern (1985), whose work drew on and elaborated upon psychoanalytic and developmental models. To date, there has been little written about nursery work with deaf-hearing dyads. This paper hopes to contribute to the infant-psychotherapy and attachment literature by looking at the special case of deaf-hearing dyads. In hearing-hearing or deaf-deaf dyads, the issue of language and communication is taken for granted. Children learn language naturally, and they share the same native language as their parents. However, in deaf-hearing mixtures, language learning is neither natural nor necessarily easy and parents and children may share different "maternal" tongues.

Of all the many functions that language serves, from the communication of information, to enhancing cognition, to self-regulation, it is as the creator/mediator of the emotional relationship between parent and child that has been the most compromised in our deaf and hearing dyads. Language helps to clarify and deepen the bond between parent and child, yet language also emerges from that bond. Language links the child emotionally to the caretaker. Recent studies in attachment point to the importance of the parents' ability to mentalize their infant as a critical factor in creating/maintaining a secure attachment. Peter Fonagy (Fonagy and Target, 2001) points out how the process of attachment includes not only physical protection (Belsky, 1999), stress regulation (Cicchetti and Walker, 2001), the establishment of attentional mechanisms (Posner and Rothbart, 2000), but the development of mentalizing capacities. By mentalizing capacity, Fonagy means that in a secure attachment, the parents' thinking about the child as a separate person whose behavior had agency and meaning allows the child to conceptualize herself as a distinct, feeling, and thinking person. "A child's awareness of the mental world arises intersubjectively, through a process of having been thought about . . . we consider the psychological self to be a re-internalisation of one's thoughts and feelings as they have been perceived and understood by the other." (Fonagy and Target, 2001, p. 8) This ability to mentalize, in turn, is dependent upon the parent being able to symbolically represent their infant's feelings and to communicate them to the infant through language. In hearing families, this dialectical relationship between language and attachment is taken for granted; working with mixed hearing and deaf family members allows us to deconstruct this relationship and look more closely at its complexity. Let me begin with a clinical example.

LOOKING AT THE PARENT-CHILD DYAD

Patty is an engaging 26-month-old toddler. She is hearing. Both of her parents are deaf. As she enters the nursery, her eye catches a sound toy. She picks it up and brings it over to her father. She presses down upon the picture of a cow and there's a "moo." Her father directs her attention to the picture and signs "cow." Patty looks intently at her father and copies his sign. They smile at each other. He then points to another picture, cat, and signs "cat." Again she follows. As I watch their interaction I note the pleasure they feel together. Patty clearly adores her father, and he beams with delight and pride at her. It is a very moving moment between them. Then Patty's attention wanders; she turns away from him goes off to play with some tools. Her father is upset; their visual line of communication is ruptured. Using his voice, which is not very clear, he calls her name, trying to (re)attract her attention. His voice is high-pitched and shrill to my ears. His facial expression is one of anger. She orients to him, but ignores his gestures to return. I wonder how she experiences his voice. What sounds unsettling to me may feel comforting and familiar to her. With a shrug of my shoulders, I sign, "she's two . . ." meaning that her behavior is typical of the short attention span of young children. The father is angry. "Bad attitude. No respect," he signs. He has read her behavior as a rejection of him. The pleasure of the previous moment is shattered. He is hurt, angry, and shamed. His worry that Patty will not respect him is linked with his own prior experience of feeling/being disrespected as a deaf man in a hearing world. He breaks eye contact with me and gazes downward. Patty cannot understand why her father's face is angry; she becomes more defiant as he increasingly demands that she attend to him and the animal pictures. My attempts to normalize Patty's behavior, as the "hearing expert," succeed only in shaming him and reminding him of the painful gulf between hearing and deaf worlds. Patty's subsequent efforts to reconnect with her father are then rebuffed by him.

Note how, when there is reciprocity in the dyad, the pleasure and sense of safety and connection between Patty and her father is clear. Once disrupted by Patty's roving attention, however, her play becomes less symbolic (putting tools in and out of a box), and her father's self-esteem plummets. Later efforts on Patty's part to re-engage her father are only partially successful. She turns to me, the hearing therapist. From my vantage point, this turning toward me is because I understand her; from the father's it is because I am hearing. This then re-enacts for the father the familiar feeling of being the only deaf person in his hearing family of origin where no one signs or understands him and he is left feeling "bad," shamed, vulnerable, and alone. This brief sequence illustrates the importance of simultaneously keeping in mind the parent-child relationship, the needs of the child, and the needs of the parent. Disruptions in any one of these three areas impact upon the other two.

Looking at the Impact of the Parents' Background

Most deaf adults have grown up a hearing family. Approximately 90 percent of deaf children have hearing parents (Meadow, 1980). The etiology of their deafness is most often genetic; maternal rubella or early childhood illnesses, two other causes, are much more infrequent. Having a deaf child in the family, as Harvey and Dym (1987) point out, places enormous external and internal stress on the entire family system:

> The deaf child influences everything, from the use of time and space, financial arrangements, travel patterns, patterns of communication among all family members, and to the family's image of itself as well or not well, competent or incompetent, nurturant or not nurturant (p. 55).

For Patty's father, Joe, diagnosis of his deafness, following a childhood illness, led to the family's immigration to the United States. Joe believes that his family relocated here from southern Italy, so that he could get a better education as a deaf person. Uprooting oneself from one's native culture is an enormous endeavor, reflecting another major loss and yet also a hopefulness for the future. Although his parents have been living here for more than 20 years, they do not speak English. Note the many potential meanings for attachment and connection in just this "fact" alone. Is their seeming refusal to learn English a continuing reflection of unresolved feelings about Joe's deafness and its impact on the family? Is there continuing conflict about coming here and the cost of Joe's deafness? Does Joe's deafness make him both specially loved and resented?

While having a deaf person in the family influences everyone, the experience for the deaf person is often one of intense isolation. Most hearing parents of deaf children do not learn to sign; 88 percent of families who have a deaf child do not use a sign language system of communication (Harvey and Dym, 1987). Hearing parents most often want their deaf children to learn spoken English so that children and their parents can participate in the hearing world and share a common language and culture. When their child's deafness is diagnosed, hearing parents need to mourn the loss of the child they thought they had (Solnit and Stark, 1961). This realization, in itself, can be a daunting process, and the parents' successful working through of this depends on many factors such as degree of loss, child's age at diagnosis, parents' own character and history, and degree of family support. Parents' reluctance to learn sign language is often the result of incomplete or chronic mourning. Yet asking hearing parents to learn another language is itself a prodigious task and sign language (ASL) is, indeed, another complete language (Bellugi, 1970; Stokoe, 1970). Imagine what it means for parent and child not to share the same language. In every interaction between them, the parents will be reminded of their child's difference from them, a realization that entails the loss of the natural pleasure and ease of communication. For a deaf person, learning to accommodate to the hearing through speaking and lip-reading is a long, arduous process, often only minimally successful. Research indicates that the best lip-reader gets, at most, a third of what is actually being said on the lips of the speaker. (Jeffers and Borley, 1964). The quality of a deaf person's spoken speech varies from clear to unclear. Lacking auditory feedback, deaf people have great difficulty modulating the tone, pitch, and rhythm of their voices; consequently, there are often enormous gaps between what the deaf person believes they are communicating and what the hearing person understands. Thus, many deaf adults have had minimal communicative contact with their hearing parents as they grew up. They were not immersed in a world rich with sound and aural meaning, and later, with the coming of words, there was little or no story-telling, signs-alongs, word plays, or talk about thoughts and feelings.

How do such "facts" as difference, isolation, and poor or at best limited communication become psychically elaborated for the deaf person? How are the hearing parents' complex feelings about their child's deafness internalized by the deaf person? Mintzer et al. (1984) point out that parents who have handicapped children sometimes experience their infants as negative extensions of themselves. Derailment in empathy, pleasurable contact, and mutual regulation may occur, and the child internalizes negative projections of himself and negative expectations regarding connectedness with others (cf. Fonagy and Target, 2000; Stern, 1985).

Moving forward in time, to the deaf parent's current experience, what does it mean for the deaf parent to have a hearing child? How is that child conceptualized by the parent? Who is the child for the parent? Lieberman et al. (2000) speak of hearing parents who misread their infants' behaviors and pathologically construct their children as being "evil," "destructive," "invisible," or "insatiable." While these misreadings may occur in deaf-child parent-child pairs as well, we also see the "responsible" infant and the "disappointing" infant. Some deaf parents tell us that they are delighted to have a hearing child—the hearing child will be able to take care of them, become their ears, and they often parentify their child and fail to read the child's age-appropriate needfulness. Other deaf parents are disappointed; the hearing child is the Other. They mourn for the deaf child they didn't have and worry about how they will communicate with their hearing child. If their mourning is incomplete or chronic, then there is a repetition of what the deaf parent experienced with his hearing family: disrupted conceitedness and negative attribution. Joe sees Patty as older and more responsible than she is. Because she is a hearing person, he attributes to her knowledge and intentions beyond her chronological age. He is proud of how smart she is. He tells me how she alerts him to the ringing of the phone or the presence of someone at the door. She should, therefore, "know" that her turning away from him is rude and disrespectful. It is difficult for Joe to realize that Patty's hearing often makes her feel scared and confused because he cannot help her understand what she has heard.

Patty and her father are again playing. Patty is quite directive. She gestures to the hula-hoops at the back of the room and indicates that he and I should lay them down on the floor to play the marching/jumping game, which we have all played before. Six hoops are placed next to each other. "Stand here," Patty gestures to Dad. "Now jump." She directs me to do the same and, together, we three jump up and down. Then we are to take big marching steps in and out of the hoops. And then we are to sit down inside them. Once seated, Joe gets the idea to pick up the hoop and pull it over his head and bring it back down again. Patty imitates. Joe then takes the hoop and taps it against Patty's. She giggles. He repeats the tap, but does it harder. She looks up at him, giggles again. This is fun. But Joe keeps increasing the pressure of the tap, and each time the sound is louder. Finally, Patty becomes frightened by the loud noise, and stops the game. He does not realize that Patty has become frightened by the loud sound. He cannot hear it. Patty gestures toward the papers and crayons and "baby" signs "(let's) draw." She wants a quieter activity. I sign, "that was a scary noise."

At the same time, Joe also sees Patty as the hearing Other. When he talks about his experience in his family of origin, it is with the belief that he was ignored, devalued, and misunderstood by its hearing members. Not surprisingly, Joe expects to be rejected and dismissed as a deaf person; these expectations also color his interactions with Patty and, transferentially, with me. Part of the work with Joe, therefore, is to support and facilitate changing notions of who Patty is. In order to do this, I must be sensitive to Joe's experience of me as a hearing person. As much as I wish to avoid these (re)enactments of helplessness, shame, and isolation, they are inevitable. My goal is to establish a strong enough alliance with him that we can explore these enactments and use them productively in our work. If I must be the hearing parent who fails, it is hoped that I can also be the hearing parent who succeeds—the hearing parent who can help him to reflect upon his own experience.

If language was an issue in Joe's family of origin where no one learned to sign, how will language be used in his own family? Joe is not especially oral. His wife, Betty, is more oral than he, although her speech is not readily intelligible. He prefers to use ASL with Patty; Betty uses more signed English with Patty, while Joe and Betty use ASL with each other.[2] Because Joe lives near his own parents and they are very involved with Patty, Patty is frequently exposed to spoken Italian. She hears spoken English from the TV, speech therapy classes, and within Betty's family of origin. Exposed to such a melange of language, Patty signs and vocalizes. What language ought I to use? Both parents want me to do total communication, to voice and sign. I am wary of this. Too often the hearing child will attend to the voice, not the sign. Since our goal is to facilitate the natural development of language between deaf parent and child—ASL—introducing voice serves to create a wedge between Patty and her parents, emphasizing our similarity and their difference.

Patty's vocalizations are often unclear. I wonder whether her words are imitations of her parents' voices and/or a representation of the mixture of languages to which she is exposed. Her sign is not always comprehensible. Sometimes she moves her hands and arms in rhyth-

---

2. ASL (American Sign Language) is a language with its own syntax, grammar, and structure, and is signed without using spoken voice. Although there are other signing systems used in teaching and communicating with deaf persons, such as Total Communication and Signing Exact English, they are based on spoken English. It should also be noted that researchers have found that deaf children acquiring signed languages do so without any modification, loss, or delay to the timing, content, and natural course associated with reaching all linguistic milestones observed in spoken languages. (Petitto and Marentette, 1991).

mic imitation of her parents' conversations; sometimes she uses "baby signs"—technically incorrect word formations that are nevertheless intelligible and precursors of more formal language—like a hearing child's use of "scetti" for spaghetti. At 28 months, Patty can code switch: she signs with voice off to her father; she talks and signs to her mother (who can often read her lips) and tends increasingly to talk with me, although I generally sign with her.

But it is not only the question of what language is being spoken, but how that language is being used. In many middle-class hearing families, the infant is very early on surrounded by language. The child's earliest behaviors are verbalized and given meaning, "Oh, you're smiling at Daddy!" For deaf parents, especially those that were raised in hearing families where communication was so limited, and/or in working-class families, language use is more restricted.[3] Parents often sign commands (stop it, sit down, etc.) or simply label objects (ball, cat, dog). More rarely do they use full sentences and elaboration such as, "Look at the big red ball. Wow, it's bouncing fast!" Attention is directed to external functions and behaviors as opposed to feelings. Thus, a deaf parent might pick up that their child was hungry and sign "eat" with a raised eyebrow, (meaning, do you want something to eat) and respond by getting the child a cookie. A hearing parent might ask "Are you hungry? Do you want a cookie?" thus labeling the inner feeling for the child. It is not that the deaf parent ignores the child's hunger; rather, it is that the language is not used to label the inner child's state.

Once again we need to go back a generation—to Joe's experience with his own parents. What was language learning like for Joe and his parents? Like many deaf clients, Joe describes how painful the process of learning language was. In hearing families, the ease of learning language is taken for granted; sound and language are

---

3. Linguist Basil Bernstein (1975) discusses how language use varies across social classes. Working class parents use what he calls "restricted codes," while middle-class parents use "elaborated codes." Labeling feelings and developing the context of a communication are aspects of middle-class language use. Similarly, research on parenting styles indicates that middle-class parents are much more likely to use authoritative parenting styles based on explanation through language than working class parents, who use more authoritarian styles based on parental authority (Baumrind, 1971). Cultural differences also contribute to differing parenting styles, with more traditional cultures using parenting styles based on authority (McGoldrick, 1983). Since many of our deaf parents were themselves raised in working class families from other cultures, much of the reaction to and meaning of their deafness needs to be understood as shaped by class and ethnic factors.

everywhere. Learning to speak is natural; vocalization and word play are fun, and they contribute to the pleasurable dance between parents and child.[4] Not so for the deaf child in a hearing family who intently watches his parents' lips as they mouth, "that's a ball, say ball." To keep the child's attention on their lips, parents often hold the child's head steady as they speak. From the deaf child's perspective, this can feel intrusive and coercive. As the language becomes more complex, deaf children may not know the meaning of what they are expected to parrot back to their parents. The deaf child does not get auditory feedback on what he says or how he says it; he cannot hear his own voice. The feedback he gets is the pleasure or displeasure read on the parents' face. This is often alienating for the child. It shifts his attention away from his own bodily, subjective experience toward the external, objective experience of the other. This, in turn, impacts on the parent-child relationship and can often set up negative expectations and contingencies for both.[5]

If Joe's capacity to mentalize and reflect is handicapped, how will this affect his parenting of Patty? How will Joe's conceptions of Patty as a separate hearing person with a unique interior life of her own be constructed from his past experience and his current experience of her? It is hoped that our clinical interventions will help him to mentalize his own experience, and to and create increasingly complex constructions of Patty. And what of Patty's experience that may be beyond Joe's ability to interpret?

---

4. Language learning for deaf children within Deaf families is as natural as that in hearing families. Padden and Humphries (1988) give an example of how peculiar spoken language appears for a Deaf family: "One day, Sam remembers . . . he finally understood that his friend was indeed odd. They were playing in her home, when suddenly her mother walked up to them and animatedly began to move her mouth. And as if by magic, the girl picked up a dollhouse and moved it to another place. Sam was mystified and went home to ask his mother about exactly what kind of affliction the girl next door had. This mother explained that she was HEARING and because of this did not know how to SIGN; instead she and her mother TALK." (p. 15)

5. It is important to realize that there are hearing parents who learn sign and that the learning of sign language, in itself, does not guarantee an unproblematic connection between parents and child. The meanings and elaboration of deafness can take on many different colorations. For example, Phyllis Skoy (2001, personal communication) details a case in which a deaf mother grew up in a hearing family where the hearing mother learned sign language so the fact of communication was not at issue between them; however, the deaf person experienced her hearing mother as withholding in other ways, and the pattern of withholding was then transmitted to the deaf woman's hearing daughter. One way to think about the issue of a common language between parents and child is that it sets up a necessary, but not sufficient condition for emotional bonding.

LOOKING AT THE CHILD

Very often, our toddlers do not know how to play with toys. They enter the nursery, pick up one object after another and flit from toy to toy. Sometimes, the parents themselves do not know how a particular toy functions, and they have difficulty encouraging their child to explore. Parents do not realize that play is "serious business" (Sutton-Smith and Sutton-Smith, 1974), nor recognize their important role as scaffolders of play (Bruner and Haste, 1987; Ratner and Bruner, 1978). This aspect of our work involves several stages of facilitation: broadening the child's ability to engage with play materials, helping the child make the transition to more symbolic modes of playing and more complex play schemas, encouraging the parents' pleasurable interaction in the child's play, and educating them about the many meanings of their child's play. Interventions here involve direct modeling of how to play, eliciting the parents' observational skills, and psychoeducation regarding what play is and how it develops. We also keep in mind what may get evoked for the parent(s) as she observes and participates in the play and we encourage the parent(s) to talk about her own childhood.

When Patty first came into our nursery at 15 months of age, Betty would sit passively and watch Patty play. If Patty picked up a toy and put it in her mouth, Betty would immediately jump to her feet, sign and voice "wrong." The toy would be taken from Patty, no explanation given, and Patty would become tearful and angry. Similarly, if Patty dumped the toys out of a basket and used the basket as a hat, mother would sign "wrong." As Betty and I developed more of a working alliance, I could begin to explore her own childhood. I learned that her mother often labeled her curiosity pejoratively and was uncomfortable with Betty exploring her environment. We speculated together that perhaps this was because her mother didn't understand how curious young children were, and perhaps her mother was worried that Betty, as a deaf child, should not do anything that marked her as more different. The need to look and feel "normal" was important. She could see that as a mother now, she worried that if her daughter did anything that did not "look normal," it must mean she wasn't being a good enough mother. Betty was reassured to learn that Patty's mouthing of objects was appropriate and a way that children explored new objects, and that using the basket as a hat was a creative act, not an inappropriate one. Betty is now much more of a participant in Patty's play. She is curious about it, better able to tolerate its messiness and confusion, and to provide some words for her (mother's) actions and Patty's reactions.

Patty's play has followed the trajectory described by Piaget (1962) and elaborated by Anna Freud's (1965) concept of a developmental line: she has increasingly gone from motor play to symbolic play; from play schemes performed on her own body (putting on a hat, combing her own hair) to schemes performed on a doll; from single instances of pretend play, such as putting dolly to sleep; to chains events, such as putting dolly to bed in a stroller, taking the stroller to the doll house, and having "visitors" (mother and myself) arrive. In the opening vignette, we could see how Patty's play regressed when the connection with her father was broken, and how she wasn't yet ready for sustained play sequences. Being older now, her concentration is more focused. At 29 months she was able to read an entire book with her mother. This book, *One, Two, Three Baby*, showed a series of infants doing various activities (one baby clapping, two babies eating, three babies playing, etc.) Mother signed the pictures; Patty looked attentively at the pictures, then at her mother, and imitated the signs. Both mother and child beamed with delight.

Discussion

Bowlby's (1969) groundbreaking work on attachment argued that children needed to form close emotional attachments to their mothers for survival. Such survival entailed not only physical safety, but also emotional comfort and stability. The infant enters the world with a physiological endowment that primes the child for connection to her caretaker. Within hearing dyads, infant research has pointed out that at four months of age infants recognize and prefer their mothers' voices to those of strangers (Mandler, 1990). The exaggerated vowels and higher pitches characteristic of "motherese" are found across cultures and languages. (Ferguson and Snow, 1977) and connect parents and their infants in playful, pleasurable ways. Background sounds often take on comforting aspects for the infant; she comes to recognize that the clip clops she is hearing are mother's footsteps in the adjacent room and signal that mother is coming to pick her up. Through audition, the connection between the mother and child can be held beyond the visual field. Such experience is not available to deaf children of hearing parents. For hearing children of deaf parents, mother's voice—however unclear—is available, but making sense of the background sounds as cues to comfort may be more problematic. Leonard Davis (2000) a hearing adult of deaf parents opens his memoir, *My Sense of Silence*, with his dread at bedtime:

> When I lay in bed at night, I did not experience what most children feel: that sense of security and comfort, of being in the lap and bosom of my family. Instead, I lay terrified and cold. I had to listen for every sound, because my parents could not hear any danger. Even were I to call them from my bed, they could not hear me. I was alone, small and helpless. (p. 1)

In an earlier vignette with Patty and her father, we saw how her father was not able to hear the loud noise that frightened her, so that he could not label her affect, nor understand her sudden shift of activity. We can only wonder what Patty's experience at bedtime might be. This gives the later vignette where Betty and Patty are reading together a special significance. Not only is this act a source of mastery for Betty, who as a deaf child had never been read to by her hearing mother, but it creates a connection through language that becomes internalized as a pleasurable experience of being-with-the-other (Stern, 1985). This internalized object relationship may then serve as a transitional experience between waking and sleeping states. Paradoxically, this internalized object relationship allows for both connection and separation, where recall of pleasurable experiences with Mommy in stressful situations provides both an emotional connection as well as a means of autonomous self-regulation.

Thus language is not simply the carrier of objective information, but constitutes a living core of subjectivity. Hans Loewald (1980) points to the inseparability of language from the early affective caretaking presence in which it was first embodied. When we first learn a word for a thing, he says:

> Much of the time, the word is not simply added to the thing, but the thing itself becomes first defined or delimited as an alive circumscribed entity. The emotional relationship to the person from whom the word is learned plays a significant, in fact crucial part, in how alive the link between things and words turns out to be. (p. 187)

Vygotsky was one of the earliest psychologists to speak of the intersubjective nature of mind, which he felt was mediated through language. Vygotsky (1931) believed that individual thought was an internalization of a social relationship between parent and child mediated through language. Where, for Piaget (1955), thought was the result of the child's own internalized activity upon the world; for Vygotsky, thought was inherently social, and the social necessarily preceded and constituted the individual or psychological. "Any function in the child's cultural development appears on the stage twice, on two planes, first on the social plane and then on the psychological" (p. 44–45). Peter Fonagy's (2001) concept of mentalization picks up on the intersubjective nature of mind as mediated through language.

In order for mentalization, or what Fongay calls the reflective function, to take place, parents must be able to attune to their child with contingency and markedness (cf. Gergley, 2001). By contingency Fonagy means that the parents' response to the child must accurately match the child's internal state; by markedness he refers to the parents' ability to incorporate into their responsiveness a clear indication that they are expressing the feelings of the child, not their own. Fonagy et al. (1994) found that mothers in a relatively high stress group were more like to have securely attached infants if their reflective function was high. Thinking about deaf children growing up in hearing families where the parents do not learn to sign, and/or where the child is not oral, poses questions. How was Joe mentalized by his parents? To what extent did their lack of a common language prevent the parent from communicating to Joe his mental states and separate personhood? And if the quality of Joe's attachment to his parents was compromised by their inability to use language to mediate connection, will the quality of Joe's attachment to Patty be similarly compromised?

There is now a body of research supporting the intergenerational transmission of attachment styles between hearing parents and children. Mary Main and colleagues (1985) working with the Adult Attachment Interview (AAI) (George, Kaplan and Main, 1985), a semi-structured interview that asks parents to narrate their own attachment history, demonstrated a strong, predictive correlation between a parent's attachment style and the attachment style they create with their own child. The interviews are scored according to linguistic criteria; what is critical is not so much what the parent(s) says as *how* the parent(s) says it. For example, parents who speak of relationships within their own family of origin in a dismissive way, often have children who score as being insecure/avoidantly attached to them. (Main and Hesse, 2000). Longitudinal data are now available that point to better social and academic outcomes for securely attached children. (Grossman and Grossman, 1991; Urban et al., 1991).[6]

---

6. There is currently work being done using the AAI with deaf parents and comparing and correlating their scores with observations from the Infant Strange Situation, although the outcome data are not yet available (Irene Leigh 2002, personal communication)

Interventions in the nursery with Joe aim to avert the (re)creation of a problematic attachment. Helping Joe to reflect on his own experience will partly depend on my ability to mirror, through contingency and markedness, his mental states. The more that I can do this through the mediation of language, the more intimate the bond between us will become, and the more possible it will be for new and more complex narratives to emerge. As Stern (1985) points out, connection is an achievement. Unlike Margaret Mahler who emphasizes psychic separation from a mother-child unity (Mahler, 1968), Stern privileges attachment. He believes that the infant enters the world having a rudimentary sense of self as separate and must be dependent upon responsive care-taking for the establishment of a self-with-other connection. While the earliest ways of attunement may be non-verbal and cross modal (e.g., the matching of vitality affects), later attunement requires language. Joe and I, deaf and hearing, begin from the vantage point of separation and difference. Our goal is connection and the bridging of differences through how and what is communicated between us.

RESEARCH IMPLICATIONS

If, as our work in the nursery suggests, mentalization is a major mediator of attachment, are there ways of facilitating its development? Are there ways in which mentalization could be highlighted? Some researcher/clinicans working with a parent-child model use videotaping of parent-child interactions and a later discussion of those interactions with the parent to help the parent reflect anew about what and how the child was feeling. (Carole Lapidus 2002, personal communication). It would be interesting to compare groups of deaf parents with hearing children who are exposed to this technique with a group of such parents without this. Had the opening vignette with Patty been videotaped and played back to Joe, would Joe have been able to see his interaction with Patty differently?

The focus on mentalization can also be seen within the context of preventing trauma. Helping Joe to reflect upon both his own experience as a deaf child of hearing parents and his experience as a deaf parent of a hearing child might alleviate the transmission of unresolved loss and mourning from one generation to the next. With this in mind, it would be interesting to administer a pre and post AAI and Strange Situation before and after a family's two-year participation in the nursery setting. Would there be significant pre and post changes in both measures, and would we find correlations between AAI and the Infant Strange Situation scores? One might also want to add another condition: comparing one group of parents who get the two-year nursery program with the extra mutual video playback piece, with those dyads who only get the nursery program.

Both of these potential research ideas call upon and use the relationship between therapist and parent as the avenue of change. Watching the videotapes, for example, provides an in vivo experience of using a relationship—that between therapist and parent—to foster the parent's ability to use language in a different way both in relationship to her child and to her own self. Hopefully, language use will shift from primarily denotative functions—as a medium for communicating expectations ("sit down," "put the toy back") and naming ("yellow," "cat," "ball")—to more its connotative functions, alive with meaning and vital dialogic experience.

BIBLIOGRAPHY

BAUMRIND, D. (1971). Current patterns of parental authority. *Developmental Psychology Monographs, 4* (1, Pt. 2).

BEEBE, B. & LACHMANN, F. (1988). The contribution of mother-infant mutual influence to the origins of self and object representations. *Psychoanalytic Psychology, 5,* 305–337.

BELLUGI, U. (December 1970). Learning the language. *Psychology Today,* 32–38.

BELSKY, J. (1999). Modern evolutionary theory and patterns of attachment. In J. Cassidy & P. R. Shaved (Eds.) *Handbook of attachment; Theory, research and clinical applications* (pp. 141–161). New York: Guilford Press.

BERNSTEIN, B. (1975). *Class, codes and control.* London: Routledge.

BOWLBY, J. (1969). *Attachment and loss, vol I: Attachment.* London: Hogarth Press.

BRUNER, J. & HASTE, H. (EDS). (1987). *Making sense: The child's construction of the world.* London: Methuen.

CICCHETTI, D. & WALKER, E. F. (2001). Editorial: Stress and development: Biological and psychological consequences. *Development and Psychopathology, 13,* 413–418.

DAVIS, L. (2000). *My sense of silence. Memoirs of a childhood with deafness.* Urbana: University of Illinois Press.

FERGUSON, C. & SNOW, C. (1977). *Talking to children: Language input and acquisition.* San Francisco: Josey-Bass.

FONAGY, P. & TARGET, M. (2001). The evolution of the interpersonal interpretive mechanism: Clues for effective preventive intervention in early childhood. Paper presented at "When the Bough Broke: Perspectives on trauma from psychoanalysis, attachment theory and developmental psychobiology. Conference of the Center for Psychoanalytic Training and Research and the Sackler Institute for Developmental Psychobiology, Columbia University, November 2001.

FRAIBERG, S. (1980). *Clinical studies in infant mental health.* New York: Basic Books.

FREUD, A. (1965). *Normality and pathology in childhood.* New York: International Universities Press.

GEORGE, C., KAPLAN, N. & MAIN, M. (1985). The Berkeley Adult Attachment Interview. Unpublished protocol, Dept. Psychology, University of California, Berkeley.

GERGLEY, G. (2001). The development of understanding of self and agency. In U. Goshwami (Ed.) *Handbook of childhood cognitive development.* Oxford: Blackwell.

GROSSMAN, K. E. & GROSSMAN, K. (1991). Attachment quality as an organizer of emotional and behavioral responses in a longitudinal perspective. In *Attachment Across the Life Cycle,* ed. C. M. Parkes, Stevenson-Hinde & P. Marris. London: Tavistock/Boutledge.

HARVEY, M. A. & DYM, B. (1987). An ecological view of deafness. *Family Systems Medicine, 5, No. 1,* 52–64.

JEFFERS, J., & BORLEY, M. (1964). *Speechreading (Lipreading).* Springfield, Ill.: Charles C. Thomas.

LIEBERMAN, A., SILVERMAN, R. & PAWL, J. (2000). Infant-parent psychotherapy: Core concepts and current approaches. In Charles H. Zeanah, Jr. (Ed.). *Handbook of infant mental health* (2nd edition). New York: Guilford Press.

LOEWALD, H. (1980). *Papers on psychoanalysis.* New Haven: Yale University Press.

McGOLDRICK, M. (1983). Ethnicity and family therapy: An overview. In M. McGoldrick, J. Pearce, & J. Giordano (Eds). *Ethnicity and family therapy.* New York: Guilford Press.

MAHLER, M. (1968). *On human symbosis and the vicissitudes of individuation.* New York: International Universities Press.

MAIN, M. (2000). The organized categories of infant, child, and adult attachement: Flexible vs. inflexible attention under attachment-related stress. *Journal of the American Psychoanalytic Association, 48,* 1055–1095.

MAIN, M. & HESSE, E. (2000). Disorganized infant, child, and adult attachment: Collapse in behavioral and attentional strategies. *Journal of the American Psychoanalytic Association, 48,* 1097–1127.

MAIN, M., KAPLAN, N., & CASSIDY, J. (1985). Security in infancy, childhood and adulthood: A move to the level of representation. In *Growing Points of Attachment Theory and Research,* ed. I. Bretherton & C. Waters. Monographs of the Society for Research in Child Development, serial no. 208, vol. 50. Chicago: University of Chicago Press, 66–104.

MANDLER, J. M. (May–June 1990). A new perspective on cognitive development. *American Scientist, 78,* 236–243.

MEADOW, K. P. (1980). *Deafness and child development.* Berkley, Calif.: University of California Press.

MINTZER, D., ALS, H., TRONICK, E., & BRAZELTON, B. (1984). Parenting an infant with a birth defect. *Psychoanalytic Study of the Child*, 561–72.

PADDEN, C. & HUMPHRIES, T. (1988). *Deaf in America. Voices from a culture.* Cambridge, Mass.: Harvard University Press.

PETTITO, L. & MARENTETTE, P. (1991). Babbling in the manual code: Evidence for the ontogeny of language. *Science, 251,* 1017–1025.

PIAGET, J. (1955). *The language and thought of the child.* New York: The World Publishing Company, Meridian Books.

PIAGET, J. (1962). *Play, dreams and imitation in childhood.* New York: W. W. Norton & Company, Inc.

POSNER, M. I. & ROTHBART, M. K. (2000). Developing mechanisms of self-regulation. *Development and Psychopathology, 12,* 427–441.

RATNER, N. & BRUNER, J. (1978). Games, social exchange and the acquisition of language. *Journal of Child Development, 5,* 1–15.

SLADE, A. (2000). The development and organization of attachment: Implications for psychoanalysis. *Journal of the American Psychoanalytic Association, 48*(4), 1147–74.

SOLNIT, A. & STARK, M. (1961). Mourning and the birth of a defective child. *Psychoanalytic Study of the Child, 16,* 523–37.

STERN, D. (1985). *The interpersonal world of the infant.* New York: Basic Books.

STERN, D. (1995). *The motherhood constellation: A unified view of parent-infant psychotherapy.* New York: Basic Books.

STOKOE, W. (1970). The study and use of sign language. In M. Sternberg (Ed.) *American sign language.* New York: Harper & Row, 1986.

SUTTON-SMITH, B. & SUTTON-SMITH, S. (1974). *How to play with your children (and when not to).* New York: Hawthorn Books, Inc.

URBAN, J., CARLSON, E., EGELAND, B., & STROUFE, L. A. (1991). Patterns of individual adaptation across childhood. *Developmental Psychopathology, 3,* 445–460.

VYGOTSKY, L. (1931). Development of higher mental functions. In *Psychological research in the U.S.S.R.* Moscow: Progress Publishers, 1966.

Symptom, Screen Memory, and Dream

The Complexity of
Mental Representation and Disguise

DELIA BATTIN, M.S.W., and
EUGENE MAHON, M.D.

The relationship between screen memory, symptom and dream is not immediately obvious. All three are mental products to be sure and therefore they must have complex connections with each other, however far apart their genetic origin may be, however discreet they may seem from each other in the mind's archival filing system. A case is presented in which "the content" of a screen memory and a symptom and a subsequent dream shared certain similarities. The "content" became the subject matter of elaborate free associative explication in the context of analytic process and transference neurosis. As all three products began to "converse" with each other in the psychological fugue known as analytic process, the seamlessness of the human mind and its complemental series of complexities unscreened itself, as illusion became its own mirror rather than an exercise in perpetual self deception. A screen memory, a symptom, and a dream were show to be only façades

Delia Battin is Supervising and Training Analyst at the New York Freudian Society; she is a member of IPTAR; she is in full-time private practice of psychoanalysis in New York City. Eugene Mahon is Supervising and Training Analyst at the Center for Psychoanalytic Training and Research Columbia College of Physicians and Surgeons; he is in full-time practice of psychoanalysis in New York City.

The Psychoanalytic Study of the Child 58, ed. Robert A. King, Peter B. Neubauer, Samuel Abrams, and A. Scott Dowling (Yale University Press, copyright © 2003 by Robert A. King, Peter B. Neubauer, Samuel Abrams, and A. Scott Dowling).

of an architectural complexity they hinted at to be sure, but without analysis were unable to reveal.

INTRODUCTION

ONE COULD ARGUE THAT PSYCHOANALYSIS, FROM ITS INCEPTION, WAS the study of disguise. When Charcot could move a symptom from one side of the body to the other through the power of suggestion showing that what seemed somatic was clearly psychologically driven, the young Freud began to see the engine of the unconscious beneath the somatic wheel of disguise. If the code of a hysterical symptom seemed easy to crack from that point on, other mental products wouldn't reveal their intricate archeology so readily, dream for instance. Only a genius could have cracked the code of dreams in 1900, with insights theoretically so original and clinically durable that they have required little emendation in more than 100 years. Screen memories, which Freud first wrote about in 1899, have also maintained their originality and freshness despite the passage of time. In this paper, we will focus on how these three mental products—symptom, screen memory, and dream—can assist the mind ironically not only in the maintenance of disguise, but, through the power of analysis, to reclaim via insight and revelation what has been repressed. It is one of the ironies of the human mind that mental products of self-deception and disguise nevertheless keep a record of themselves which in the free associative process of disclosure can effect their own undoing. One is reminded of Freud's similar statement on transference: that it is all at once an act of revelation and disguise.

The mind is obviously a seamless psychological entity, a fact we lose sight of often, when we divide it theoretically into its component parts, reifying the imaginary divisions our theories have proposed. In this paper we address this seamlessness, as we attempt to show how mental products, such as symptom, screen memory, and dream, which seem to come from such different strata of mind temporally, structurally, and topographically speaking, can be seen nonetheless to reside in seamless unconscious contiguity when the free associative linkages between them have been identified. That there is no time in the unconscious, as Freud argued, is perhaps another way of saying that the mind is an unrelenting historian of itself and cannot do otherwise as long as memory insists on being true to itself. If the return of the repressed is a symptomatic depiction of the doggedness of memory in pathology, unrelenting memory as witness of its own recovery is the essence of psychoanalysis and mental health, or so we will argue as we attempt to show how symptom, screen memory, and dream can form a seamless coalition that explicates the dynamic history of the mind, especially the unique mind our clinical exposition and theoretical argument will focus on.

THE PSYCHOANALYTIC PROCESS

Leonora was 31 when she sought help for a variety of reasons, some obviously psychological and some "physical." As the analysis proceeded, the physical ailments receded dramatically and Leonora became more convinced than ever that mind and body could not be thought of as such separate compartments. The psychological issues that Leonora wanted to address were her passivity, her depressive moods, her sexual "timidity" (she couldn't reach orgasm very often), and a sense that aggression for her was an intellectual concept rather than an affect or an attitude she could embrace wholeheartedly and be comfortable with its integration into the fabric of her personality.

A screen memory had puzzled her for years, but her intellectual curiosity about it would develop only as the memory took hold of the transference in a most dramatic way as the analysis deepened. In the screen memory Leonora reports: "I'm learning how to swim. I'm breathless, floundering, frightened. My older sister supposedly helping me is actually drowning me." While the memory had the lucidity of delineation, so characteristic of this genre of "record keeping," Leonora had some skepticism about its historical accuracy, an assessment that would prove to be borne out when, as we will report in more detail later, toward the end of the analysis Leonora checked her own genetic record with her mother's version of actual childhood events and was surprised by the disparity!

Leonora sensed that a symptom that had compromised her sense of well-being for years was in fact connected in some mysterious way to the screen memory, but more insight than that seemed to elude her. The symptom in question, as already stated, involved bouts of fatigue and shortness of breath, as well as inability to reach orgasm: "As if all my energy were suddenly drowned out," Leonora once commented, not aware of the irony her verbal imagery had stumbled on. Leonora at times felt she was being hypochondriacal and at other times that the shortness of breath, fatigue, and sexual dysfunction were leftovers of a bout of childhood rheumatic fever, which cleared up after the initial assault, but perhaps had left these sequelae. The total disappearance of these symptoms as analytic process expanded psychological awareness and diminished somatic expression was striking: timidity, fatigue, and breathlessness were replaced with robust athletic endurance and engagement.

It was the analytic process of transference interpretation and the integration of insight into the reshaping of character that made the achievement possible obviously and if we focus on screen memory, symptom, and dream, we do not mean to ignore or neglect the constant matrix of transference and its interpretation that made it possible for discrete products such as these under study to be explicated.

If screen memory and symptom are static mental products, the manifest tips of psychological icebergs that do not always reveal their contiguity and relevance to the latent depth psychology they conceal, analytic process, and especially perhaps dream analysis, focuses on a product that does invite free associative explication. When a dream seems to manifestly echo the "content" of the symptom or screen memory, the latent process that informs all three brings genetics and current "residues" into a focus that is nothing but thrilling for both analyst and analysand. But we have gotten ahead of ourselves. In mid analysis, a symptomatic reenactment on the couch was followed by a most significant dream. They both emerged out of a deepening transferential process that will first be described. At that pivotal time, Leonora's sense of intimacy with her analyst was intense. She was allowing herself to be more and more sexual in her associations, more aggressive in response to analytic silence and the whole atmosphere of conflict the neutrality of the analytic situation generates and thrives on. Pre-oedipal thirst for the seemingly stony breasts of the mother could coexist in transferential time with hatred of the mother's pathological deprivations, not to mention the analyst's. Oedipal desire for the analyst to spank her for the naughty sexuality transference was "extracting" from her, the brazen sexual womanliness analysis was tempting her to reclaim was daring to bare its flesh more and more in the sanctioned exhibitionism that the couch was fostering. In this climate, in mid session, Leonora began to suffocate, to choke on her words, to gasp for breath, to cough repetitively and alarmingly. The analyst had the presence of mind to "keep her cool" and comment sympathetically and genuinely: "You are trying to tell me something." Symptomatically, rather than verbally was the implication of the analytic intervention and the analysand "got it" immediately. In one breath (ironic pun intended) she asked herself whether the fatigue and dyspnoea were not transformations of desire and aggression, a respiratory knot that desire and aggression had "choked" her with, rather than promoting her voice, a knot that could now perhaps be opened, a throat that could develop its decibel reach rather than stifling itself. She began to weep, but the tears did not interfere with expression, on the contrary they rather enhanced it. Screen memory and symptom now came together more convincingly than ever, as if they had been waiting for years for transference, like a go-between to bring them together. "I am drowning, choking, breathless, voiceless in both of them," was the synthetic achievement of her new readiness to integrate psychic elements that needed to be kept apart until transference made it safe to unite them. Bringing them together in this new insightful rendition of memory and symptom did not completely elucidate the dynamic, strategic functional structure of both, but it paved the way for the subsequent analytic work out of which the previously mentioned most significant tripartite dream emerged.

> Awful dream! I was torturing people . . . leaving them after wiring them so that if they moved, they would experience an electric shock . . . lots of people I knew . . . later, I couldn't identify them . . . (then I did identify some). I felt pleasure doing that . . . awful! And in another part of the dream I was drowning and people couldn't reach me . . . their arms weren't long enough . . . they looked so sad . . . I felt sad for them . . . the undertow was throwing me to the bottom of the ocean . . . I called out . . . then couldn't anymore . . . I was like in a pocket of very rough ocean . . . if people went in there, they would be caught too. There was a third piece to this dream . . . I was also drowning . . . the ocean was rough . . . people were close to me in space but couldn't touch me, couldn't hold me, they didn't care . . . I felt angry . . . I was watching children being held by other people in warmer water . . . where I was, the water was cold . . . the people next to me were stronger . . . obviously they could hold out in the ocean, they had no feelings . . . I felt hopeless, I didn't call out . . . I couldn't get air, I gave up.

Leonora's first association was that the sequence of the dream parts was not the way she told them: the last part came first, then the first, and then the second. The telling of the dreams out of sequence was significant in the sense that the most sadistic elements seemed to rush to the fore, ignoring sequential etiquette so to speak. The dream's tripartite structure seemed to the analyst to represent the original screen memory sliced in two with the sadistic portion about the "wires" sandwiched between the other two. But it was the free associative and collaborative work on the dream over the next weeks and months that "opened up" Leonora's genetic and current sense of herself rather than countertransferential intuitions or poetic leaps (not that the two are mutually exclusive, but in fact are complementary in ideal collaborative process). In the collaborative work over the years Leonora had learned how to neglect no detail of a dream, the neglect itself always loaded with dynamic defensive significance. The conflicted pleasure she could allow herself to feel in wiring the dream protagonists so that if they moved they would experience a shock was perhaps, if not the greatest analytic achievement to date, certainly the most dramatic. Leonora was aware of the deep genetic as well as the current transferential meanings: as a child, she felt not only bed ridden by virtue of her rheumatic fever but also bound and wired so tightly by the stifling parental atmosphere that seemed to choke the playful spirit out of her. On the couch, she also felt confined by the analytic etiquette that allowed the analyst the freedom to "sit up" while she was "trussed" like a sacrificial victim, an Iphigenia in some Greek or Freudian play the analyst was writing. As she came to understand more and more that this was her own unconscious script, she began to bristle at the masochistic ink she felt obliged to write with for most of her life. "I was drowning and people couldn't reach me: their arms were not long enough. They looked so sad. I felt sad for them. Why did I set the dream images up that way?" Leonora mused as she examined the dream piece by piece. "I must have wanted to drown them. I disguised it instead. Their arms weren't long enough," she scoffed sarcastically. "Maybe I had cut them down to size, chopped off a few joints. They were sad. I felt sad for them. The hypocrisy is sickening. You know where the word hypocrisy comes from? From Greek, it means a stage actor. That's what I was, that's what they made me, a tragic actor in a play I didn't realize I had written for myself, with plenty of help from them!" she hissed. "No wonder I wanted to finally electrocute them. My anger drove the sadness out for a while, but it returned." Leonora reflected on the dream imagery about the children in warmer water being held by people, whereas she was in cold water and untouchable: "People were close to me in space, but couldn't touch me." The genetics and the current transferential climate were now accessible to Leonora almost simultaneously. "It's like here. You are so close to me, but you won't touch me or hold me. You're not supposed to, but they were. They were so strange, weren't they, yet so familiar? In the dream I gave up on them. I felt hopeless. I couldn't call out. I couldn't get air. I gave up." The anger returned at such moments drowning out the sadness momentarily. "Maybe I didn't want to breathe the same air they were breathing, maybe my breathlessness isn't so passive, maybe I'm holding my breath not to be contami-

nated by the stench of their stupidity, their incompetence." The tears
would return at such moments when Leonora realized that she loved
them of course and needed them no matter how incompetent they
were, the incompetence increasing the need, rather than meeting it.

Now that the manifest sadism of the dream in which people were
wired and shocked no longer made Leonora turn away from its serious implications, her new "genetic" grasp of herself seemed more
real. She knew she was deeply hurt and deeply angry for as long as
memory kept records (and even beyond that, "further back than
that," she could now quip given her understanding of repression).
What she was only beginning to recognize was the complexity of psychological disguise that used every "trick" in the unconscious book to
make truth seem too dangerous for conscious insight to call its own.
It was as if truth needed dream, symptom, and memory to screen itself from a psychological reality it couldn't bear to face. Ironically of
course it was the analysis of dream, symptom, and memory that finally allowed the hidden truth to emerge! Leonora as torturer in the
sadistic dream was an image she no longer needed to be afraid of,
since she knew she was simply turning the tables on the puppeteers
of childhood who had made her feel wired like a puppet whose actions were controlled beyond, and in flagrant neglect of the wishes of
the self. Leonora's vision of herself in the dream sequence in which
she was out of her depth, unable to be reached by the arms of the
would be rescuers, was of course analyzed as the opposite side of the
unconscious coin as if the dream calculus could allow her to be torturer in one instance, but then demanded her to be victim in another. The act of interpretation, by rescuing the hidden affective
meanings in either instance, did of course eventually allow her to be
emotionally self possessed in both. In such a newly balanced state of
mind, Leonora could reflect from a complex perspective that had
eluded her when she was "a mere puppet." Analysis had made her
physical symptoms unnecessary and the total absence of fatigue, dyspnoea, and muscular "weakness" made her more convinced than
ever that her new found mental "agilities" released energies that
made fatigue and shortness of breath "laughable" and dismissible,
even though the symbolic meaning could continue to intrigue: Why
had she "chosen" the respiratory as the avenue of expression? Why
did dream and screen memory depict drowning? Why did all three
"products" seem connected by invisible unconscious threads? It was
at this point in the analysis that Leonora began to question certain
genetic assumptions. Did the screen memory depict an actual event
at all? Could the "unreliable" mother be relied on to provide the "ac-

tual" historic events that screen memory may have subsequently amended (doctored) for dynamic reasons? The mother's rendition of the historic record did challenge the testimony of the screen memory, calling memory as witness into question, as Freud so ingeniously hypothesized in 1899! The mother's version of the reality exposed the screen memory's cover up tactics rather glaringly: the older sister had tried to strangle the younger (Leonora) and might have succeeded were it not for adult intervention! This was a bomb shell and led to a most productive period of analysis in which the "psychotic" character of certain aspects of Leonora's childhood could no longer be ignored.

Not only was the older sibling's behavior a constant irrational element in Leonora's childhood, the mother's bizarre and unreliable care-taking (she would mysteriously disappear from family life for periods of time, no explanations offered) came to light as Leonora's less dumbfounded ego became capable of processing it. Nor were the father's contributions any less noxious, which became clear as the ego tried to master the whole historic record. When Leonora was able to let herself recall his declaration to his children that if any one of them was kidnapped, he would never pay the ransom, she winced until she came up with her own counter-declaration: "He was an ass, but of course to a child he was my king." The king, like all kings could be aggressive and irrational: Leonora remembered a dispute between her and a housekeeper in which the king sided with the housekeeper against his own daughter. Leonora was spanked on bare buttocks, an assault which produced orgastic feelings and a childhood memory that colored adult sexual fantasies with her husband until analytic process allowed her a more expansive sexual repertoire: as analysis proceeded, she could allow herself the freedom to be not only a spanked child in sexual fantasy, but a full-blooded woman as well. As Leonora put it, exploiting a double entendre for all it was worth, "If I can just get the past out of my bed, the present will take care of itself!" Ironically it was putting the past on the Freudian bed of the analytic couch that had made this current freedom possible.

DISCUSSION

MIND AS FUGUE

We have bent the complex process of one long analysis to our purpose as we focus on three of the mind's many products. Our purpose has been to show how three mental products forged at three very different moments in the complex psychological history of one mind have a timeless, seamless quality nevertheless, when the alchemy of analytic process brings the most seemingly disparate elements together in the new alloys of insight. If we have neglected a full exposition of the transference-countertransference choreography, resistance, and all the pains-taking piecing together of free associative process that informs analytic collaborative labor, it is not out of a lack of awareness of complexity, but merely to emphasize one insight that formed the starting point of our argument: human conflict is like a fugue—what was wrestled with at first as screen memory can later be taken up in a symptom and eventually end up in a dream as the mind, like a complemental series, to take a Freudian idea out of context, addresses the unresolved again and again in its search for relative closure or mastery. In earlier communications (Mahon and Battin, 1981, 1983) we even suggested that the subjective assessment of a screen memory's "appearance" over time can be a gauge of analytic process, some screen memories shedding their "luminosity" as psychoanalysis nears termination, as if the repressed energies that gave screen memories their heightened luminous qualities had become dissipated as new mental organizations recycled the raw material of earlier strategies. This quantitative assessment of psychic change is hardly popular as "modern" psychoanalysis weans itself from old fashioned concepts of libidinal cathexes and hydraulics, and so on, and yet screen memories and symptoms, as subjective phenomena, do have "a feel" or "a hold" on psychic life that lends itself to metaphoric images of quantity or weight that invite measurement by subjective assessment. Surely this kind of subjectivity cannot be ignored in an enterprise that is after all a complex dissection of the whole fabric of subjectivity, with as much objectivity as self scrutiny can muster! A symptom such as dyspnoea or breathlessness or fatigue has an obvious somatic component, as if psychic conflict, unable to stay within the framework of the psychological, as the mental forces clashed with each other, reached for a somatic foothold to anchor itself with, in a kind of physical time-out from endless unconscious bickering. This way of describing psychic conflict and somatic compliance may be too dramatic or energic for some tastes, but it is certainly the way some patients in analysis describe their conflicts. Language has always leaned on the body to fully express itself: "to kick ass," "he's a prick," or "a shit," "she's a cunt," "it sucks" are expressions that reveal the indebtedness of everyday speech to a palette of anatomy and physiology that lends it color. The only point being stressed here is that if screen memories have a luminosity, a kind of "aura" that may reflect the quantity of psychic energy the infantile amnesia has invested them with, "forced upon them" so to speak (Freud believed that behind the screen of the screen memory the whole emotional history of childhood lay hidden perhaps if only we could detect it!) symptoms reveal an avoir du poids, a somatic bulk that makes the "weight" of psychic conflict almost measurable, for once, given this kind of physical extension of its provenance. This is illusion of course if mind-body is thought of as seamless, but illusion, metaphor, self-deception is the raw material of analysis that eventually leads to the irony of its own undoing as truth and insight are arrived at by very circuitous routes.

If screen memory and symptom can serve as log-jams where some excess psychic lumber can be detained for a period, as the developmental currents sweep by, dream on the contrary would seem to be a psychic product with all its receptors ready to engage the free associative "flow" of investigation all the time. This is an overstatement surely, since dreams are forgotten, certain parts resisting analysis more than others, depending on levels of resistance and so on. In pre-Freudian times, dreams seemed as opaque as screen memory or symptom, quite dismissible with the exclamation, "it's only a dream!" But in a climate of free-associative collaboration there is no facet of a dream that need be neglected, whereas a screen memory or a symptom may be encapsulated and resist all attempts to fathom what is obligatorily repressed by virtue of its structure.

CONFLICT RESOLUTION: UBIQUITY VERSUS SPECIFICITY

We are trying to conceptualize screen memory, symptom, and dream as psychic strategies that, like all mental acts, must partake in, and reflect conflict and compromise. If conflict is ubiquitous, how it is dealt with obviously is not uniform, and different psychic organizations will have their own unique ways and means of processing and resolving. If we knew every component of such intricate psychic manifestations as screen memory, symptom, or dream, we would be able to differentiate the "machinery" of one from the other and have a better understanding of how it works, and what precisely is the service the mind is expecting it to accomplish. One is reminded of William Carlos Williams' depiction of a poem as a little engine constructed quite precisely according to placement of certain words, metaphors, verbs, and so on, an engine that, if constructed properly, gets the aesthetic job done. A screen memory, a symptom, a dream must be similarly constructed out of certain psychic raw materials that ideally could be identified by analysis and discussed scientifically. One of the recurring arguments of this paper is that as analytic process unfolds, the demarcation between dream, screen memory, and symptom slips away, as if the free associative enthusiasms of transference neurosis makes bed fellows out of the most unlikely characters. As Leonora, musing on the tripartite dream, shifted her free associative attention from screen memory to symptom to various details of the dream imagery, the imaginary lines of demarcation that separate mental products from each other began to blur, creating the alternate impression that in the creative flux of intense analytic process something akin to Keats' "negative capability" gets invoked: the state of mind that Keats' celebrated phrase refers to, is the facility Shakespeare possessed so uniquely "when man is capable of being in uncertainties, mysteries, doubts, without any irritable reaching after fact and reason." Leonora was not especially creative as artist or poet, but the fluidity of free associative thought, that "regressive" (in the most progressive Hartmann sense) collaborative analytic process exploits in the interest of adaptive, proactive mental health, can be compared perhaps to the flux out of which creative products are plucked by the judicious artistry of poet or playwright. Another way of approaching this regressive seamlessness would be to examine the discrete resistances to its existence, to describe the functioning of the imaginary wall that a symptom or screen memory seems to be surrounded by, until by Jericho the trumpets of analytic process make the walls come tumbling down. Why is a screen memory so discreet, so cut off from the "ordinary" flow of historic memory? Are the unconscious record keepers making a point of underlining this event surrounding it with a luminous halo, not only in the interest of memorial accuracy, but for tendentious reasons, as Freud argued? The free associative process does not readily "infiltrate" the membrane of the screen: as Greenacre pointed out, only late in the analytic process can some "metabolism" of the screen be expected. In dynamic psychoanalytic language, this suggests that the compromise called screen memory resists interpretation with a force that packs as much, if not more, psychological clout than defense, character trait, symptom, mood, dream, and so on. The "architectural" walls that these mental products come with may define the essence of their identity. Resistance may define the clinical feel of these walls in the ferment called analysis, but resistance of course is not only a wall but a window that can reveal interiority when rapport disarms mistrust. As rapport disarmed distrust in Leonora's case, she began to think of her mental life as "a titration of illusion." She may never have read Winnicott, but, in any case, her insight seemed to have an even greater provenance than Winnicott, who might confine the illusory to the transitional world, whereas Leonora seemed to be referring to the totality of her mind and all its structures and products.

Taking Leonora's lead and going beyond Winnicott somewhat, could one argue, à la Brenner, that all mental conflict can be thought of as titration of illusion, depending on which subtlety of compromise the mind is exploiting at any given unconscious moment? The illusion being referred to in the context of this paper would be the one that makes screen memory or symptom seem so foreign to the totality of mind they have estranged themselves from. Dream also, certainly in a pre-Freudian universe, seemed like a mental aberration, a nocturnal mystery that could be dismissed in the light of morning as not very significant. In the midst of intense analytic process, these illusions of demarcation are willing to renounce their snobbish exclusivities, as if members of the screen memory club are now willing to consort with the members of the dream club or the symptom club, without losing any of their psychic social status. This is perhaps too simple minded a way of describing dynamic subtleties. In a way, this is merely a basic psychoanalytic hypothesis about the nature of instinct, defense, and insight: when defense becomes aware of the affect or instincts it previously needed to obfuscate, insight, armed with its new information about the mind's strategic illusions, is the beneficiary. Smaller units of defense and instinct are perhaps easier to discuss scientifically or dynamically, but surely the same principle applies nevertheless to larger units, such as screen memory, symptom or dream.

If we return to William Carlos Williams' image of poem as engine, an insight can perhaps be extracted from it that will assist us also in our consideration of screen memory, symptom, and dream. A poem is an aesthetic engine to the extent that it operates on a manifest and latent level all at once. If we consider a poem like "Fern Hill" by Dylan Thomas with its haunting lines, "Time held me green and dying, though I sang in my chains like the sea," the engine of communicative meaning that ignite the poet's sublimated anxieties about the existential terrible beauty of the human Yeatsian heart "fastened to a dying animal," seems to ignite a similar resonance in the soul of the reader. The aesthetic engine that commands such conscious and unconscious resonance, is a classic canonical engine when it commands such resonances "for the ages" (century after century). The skill of the poet has woven the manifest and the latent, the conscious verbal reality and the unconscious surreal with such artistry that a timeless communication is forged that cannot be completely explicated or understood. If we now compare screen memory, symptom, and dream to the aesthetic engine of the poem, a similar impressive complexity will be obvious, even if compromise and conflict resolution are the raison d'être of these mental products rather than aesthetic pleasure. In the case of screen memory, symptom, and dream, the three engines have distinct features that on close examination reveal certain facets of mental functioning that might otherwise go unnoticed.

MIND AS ENGINE

Let us examine the engine of screen memory first. Bronowski (1978) suggests that a first encounter with any human artefact always raises two questions: what is it for, why was it made in a particular way? In other words, what is the form and function of the psychic artefact called screen memory? When first encountered, we would suggest that screen memories are discarded or discounted as curiosities that reflect something about childhood, about the past, but so isolated, so distant emotionally from current reality as to be without useful accessible context or heuristic meaning. Since Freud's 1899 paper, the concept of screen memory insists on being taken seriously, Freud's hypothesis that the whole of childhood emotion and conflict lies behind the screen if only human instruments could detect it! So, if we examine this curious engine with Freudian eyes what do we detect? The whole of childhood is being represented by one snapshot that usually has a luminous halo surrounding it, a sphinx-like image that is often affectless, a pale ghost indeed of all the rambunctious activities and emotionalities of childhood. What kind of an engine is this that seems stalled, motionless, like a ghost-town relic at the still center of what once must have been an affect-teeming, bustling, childhood metropolis? The motionless, stalled engine of memory does bring to mind another Freudian image: the motionless wolves in the Wolf man's dream, whose very absence of motion signified to Freud the fierce activities they must be hiding. Perhaps we need to apply Freud's ingenious explication of dreams' mysteries if we are to understand the mechanics of an engine called screen memory. In other words, let us turn to the engine of dream first and use our examination of one engine to explicate the other.

A dream could be thought of as a structure made of manifest and latent elements, a condensation of the visible (visually jumbled imagery) and the invisible (latent meaning). The primary processes (symbolism, condensation, displacement) have constructed an architecture of disguise that houses and essentially obfuscates the interior secret meanings. A Freudian analysand, who has developed free-associative skills, is able to get this oneiric engine revved up so that it can reveal its secrets. Non-Freudians are inclined to dismiss this fantastic engine as silly: "it's only a dream." One could picture this fantastic engine (what makes it seem so fantastic is Freud's description of the regression that magically transforms verbal secondary process language into a sort of Orwellian dreamspeak that speaks in outlandish visual images rather than in words) as a container of secret meanings totally disguised with a manifest chassis of condensations, displacements, and symbolism, like a car, so totally covered with stickers, nothing can be seen besides the exterior "billboard" of disguise. (This mixed, even jumbled metaphor hopefully captures the zany complexity of our topic.) The car's engine is loaded with irony however, since each sticker, each item of disguise on the exterior "billboard" will promote free-associative allusions that eventually strip the car of all disguise and reveal the workings of the engine and all its primal parts and meanings. The royal road to the unconscious Freud called this vivisection of the dream that revealed the anatomy of desire, the engine of instinct at its most elemental.

With this sketch of the dream engine to guide us, let us try to imagine screen memory and symptom as psychological engines. This exercise has become undoubtedly tiresome and, to avoid the risk of sounding more like used car salesmen rather than analysts, we will proceed with as much brevity as possible to illustrate our point. A screen memory has a dream-like structure one could argue, a manifest luminous image that attracts attention to itself but seems to hide more than it reveals. If dream seems to wave its billboard of stickers at the free-associative collaborative inquiries of analyst and analysand, thereby eventually uncovering its secret trove of unconscious meanings, a screen memory seems to be an abandoned engine, a dream that cannot be associated to, a burnt out psychological star. This is not entirely true, as Leonora's case makes clear, analytic process eventually jumpstarting the engine of the screen memory and exploiting its dormant horsepower to further accelerate analytic process. But the image of the screen memory as inert engine does have clinical relevance throughout a substantial period of analysis.

Symptom viewed as engine strikes one as different from screen memory or dream, given that the somatic compliance makes the engine seem more mind-body crafted than the purely psychological screen memory or dream. A symptom, in other words, demands a somatic expression, as if the engine of the mind insisted on dragging the body along with it, giving the body a work out also, so to speak. The symptom, in more Freudian language, reveals very clearly that instinct, as psychoanalysts use the concept, is the representation in the mind of the body's urgencies. The body's urgencies may also be represented in screen memory and dream, but the subtlety of their expression hides the connection to the body completely. In fact, EEGs of sleep architecture show that in the REM stage in which dreams occur, body motion is inhibited, so that dreams "cut off" from the body's activity cannot act out their wildest wishes. Similarly, a screen memory seems to have no connection whatsoever to somatic activity or behavior, the memory as inert as a forgotten tome in an abandoned library until analytic process insists on using its library card again, revisiting the dust covered books of the past.

Now that we have belabored this engine metaphor, can we put it to use as we seek to comment on Leonora's analysis? The description of screen memory, symptom, and dream as discrete engines does suggest that each of them is on a separate track, on its own journey, with its own agenda. The Hartmannian way of discussing them would be to suggest that each is a separate "structure" defined by its unique functions. The function of dream, according to Freud, would be to deploy enough primary process distortion to disguise the infantile wishes at the core of dreams, thereby securing a good night's sleep for the dreamer. The function of symptom would seem to be a compromise between the mind's agenda and the body's, so that, through an elaborate condensation of primary gains and secondary gains, the needs of mind and body are ambiguously met. The function of screen memory would seem to be to freeze the infantile amnesia in place by offering consciousness the barest reminder of all that's been repressed, a memorial consolation prize, a nostalgic reminder of a lost childhood.

Describing the three engines and their functions in such shorthand does violence to their complexities, but it does allow us to see more graphically perhaps what transference neurosis and intense analytic process achieve: it eventually, through free-associative cross fertilization, holds a sympathetic mirror up to every illusion, lends an understanding ear to every self deception, so that truth can eventually recognize its own reflection and the mind becomes one engine generating its own unique meanings as it takes the measure of experience and the phenomenal world. The titration of illusion, as Leonora might have said, is only sleight of hand until the magician sets aside his tricks and makes peace with the frail, sturdy, resourceful, conflicted human engine that maps its complex course between life and death.

MIND AS THEATER

We believe we have been using metaphors (engines) trying to exploit their dramatic imagery, at first, to lead to what now perhaps can be stated more theoretically. If mind, as a grand scheme, can be thought of as instinct and defense, mind, like a superior dramatist, senses that the two main protagonists, instinct and defense, cannot be center stage throughout every scene and act of the drama, or the audience, saturated with the obvious, un-amused by the playwright's meager command of aesthetic artifice, will pile out of the theater at intermission or sooner. If mind and audience are thought of not as two separate entities, but as the reflective self and its mirror, instinct ashamed or afraid of its own image in the looking glass of conflict, the need for sub plots, minor characters, red herrings, and such, will be obvious as development ambles toward denouement. Another way of stating this would be that if instinct is devious in its program of desire, defense is equally devious in its mastery of disguise. It is only at the end of analysis perhaps that both become partners in an enterprise called mental health, whereas earlier they act like strangers or rivals as neurosis rules the roost.

Analysis is essentially the study of this elaborate deviousness that the free-associative process never ceases to unravel and marvel at. A screen memory, for instance, keeps a record of certain childhood events, but distortion may be the rule rather than accuracy. Why? To protect the hegemony of infantile amnesia perhaps. Why is infantile amnesia so obligatory in the first place? The memories of the first six years of a human's life have to be shredded or, if not shredded, filed away so bureaucratically they can never be retrieved. Why? Childhood schizophrenia has been characterized, too simply perhaps, as a mind that is unable to repress: the undefended mind, at the mercy of massive instinctual energies, becomes psychotic. Luria's description of the mind of a mnemonist is a moving depiction of a mind that remembers everything, and the great sorrow this overload brings in its wake. The man became a "circus act," a stage performer of fantastic memorial exploits, but his life as a social entity was a catastrophe. The only point we wish to extract from these tragic clinical examples is that amnesia ironically may be the only way to protect memory from itself so that instead of being a totally unrepressed renegade, it civilizes itself, prunes itself of excessive details and record keeping, so that it can function in society as an instrument of communication, rather than an instrument of endless self reflection, self torture, self referentiality. The screen memory in that sense is a kind of tombstone, infantile amnesia's monument to itself, a remnant of necessary grief, as the mind de-centers itself from total memorial narcissistic obsession and allows development to move the wheels of social progress forward. The irony of course is that total repression is as impossible to imagine as total recall and probably just as detrimental to mental health. If there is tragedy in the mind of a mnemonist, as Luria warns, there is certainly tragedy in total repression, as Freud has made abundantly clear. Screen memory, in this light, could be viewed as the mind's first great tribute to an act of compromise, so all encompassing, that memory, astonished by its own daring act of self pruning, never quite gets used to the new version of itself. The "unrememberable and the unforgettable" in Alvin Frank's felicitous phrase, will haunt its conflicted architecture forever after, like a cornerstone erected on a sacrificial piece of the self that threatens to pull the building down around itself, even as it knows how securely, how crucially, it holds it up.

If man eventually has to process his own death, integrate a sense of morality into a narcissistic fabric that insists on immortality, perhaps this childhood act of coping with the death of memory infantile amnesia insists on, is an early exercise in self renunciation that prefigures and perhaps paves the way for the ultimate act of renunciation Nature has in store for all of us. If "all flesh is as grass," as Ecclesiastes puts it, man however is "a reed that thinks," according to Pascal, and it is the complexity of this reed and its thoughts and its disguises that we have been emphasizing.

If infantile amnesia is the most impressive demonstration of the power of repression and so clinically palpable at such an early age (in child analysis, one can only marvel at times at how totally amnesic a 7-year-old has become to analytic process that at age 5 seemed so turbulent and unforgettable), one cannot but be curious as to where the instinctual energies have been secreted. "Where raw instinct was, developmental fuel shall be," would seem to be the maxim of latency, as Eriksonian "industry," a passion for learning transforms the naked energy of oedipal passion into a readiness for education which makes the transmission of culture possible throughout the school years from ages 7 to 14. Ego development, character development, and experience are a few of the variables that a developmental sketch such as this can only allude to without getting into the intricacies of motivation and compromise, the perpetual context of conflict, out of which all this has emerged.

As Lustman (1962) has pointed out, in his most insightful paper on symptom and character, the two are not as discrete as theory and definitional precision would seem to imply. If character is defined as a predictable unconscious cluster of automatic strategic responses to conflict resolution manufactured over time, reflexive almost in its operational finesse, it does cover its developmental, conflictual tracks so well so as to make its psychological sibling, symptom, seem almost clumsy and obvious in its attempts to resolve conflict. If character has developed a smooth, almost invisible diplomacy in dealing with psychological disputes, symptom can perhaps be compared to a gauche hysterical ingénue in the poker game of conflict resolution, showing its hand too readily, as somatic display is unable to keep the mind's secrets hidden! It's the symptom's transparency that we wish to stress, a transparency that allowed us after all to see its connection to the screen memory that may have antedated it by many years. Leonora's wish to drown her mother, her sister, her father, in positive and negative expressions and variations of her conflicts, had to be disguised in complex ways, such as by reversal (she was the one being drowned), reaction formation (her sweetness of character made her seem too good to be true even to herself, as analytic process constantly reminded her), repression and a whole host of other defenses and character traits. Out of all this complexity, we have chosen to focus on screen memory, symptom, and dream, and on the continuity of imagery that hinted at the hidden connection between all three. The connection between dream and character, for instance, would have been more difficult, if not impossible, to explicate, since the "connective transparency" which may well exist unconsciously is nonetheless impossible to see, to exploit or to expose. An investigator finds a window or a door, some point of entry into the architecture of the mind, where one can. One cannot walk through walls.

Leonora's symptoms (breathlessness, fatigue, and inability to have orgasm) can be viewed as somatic expressions of their psychological correlatives (self-imposed assault on the body as punishment for imagined oedipal and pre-oedipal crime). The lungs (breathlessness), the musculature (fatigue), and sexual organs (frigidity) were the targeted areas and it is not too speculative perhaps, to view these symptoms as emanations from a primal scene (the drowning of mother by father or vice-versa in the breathless, "fatiguing" tumult of sexual intercourse, all seen through the distorting lens of course of a child's primal imaginings). Choice of symptom and the precise genetics that spawned it have confounded analysts since Freud's time, but the formal properties of the symptom in this case are highly suggestive of their primitive sexual origins. The symptom, seen as a regressive act, could be characterized as a depiction of the psyche's failure to master the over stimulating ingredients the child was struggling with. The symptom, seen as a more adaptive psychosomatic expression, could be characterized as the mind's strategic use of the body to find its bearings in turbulent, sexual, conflictual waters, to learn how to swim slowly so to speak, rather than drown in precocity and overstimulations that throw the mind into the deep end of the developmental pool, before it has learned how to doggy paddle in shallower developmental waters. If screen memory is a monument to the absolute power of repression, symptom on the other hand is an expression of the organism's developmental struggles, a refusal to let repression drown out all developmental desires, a kind of tentative courage in which the mind takes the body's hand and isn't ashamed to ask for assistance. The developmental crutch can be tossed aside later, as Leonora's analysis makes clear, when the mind has assumed its full stature!

If the relationship between screen memory and repression seems more absolute than symptom's relationship to defense, dream is perhaps the most puzzling of all, since, royal road to the unconscious as it may be, it is such a complex knot of primary processes and obfuscations that its royalty as a portal of entry into the kingdom of the unconscious had to await the genius of Sigmund Freud for recognition. As we examine the progression from screen memory to symptom to dream, an artificial progression to be sure constructed for the elucidation of our thesis, one could argue that if there is a complemental series of aetiological events that "construct" the complexity of the mind's pathologies, there must be an analogous complemental series of developmental events or psychological events that "construct" the reality of insightful adaptation. We would like to suggest that dreaming and the opportunity it affords the mind to reflect on itself, "in a glass darkly" to be sure, is nevertheless still a looking glass that, if held up to the nature of the unconscious, can reveal the dark side of truth to itself, thereby making it whole. If screen memory and symptom hinted at what Leonora had hidden from herself, her dreams dared her to decode their unconscious communications, a challenge she was able to meet in the analytic situation, as she assumed her full psychological stature. Dream analysis made it possible for Leonora to recognize and reclaim her wish to "wire" her "enemies," electrocute them, torture them until the thirst for revenge was requited, as deeply as the original thirst for love had been disappointed. It made it possible for her to understand why she needed to see herself as a psyche floundering in waters that the hands of love were too short to reach. She could understand that these masochistic metaphors were of her own making, unconscious hatred and love bent out of shape in the interest of defense, self deception, development, pathology, and adaptation. She could see that self deception is a necessary stepping stone as truth stumbles toward the insights that allow courage to replace fear as the mind's cornerstone. "Sympathetic insight" was her way of describing the process of analysis, a kind of revised insight that can change one's outlook on the complexity of life. The dreaming process, a life long recycling of unconscious imagery and conflict seems to have more fluidity than the seemingly more static screen memory or symptom. The static, repetitive nature of the structure of screen memory and symptom is suggestive of the compulsive repetitious recycling of the same image in traumatic neurosis, a commentary on the traumatic genetics of childhood screens and symptoms perhaps, which would differentiate these mental phenomena from the non-static interplay of manifest content and latent content that is the hallmark of dream. If the mind is depicted as drama, screen memory and symptom could be thought of as early mise-en-scènes of the playwright's intentions, the early scenes that introduce the gist of plot and character, whereas dreams are all about denouement and ultimate exposition when the loose ends are shown to be crucial threads in the total majesty of a fabric that could only be partially glimpsed at first. When symptom, screen memory, and dream recognize each other as interlocking facets of the meaning of the whole, the curtain can come down on the stage lights of self deception as the house lights of reality are turned up.

BIBLIOGRAPHY

BRONOWSKI, J. (1978). *The Visionary Eye: Essays in the Arts, Literature and Science.* Boston, Mass.: MIT Press.

ERIKSON, E. H. (1950). *Childhood and Society.* New York: W. W. Norton and Company.

FRANK, A. (1969). The unrememberable and the unforgettable. *Psychoanal. Study Child,* 24:48–77.

FREUD, S. (1899). Screen memories. *S.E.,* 3:301–322.

——— (1901). Childhood memories and screen memories. *S.E.,* 6:43–52.

LURIA, A. R. (1987). *The Mind of a Mnemonist: A Little Book about a Vast Memory.* Cambridge, Mass.: Harvard University Press.

Lustman, S. (1962). Defense, symptom and character. *Psychoanal. Study Child,* 17:216–244.

Mahon, E. & Battin, D. (1981). Screen memories and termination. *JAPA,* 29:939–942.

Mahon, E. & Battin, D. (1983). The fate of screen memories. *Psychoanal. Study Child,* 38:459–479.

IN MEMORY OF
DONALD J. COHEN, M.D.

In Memory:
Donald J. Cohen, M.D.

LINDA C. MAYES, M.D.

MORE THAN A YEAR HAS PASSED IN OUR MOURNING OF OUR FRIEND
and colleague, Dr. Donald Cohen. As we count the calendar days that
he has not been a daily, collegial presence in our lives, the year and
months have been remarkably long and soberly filled with our missing him. But in memorial time that keeps him alive and present in
our minds, it seems only yesterday that we were together in one of his
signature interactions with so many of us—a knock at an office door
or an impromptu telephone call just to check in or go for a quick
walk, going to the hospital together to see a patient, co-teaching a
seminar, having dinner with new fellows, finding an extra few minutes to connect a student with just the right mentor, writing a paper,
imagining a book, talking about friends, family, children and grand-
children, vigorously arguing science, religion, philosophy, death,
and life. In each and every one of these moments in their real time
and now in their memorial time, there is Donald's characteristic urging—celebrate life, look to the future, be curious, give of ourselves to
the children and families coming to us for care, always keep in mind
those who have come before and will come after us. Donald's curiosity was boundless in its depth and breadth. He was a world-class scientist, compassionate clinician, ever-present teacher and mentor, confident, caring administrator, devoted humanitarian, and a loyal friend
of psychoanalysis. His psychoanalytic identity is seamlessly woven
with his role as scientist and academician. Each informs the other,

Arnold Gesell Professor of Child Psychiatry, Pediatrics, and Psychology in the Yale
Child Study Center; Faculty, Western New England Institute for Psychoanalysis.

The Psychoanalytic Study of the Child 58, ed. Robert A. King, Peter B. Neubauer,
Samuel Abrams, and A. Scott Dowling (Yale University Press, copyright © 2003 by
Robert A. King, Peter B. Neubauer, Samuel Abrams, and A. Scott Dowling).

and his academic, investigative life at the Child Study Center is an integral part of his psychoanalytic life.

As director of the Yale Child Study Center from 1983 to 2001, and a member of the Center's faculty since 1972, Donald strengthened the Center's developmental research programs, maintained its strong psychoanalytic tradition, and expanded its collaborations into an international network of scholarly colleagues and friends, all committed to bettering life for the world's children. In his tenure as chairman, the Child Study Center became internationally recognized for its multidisciplinary programs of clinical and basic research, professional education, clinical services and advocacy for children and families. Building on the psychoanalytically informed family studies of his mentors, Al Solnit, Sam Ritvo, and Sally Provence, Donald emphasized research programs that also involved committed service to families who participated as long-standing partners in the research programs. Indeed, many of the studies in the Center are now in the third generation of families and investigators with the fourth just being born.

There are so many programs of research and scholarship that bear Donald's creative stamp. His work with children with the most serious childhood psychiatric disorders such as autism, pervasive developmental disorders, and chronic motor and vocal tics integrated biological, psychological, and behavioral perspectives into multidisciplinary, world-class programs combining research and clinical care. His leadership in studies of the impact of violence and trauma on children and families in the United States and abroad created a worldwide network of collaborators in innovative programs to respond to the mental health needs of families caught in war and community violence. His interest in the earliest phases of development fostered the Center's programs in the developmental behavioral neuroscience of early emotional life in which clinicians and scientists work side by side to understand how behavior and brain development are influenced by stressful experiences during and immediately after pregnancy and during the preschool years.

All of Donald's research interests centered on questions at the interface of biology and psychology, brain and mind. His grounding in philosophy (with a particular interest in Wittgenstein) informed his science and his training as a child psychiatrist and a child and adult psychoanalyst. In his own words, he was concerned with the "most intimate human activities—the forming, sustaining, repairing, and terminating of our closest relationships."[1]—and in understanding the

---

1. Cohen, D. J. (2000). Into Life: Autism, Tourette's Syndrome and the Community of Clinical Research. Sterling Lecture, Yale University, February 2000.

basic biology of relatedness, how that biology becomes psychology, and vice versa. He fostered a unique model in which experienced clinicians work side by side with behavioral neuroscientists to translate new knowledge into sophisticated clinical services that recognize and address simultaneously patients' biological and psychosocial adversity.

In the last year of his life, Donald wrote about his own development as a scholar of autism and related early developmental disorders and about the moment when his research interests crystallized. All of us who were his close friends and colleagues knew about his intellectual gifts, but we did not quite conceive how early he had declared himself a child psychiatrist and a scientist with an abiding interest in individual life histories. As he told the story, when he was a young boy, he noticed a gardener at the Garfield Park Conservatory in Chicago. Fascinated by the gardener's attentive, methodical care of the surrounds and his calm, gentle demeanor, Donald, at 8 years old, decided to do an interview for the school newspaper he was editing. Looking back on that first publication, he wrote:

> The interview . . . constitutes one of the earlier reports, though less widely circulated than that of Kanner and Asperger, on the central phenomena that still intrigue our field. . . . This is the verbatim interview: "I was a shy and frail child. Therefore I decided to become a gardener." This early report on a socially dysfunctional adult identifies constitutional factors, shyness, and possible biological correlates, frailty, with long-term prognosis in a career that was socially isolated: the gardener represents an optimistic adaptation to an underlying disability in social orientation.[2]

Here even in retrospective account is Donald's remarkable mind at work. He had an eye and ear for the novel and for asking questions that sparked others' energy and curiosity. His ability to bridge and blend disciplines gave him a creative edge on formulating research questions that brought together scientists and clinicians not accustomed to working collaboratively and encouraged them to think of different methods to approach the problem. Donald's interest in Tourette's syndrome emerged with the same spontaneity and curiosity as his early observations about social disabilities. The problem of multiple tics was central to his interest in the mind-body interface. In his own words:

2. Cohen, D. J. (2001). A Lifetime of Research on Autism. Lecture on the Occasion of the Lifetime Award for Research in Autism. International Meeting for Autism Research, November 2001, Los Angeles.

Unlike those with autism, the children with tics are fully aware that
their symptoms cause their parents terrible pain and lead to their
own social isolation. These children suffer an excruciating sense of
the loss of self-control—of the capitulation to inner impulses that
hover between consciousness and the preconscious. Like young
philosophers, they develop theories about what is voluntary and what
is involuntary, what is psychological and what is neurological; they
know there is a broad, indeterminate domain in-between these contrasting categories; and they think about the mysterious leap from
body to mind, mind to body, inside themselves. They also long to be
in the mainstream of society—and with real courage and the use of
all their talents, including their psychological sensitivities, they often
achieve their goal.[3]

Here is Donald, the consummate scientist, thinking about a child's
inner experience and emerging sense of self as defined by a set of
symptoms—the voice of Donald as a master clinician, and intuitive
observer. He felt it was a "special, privileged position that is offered
to us to study whole persons, children and adults, in their most private lives, because of our commitment to offer care and reduce suffering."[4] He taught his students and colleagues always to look beyond
the tics and other symptoms and to build on the strengths and potentialities of the children affected.

Each of these research themes also bears the stamp of Donald as a
psychoanalyst—his concern for children's inner worlds, fantasies,
worries, and desires. Donald's contributions to psychoanalysis are
given voice in his papers with his colleagues about the meaning of
play in oedipal-aged children, depression and mourning, children's
imagination, aggression, and emerging theory of mind. For Donald,
child psychoanalysis was a process of understanding and asking questions with a primary emphasis on the emergence of a child's inner
experiences, an internal world, and the process of symbolization. He
admired the early child analysts especially for their observational
skills and bold creative leaps and for their engagement with children
in the real world—nurseries, orphanages, war-torn cities, juvenile
gangs and homes, hospitals, schools for the blind and the deaf. As a
training and supervising analyst at the Western New England Institute, he pushed candidates never simply to accept a psychoanalytic
concept without debate and playful, probing skepticism. Only Donald could have thought of turning Winnicott's Piggle into a three-act

---

3. See footnote 1.
4. Ibid.

play complete with Melanie Klein as narrator as a way of urging candidates to study the text up close.

But perhaps even more important than his published psychoanalytic work was Donald's insistence on the possibilities of creating a freely traveled bridge between other developmental, empirical perspectives and psychoanalysis as a theory of mind and a therapeutic endeavor. In the last year of his life, together we were working on a reappraisal of the status of child psychoanalysis and a challenge to all of us as psychoanalysts to take on a new and synthetic developmental psychoanalytic epistemology. Our hope for psychoanalysis is that as a field, it might embrace again the original creative spark and the spirit of inquiry and discovery that infused the earliest practitioners Donald so admired. And by so doing, psychoanalysts might look outside the field's formalized training and practice structures to see those individuals who cannot adjust their lives to the rigors of the usual analytic parameters—single parents struggling to make ends meet to raise their children, teenagers caught up in the grinding stress of community violence and poverty, the chronically ill child or adult.

Donald worried about psychoanalysis becoming progressively isolated from different developmental epistemologies and a working intellectual collaboration with other disciplines struggling with these basic questions about how children enter the fullness of human relationships. In his view, if psychoanalysis does not begin to build these bridges, it will face a profound irony: A field that concerns itself with those truths that cannot be known, with the survival and adaptation that can come from illness and loss, and with the awful unpredictability of life may become increasingly isolated and cut-off from those most powerful conditions, ideas, and situations that people often willingly die for. A field about those very passions that give life meaning may find itself increasingly isolated from those passions in the rough and tumble crucible of day to day existence, family life, and children's growing up.

For Donald, these challenges to psychoanalysis were the essence of what it means to live a psychoanalytic (and spiritual) life—a continual effort toward reflection, self-scrutiny and understanding whether within the individual or within the field. Engaging in systematic personal or professional inquiry means accepting the possibility of being surprised, distressed, doubtful, and disappointed as well as satisfied, secure, and knowing. He taught us that in embarking on any investigation, we acknowledge the risks of what we might learn as well as the excitement of discovery and satisfaction of confirmation. There is an inevitable and necessary tension between the empirical, the rigorous science of measurement, and accepting the sometimes unknowable complexity of what it means to be human, to love and to hate, to mourn or rejoice. In these matters of head and heart, soul and mind, Donald was our surest guide. He modeled a life of relentless inquiry balanced with one of reverence for what we cannot easily understand or accept—balancing the spiritual and the empirical, the sacred and the profane. In the fullness of his relationships, Donald passed on his highest values in the shared pursuit of understanding wherever it may lead, and this is perhaps Donald's most enduring legacy to us as his students, colleagues, and friends. It sustains us through the unexpectancies of life—its losses and its gains, friendships ended in one time but enduring in another—and grants us the solace of never-ending wonder.

In Tribute to Donald J. Cohen: Some Thoughts on Childhood Trauma

STEVEN MARANS, Ph.D.

INTRODUCTION

HAVING COMPLETED MY TRAINING AND WORK AT THE ANNA FREUD Centre in 1984, I was recruited by Donald Cohen to join the faculty at the Yale Child Study Center. While we had extensive discussions during this process, I began to get a better sense of Donald with our first brisk walk across the Yale campus following a planning retreat for Center faculty members. As I tried to keep up with his determined, quick pace, I was introduced to Donald's intellectual intensity and spirit of scientific inquiry as he questioned me about Anna Freud's concept of developmental lines and about the use of the Hampstead Clinic's Diagnostic Profile. Discussing the difficulties of moving from child psychoanalytic concepts to systematic research, Donald issued what would become a very familiar challenge to action in his statement, "We have a lot to learn." Around basic child analytic concepts, this challenge would lead to studies of play and the analytic interview with young children (Cohen et al., 1987; Marans, Mayes, Cohen, et al., 1990; Solnit, Cohen, and Neubauer, 1993) and a range of psycho-

---

Harris Associate Professor of Child Psychoanalysis and Psychiatry, Child Study Center and Department of Psychiatry, Yale University, School of Medicine.

This paper was presented at the Donald J. Cohen Symposium on Child Psychoanalysis, Tuesday, June 17, 2002.

The Psychoanalytic Study of the Child 58, ed. Robert A. King, Peter B. Neubauer, Samuel Abrams, and A. Scott Dowling (Yale University Press, copyright © 2003 by Robert A. King, Peter B. Neubauer, Samuel Abrams, and A. Scott Dowling).

analytic studies that included the examination and integration of psychoanalytic theories of development with advances in neuroscience and developmental psychopathology (Leckman and Cohen, 2002; Cicchetti and Cohen, 1995; Mayes and Cohen, 1996; Marans and Cohen, 2002). The challenge would also be applied to Donald's deep concerns about the impact of adversity on children's inner lives and adaptive capacities. Investigation and action were equally reflected in his research pursuits, in his leadership in developing innovative clinical services and programs, and in his role in advancing social policy. In this area of violence and trauma, so central to psychoanalytic traditions of inquiry, Donald initiated our intensified efforts to look, learn, and act. He said that we could offer very little to children and families at greatest risk for symptoms and developmental deviations that were secondary to violent traumatization if we never saw them or saw them too late. Donald also recognized that we might have a great deal to learn from another group of professionals, the police, because they almost always saw the witnesses, victims, and perpetrators of violence. The Child Development Community Policing Program (CDCP) grew out of these basic observations. In considering the best ways of responding to the effects of violence exposure and trauma, we have looked to the broadest contexts of experience—of inner lives and external worlds, of biology and cognition. We have broadened the scope of our sources of data—from the consulting room to the living room to schools and neighborhood streets. As the CDCP Program has developed, so too has our appreciation of the broad range of partners whose professional activities might play a role in ameliorating the effects of violent trauma—clinicians, police officers, parents, teachers, domestic violence advocates, juvenile probation officers, child welfare workers, pediatricians, emergency room physicians, and others concerned about the effects of violence on children that occurs in homes, neighborhoods, schools, and in the warfare between countries. Throughout this process of learning, we first needed to observe and to listen.

PHENOMENOLOGY OF CHILDHOOD TRAUMA

We can all recall the experience, as children, of waking from a nightmare. Accelerated heart-rate, increased respiration, and confused thinking—desperately trying to locate the boundaries of experience; trying to determine what is real of the terror/threat that has awoken us. We automatically sought sources of safety. Sometimes we looked for it in the presence of others and stood stricken, wordless in front of parents who may have asked solicitously about the bad dream we must have had before sending us back to bed. With few other words available, we may have repeated, manta-like, their reminder: "it was only a dream" and returned to our rooms. We did the best we could, turning lights on, staving off a return to sleep and the dreams where our terror resided. Vigilant to hopeful reminders of reality and the remaining uncertainty that perceived threats were really only in our minds, we did everything we could to change the channels, and disable the instant, involuntary replay. The specific scenarios, though highly individualized and varied, shared underlying themes and terrifying effects.

As child analysts, we know something about the internal dangers and fears that can be powerful enough to disrupt sleep, leave children speechless, feeling unsafe in their dreams of their immediate worlds. We are regularly reminded in our clinical work—and in our own lives—of the most prominent sources of danger and fear: (1) loss of life and the lives of those we love and upon whom we depend; (2) losing the love of others and the love of ourselves; (3) damage to our bodies and impairment of functioning; (4) losing control of impulses, affects, and integrative thought; and, (5) losing the external structure and order that provides the basis for anticipating, planning and responding to the new challenges.

As we know all-too-well, these fears that fuel our nightmares also lurk in the background of numerous situations in our waking lives. While we are not always pleased with our solutions, the signals of anxiety and concern alert, prepare, and enable us to take protective action. In the aftermath of the nightmare, fear and arousal are diminished as reality reasserts itself and sleep can once again provide the opportunity for multiple narratives that afford pleasurable alternatives to dreaded aspects of our imagination. Freud recognized that the dangers that each of us hope to avoid are the ones that we have experienced in the past and that when they materialize in the unexpected events of the present, internal threats and external, real dangers converge and overwhelm the unprepared ego (Freud, S., 1926).

In the traumatic moment our worst nightmares are realized and basic patterns of cognitive, affective, and physiological processes are severely disrupted and compromised (Marans, 2000; Pynoos et al. 1999; Ehlert et al., 2001; Heim and Nemeroff, 2001; Shale, 2000; and Yehuda, 2001). The traumatized child and adult are often unable to recognize, identify, or articulate discrete affects; orient experience in time and space; control somatic expression of hyper-arousal/overstimulation; or maintain integration of stimuli that is required for ex-

ecutive decision making and defensive reaction. In our clinical practice we regularly observe the fundamental need to reverse the experience of helplessness that confronts individuals when traumatic dangers are not only present and real but also arouse and vivify the most
threatening sources of danger that always reside in the unconscious
realms of our imagination. In the aftermath of traumatic situations,
perhaps the greatest challenge to regaining a semblance of control is
in the recognition that we have lost it—that we are not as powerful or
immune to the effects of danger—especially when real events converge with our worst nightmares. Consider the following vignettes.

*A group of 5-year-old children witnessed a classmate wounded by gunfire
when their school bus was caught in a cross-fire of rival drug dealers. In the
immediate aftermath, they clutched their knees, stared off into space, and
rocked themselves; they could not speak of what they had seen or felt. Slowly,
through drawings and later, play they would teach us that their attempts to
master normative concerns about bodily integrity and damage and their efforts to establish increased sense of mastery of a predictable world were dramatically undermined with realization of their worst nightmares. We would
learn that the sight of their friend's injuries and the dramatic disruption of an
expectable bus-ride from school was also an assault on the reassuring connection to parents that ordinarily ensures a basic sense of safety. Given the phase-
specific context of normative concerns, it was perhaps no surprise that in the
weeks that followed the shooting, the most prominent symptoms to emerge were
clinging behavior and somatic complaints. The stomach-aches, school avoidance, demands to sleep with parents, not leave their sides, located children's
central areas of concern affording them the opportunity to anticipate and seek
control of the most frightening aspects aroused by the original event: loss and
bodily harm.*

*A 15-year-old girl shook and hyperventilated but was unable to find words for
what had happened or what she felt immediately after being threatened at
gun-point and robbed. Once in psychotherapy, she would report that immediately following the event, she felt that she couldn't control her body or locate
any thoughts. Over the ensuing weeks, she would not go into any rooms in her
house unaccompanied, refused to go outside or to school, and fought frequently with the same mother she could not separate from. Her symptoms
would resolve with her awareness and appreciation of the multiple meanings
of her traumatic experience. It would emerge that for her the traumatic moment consisted of the fantasy that she would be raped. The fear was especially
powerful not only because it might have been in the realm of possibilities. This
particular fear was also potentiated by feelings of danger and vulnerability*

that she associated with the trepidation that accompanied the normal excitement she felt about sexual experimentation with a first boyfriend. In addition, she would later explain her need to fight with her mother as an attempt to reverse what she experienced as babyish in the fear and helplessness generated by the robbery.

An 11-year-old girl in Bedford-Stuyvesant talked about the impact of watching the World Trade Center towers collapse to a group of children and parents who met several weeks after the attacks of September 11, 2001. She did not want to elaborate on what she saw, but volunteered that since September 11, she was frightened to go outside or to school. She had frequent nightmares and was especially worried about burglars coming into her house. When asked what connections she thought there might be between her new worries and the attack on the WTC, she surprised her parents and perhaps everyone else in the room. She explained: "You see, the CIA, FBI and the police all kept their evidence in the World Trade Center. When the Towers went down, they had to release all of the criminals onto the streets of my neighborhood." Now, she added, whenever she hears sirens, she is both reminded of her concerns and believes that they are being confirmed by the supposed police activity. Her parents had assumed that her symptoms were related to 9/11 but, until this meeting had, by their own account, been so preoccupied with their own distress and worry about the attacks, they had not inquired about the specific nature of their daughter's experience.

When the ego is overwhelmed, when repression and supporting defenses are dramatically disrupted, the ability to relegate the most powerful sources of fear to the realm of the unconscious is lost. As with the nightmare, the traumatized child seeks to protect himself, to undo the original experience of helplessness by assuming a vigilant stance toward the external world, externally "locating" the source of danger in an effort to develop strategies to avoid its repetition. With the aim of reversing the dramatic experience, the child attempts to take control by reinstating signal anxiety and assigning threat to an identifiable source. If danger can be located and anticipated, action can be taken to avoid being rendered passive once again. As we know, however, the symptoms of avoidance and bids for control bring their own heavy prices as children attempt to turn away from the primordial fears that have been aroused. The challenge to regain a sense of personal control is exacerbated as original event-related experiences of traumatic loss of control are revisited when physiologic changes— particularly dysregulation of the noradrenergic system—make bodies more vulnerable to lower thresholds for startle, rapid changes in

heart-rate and respiration. These somatic symptoms may be especially distressing when individuals are unable to consciously locate
the traumatic reminders or triggers (Pynoos et al., 1999) that give
rise to them. Multiple factors including physical proximity to both
observations and immediate personal threat of dangers; degree of
emotional threat; pre-existing vulnerabilities in psychological functioning; previous traumatic loss or events involving overwhelming
danger; degree of recognition of distress by adults and the availability
of family and other social supports all contribute to the extent to
which frightening events reach traumatic proportions. Additionally,
Toren and colleagues point out that the challenges of recovery in
children are further complicated when the events themselves are (a)
unremitting, (b) disrupt the predictability of daily life, and (c) trau-
matize and disrupt the capacities of parents and entire communities
of adults to provide psychological mediation and climate of emotional stability, strength, and safety (Freud, A. and Burlingham, 1973;
Toren et al., 2002).

For some children and families, the opportunity to quickly recognize the fact and effects of the traumatic nature of events occurs with
acute, brief psychotherapeutic intervention. Helping parents to recognize the ways in which their children demonstrate the impact of
overwhelming events of danger and to appreciate the range of specific fears that are aroused can create the scaffolding of ego support
that they and their children need in order to recover. Providing children with the opportunity to find words and organized representation of the traumatic experiences that arouse the current and past
conflicts and fears allows them to return to what Anna Freud described as the "optimal path of development" (Freud, A., 1981). For
others, the acute point of therapeutic involvement affords an opportunity to recognize the broader context of developmental derailment
in which the child experiences the most immediate traumatic events.
Psychoanalytic treatments have allowed us to understand the detailed ways in which acute episodes of trauma are woven into a fabric
of compromised development and increasingly intransigent psychopathology. Longer-term psychoanalytic investigation and treatment can help unlock the stranglehold on the complex relationships
between trauma, inadequate conflict resolution and pathological
adaptations that interfere with negotiating age-adequate tasks of development. This was especially the case in the life of a 15-year-old boy
whose maladaptive responses to multiple episodes of violent trauma
led to persistent and destructive distortions in his character development.

Psychoanalytic Case Material[1]

Dean J. was 15 years old when he entered psychoanalytic treatment. His history was marred by exposure to domestic violence, his own beatings at mother's hand and mother's chronic depression, suicide attempts, and repeated psychiatric hospitalizations. In addition to the visits from the police, Dean also had to contend with his father leaving the home for several days at a time after marital fights. Following the parents' divorce when he was 2½, Dean saw father only sporadically until he was 8 years old. At that time, he went to live with father and step-mother just after his mother's most dramatic suicide attempt in which she cut her wrists in front of her son. In his second year of treatment with me, Dean spoke of this event for the first time. He could only remember seeing her as she was being brought out of her trailer on a stretcher. He broke away from a neighbor who had been trying to hold him back, and ran to his mother before she was placed inside the ambulance. "The last thing I remember best is her yelling at me: 'This is happening because you are such a bad boy!'" Dean added that at age 8, this was the last time he could recall crying about her.

Dean arrived in Connecticut malnourished, withdrawn, and severely depressed. He was only able to talk minimally with his father and actively attempted to avoid any contact with the woman introduced as his new mother. While his appetite improved gradually within the first several months in his father's home, he continued to sleep fitfully and had frequent nightmares. However, the picture of the quiet and depressed little boy quickly and dramatically changed. He began to get into daily fights with classmates, repeatedly attacked the family dog, lied about his destruction of property, stole money, and made several attempts to run away. His father and stepmother sought a psychiatric evaluation. While very concerned about his aggressive behavior, father and stepmother were especially struck by Dean's denial of any thoughts or feelings about having left his mother and by the apparent absence of any remorse about any of his difficult behaviors. They were equally concerned that whenever anything independent of him went wrong, Dean became very anxious that he was the cause of it. When his step-maternal grandmother died after a long illness, Dean became very upset and repeatedly asked, "Why did she die . . . haven't I been a good boy?"

---

1. A fuller discussion of "Dean" appears in the *Psychoanalytic Study of the Child*, vol. 55, 2000.

Dean received once-weekly out-patient psychotherapy for several months but his symptoms continued to escalate. His father and stepmother were unable to manage him at home even as his out-patient care was intensified with more frequent sessions, medication trials, and increased parent guidance. He was referred for residential treatment where he remained until he transferred to an adolescent group home whose requirements included out-patient psychotherapy.

He began his evaluation and subsequent treatment with me by regaling me with accounts of his exciting, anti-social behavior that ranged from fighting, to drinking and drugs, to burglaries and destruction of property. He craved an audience and readily accepted the idea of coming for treatment several times a week. Two themes began to emerge in these hours. I began to point out that he described each of his examples of delinquent or disruptive behavior as stupid and suggested that while he criticized himself after the fact, there seemed to be some compelling reasons for engaging in them. While first protesting that there couldn't be any good reasons for these "stupid" acts that only got him into trouble, Dean began to describe the buzz he got when engaged in them. "It's like when I'm doing stuff, I feel . . . well . . . powerful . . . like nothing can touch me, nothing can hurt me." Fights in school invariably started when "some kid who thinks he's a bad-ass bumps into me or looks at me funny." He explained that even though he knew that the fights were pretty stupid, they let off steam and made him feel strong. At this point, the analytic process was well on its way.

During the fourth month of treatment, after one of the typical fistfights that occurred in school, Dean arrived to his session looking sullen. He glared at me and angrily warned that I better not start with any of the psychology crap about why he fights. It was a good moment to say nothing. After a few minutes, he told me about a tough kid at school who had stuck out his foot trying to trip him and make him look like a fool. "If I had let him get away with it I would have looked like a pussy . . . like a scared little kid." I tentatively suggested that if this guy was so tough, perhaps it made some sense to be a bit scared. Before deciding to leave the session 10 minutes early, Dean scowled and shot back, "Ok, ok I was scared . . . big fucking deal!"

In the following hour, Dean arrived ready to do battle with me. He sat with his arms folded, scowling as he looked about the room. He focused on a Monet print of water lilies that hangs on my wall and with a snarl demanded, "What kind of bullshit picture is that anyway!?" To my question about what he saw in it, he replied, "A bunch of stupid colors." I told him a story about a guy about his age who went to an art gallery and asked a curator—in a similar tone—why anyone would be interested in a bunch of colors splashed onto canvas. The curator suggested that this guy sit down, look at the painting for a while and then she would come back and they could talk. This guy began to describe the feelings the dark, brooding colors on the canvas gave him. When the curator pointed out that this particular painting—by Rothko—was one of the last in a series by the artist before committing suicide, the painting no longer seemed so ridiculous. Dean smiled, pointed at me and said, "That guy was you, wasn't it?" When I returned the smile, Dean looked away and said he wanted to tell me something he'd never told anyone before. "It's really stupid, but I use some of my clothes money (allowance from the state) to buy crayons, markers and coloring books. Late at night I color . . . isn't that stupid?" You mean like a little kid? I replied. Without any more words or smile, Dean just sat there and nodded. After a few minutes with a knowing smile he said, "You think I need to get into fights and stuff so that I don't feel like some little kid don't you!?" I asked what he thought. "You may have something there . . . wow, maybe you do."

In the second year of treatment, as we prepared for a holiday break, Dean asked where I was going for my vacation. When I asked for his ideas, he imagined that I was going on a plane with my family to someplace warm. With the first expression of genuine sadness, he recalled his last plane trip at the age of 8 when he was being sent to live with his father and stepmother. He described feeling alone and afraid as he got onto the plane but said he felt much worse when he had to return to his mother for an additional two days because the plane was unable to land in Connecticut due to snow. "God, I hate thinking about that shit . . . you know I haven't spoken to her in over a year, but I guess I've been thinking a lot about her lately." After a pause, he said that he'd forgotten to mention that he almost got into a fight the previous day. The scenario was familiar, only now, Dean posed the rhetorical question: "Do you suppose there's some connection?" When I suggested that perhaps his feelings about not seeing me stirred up some of those alone and helpless little kid feelings, Dean first insisted that that was ridiculous, that he hoped I would have a great vacation. But then with a nervous laugh he said, "Well, maybe just a bit."

In the course of Dean's treatment, we were able to get a glimpse of an internal view of a young man who equated sad and frightened feelings and the longings of the younger child with impotence and dangerous vulnerability. In response to those feelings, Dean sought recourse in the excitement and power of aggressive acts. As we were able to explore and make conscious his defensive use of aggressivity, Dean's tolerance for fearful and depressive affects deriving from the past and present increased. As a result, there was a significant decrease in the incidence of fighting and other provocative behaviors that had invited multiple detentions and privilege restrictions. He began to spend most weekends at home with his father, stepmother, and younger brother. Eventually, in the beginning of his third year of treatment he moved back completely. At school, he was moved up into a section for kids who did not present with behavior problems.

Staying out late, getting into struggles about the use of his father's car and about compliance with house rules, and missing more sessions with me than he attended served the more recent version of Dean's compromise solutions. We could begin to recognize the ways he at once punished father/me while also satisfying an enormous appetite for attention—even if that attention took the form of a struggle. This situation emerged most clearly, when, after an absence of over two weeks, Dean arrived early for our session. He began by laughing anxiously, asking, "So, were you worried about me?" I replied by saying that whatever I said might be problematic for him. If I told him of my genuine concern, he might be both gratified and *frightened* by the pleasure that could reveal his "babyish" longings. If I said nothing, I would be joining him in a re-enactment of an earlier drama of disappointment, pre-emptive rejection and vengeful rage. He was at first startled, muttered something about psycho-bullshit and remained quiet. After several moments he said in typical Dean fashion, "I know. You think all this stuff with you and my Dad is really connected to my mother don't you?" For the first time Dean began to elaborate on sketchy memories of time with his mother.

While he referred to her beatings and her hospitalizations, what repeatedly plagued Dean was the question: "What could I have done to make her forget about me. . .?" He trailed off and with tears in his eyes added, "I could never get the answer." During the course of the next several months Dean would work energetically at making a connection between his inability to recall details of his mother and early years with her and the only answer that he had been able to construct: If being a "bad boy" could explain her rejection then he might finally establish some semblance of control over the experiences of trauma that had occurred. If he was responsible for her feelings and behavior, then he could hold onto a vestige of the wish that he alone might be finally able to secure her love.

As his situation continued to improve and stabilize, in the middle of his third year of treatment Dean introduced the idea of stopping. He pointed out that school was going well, struggles at home were minimal and in slightly embarrassed tones, indicated that his involvement with a "real girlfriend was eating up" a lot of his time. After much discussion and sessions that were often taken up with descriptions of pleasure and trepidation about his new relationship, we agreed that for now, he needed to stop. We set a date for our last meeting. In our last hour, Dean spoke of his mixed feelings and the poignancy of stopping. He said that it felt different to decide to end rather than quitting. Just before leaving the session, Dean smiled and said, "I've got your number if I need it." With some anxiety and a chuckle, he quickly added, "You aren't going anywhere are you!?!"

The last time I heard from Dean was in the year following the end of treatment and his graduation from high school. He called asking for a letter of recommendation for a local community college program. He was still thinking about drafting but was no longer certain about what he wanted to pursue. We chatted briefly and he told me that he'd been working in a garage and was still living at home. Things had not worked out with his first real girlfriend. I carefully reminded him that I'd be happy to see him to catch up more fully. He declined and recognizing my efforts to temper my concern with caution/tact, added, "Don't worry I'm okay . . . I'll keep you posted."

For Dean, characterologic patterns of defense were crafted in response to views of himself and others that persisted from his earliest years. These early views and expectations, fraught with experiences of traumatic violence and loss and the dangers associated with inconsistent and volatile relationships limited the range of adaptations and experiences in his current life. For Dean, conflicts and patterns of primitive defense were as tenacious as were internal convictions about himself and others that derived from the past. For a long time, in the face of these powerful convictions, Dean was simply unable to see himself in a world that was, in fact, no longer characterized by the trauma and dangers he had experienced as a small child but rather, filled with possibilities of safe relationships and the satisfaction of personal achievements. In treating children like Dean, we are particularly interested in the extent to which beliefs about the self and others fit the current reality. When there is a significant gap between beliefs and reality, our psychoanalytic task is to help the patient appreciate the difference and put the views of the world deriving from the past in their proper place.

CHILD PSYCHOANALYSIS AND THE CHILD STUDY CENTER

It has long been the best of psychoanalytic traditions that the complexity of personal experience has been embraced as the basis for considering a range of interventions that will benefit children. There is a long history of the central involvement of child analysts at the Yale Child Study Center—Alice Colonna, Wayne Downey, Robert Evans, Ernst and Marianne Kris, Mel Lewis, Seymour Lustman, Sally Provence, Sam Ritvo, John Schowalter, Al Solnit, and collaborators like Anna Freud, and Sonia and Joe Goldstein. The list is long and getting longer as the next generation of child psychoanalysts at the Center—Steven Berkowitz, Phyllis Cohen, Kirsten Dahl, Bob King, Jim Leckman, Linda Mayes, Barbara Nordhaus, Janet and David Szydlo, Fred Volkmar—apply their psychoanalytic training to the broadening field of research, program development, and treatment approaches. What each of these Child Study Center colleagues shares is the notion that exploring and appreciating the details of individual experience is crucial to understanding clinical phenomena. It is the application of this central psychoanalytic principle that informs the Center's work with a broad range of clinical problems affecting children and families. Donald Cohen, who led and embodied the traditions of the Center, articulated the best of our psychoanalytic perspectives that have informed these traditions. In his lecture, "Life Is with People," on the occasion of his appointment as Sterling Professor at Yale University in 2001, he wrote:

> The process of self-understanding—the task to which so much of our mental energy is directed throughout life—goes on from moment to moment, epoch to epoch. Its product is an increasingly nuanced self portrait—including thoughts, feelings, motivations, actions, reactions, memories—that is tested in lived experience. When this self-understanding proves trustworthy, we feel more certain in knowing who we are and with whom we are living, we can make wiser decisions with recognition of consequences, and we are not so easily surprised. Our theory of our own minds and minds of others becomes more reliable, a firmer basis for expectation. Yet the story of a life—this rich construction built of feeling-filled memories—remains, at least in part, tentative and open to renovation. Its tone and narrative are dependent not only on what has transpired in the inner and outer worlds, as felt and seen by the person, but also on the moment in time it is created.

Donald's absence is felt especially deeply by his family. He is also missed by his colleagues and friends at the Child Study Center and in the broader world in which he lived and worked. Personally, I am very aware of his absence and constantly reminded of his presence and of my great fortune to have known him as a colleague, mentor and, most important, as a friend. His values, achievements, and the continuation of work that he initiated, inspired, and guided are his gift and his legacy.

One of the greatest gifts that Donald gave to so many of his younger colleagues was his investment in their developing skills. Whether in the fields of genetics, neurobiology, medicine, education, or psychoanalysis, he encouraged and, at times, implored us with the words: "Find your own voice." He inspired and challenged each of us to explore new ideas, new approaches to our research and clinical endeavors, because, as he would say, the questions are so fascinating and the answers so important to the communities in which we work and live. For Donald, successful training and mentoring afforded more opportunities for solving the problems that children and families face. Success could also yield the enormous pride he took in hearing his younger colleagues find their voices, telling the stories of their work. And, no matter how much we learned, Donald continued to inspire, challenge, and to join us in learning more.

As we continue to work in our own community with children and families involved in traumatizing violence and terror, the Child Study Center is now the home of the National Center for Children Exposed to Violence, established in 1998, by the White House, the U.S. Department of Justice, and Congress. As a result, the work of implementing and evaluating the Child Development-Community Policing Program around the country continues and as do efforts to increase public awareness about the developmental implications of children's exposure to violence and trauma. This is Donald's legacy.

An entire nation continues the work that he implemented at the Child Study Center and that he inspired throughout the country. In 2000, the U.S. Congress authorized the Department of Health and Human Services to inaugurate a network of centers around the country devoted to research, program development, and consultation resources around issues of childhood trauma. The Child Study Center was chosen as one of the sites and plays a central role in this network particularly with regard to violent trauma. In 2001, Congress voted and the President signed an amendment changing the name of this legislation and the network to the Donald J. Cohen National Childhood Traumatic Stress Initiative. This is Donald's legacy.

Donald never turned away from problems, he embraced them. His humility informed his scientific approach to inquiry and his humanity helped to contain the pain associated with disturbing cases. It is this combination that has set the tone of our responses to violent trauma where close engagement and enduring curiosity are essential ingredients in being of help to the children and families whose burdens are far greater than our own. Donald knew, however, that providing care for others required support for ourselves. His door was always open. As I waded into the most difficult experiences of violence and acute trauma that involved a mixture of the most primitive and the most altruistic of human behavior, Donald was always available to listen, think, and learn with me. If there wasn't time during the day, Donald meant it when he suggested that you could call him at home late at night and proved it by often initiating the calls himself. Working late at night also spread the range of his attention to problems of children and families around the world. This was especially the case in his work with Nathaniel Laor and colleagues in Tel Aviv but equally true in his responsiveness to colleagues in the West Bank and throughout the Middle East. He provided ideas, clinical consultation, brokered unlikely relationships, and garnered support for efforts on behalf of children and families living in the midst of cycles of violence and despair. For Donald, scholarship, basic science, and psychoanalytic exploration were all instruments for advancing efforts to find words and explanations for challenges to the mind, body and spirit that too often leave individuals, communities, and entire nations unable to wake from their nightmares. When there are no words and no one to listen, immobilizing feelings of fear, isolation and helplessness remain. Recently, the Cohen-Harris Trauma Center was established in Tel Aviv to continue this work. This is also Donald's legacy.

When the attacks of September 11th occurred, it was no longer possible to strategize with Donald, to think with him about the ways in which we could be most useful to our patients, our colleagues, our community, and our country. In some ways, the inability to collaborate with Donald in response to this national crisis was further preparation for confronting so many challenges that now we would be meeting without him. Immediately, after his death, I was aware of the many hours the trauma team was working in the wake of the terrorist attacks. We were exhausted but also impelled, to do as much as possible—to say yes to any requests for help from New York, Washington, D.C., Connecticut, and from around the country.

At one point in the weeks following September 11th, I was reminded of one of Freud's wonderful observations about mourning. He suggested that the most immediate response to the loss of someone close is to maintain a sense of connection by identifying, in concrete ways, with aspects of the person who has died (Freud, S., 1917). There were certainly many times during this period when I found myself hearing Donald's words, imagining conversations we might have had about the events themselves, concerns and speculation about events to come, about psychological responses and about how to deploy our resources and how to think clinically, psychoanalytically about the work that was needed. However, at one moment I also became conscious of another important, behavioral characteristic of my friend: Donald simply never seemed to need as much sleep as anyone else. He was indefatigable. And, most important, in the face of daunting odds and upsetting facts, Donald always responded by thinking, acting, and moving from "strength to strength." Continuing our work, exploring, learning and acting in response to tragedy and trauma in the lives of children and families is but one way of honoring and celebrating Donald's life and his achievements. A psychoanalyst, scientist, teacher, leader, mentor, and friend, Donald remains a presence at the Yale Child Study Center and in the world, as we strive to achieve his spirit of excited scientific inquiry and compassionate engagement in the work that needs to be done.

BIBLIOGRAPHY

CICCHETTI, D. & COHEN, D. J. (1995). Perspectives on developmental psychopathology. In: *Developmental Psychopathology: Theory and Method,* Vol. 1., Chap. 1. D. Cicchetti, D. J. Cohen (eds.). New York: John Wiley & Sons, Inc., 3–20.

COHEN, D. J., MARANS, S., DAHL, K., MARANS, W., & LEWIS, M. (1987). Analytic Discussions with oedipal children. In: *Psychoanalytic Study of the Child,* Vol. 42, Solnit, S. and Neubauer, P. (eds.), New Haven, Conn.: Yale University Press, 59–84.

COHEN, D. (2001). Lecture—"Life Is with People" Yale University School of Medicine, New Haven, Conn.

EHLERT, U., GAAB, J., & HEINRICHS, M. (2001). Psychoneuroendocrinological contributions to the etiology of depression, posttraumatic stress disorder and stress related bodily disorders: The role of the hypothalamus-pituitary-adrenal axis. In: *Biological Psychology.* 57(1–30) 1–141–52.

FREUD, A. & BURLINGHAM, D. (1973). Infant without families. In: *Writings of Anna Freud,* Vol. 3. New York: International Universities Press, 563–664.

FREUD, A. (1981). Child analysis as the study of mental growth, normal and abnormal. In: *The Writings of Anna Freud,* Vol. 8, 1970–1980, *Psychoanalytic Psychology of Normal Development.* New York: International Universities Press, 119–136.

FREUD, S. (1926). Inhibitions, symptoms and anxiety. *SE*, 20:77–174.

FREUD, S. (1917). Mourning and melancholia. *SE*, 14:289–300.

HEIM, C., & NEMEROFF, C. (2001). The role of childhood trauma in neurobiology of mood and anxiety disorders: Preclinical and clinical studies. In: *Biological Psychiatry*, 49(12):1023–39.

LECKMAN, J. F., & COHEN, D. J. (2002). Tic Disorders. In: *Child and Adolescent Psychiatry*, Fourth Ed., M. Rutter and E. Taylor (eds.). Oxford: Blackwell Scientific Publication.

MARANS, S. (2000). That's what my imagination says: A study of anti-social behavior in two boys. In: *Psychoanalytic Study of the Child*, vol. 55. New Haven, Conn.: Yale University Press, 61–86.

MARANS, S., & COHEN, D. J. (2002). Child psychoanalytic theories of development. In: *Child and Adolescent Psychiatry: A Comprehensive Textbook*, 3rd Edition. Lewis, M. (ed.). Baltimore, Md.: Lippincott, Williams and Wilkins, Inc.

MARANS, S., MAYES, L. C., CICCHETTI, D., DAHL, K., MARANS, W., & COHEN, D. J. (1990). The child psychoanalytic play interview: A technique for studying thematic content. In: *Journal of the American Psychoanalytic Association*, 39(4):1015–1036.

MAYES, L. C., & COHEN, D. J. (1996). Constitution. In: *Psychoanalysis: The Major Concepts*, B. E. Moore and B. D. Fine (eds.), Chapter 21. New Haven, Conn.: Yale University Press, pp. 271–292.

PYNOOS, R., STEINBERG, A., & PIACENTINI, J. (1999). A developmental psychopathology model of childhood traumatic stress and intersection with anxiety disorders. In: *Biological Psychiatry* 46(11):1542–1554.

SHALE, A. (2000). Biological responses to disasters. In: *Psychiatric Quarterly*, 7(3):277–288.

SOLNIT, A. J., COHEN, D. J., & NEUBAUER, P. (1993). *The Many Meanings of Play: A Psychoanalytic Perspective.* New Haven, Conn.: Yale University Press.

TOREN, P., WOLMER, L., WEIZMAN, R., MAGAL-VARDI, O., & LAOR, N. (2002). Retraumatization of Israeli civilians during reactivation of the Gulf War threat. In: *Journal of Nervous and Mental Disease*, Vol. 190(1):43–45.

YEHUDA, R. (2001). Biology of posttraumatic stress disorder. In: *Journal of Clinical Psychiatry*, Vol. 62 Supplement, 17:41–46.

Donald and His Coat of Many Colors: An Appreciation

T. WAYNE DOWNEY, M.D.

DONALD COHEN HAS BEEN MUCH IN MY THOUGHTS SINCE HIS DEATH, particularly as I pondered his ending and wondered what my own would be like. I think of him often, during the Education Committee meetings of the Western New England Psychoanalytic Institute, which we both attended monthly for many years. Memories of Donald come to me whenever I enter this new building. More have been evoked over the past several months as I have been pouring over his many papers on analytic topics in preparation for this talk. That exercise further stimulated thinking about Donald and his fine qualities and talents.

So, I was interested but not particularly surprised that, several weeks ago, when my oldest granddaughter, Hailey, started to tell me about her latest musical infatuation, I once again started to link what she said with memories of Donald. I add parenthetically that Hailey is now seven. For most of the past four years she has been in love with one video musical after another. It all started, as it seems to for many kids these days, with "The Sound of Music." After an eternity with the von Trapps, her interest shifted to the Disney animated musicals. Currently she is making her way through Shirley Temple films from

Clinical Professor of Psychiatry and Child Psychiatry, Yale School of Medicine and Yale Child Study Center; Training and Supervising Analyst, The Western New England Institute for Psychoanalysis, New Haven, Connecticut.

This paper was presented at the dedication of the Donald J. Cohen, M.D., Auditorium at the Yale Child Study Center, 18 June 2002.

The Psychoanalytic Study of the Child 58, ed. Robert A. King, Peter B. Neubauer, Samuel Abrams, and A. Scott Dowling (Yale University Press, copyright © 2003 by Robert A. King, Peter B. Neubauer, Samuel Abrams, and A. Scott Dowling).

the thirties. However, when we visited her in early May, her excited interest was consumed by "Joseph and His Amazing Technicolor Dreamcoat." She had just been in a school production of this musical. As she recounted the story and sang along to the music, I thought immediately of Donald, not because of any particular similarities in the storylines between the life of Donald and the legend of Joseph. I know little of Donald's personal history. In the 30 years that I knew him, our relationship was primarily a collegial one, centered on our mutual interest in Psychoanalysis and children. For me, Joseph and Donald both exhibited special gifts in their many colored, multi-faceted traits and talents. In their ways, they were steadfast in their faith, compassionate toward the afflicted, wise in their abilities to lead and preside. Both exhibited a deep and ultimate love for family. In Donald's case, what set him even more apart was his keen mind. He possessed and exercised a restless searching intellect. He was in a constant quest to establish a science that encompassed psychobiology, mentation, and human relatedness. Finally, of course, I was also drawn to the ways in which Joseph and Donald, each in their own unique ways, were interpreters of dreams. Not only that, they were able to take that unusual talent and bring dreams to realistic fruition in the midst of a life lived.

In the course of a life that was brilliantly creative and unexpectedly shortened, Donald brought his great gifts for thinking and healing to bear upon many different people. As the plaque gracing this auditorium indicates, he achieved great distinction in becoming Sterling Professor of Child Psychiatry, Pediatrics, and Psychology as well as the Fourth Director of the Yale Child Study Center. More than these titular positions, his multi-colored persona brought together the roles of physician, humanitarian, scientist, clinician, psychoanalyst, teacher, and mentor. Each of these facets of his being might be present alone or might overlap with others at the same time. Beyond and perhaps above these roles he was, in the tradition of one who studies natural science, an observer and investigator, an advanced late twentieth-century proponent of a frame linking psychoanalysis and science.

I struggle to capture the essence of a man who was also husband, father, and grandfather. Overall perhaps I should borrow from a description that I first heard applied to Ralph "Romi" Greenson, the outstanding west coast analyst from the borough of Brooklyn. When Greenson entered the Senn Room of the Center back in the late 1960s, he was identified by the person sitting next to me as someone whose presence could fill a room. Donald, like Ralph, could "fill a room." It was Donald himself who also interpreted for me another term that perhaps I am permitted to apply to him because of its provenance. He was a "mensch." His curiosity embraced the world and the world embraced him as an individual of global presence and deeply spiritual perspectives. In the vernacular of my reputed Native American origins he would be described similarly as a "human being."

Donald asked hard questions that often started out as deceptively simple inquiries. These led to complex and multi-variant answers. Intellectually he combined the erudition of a philosopher with the healing sensibilities of a physician, the leadership capacities of a statesman, and the introspection of an artist. The coat symbolizing his many capacities indeed had many colors and perhaps in keeping with his contemporary, cutting edge orientation, calling it a Technicolor Dreamcoat is not so far off.[1]

Pre-eminently, Donald was a writer and a scribe. He wrote not only in English but also in Hebrew and French. Whatever his subject, he told a good story and he told it well with sophisticated, but direct prose. He was also a scribe in the classical sense of the term. These are the hues, so to speak, among the many I have mentioned and the many more that I have not chosen to highlight. He made significant contributions both in psychoanalysis proper and in applied psychoanalysis. He was a man of science, writing about his attempts to understand the inner man and the outer man. He was interested in the synthesis of the self that comprised the inner man of fantasy and feeling and the outer man of community. He worked long and hard to conceptualize the resulting person. His excursions often started with particularly vulnerable people who struggled with special dilemmas. Their plight arose from their exposure to the "experiments of nature" that can accompany the challenges of self as refracted by the processes of socialization, parenting, or genetic endowment.

As a scribe, Donald's production was prodigious. Over a period of almost 40 years he wrote, co-wrote, or assisted in the production of 318 papers at most recent count. What strikes me in reviewing his production is, in addition to the volume, the quality of the curiosity and thought that he put into advancing new knowledge in his areas of science. It was his drive and his awesome work ethic that produced

---

1. Donald, no doubt, would have been quick to point out that the King James' translators' phrase, "coat of many colors," was simply an inspired guess at an obscure Hebrew phrase apparently meaning something like "ornamented (or striped) tunic of distinction."

the sort of numbers Donald put up in the academic game that is known as "publish or perish." I think that paradoxically, it fell to his reviewers to survive the inundation of his writings. It is of note that in cross-checking dates and papers, I found that his CV could not keep track of his output. As far as I could determine, several of his papers on play and on Tourette's syndrome are not included. On second thought, perhaps I am the one who cannot keep track, even when given the manual of his publications. He posted big numbers in the column for book chapters written as well. Between 1970 and 2001 he participated in the writing of 159 chapters. Doing the math on these numbers, we come up with an output of more than five chapters a year to go with the production of something over eight papers per year. As a struggling wannabe writer with less than twenty papers to my credit, I blanch and go faint in the presence of such a phenomenal output. He gave new meaning to the term "burning the midnight oil." Depending upon your perspective, he worked late into the night or until the early morning hours. He wrote or edited twelve books and four monographs. This is just the visible part of the iceberg of Donald's work. He was constantly involved in grant writing, an activity that was below the surface, but which served as an invisible accompaniment to his scholarship. Lastly, he handled with great aplomb many years as Chair of the Publications Committee of the Yale University Press.

Donald's first paper was published in 1962 in the appropriately named journal *Child Development*. It was titled "Justin and His Peers: An Experimental Analysis of a Child's Social World." The wording in the title is notable: a boy Justin, his age mates, experimental (that is, scientific), analysis, social, world. Many of the "fixins" are there in this first formal step toward what was to become a lifelong quest involving science, analysis, and the multiple determinants for development in the inner and outer worlds of the child. In that paper he used a skinnerian operant conditioning paradigm to examine competition and mutuality in social exchange. At the end of his arc of scientific investigation and writing, in his last paper to date (2001), he focused his attention on brain morphology in Tourette's Syndrome as determined by state of the art magnetic resonance imaging data. The primary author was B. Peterson, followed in the author's banner by L. Staib, L. Scahill, H. Zhang, C. Anderson, and J. Leckman. Following them were D. Cohen, J. Gore, J. Albert, and R. Webster. Here we have many of the major players in Donald's research shop. The paper was titled "Regional Brain and Ventricular Volumes in Tourette Syndrome." It appeared in *The Archives of General Psychiatry*. What impressed me once more in this paper was that Donald's presence again reflected his implicit and explicit roles as mentor, investigator, cross-collaborator with people from many fields of interest, as well as his function as designated learner.

Today, after this overview of Donald's writing, I want to focus more closely on Donald's papers that have to do mostly with Psychoanalysis, Applied Psychoanalysis, and always, Science.Over the past twenty-year period in which they were mainly written, he brought together his many colors as physician, philosopher, psychoanalyst, and scientist in an increasingly mature, always thoughtful, manner. Prior to this period his investigative arc gathered information about twins, serotonin, and other neuro-chemicals in the brain. He pondered the incessant agony of children with raging eczema. He went places that few scientists had been as he studied children of empty object states afflicted with autism, and the children with Tourette's Syndrome possessed by involuntary spasms of their muscles and their minds. In the most recent period, roughly since 1980, Donald's analytic writing reflected his excursions into the inner world of loss and depression in children and adults. It led to profound questions both empathic and cognitive, about how one mind knows another mind and, furthermore, how one mind comes to establish the existence of another mind. To this mix, he added questions about the manner in which the development of children and their parents is shaped by their interactions with genetics, trauma, war, police, and poverty.

As he coursed along this developmental arc, he not only employed the formal tools of Science, he inter-mixed a longstanding tradition of psychoanalysis and natural observation, particularly in its applications to the mental life of the individual, and he partook of a renewed emphasis on a developmental model. This is a perspective that is shared with other natural sciences such as psychology, sociology, anthropology, and astronomy, and geology in some of their editions. One early example is from 1909 when Freud reported on the case of Little Hans, in which a father relayed his observations on his pre-school son's behavior and communications to Freud. Freud took these reports and inferred from them certain patterns of meaning and mental dynamics. However, it was almost four decades later before similar observational exercises and applied psychoanalytic data started to occupy a place in psychoanalytic thought that went beyond the occasional case study. With the publication of Anna Freud and Dorothy Burlingham's monographs *War and Children* (1943) and *Infants Without Families* (1944), a new era of child observation and inference was initiated. Spitz's papers on object loss in infancy and anaclitic depression followed several years later. Spitz's data was derived from children that he observed in nurseries and in the hospital. As time passed, Donald came to be very much at the forefront of this way of collecting psychoanalytic data by less direct means, using analytic ways of thinking rather than the direct analytic method.

In 1950, Ernst Kris wrote about the various challenges posed to psychoanalytic child psychology by problems of determining causation. As he put it, causation in behavior could be tested by the convergence of two sets of data—those gained by analysis and those assembled over many years and tested by predicting short-term steps. He went on to state:

> Moreover . . . we shall sooner or later have to include the problem of hereditary factors in our investigation. Again, if the double approach, psychoanalytic and observational, were systematically directed toward a study of identical twins, in both similarities and differences that according to some preliminary impressions seem not unrelated to parental preferences—we would have advanced further toward what we take to be our goal: The integration of data and approaches in developmental psychology around a center rooted in the thought of Freud (p. 79).

In this essay, Kris was contemplating the design of the groundbreaking research project, "The Longitudinal Study of the Child," which he directed here at the Child Study Center until his death in 1957. His cadre of investigators included Drs. Ritvo, Solnit, and Provence. I quote his remarks on identical twins because they served as a platform for Dibble and Cohen's longitudinal study of twins. It was cited in their article, "Personality Development in Identical Twins." This was Donald's second publication in the *Psychoanalytic Study of the Child* (1981). He and Eleanor Dibble presented a systematic, methodical and thoughtful account of their longitudinal study over a ten-year period of eight sets of monozygotic twins, six sets of boys and two sets of girls. It was the first reported study of twins from gestation to latency, taking advantage of what amounted to, in Donald's oft used idiom, "fruitful experiments of nature." It also attempted to account for nurture and accidental events, I might add. The paper is splendid in its delineation of the emergence of individuality amidst the experience of the apparent simultaneity of twinship. The point is made that the four sets of twins treated as "the twins" displayed a remarkable similarity in competence styles, either high or low, over the period of the study. This suggested to the investigators that, approached as dyads, rather than monads, a pressure against individualization was present. The non-linear factors in development were also invoked around issues of competence and vulnerability. Accidents and illness in one or another of the twins became stable markers for the onset of individual differences. The stressful nature of ordinary, comfortable families was pondered as well. Moves, divorce, illness, the stuff of everyday life, were commonplace in the group. As Donald remarked, "Perhaps the relatively gloomy picture of the first decade of these twins' lives reflects some aspects of self-selection in this population; yet, we tend to doubt this. Instead, our experience suggests the broad range and frequency of life stresses to which children are exposed, the normative nature of change and difficulty, and the multivariate nature of the determinants of competence and emotional disorder."

You will note that I started this section of the review with Donald's second psychoanalytic work, rather than his first. I did that to dramatize another of Donald's points, that one should not be a slave to a sequential developmental chronology, at the risk of overlooking or misinterpreting spontaneous contributions to psychological growth that add a more fulsome, if complicated intellectual picture. The psychoanalytic thought of his twins' paper predates that of his first. It directly established the intellectual linkage between Donald's thinking and research over the past twenty years and the earlier heritage of the Freuds, Spitz, and Kris.

In 1980, Donald wrote a paper published in *The Psychoanalytic Study of the Child* titled "Constructive and Reconstructive Activities in the Analysis of a Depressed Child." In it he credited his psychoanalytic progenitors, mentors, and companions, Drs. A. Solnit, S. Ritvo, S. Leavy, S. Van Amerongen, H. Loewald, and Phyllis Cohen. The paper provides a model for approaching Donald's thought as a solitary analyst. It is also a marker for the subsequent development of his analytic thinking, and as such, it will have to stand for the many co-authored psychoanalytic papers with Steven Marans and Linda Mayes that time does not permit delving into. Donald's writing, so rich and evocative, caused me long ago to give up my initial plan to present an overview for you of Donald's psychoanalytic works. Rather, now, I will humbly settle for trying to illustrate a few parts that may stand as representatives of the whole of his writing in this area. It was a struggle to find a way to capture both the scope of these analytic writings and the particular qualities of the man who wrote them. In my attempt to accomplish this, I am going to report on Donald's story of his analysis of Andrew, and the stages of his psychological resuscitation, in some detail. This is also the journal of Donald's construction and reconstruction of his three years of analyzing Andrew, from ages seven and ten. Andrew is described as a child both loaded with, and beset by, sadness and depression. The contributions from both his parents provided Andrew with an enormous genetic load for depression. Looking at all the data, I would speculate that Donald's analytic intervention may have prevented Andrew's condition from blossoming into a full scale affective illness in adulthood. This speculation was subsequently confirmed by Phyllis Cohen in a personal communication. This is a contribution of child analysis that has been partially documented by Fonagy and Target (1996), but which requires further examination and emphasis.

Getting back to Andrew, he had gained and lost on multiple occasions a good connection to a mother who repeatedly frustrated and disappointed him as a consequence of her own psychotic disorganization and absences. Lack of even minimal environmental support for healthy development was also a factor. The psychoanalytic narrative is a model for describing the multi-modal communication that occurs in child analysis through speech, silences, presence, new and old relationships in new and old forms of play. Donald sets the stage for engaging Andrew around his deep anaclitic depressive issues. This permitted him to empathically confront this poor child around his withdrawal into a starved state of relations in which a desert of defensive loneliness and isolation confirmed and obscured any possibilities that the world offered opportunities for connectedness and nurture.

As presented, Andrew's state reminds me of the story of the mariners adrift on the ocean some miles off the estuary of the Brazilian river, the Amazon. Assuming that because they were at sea, there was salt water floating their raft, they died of dehydration. Because of their presuppositions, they had not attempted to drink from what was at that point a fresh water stream. This is a cautionary tale that also applies to neurosis, where early childhood choices for adaptation become the maladaptive state of semi-survival, semi-comprehension, and semi-functioning in adulthood. It exemplifies the inflexible neurotic distortions that may lead any of us to stalemated and destructive ends. In Andrew's instance, he presented himself to Donald, in the first phase of his analysis, in an emotional drought. At the time of initial engagement, he was starving himself and his analyst of interpersonal stimulation and verbal communication by his unconscious characterological assumptions so that attempts at contact and communication would only be excruciatingly painful and toxic. Only gradually did the actual and symbolic sources of succor arise as he partook with Donald on dark, cold mornings of milk warmed with coffee and cookies. This was the making of a particular dyad, the longed for mother-child dyad, where the feast is in terms of contact and presence rather than words. Rather than "My Dinner with Andre," it was "My Breakfast with Donald," the silent version. No doubt this drama, on some deep forgotten level, brought with it early memories, more grounded in the memory of the body, rather than the memory of the mind.

Andrew moved on to use Donald's Polaroid camera, as a toy and an engine for capturing Polaroid moments of continuity, stability and progression. He captured the construction of a building taking shape next door. Donald sparingly interpreted, for readers of the paper, and we assume, at some level for Andrew, how this picture taking also preserved the growing development and direction of their relationship in a way that words could never have supported at that time. In the progressive shift from regular relationship, to memory machine, to play, this downcast boy discovered the wooden implements of serial breakfasts with Donald, the stirrers that he had used to mix warm coffee with milk. He re-invented them as play materials. They were used to shape a life raft on the open sea before morphing into a wall of a pioneer cabin on the western frontier. As Donald pointed out so poignantly, these play events contained vast metaphorical meanings in terms of Andrew's longstanding experience of living in extreme circumstances and his non-verbal, but growing expectation that from such experiences on the edge of affective existence, he and Donald might build a meaningful life in which salt water is discovered to be fresh and, to mix metaphors, the desert comes into bloom.

Every day, Andrew awoke, starved for care but unable to say so. In Andrew's inner world, not knowing and not caring were cognitively better options than acutely registering what had actually gone wrong in his young life. He was cognitively fixated and regressed. Having painstakingly and primarily non-verbally gathered the intimate details of Andrew's inner life, Donald began a process of active interpretation. While he doesn't remark on it, I would guess that his interpretational activity was cued, couched in, and guided by, an alert monitoring of his little charge's non-verbal responses, the social cues of right or wrong emphasis, shifts in posture, changes of expression, surges and diminutions in the energy of the eyes. These are the subtleties of silence that lead us to intuit path, direction, and depth of interpretation. The stream of meaning that Donald presented carried in it a message about what it might be like to live an emotional life of deprivation and longing. He delivered to Andrew an empathic course on the dysphoric affects that accompany feelings about loss of love, abandonment, fear, rage, and self criticism. I would surmise that all of this was delivered in a manner that communicated to Andrew that his analyst knew deeply about loss, and understood it in ways that he could learn from. Andrew must have grasped from Donald that he was part of a community of lost souls, not a solitary figure, as he had experienced it when he huddled on the living room floor, wordlessly clutching his pillow and sucking his thumb for meager comfort and survival.

As I read Donald's stirring account of the use of coffee stirrers, I felt drawn to offer my own commentary, but that would not fit this occasion. Given Andrew's early lack of stimulation and interaction through speech and talk and his cognitive regression, Donald's tack with Andrew showed a brave and imaginative adaptation of analytic technique to person, rather than the other way around. It provided this lad who was both verbally and mentally mute and "aphasic," some mental food for thought. Donald addressed a cognitive gap that consisted of both defensive absence and developmental defect. In doing so, he delivered ideas to play with as well as an invitation for Andrew to develop self-understanding on a new interpersonal platform of object relations and thought.

As we often see, this type of interpretation of loss, when it works, can break through depressive defenses and experiential fixation and lead to the beneficial saline of tears. With Andrew, drawing sprouted as the medium of expression. His breakthrough drawing was of a teardrop. This nadir event, as captured by Donald, is packed with feeling and meaning. "Andrew's teardrop, *drawn with me,* ignited a spark of life. (p. 243)" At that point, Donald understood and felt a new harmony with his little patient. The phrase, "drawn with me" implies a physical, emotional, and psychological presence of the analyst that exists in an area somewhat beyond words. It provides the medium for the growth of self-acceptance and self-understanding into which words can then be added. The image of a teardrop became what ultimately turned into a scroll of Andrew's life. It seems as though the scroll were his very own, analytic torah. When unrolled it stretched from session to session, and drawing to drawing, over much of the next year. The ever-growing scroll depicted a fantasy mastery over the bitter happenstances, threats, and tragedies of loss, separation, and misfortune that had dogged his life, and that he anticipated sipping again in any misguided search for sustenance that he might launch. The construction of the scroll ended with its highway finally reaching the shore of the ocean where it stopped, at a boat with his mother's name.

In the third year of his analysis, Andrew had a re-defining moment that reactivated previous self-limitations and took the momentum out of what had been a very creative process. Donald thought that if circumstances had not squelched his anger, if he had been able to safely vent his rage, Andrew might have, in spite of genetics and environmental loading, been able to emerge from his analysis in a healthy state of mind. However, Andrew's real time, real world experience of finding a new mother in his father's new girlfriend, Lucy, fizzled. Energized by the ember of hope that became a flame in his new object relationship with Donald, Andrew discovered a new mother in Lucy, only to have her crush his hope, indirectly, by turning away from his father and leaving. The therapeutic work opens the child up to risk pain and feelings that were previously experienced as intolerable. But too much pain of the wrong dosage and kind restricts or interrupts the developmental gains.

Donald concludes this paper with a discussion that differentiates various areas of his analytic interest and of his treatment of Andrew. They consist of affective development, constitution and experience, technique, and the analytic process, all areas that he would continue to think, write, and expand his understanding. As he said many times, under ideal circumstances, life is for, and about, understanding. Under the heading of affective development, he enumerates the "two simultaneous and intertwined developmental processes which radiate from the child's engagement with his primary caregivers." The first is in relation to the *actual* world of everyday life as it is laid down through emerging cognition and the understanding of human relationships. Simultaneously there is a delineation of the inner world and the sense of self that is largely *virtual*. It is virtual in the sense that it is contingent upon both the child's capacities for taking in many levels of learning from the world, and it is also contingent upon the sense of self as it is defined by the learning represented in fantasies arising in the matrix of early parent-child interaction. This section ends with the statement that "Andrew clearly showed the wounds of self and object representation that were never left alone long enough, in a caregiving world, to be able to heal." (p. 257) This is Donald's accurate, conservative assessment of Andrew at the time of the report. Later on Donald would report in personal correspondences that further healing did occur, albeit in a more diffuse developmental context over many years and through many trials. Throughout the years it seems to be that Andrew was able to marry, work, and recover as he did through the continuing discovery and use of Donald as a new object (Downey, 2001).

As we are also aware, Donald was very preoccupied in his thinking and occupied in his research in teasing out the elements of constitution and experience that affect us all. He described Andrew as a double victim of both genetic familial contribution and of being the recipient of scant amounts of "joyful, pleasurable, soothing, unambivalent, and appropriately timed 'good enough' mothering." In other words, all the relational elements that we understand are necessary to foster healthy development and positive personality organization. And yet he also kept in his view a select group where the harsh vicissitudes of life might overwhelm any positive factors of genetics and early experience.

In his section on technique, Donald addressed the imperfections of life and the limitations of child analysis in completely opening up the gates of revisited traumas and recovery. His vision is sober and square as to the measure of his work with Andrew. He is clear about the role that Andrew's father, affectively limited though he was, was able to play in his son's recovery, directly and indirectly. Donald's lesson here is that analytic love in the form of the analyst's attempts at being witness to the child's pain, must always fall short, at least for the moment, if the root rage and pain remain relatively inaccessible. The analyst's respectful attempts at understanding and his implicit offering of hope and mastery may carry the process a far distance. Relief may remain partial and deferred, rather than becoming permanently withered. Life-giving potentials may bloom later in the context of relief from emotional drought. As Donald noted, the mind's capacities for conservation of experience may retard or otherwise may delay development until a later time when internal and external factors are more propitious for the exploration of the virtual internal mental world.

Donald ended this paper with a few comments on the analytic process which, for Andrew, as we have learned, centered around the construction of physical objects that were play vehicles for his affective recovery. This process was accompanied by the co-construction of regular, predictable, rhythmic routines that expressed and addressed the need for Andrew to internalize benevolent and predictable, "constant" objects in a world previously defined by malignant instability. Donald ended with a strong statement supporting an interactional model for child analysis where the analyst cannot and should not "keep his hands clean" if he is to respectfully use and respond with all the modes and dialects of communication in which the child addresses him. He ends by warning about the problems of Andrew and how they may relate to the dilemma in analysis twenty years ago that is still being resolved today. That is, that a sharp split in developmental epochs in the child or in the procedures of analysis is equally impoverishing in either the practice of analysis or in the organization of a life. He connects this directly to the exchange of information and the flow of ideas. Blocks to data should be removed. Information should be inter-scholastic and inter-disciplinary. It should be received from whence it came, and the result will inevitably be the growth of an open child or an open mind. He followed his Andrew paper up with one in 1990 titled "Enduring Sadness: Early Loss, Vulnerability, and the Shaping of Character." This is a report on Andrew, ten years later. It included data about an adult patient of his, Quentin. Here he expanded and revised his thinking about character and development. His emphasis shifted to the idea that "character is forged in the furnace of aggression" (p. 175) and he suggests that "we think of character in terms of fantasy configurations fueled mostly by aggression and modulated by love." In this he resonated with a similar concept that I put forward in 1984 for understanding the role of aggression in mental life and in relation to love.

Before ending, I must mention Donald's classic synthesis of psychoanalytic and biological perspectives on Tourette's syndrome that appeared in the *International Review of Psychoanalysis* in 1991. It is a beautiful account of his patient, compassionate treatment into adulthood of child patients, in particular one man Bruce, whose lives, personal meaning, and sense of agency were initially subject to being destroyed by their tic disease. It also demonstrates the understanding at the time of the sometimes thin red line between body and mind, particularly bodies at war with minds. In that paper he also returned to the intertwined themes of aggression, character, and development many times. With Steven and Wendy Marans and Kirsten Dahl, he explored it in a compendium on the many meanings of play (Solnit et al., 1993). He continued this examination in a paper, written with Linda Mayes and published in the *Psychoanalytic Study of the Child* in 1993, "The Social Matrix of Aggression." Donald and Linda published a lot together in the 1990s. Much of their collaboration centered about exploring theories of mind and of the mind's development of self-perspective and perspective on others' minds through various forms of empathy. Their 1996 paper on "Children's Developing Theory of Mind" is an example. Also, in 1996, they published an assessment of Anna Freud's psychoanalytic developmental psychology. In that paper they again address the interactive gossamer boundary between mind and body in the life of the child. They use Anna Freud's prompts to follow paths for increasing catholicity in child

analysis and increasing openness to all forms of child research in order to increase the base and sway of the analytic area of knowledge.

As I go through these citations there is a sense that I am leaving
much out and with Donald's death, much is missing. He collaborated
with Jim Leckman, Fred Volkmar, Sara Sparrow, and John Schowalter
on many projects over the years. He wrote several notable pieces with
Steven Marans. One that stands out is their chapter on Psychoanalytic theories of child development in Mel Lewis's textbook of child
and adolescent psychiatry (1991). My sense of Donald's collaborations is that they were part and parcel of his life long program for developing self understanding in the context of social exchange. He
wanted and needed the company of others. He needed them to
bounce ideas back and forth and to brainstorm with. It also seems
that he needed a constant series of collaborators, people who would
select from the fountainhead of his erudition and ideas those that
fascinated them. They might then work out the details. Here, might I
playfully suggest, that at times anyway, Donald was like Tom Sawyer to
many Huckleberry Finns. He attracted many helpers to paint his
fences in many colors and to help him complete his projects and his
work to the satisfaction of all.

Donald's farewell address was delivered in February, 2001. It was
upon the occasion of his becoming Sterling Professor. He titled it
aptly enough "Life Is With People." It is another model of synthesis
in the overview that it gives of his life's work. His tone was of quiet
self revelation and deep reflection. It serves as a portent of what the
next years might have brought him had the arc of his inquiry into
life's meanings not been interrupted. From his words, as well as the
way he was wording his work, there is an implication that his intellectual voice was coming into full maturity. If we are fortunate, development never stops. He seemed prepared to journey to new levels of assessment and knowledge. And yet, can there ever be a time when we
feel that our work has come to closure? As his analyst and mentor,
Hans Loewald, commented as he approached retirement: ". . . and to
think, just when I was beginning to really understand what I was doing."

I will end on a sentimental and chauvinistic note with a variation of
the local slogan, "For God, For Country, and For Yale." Donald progressed in ways that were both revolutionary and evolutionary, a difficult tension to maintain. The Slifka Center for Jewish Life at Yale exists in part, perhaps in large part, because of Donald's dedication to
his God and his faith. The national initiative to bring children and
police together communally to thwart the horrors of violence is in

part a monument to his commitment to his Country. The Harris building and the Donald J. Cohen auditorium are a lasting legacy of his life at Yale. I am told that in Buddhism, when we die, the next life appears in colors of red and gold. I imagine that by this time Donald's Technicolor Dreamcoat must contain predominant hues of Eli blue and white.

BIBLIOGRAPHY

BURLINGHAM, D., & FREUD, A. (1943). *War and Children.* New York: Medical War Books.

BURLINGHAM, D., & FREUD, A. (1944). *Infants Without Families.* London: George Allen & Unwin.

COHEN, D. J. (1962). Justin and his peers: An experimental analysis of a child's social world. *Child Development,* 33:697–717.

—— (1980). Constructive and re-constructive activities in the analysis of a depressed child. *Psychoanal. Study Child,* 35:237–266.

—— (1990). Enduring sadness: Early loss, vulnerability and the shaping of character. *Psychoanal. Study Child,* 45:157–178.

—— (1991). Tourette's Syndrome: A model disorder for integrating psychoanalysis and biological perspectives. *Int. R. Psychoanal.,* 18:195–208.

—— (2001). Life is with people: Autism, Tourette's Syndrome and the community of clinical research. Unpublished.

DIBBLE, E. D., & COHEN, D. J. (1981). Personality development in identical twins: The first decade of life. *Psychoanal. Study Child,* 36:45–70.

DOWNEY, T. W. (1984). Within the pleasure principle. *Psychoanal. Study Child,* 39:101–136.

DOWNEY, T. W. (2001). Early object relations into new objects. *Psychoanal. Study Child,* 56:39–67.

FONAGY, P., & TARGET, M. (1996). Predictors of outcome in child psychoanalysis: A retrospective study of 763 cases at the Anna Freud Centre. *J. Amer. Psychoanal. Assn.,* 44:27–76.

FREUD, S. (1909). Analysis of a phobia in a five year old boy. *Standard Edition,* 10:3–149.

KRIS, E. (1950). Notes on the development and on some current problems of psychoanalytic child psychology. *Selected Papers of Ernst Kris.* New Haven: Yale University Press, 54–79.

MARANS, S., COHEN, D. J. (1991). Child psychoanalytic theories of development. In: *Child and Adolescent Psychiatry: A Comprehensive Textbook,* M. Lewis (ed.). Baltimore: Williams & Wilkins, 129–145.

MAYES, L. C., COHEN, D. J. (1993). The social matrix of aggression: Enactments and representations of loving and hating in the first years of life. *Psychoanal. Study Child,* 48:145–169.

MAYES, L. C., COHEN, D. J. (1996a). Children's developing theory of mind. *J. Am. Psychoanal. Assn.,* 44(1):117–142.

MAYES, L. C., COHEN, D. J. (1996b). Anna Freud and developmental psychoanalytic psychology. *Psychoanal. Study Child,* 51:117–141.

SOLNIT, A. J., NEUBAUER, P., & COHEN, D. J. (EDS.). (1993). *The Many Meanings of Play in Child Psychoanalysis.* Aggressivity in play: Discussions with oedipal children, Marans, S., Dahl, K., Marans, W., Cohen, D., New Haven: Yale University Press, 275–296.

Being Mindful of Minds: A Homage to the Contributions of a Child-Analytic Genius

PETER FONAGY, Ph.D., F.B.A., and MARY TARGET, M.Sc., Ph.D.

IT HAS BEEN ONE OF THE GREATEST PRIVILEGES OF OUR PROFESsional lives to be repeatedly "set straight" by Donald J. Cohen. Even as he was performing these rather painful operations on our minds, reminiscent of the most uncharitable readings of Freud's classical surgical metaphor for psychoanalysis, one knew that it was an honor for a mind as great as his, to take time to put one's own thinking in order. Here we shall describe how he personally and through his writing straightened our thinking specifically about child analysis, but also about psychoanalysis in general, and even more broadly about issues of epistemology and mind-brain relationship. We feel that the best way we can honor him is by reviewing those of his ideas that have been formative in our own intellectual development.

Perhaps Donald's clearest exposition of his view of psychoanalysis and the psychoanalytic model of character is his paper in the *Psychoanalytic Study of the Child*, dedicated to Al Solnit on his seventieth birthday, "On Enduring Sadness" (Cohen, 1990). For those of you

Peter Fonagy is the Freud Memorial Professor of Psychoanalysis, UCL; Director of Research, The Anna Freud Centre; and Director, Child and Family Center, Menninger Foundation. Mary Target is Senior Lecturer in Psychoanalysis, UCL; Deputy Director of Research, The Anna Freud Centre.

This paper was a speech given at the Dedication of the Donald J. Cohen Auditorium, Child Psychoanalysis Session, 18 June 2002.

The Psychoanalytic Study of the Child 58, ed. Robert A. King, Peter B. Neubauer, Samuel Abrams, and A. Scott Dowling (Yale University Press, copyright © 2003 by Robert A. King, Peter B. Neubauer, Samuel Abrams, and A. Scott Dowling).

who have not recently read this brilliant essay that contains some of the best examples of his intellectual virtuosity, in it he described two cases he treated: Andrew and Quentin. Andrew was seven when he first came into treatment, whilst Quentin was 31. Andrew was struggling at school and ultimately came to manage a firm that crafts fine furniture. Quentin was an academic medievalist who in the course of his treatment overcame some of his difficulties with becoming a productive scholar. Both were driven to analysis by their depression, which had both environmental and genetic roots.

We are going to try and use Donald's description of his treatment of Andrew, and the questions it raised, as a framework for highlighting some of his many contributions to child analysis, a subject to which he had deep emotional as well as intellectual commitment. Before re-introducing you to Andrew, we should point out that many of Donald's major and lasting contributions to child analysis were collaborative with his colleagues at Yale: Phyllis Cohen of course, Kirsten Dahl, Al Solnit, Alice Colonna, Sam Ritvo as well as Peter Neubauer, Sam Abrams, amongst many others. Two co-authors in particular stand out in the last decade: Steven Marans (see Steven Marans' paper in this volume) and Linda Mayes (see also Mayes' chapter here). I shall emphasize the extraordinary contribution that Donald's collaborative work with Linda generated throughout the 1990s.

But for the moment back to seven-year-old Andrew who, I guess, was treated in the 1970s. Andrew's early years were blighted by his mother's psychotic depression, repeated hospitalizations, marital crises and then separation, his father's somber character and his departure from the family when Andrew was four, multiple forms of parenting boundary violations, including being used in bed as his mother's comforter. Later his mother abandoned Andrew, to him forever inexplicably, to go overseas. Andrew is failing by age seven, is deeply regressed, lies on the floor sucking his thumb, eats with his hands, crawls and barks like a puppy dog.

Not surprisingly, upon entering treatment, sad, failing Andrew cannot take advantage of the analytic help he is offered for a considerable time. But after some months, I guess through the extraordinary intuitive understanding of his analyst, he "happens to find" a Polaroid camera in the consulting room. He starts taking photographs of the consulting room and the building being constructed outside. Intriguingly, this sets the analytic process going and an album of photographs is put together over the first years of the treatment. In his 1990 paper, Donald did not comment on this turning point and in the original report on the case, ten years earlier (Cohen, 1980), he simply links the closely observed construction of the building to "a symbol of the mother's return and of the search for inner strength and reunion." (p. 241)

We have to wait until his paper with Linda in 1996, "On Children's Developing Theory of Mind" to arrive at an explanation for why taking pictures per se might have been of such significance to Andrew (Mayes and Cohen, 1996b). This latter paper traces the unfolding of "representation" in the mind, where representation means "allowing something or someone to stand for something else." (p. 120) Theory of mind thus concerns the representation of representations, or metarepresentations. Photographs are representations, and psychoanalysis with young children is seen as having a key function in organizing representations of mental states. Within the framework suggested by the theory of mind paper (and the companion paper published three years earlier on "Playing and Therapeutic Action in Child Analysis," Mayes & Cohen, 1993), we can see Andrew's album of photographs in which he and his analyst patiently archive the progress of the building works as itself a representation of the analytic process. Donald's frequent interpretations in the early phase of the analysis, which he himself calls "vigorous" (p. 159), are like instant photographs of Andrew's mind as he painfully struggles to build up within himself a sense of coherence about experiences inside and outside. Up to this point these experiences were, for Andrew, beyond understanding and therefore beyond effective representation.

The interpretations that help Andrew organize his subjectivity also gradually allow him to be more and more clear in his communications, which makes the analyst feel that he can "read better and better Andrew's inner life" (p. 159). This creates a virtuous cycle of increasingly apposite analytic commentary reacted to in a way that becomes easier and easier for the analyst to understand. Mayes and Cohen (1996b) point to this when they describe the interdependence of the quality of the matrix of the child's social relationships and his developing understanding of his and other minds. They write: "The capacity to observe, appreciate, react to, and reflect upon one's own and others' mental world is intertwined with the emerging understanding of other persons as separate and distinct (McGinn, 1982), and the early interactions between parent and infant (Hobson, 1991; Mayes, Cohen, and Klin, 1993)" (p. 135). While Andrew could not conceive of feelings as "feelings" he feared, as Donald noted, that "he would be flooded with sadness and anger that he could not control." (Cohen, 1980, p. 243)

Mayes and Cohen in their work link the traditional psychoanalytic understanding of affect regulation, via signal anxiety and other ego capacities, with emerging findings in developmental psychology, concerning the centrality of the representation of mental states. They generate a compelling model of how these capacities, present from the third and fourth year of life, underpin the maturational regulatory process. In a series of papers in the last decade of his life, Donald with Linda thus wonderfully enriched psychoanalytic understanding and clinical work, at the same time adding another dimension to the cross-fertilization between psychoanalysis and neurocognitive study, to which both Donald and Linda have contributed enormously.

Thus Andrew's analysis is understood to be effective at least in part because his ability to hold on to and manipulate "snapshots" of his internal world improves. Facilitated by his analyst's energetic interpretative work, Andrew's symbolic capacity takes giant steps forward. Andrew's first drawing depicts that important state of mind that he had been unable to represent and therefore to verbalize to his analyst over the course of the initial months of his treatment—his profound sadness. He draws a raindrop, a tear. The tear turns into a suburban scene, and the scene over the days and months of his treatment turns into an epic, a scroll where one scene after another depicts a journey—through the full spectrum of human experience: "the experience of being held and falling; of searching for someone and trusting and not trusting; of finding and not finding pleasure, fun, security, and inner calm" (p. 160). What is being illustrated here is what Mayes and Cohen more fully describe in their 1994 paper linking studies of autism to the psychoanalytic theory of social development (Mayes and Cohen, 1994); in concluding that paper they write "with the achievement of an understanding of mental states, of the relation between mind and action, the child has opened to him a vastly enlarged world not only for fantasy, but also for deepened relationships with others" (p. 214). Indeed in the treatment of Andrew we do observe that Donald's persistent interpretation of Andrew's experiences through his 32-episode journey leads Andrew to a qualitatively different relationship between him and his mother of imagination and between him and his analyst.

Andrew's scroll ends at the ocean. A boat, which bears Andrew's mother's name, is depicted as unable to leave but we know that the reality is different, that Andrew's mother actually abandoned him, went overseas, in reality never to return. Andrew draws a child cast adrift on a raft, exposed to threats from beneath the waves and deeply uncertain about the safety of the raft. It is easy for us to empathize with Andrew's reluctance to represent his feeling states, a reluctance which undermines his system for meta-representation. Andrew's analyst notes with sadness how, after the mother/boat was drawn, there was no space for further journeys. He had arrived at the point of his experience of rejection, the state of mind that was too unbearable to symbolize. Andrew's analyst, with exquisite sensitivity and a gentleness of touch that emerges despite the constraints of black and white print, can begin to talk about these experiences in the "quiet, tentative and short-phrased speech that was now available to Andrew." (p. 160)

Those whose training is in child psychoanalysis will, of course, be able to guess what Andrew's last project in his analysis turned out to be. We find him building boats out of scrap, building a mother out of the experiences he had with his analyst. There is something poignant about the conjunction of junk and the object of Andrew's greatest desire. The loss which fueled Andrew's depression could be met by a helpful, supportive adult, but ultimately Andrew's experience was of something of "limited value." (p. 161)

Andrew's last sculpture was free-form, juxtaposing peculiar shapes with realistic figures, a man with a cigar walking a dog and a fish swimming in manic lightness through sky. Andrew calls this "the thing," and it is constructed during the final days of termination. It probably depicts his experience of the analysis as well as, as Donald movingly pointed out, all of our experiences of life. Donald wrote: "it was a monument to the possibility of the potential for play, especially within psychoanalysis, to represent existential absurdity—the experience, shared by all of us, of living a life in a world which is not rational and which we make our own by trying to understand" (Cohen, 1990, p. 160). We think this is the most eloquent description of Winnicott's (1953) "transitional space" concept that has ever been written in psychoanalysis.

In a later paper on "Playing and Therapeutic Action in Child Analysis," Linda and Donald discuss the dialectic in child analysis "between creating a space that facilitates the child's efforts to play and the overall analytic goal of verbal interpretation to make explicit unconscious wishes and conflicts" (L. Mayes & D. Cohen, 1993, p. 1236). The important case they make in this paper is that the process of enactment through fantasy play in the space of the analysis is, in and of itself, "developmentally restorative." (p. 1236) This is so, because through play a varied set of mental processes are activated, past experiences and current feelings and desires can be integrated, and the inner world can be explored at the same time as relationships with others. They write: "Play provides children with the earliest version of a self-reflective capacity" (p. 1241). Citing a chapter from a very different mother-son dyad (a chapter co-authored by Donald's wife and older son, Cohen and Cohen, 1993), Linda and Donald point out that interpretation is not invariably necessary for this facilitation to proceed. It seems that this might have been the view that Donald took about Andrew's creation, "the thing." In his termination sculpture, Andrew condenses much of his experience that could not be verbalized in the course of the analysis, which nevertheless goes on to have an impact on him in subsequent phases of development. The figure of the analyst with a cigar, walking his pet dog patient and the re-emergence of the ocean theme, but this time in the sky, concretely at the level of Andrew's head, leaves both patient and analyst with what Donald describes as a "moving sense of ending but also of foreboding" (p. 161). Andrew was a good puppy dog during the analysis (he started analysis not even barking words and ended it talking sentences) but he also knew that because of his burning need for his mother he had to be kept on a leash, he would not be able to contain the desire on his own.

Andrew's improvement was marked. At the end of treatment he is no longer depressed and his clumsiness and school failure are no longer issues. But Andrew's rage at his abandonment remains beyond words. We are not surprised to be told that Andrew gets arrested at age fourteen for stealing tapes of love songs, which prompts a new period of therapy. Again he is difficult to engage. But his astutely tolerant analyst can eventually depict for him the sense of terrible emptiness for which no words can be found and which presents him with inter-personal and intra-psychic problems to which criminality was the only solution.

The final episode of Andrew's story is perhaps the most moving. At seventeen he is arrested again for being part of a group who stole some money and merchandise. He remains silent both in the police interviews that follow and when he returns to see Donald once more. His silence covers a deep emptiness, which comes to be addressed this time not by further interpretations but by helping him accommodate to events in external reality. His father finds a partner that Andrew can also relate to, and his mother dies in an accident (under circumstances suggestive of suicide).

Of course Donald was quick to point out in the paper that both these events were actually fortuitous in helping Andrew move forward from adolescence to adulthood. But one suspects that without his analyst's capacity to transform these experiences to Andrew's advantage they could just as easily have turned into two further disasters in the rocky road of his passage through life. Donald offers family sessions to Andrew's father and new partner, where Andrew's hopes and fears about this new relationship can be voiced and where Andrew's long-awaited substitute mother can experience the surly, over-cautious adolescent without taking offense and withdrawing from the encounter. The gentle understanding of him that, up to this point, was restricted to the analysis, can now also characterize his home. Further, Andrew is allowed to grieve for the mother who was only ever truly available to him in fantasy and with whom he will now never be reunited.

Donald's description of these events is brief, almost laconic, but the emotional intensity for all those who are part of this story nevertheless shines through. As any clinician knows, it is the interface between the internal and the external that is so hard to manage at moments of emotional crisis. Yet Donald, under fire, remains the epitome of therapeutic neutrality as Anna Freud defined it—equidistant from the demands of reality (the ego), desires and wishes (the id), and internalized demands of society's morality (the superego) (Freud, 1936). The few lines of text where these events are portrayed in the paper depict clearly Donald's pragmatic stance as a clinician, his capacity to use his insights from child analysis to intervene in the way he perceived would be most likely to work. The application of child analysis to other modes of intervention was a constant theme of Donald's clinical thinking (again, see Steven Marans' chapter in this volume).

In his work with Andrew, as in all his other work and the work he fostered among his colleagues, Donald constantly celebrated the complexity of the diverse influences on development. In their tribute to "Anna Freud's Contribution to Developmental Psychoanalytic Psychology" (Mayes and Cohen, 1996a), Linda and Donald highlight Anna Freud's observation about development: "as an intricate pattern which owes its unfolding to the integration of the most diverse influences with each other." (Freud, 1978, p. 342) Andrew is not arrested again. He progresses to a social position that may be less prestigious than his capabilities or his parents' occupations might have suggested, but it is unequivocally his own.

Donald's primary focus in writing the "Enduring Sadness" paper was to bring together a way of looking at genetics and early experience as the principal forces shaping the inner worlds of longings and fears, which our psychoanalytic work privileges us to be able to study.

This could be seen from his early psychoanalytic studies, such as his in-depth description of the development of eight pairs of twins, in his paper with Eleanor Dibble (Dibble and Cohen, 1981); here they showed in a very compelling way the intertwining of medical, environmental, and relationship influences on the development of these identical twins. The recognition of the importance of each parent's own attachment history on the ways in which they experienced the twins' personalities and roles in the family foreshadowed the work that Donald has helped us to continue at the Anna Freud Centre.

In relation to the case of Andrew (and Quentin) an intriguing theory of the interaction of constitution and environment unfolds. In brief, Donald's argument is that genetics, through determining numerous and subtle characteristics of the body, poses a unique patterning of problems to each of our minds which might indeed serve as a mediator of some genetic vulnerabilities or resilience. The grounding of the psychoanalytic model of character in the body remains from this point of view still insufficiently explored with the exception of work by his eminent colleagues, particularly Bob King and Jim Leckman, at the Yale Child Study Center. Individual differences could exist in how the gastro-intestinal tract works, sensitivity of the skin, flow between sleep and wakefulness, and so on. As the *mind creates itself,* these features of the body may be determining and, as Donald says, "bridge" (p. 175) the biological and bodily with the "highest ethical activities" (p. 174) that human social functioning can entail.

Rooted in this dialectic, the "Enduring Sadness" paper asserts that "how the mind appreciates its own aggression" (p. 175) determines key features of character. Is aggression, as it is emanating from the body, linked to sexuality? Is it habitually attributed outwardly into the social environment? Or does it remain unbound as "an ethereal and yet powerful reservoir of gloom"? (p. 175) More generally, he is suggesting that in aggression or any other powerful force emanating from within the body "we can see fantasy as an expression of those vital forces of life which represent the mind trying to understand an integrated self." (p. 175) This is a majestic idea which puts flesh upon the traditional psychoanalytic claim of mind arising out of body— "the ego is first and foremost a body ego" because it is the primary task of mind to re-present, give meaning to and appreciate its own constitutional demands and experiences of physical desires.

In the "Social Matrix of Aggression" paper with Linda (Mayes and Cohen, 1993), it is fully explained where the ideas for interpreting these bodily states come from: the interaction with the primary caregivers. In "Enduring Sadness," Donald discussed Andrew's failure to create a template of the caregiving other, which could then become a constituent part of the self through the process of internalization, so a frame of reference can be created for the interpretation of internal states. In the 1996 "Theory of Mind" paper with Linda (Mayes and Cohen, 1996b), this is further explained when the authors distinguish between internalizations of an other who is perceived as capable of mental life versus an other who merely behaves. The internalization of a thinking, feeling, what we might call mentalizing object has the capacity to enrich the child's internal world as now the relationship representation or schemata through which all experience is filtered, contains a self-other relationship where both are concerned with the internal state of the other.

Donald refers to Andrew's failure of internalization as "an acquired error of metabolism" (in contrast with the autistic child's inborn error). If there is no space in his mind for a person who thinks kindly of him, it is hardly surprising that it takes little Andrew some time to give up his suspicions about his analyst. As Linda and Donald wrote: "Internalized traumatic or neglectful early experiences and expectations may limit children's use of their capacities to represent the mind of the other and, in turn, the deepening of their capacity for developing deep and enduring relationships with others." (Mayes and Cohen, 1996b, p. 137)

Two developmental issues were raised by the intriguing formulations of psychoanalytic character formation, which Donald put forward in "Enduring Sadness." The first concerns the nature of aggression and the second the issue of the status of mental representations of mental states as these change through development. Both of these have been addressed in Donald's child psychoanalytic writings with Linda and others. In the paper in 1993 on the "Social Matrix of Aggression" Linda and Donald (Mayes and Cohen, 1993), referring to Anna Freud, point out that "aggression looms larger than sex in child analysis, dominates the child patient's acting out and transference behaviour." (Freud, 1972, p. 168) The capacity to attribute mental states to others and the self contributes to the transformation of aggressive and loving feelings into the balanced form essential for mature object relations, thus linking the theory of mind concept with the concept of the depressive position (see also Spillius, 1992). Using the work of Loewald (1978) as their starting point, they point to the reaction of the caregiver to a child's aggression as a key factor in determining the child's own experience of the meaning of his internal state. "When the 4-month-old infant vigorously sucking at the breast abruptly bites, how much the mother reacts to her unexpected pain as an aggressive attack versus a surprising but notable measure of her child's assertiveness and mastery will influence how the infant experiences such moments later on." (p. 152) This notion was restated three years later more formally in an important paper by Gergely and Watson (1996) as the social bio-feedback theory of parental affect-mirroring. What Mayes and Cohen imply in 1993 and Gergely and Watson explicitly state is that the caregiver's mirroring reaction is internalized by the child to form the core of the second-order representation he has of his own reaction. Two properties of the mother's mirroring reaction turn out to be critical: contingency and markedness. Contingency refers to the extent to which the mother's reaction is congruent with the infant's constitutional (or what Donald might have termed "bodily") emotional experience. Markedness concerns the extent to which she is able to indicate to the child that the emotion she is expressing is a mirroring of the child's feelings rather than an indication of her own dispositional state. Our own work, as well as that of other labs, has demonstrated that the markedness of mirroring is ensured by combining a congruent affect with an incongruent one (e.g., mirroring sadness by mixing its expression with irony is more soothing than reflecting sadness on its own).

"The Social Matrix of Aggression" highlights an issue that the Gergely and Watson paper and other work on mirroring do not deal with—namely, the particular developmental challenges which confront the infant or child as it is in the process of attempting to develop second order representations of anger and aggression. "In a very real sense, understanding aggressive states of mind and intentions is a more difficult . . . task in the child's developing and expanding relationships with multiple others." (p. 163) It may be expected that there would be particular challenges in the internalization of mirrored aggression. Markedness may be particularly hard to achieve on the part of caregivers who have difficulties in controlling their aggression. Contingency or congruence will be less likely on the part of caregivers who, because of their own conflicts about aggression, might be inhibited in mirroring the child's aggression or are less able to recognize it.

It is most likely that Andrew was disadvantaged on both these counts, with a mother whose illness would have undermined her capacity to focus on her infant's state of mind and whose expressions of affect are likely to have been extremely poorly modulated and whose pathology quite probably involved conflicts over aggression. He had no second order representation of aggression. No wonder, then, that

Andrew had such difficulty in becoming aware of his aggressive feelings, even when these were repeatedly put to him by a gentle and careful analyst. It follows from the wonderful descriptions presented by Linda and Donald in the "Social matrix" that Andrew had at best the most rudimentary representations of the rageful feelings experienced within a constitutional, bodily self-state.

There is a second aspect of the paper that is pertinent here and to which Linda and Donald vitally drew attention. If the child is exposed to violence in the home in the way Andrew had been, there is likely to be a general destructive effect on his capacity to represent mental states. Linda and Donald note: "relationships with important others that are marred by explicit violence and abuse may bring the child face to face with the mind of another that is too frightening and dangerous to try to understand. In such cases, despite maturational readiness, the capacity to understand others' minds and different states of aggressive intention may be seriously impaired." (p. 164) The clinical picture initially presented by Andrew is, of course, explicable in terms of this model. He was withdrawing from human activity, from social interaction altogether, feeling minds to be too dangerous and experiencing safety only with the identity of a dog. One would not be surprised if his second order representation of aggression at that stage was more closely linked with a dog's bark than the chaotic set of human reactions that confronted him whenever he had actually felt anger.

The second developmental issue with which the case of Andrew, as understood by Donald, Linda, and their colleagues at Yale, confronts us, links psychoanalytic treatment to our understanding of play. In yet another important paper that appeared two years after the Enduring Sadness article, Linda and Donald delineated the neurocognitive preconditions for an imaginative capacity (Mayes and Cohen, 1992). In this particularly beautifully crafted paper, they establish a crucial link between the awareness of having a mental world and the exercise of imagination or fantasy and play. They provide a developmental line for imaginative capacity which is seen "to develop in tandem with the child's increasing differentiation and separation from others and provides a way for the child to be a separate individual while at the same time creating an inner world filled with others." (p. 44)

At this point, they link a longstanding interest in the nature of play and playfulness by many distinguished child analysts here at the Child Study Center and elsewhere with the development of second order representations of internal states (Cohen, Marans, Dahl,

Marans, and Lewis, 1987; Marans, Dahl, Marans, and Cohen, 1993; Marans et al., 1991). They point out that children with a marked incapacity to play have profound dysfunctions in the capacity to represent mental states. In the 1994 paper on experiencing self and others, Linda and Donald particularly draw on studies of autism in tracing the interaction between the creation of an internal sense of self and the attribution of meaning to the actions of others (Mayes and Cohen, 1994). Playfulness turns out to be critical in the acquisition of a theory of mind. In studies from the Yale laboratory, the spontaneous use of belief-based explanations was advanced by introducing humor into the false-belief situations (Mayes and Cohen, 1996b). In pretend play there is a decoupling of internal and external reality. The state of pretending makes what is external less compelling. It seems clear from the body of theory which Donald, Linda, and their colleagues constructed, that playfulness will facilitate the development of representations of mental states in that the playful attitude encapsulates the crucial understanding that mental states are real and unreal at one and the same time.

Here we come to understand the theoretical justification behind Donald's delightful way of working with Andrew. In both the 1980 and the 1990 report it is clear that analysis was something that the two of them took enormously seriously but nevertheless played at, at the same time. We see Donald eating crackers and drinking tea with Andrew and there is humor from the very first Polaroid shot taken to the poignant termination of the treatment where ten-year-old Andrew re-presents himself, not without irony, as the dog of the man with the big cigar. There is a lightness of touch in this work which, knowing Donald, I feel certain was deliberate and consciously or unconsciously derived from Donald's understanding of the developmental difficulties emerging during the first year of life of individuals whose symptoms and natural histories in certain ways resemble those with autism but "rather than the impoverished social relations shown by autistic individuals, these children show atypical social relations and have been given a variety of diagnostic labels including borderline, atypical development, or, more recently, multiplex developmental disorder" (Cohen, Paul, and Volkmar, 1986; Dahl, Cohen, and Provence, 1986). Andrew certainly fits these descriptions.

We have thus arrived at what I hope is an adequate review of key aspects of Donald's contribution to child analysis, which includes a profound formulation of pathology such as Andrew's and the description of a successful treatment model at least in the hands of this unique clinician. One question remains outstanding, which is only implicitly addressed in "Enduring Sadness," which preceded the most productive phase of Linda and Donald's collaborative work. That is: What is the relationship of Andrew's and Quentin's enduring depression to the development of an awareness of minds? What is the nature of depression from the psychoanalytic developmental point of view, which Donald with Linda so energetically advanced? Let us make a suggestion of our own here to join Donald's wonderfully rich clinical description and magnificent theory with the structure of psychoanalytic understanding which he went on to evolve with Linda.

The concept of theory of mind can illuminate the cognitive impairments associated with depression. Depressive beliefs are not experienced as mental states but rather as direct representations of reality—as if they are perceptual rather than conceptual. It seems to us that Donald's profound idea in "Enduring Sadness" was that most mental disorder could be seen as involving one or other form of specific theory of mind dysfunction. *Psychopathology is the mind misperceiving and misrepresenting the status of its own contents and its own functions.* While multiplex developmental disorder may be seen as a fear of minds, depression entails an over involvement with and concretisation of mood related ideation. It follows from this formulation that an important common component of effective psychoanalytic therapy must be the restoration of a normal relationship with one's own mental world. But Donald wrote more eloquently of this than we can, and we would like to end with a passage from this paper:

> The most fundamental concerns of psychoanalytic theory of character are the processes of mental functioning which create what we mean by being a person, including continuity of experience, intentionality, and the growing sense of personal responsibility. . . . Yet, there remains a mystery . . . in the process by which I come to appreciate that I am an I, across different states of arousal, while calm and distressed, in my mother's arms and while alone. The self is not created inductively. From constitutionally given competencies and temperament, from the undifferentiated state and the mother-child matrix, the mind emerges and new functions and structures evolve; the mind as seen by psychoanalysis builds itself, in response to its own experiences and discoveries about its urges, fears, and capacities. In this process of self-creation, narcissism and concern for others are delicately balanced; both have their origin soon after birth, are progressively expressed in fantasy and act, and mature in close interdependence. (p. 173)

Donald was a genius of many professions. If we were more able, I feel sure he could have set us straight in our thinking also in other fields of knowledge. In this brief review, we merely wished to underscore the immense significance of his contributions to the fields of child psychoanalysis and psychoanalytic developmental psychology. That these may not have been his most important contributions from certain standpoints is just a measure of the man. For us, these ideas and his philosophical approach were the most important guides to our work over the past decade, even when we appeared not to be following them in all the ways that he would have wished. As it is, we are honored to acknowledge that we share with Andrew a gratitude for being directed with firmness and humor, immense conviction but above all a combination of intelligence and mindfulness that we know can never come our way again. For Andrew's sake and ours, let's hope we have taken enough from him. If we did not, it was never his fault for not offering.

BIBLIOGRAPHY

COHEN, D. J. (1980). Constructive and reconstructive activities in the analysis of a depressed child. *Psychoanal. Study Child, 35,* 237–266.

COHEN, D. J. (1990). Enduring sadness. Early loss, vulnerability, and the shaping of character. *Psychoanal. Study Child, 45,* 157–178.

COHEN, D. J., MARANS, S., DAHL, K., MARANS, W., AND LEWIS, M. (1987). Analytic discussions with oedipal children. *Psychoanal. Study Child, 42,* 59–83.

COHEN, D. J., PAUL, R., AND VOLKMAR, F. R. (1986). Issues in the classification of pervasive developmental disorders. In D. J. Cohen and A. Donnellan (Eds.), *Handbook of Autism and Pervasive Developmental Disorders,* (pp. 20–40). New York: Wiley.

DAHL, E. K., COHEN, D. J., AND PROVENCE, S. (1986). Clinical and multivariate approaches to nosology of pervasive developmental disorders. *Journal of the American Academy of Child Psychiatry, 25,* 170–180.

DIBBLE, E., AND COHEN, D. J. (1981). Personality development in identical twins—The first decade of life. *Psychoanal. Study of the Child, 36,* 45–70.

FREUD, A. (1936). *The Ego and the Mechanisms of Defence.* New York: International Universities Press, 1946.

FREUD, A. (1972). Comments on aggression. *International Journal of Psycho-Analysis, 53,* 163–171.

FREUD, A. (1978). Inaugural lecture for the Sigmund Freud Chair of the Hebrew University, Jerusalem, *The Writings of Anna Freud* (Vol. 8, pp. 340–343). New York: International Universities Press, 1981.

GERGELY, G., AND WATSON, J. (1996). The social biofeedback model of parental affect-mirroring. *International Journal of Psycho-Analysis, 77,* 1181–1212.

HOBSON, P. (1991). Against the theory of "theory of mind." *British Journal of Developmental Psychology, 9,* 33–51.

LOEWALD, H. W. (1978). *Psychoanalysis and the history of the individual.* New Haven: Yale University Press.

MARANS, S., DAHL, K., MARANS, W., AND COHEN, D. J. (1993). Aggressivity in play: Discussions with oedipal children. In A. J. Solnit and D. J. Cohen (Eds.), *The Many Meanings of Play: A Psychoanalytic Perspective* (pp. 275–296). New Haven, Conn.: Yale University Press.

MARANS, S., MAYES, L., CICCHETTI, D., DAHL, K., MARANS, W., AND COHEN, D. J. (1991). The child-psychoanalytic play interview: A technique for studying thematic content. *J. Am. Psychoanal. Assoc.,* 39(4), 1015–1036.

MAYES, L., AND COHEN, D. (1993). Playing and therapeutic action in child analysis. *International Journal of Psycho-Analysis, 74,* 1235–1244.

MAYES, L. C., AND COHEN, D. J. (1992). The development of a capacity for imagination in early childhood. *Psychoanalytic Study of the Child, 47,* 23–48.

MAYES, L. C., AND COHEN, D. J. (1993). The social matrix of aggression. Enactments and representations of loving and hating in the first years of life. *Psychoanal. Study Child, 48,* 145–169.

MAYES, L. C., AND COHEN, D. J. (1994). Experiencing self and others: Contributions from studies of autism to the psychoanalytic theory of social development. *Journal of the American Psychoanalytic Association, 42,* 191–218.

MAYES, L. C., AND COHEN, D. J. (1996a). Anna Freud and developmental psychoanalytic psychology. *Psychoanal. Study Child, 51,* 117–141.

MAYES, L. C., AND COHEN, D. J. (1996b). Children's developing theory of mind. *Journal of the American Psychoanalytic Association, 44,* 117–142.

MAYES, L. C., COHEN, D. J., AND KLIN, A. (1993). Experiencing self and others: A psychoanalytic perspective on theory of mind and autism. In S. Baron-Cohen and H. Tager-Flusberg and D. J. Cohen (Eds.), *Understanding Other Minds: Perspectives from Autism* (pp. 450–465). Oxford: Oxford University Press.

MCGINN, C. (1982). *The Character of Mind.* Oxford: Oxford University Press.

SPILLIUS, E. B. (1992). Discussion of "Aggression and the Psychological Self" (shortened version of present paper), given at scientific meeting "Psychoanalytic Ideas and Developmental Observation" in honor of George S. Moran, London, June 1992.

WINNICOTT, D. W. (1953). Transitional objects and transitional phenomena. *International Journal of Psycho-Analysis, 34,* 1–9.

Index

Castration anxiety, 26–27, 200
CDCP. *See* Child Development Community
  Policing Program (CDCP)
Character, 263, 303
Charcot, J., 247
Child abuse, 281–85, 317
Child analysis: analyst's playing with child
  in, 190, 309, 311–12; anger at analyst
  during, 43, 46–48, 58, 149–50, 152, 157;
  applications of developmental research
  for, 139–41; co-constructing in, 146,
  155–56, 182; co-creating in, 145–46,
  156, 182; co-discovering in, 145, 155–56,
  182; Cohen's analysis of depressed child,
  226, 297–303, 307–20; developmental
  considerations in, 134–37, 172–86, 273;
  developmental object role of analyst in,
  146, 150, 154, 156, 173, 184, 189–211; of
  developmentally delayed girl (Sandy
  case), 89–110, 112–22, 179–82; and divided consciousness of analyst, 121–22;
  factors beyond verbal interpretation in,
  190–91; A. Freud on, 136, 190, 297,
  303–4, 313, 315; and gender conflicts,
  12–15, 16, 23–31, 37–84; limit setting in,
  206–7; narrative building in, 133–58;
  obstacles encountered by study group
  on, 173–79; real object role of analyst in,
  146, 173–74; study group on integration
  of developmental process with, 172–86;
  therapeutic action in, 157; transference
  object role of analyst in, 146, 156–57,
  207–8; transformations in, 178–79, 185.
  See also Countertransference; Play; Termi-
  nation; Transference; Transformations
Child Development Community Policing
  Program (CDCP), 276, 287
Child sexual abuse, 67
Children of deaf parents, 228–43
Children's developing theory of mind, 110,
  138, 303, 309–10, 315
Chodorow, N. J., 15
Chused, J., 7, 191, 209
Cicchetti, D., 230, 276
Coates, S., 7, 204
Co-constructing, 146, 155–56, 182
Co-creating, 145–46, 156, 182
Co-discovering, 145, 155–56, 182
Cognitive psychology. *See* Mind
Cohen, D. J.: on aggression, 203, 204–5,
  303, 314, 315–17; on analysis of de-
  pressed child, 226, 297–303, 307–20;
  and Andrew case, 297–303, 307–20; on
  autism, 270, 271, 310, 318; and chil-
  dren's developing theory of mind, 110,

138, 303, 309–10, 315; colleagues of and
  collaborations by, 294–95, 304, 308; contributions of, as psychoanalyst, 272–74,
  297–303, 307–20; as director of Yale
  Child Study Center, 269–76, 286–89,
  292, 296; on A. Freud, 303–4, 313, 315;
  on genetics, 314; on imagination in early
  childhood, 317–18; and Justin case, 294;
  longitudinal study of twins by, 296–97,
  314; on play in childhood, 303, 317–18;
  on playing in child analysis, 190, 311–12;
  and Quentin case, 308, 314, 319; research interests of, 269–72; and Slifka
  Center for Jewish Life, 304–5; as Sterling
  Professor, 292, 304; on Tourette's Syn-
  drome, 272, 294–95, 303; at Western
  New England Institute, 272–73; writings
  by, 293–304, 307–19; and Yale Univer-
  sity, 304–5; and Yale University Press, 294
Cohen, J., 137
Cohen, N. A., 225
Cohen, P., 207–8, 286, 297, 298, 308, 312
Cohen-Harris Trauma Center, 288
Colonna, A., 172n1, 286, 308
Compliance, 23
Compromise formation, 32, 226
Compulsive overeating, 223, 224, 225
Compulsivity and gender conflicts, 10, 22
Contingency, 316
Continuity fallacy, 166
Controlled regression of the ego, 70
Countertransference, 41, 44, 205

Dahl, K., 7, 286, 303, 308, 317–18
Davis, L., 240
Deafness, 228–43, 235n2, 237nn4–5
Dean J. case (trauma), 281–85
Death, 71–72, 150, 262, 281
Death drive, 130
Defense mechanisms, 12, 20, 27, 28, 32, 58,
  91, 96, 104–5, 110, 116, 119, 121
Delay ability, 106–7
Depression: Andrew case, 297–303, 307–
  20; cognitive impairments of, 319; Co-
  hen's analysis of depressed child, 226,
  297–303, 307–20; and gender conflicts,
  5, 8, 10, 11, 13, 57, 60–84; Leonora case,
  248; Mona case (gender conflicts), 60–
  84; Quentin case, 308, 314, 319. *See also*
  Mourning and sadness
Development: Abrams on, 135; and affect
  regulation, 204–5; analytic applications
  of developmental research, 139–41; and
  anxiety, 126; aspects of, 124; British
  School on, 124–25; child analyst's role as